D1541476

The International Protection of Internally Displaced Persons

Despite the fact that there are up to 25 million internally displaced persons around the world, their plight is still little known. Like refugees, internally displaced persons have been forced to leave their homes because of armed conflict and human rights abuses, but they have not left their country. This has major consequences in terms of the protection available to them. This book aims to offer a clear and easily accessible overview of this important humanitarian and human rights challenge. In particular, it seeks to provide an objective evaluation of UN efforts to protect the internally displaced. It will be of interest to all those involved with the internally displaced, as well as anyone seeking to gain an overall understanding of this complex issue.

CATHERINE PHUONG is a Lecturer in Law at the University of Newcastle. She studied law, politics and economics at the Institut d'Etudes Politiques de Paris (Sciences Po), and received her Master of Laws from the University of Durham and her Doctorate from the University of Nottingham. She has been Visiting Professor at the University of Lyon II, and Visiting Research Scholar at the University of Michigan.

CAMBRIDGE STUDIES IN INTERNATIONAL AND COMPARATIVE LAW

Established in 1946, this series produces high quality scholarship in the fields of public and private international law and comparative law. Although these are distinct legal subdisciplines, developments since 1946 confirm their interrelation.

Comparative law is increasingly used as a tool in the making of law at national, regional and international levels. Private international law is now often affected by international conventions, and the issues faced by classical conflicts rules are frequently dealt with by substantive harmonisation of law under international auspices. Mixed international arbitrations, especially those involving state economic activity, raise mixed questions of public and private international law, while in many fields (such as the protection of human rights and democratic standards, investment guarantees and international criminal law) international and national systems interact. National constitutional arrangements relating to 'foreign affairs', and to the implementation of international norms, are a focus of attention.

The Board welcomes works of a theoretical or interdisciplinary character, and those focusing on new approaches to international or comparative law or conflicts of law. Studies of particular institutions or problems are equally welcome, as are translations of the best work published in other languages.

General Editors	James Crawford SC FBA *Whewell Professor of International Law, Faculty of Law, and Director, Lauterpacht Research Centre for International Law, University of Cambridge* John S. Bell FBA *Professor of Law, Faculty of Law, University of Cambridge*
Editorial Board	Professor Hilary Charlesworth *Australian National University* Professor Lori Damrosch *Columbia University Law School* Professor John Dugard *Universiteit Leiden* Professor Mary-Ann Glendon *Harvard Law School* Professor Christopher Greenwood *London School of Economics* Professor David Johnston *University of Edinburgh* Professor Hein Kötz *Max-Planck-Institut, Hamburg* Professor Donald McRae *University of Ottawa* Professor Onuma Yasuaki *University of Tokyo* Professor Reinhard Zimmermann *Universität Regensburg*
Advisory Committee	Professor D. W. Bowett QC Judge Rosalyn Higgins QC Professor J. A. Jolowicz QC Professor Sir Elihu Lauterpacht CBE QC Professor Kurt Lipstein Judge Stephen Schwebel

A list of books in the series can be found at the end of this volume.

The International Protection of Internally Displaced Persons

Catherine Phuong

University of Newcastle

CAMBRIDGE
UNIVERSITY PRESS

PUBLISHED BY THE PRESS SYNDICATE OF THE UNIVERSITY OF CAMBRIDGE
The Pitt Building, Trumpington Street, Cambridge, United Kingdom

CAMBRIDGE UNIVERSITY PRESS
The Edinburgh Building, Cambridge, CB2 2RU, UK
40 West 20th Street, New York, NY 10011–4211, USA
477 Williamstown Road, Port Melbourne, VIC 3207, Australia
Ruiz de Alarcón 13, 28014 Madrid, Spain
Dock House, The Waterfront, Cape Town 8001, South Africa

http://www.cambridge.org

First published 2004

Printed in the United Kingdom at the University Press, Cambridge

Typeface Swift 10/13 pt.   *System* LATEX 2$_\varepsilon$ [TB]

A catalogue record for this book is available from the British Library

Library of Congress Cataloguing in Publication data
Phuong, Catherine.
The international protection of internally displaced persons / Catherine Phuong.
   p.   cm. – (Cambridge studies in international and comparative law ; 38)
Includes bibliographical references and index.
ISBN 0 521 82686 1 (hardback)
1. Refugees – Legal status, laws, etc.   2. Civil war.   3. Refugees – International
cooperation.   4. Humanitarian law.   I. Title.   II. Series.
KZ6530.P49   2004
341.4′86 – dc22   2004049738

ISBN 0 521 82686 1 hardback

A mes parents
Pat et Louis

Contents

Acknowledgments

This book would not have been written without the assistance and support of a number of people, of whom there are too many to list here. It started as a doctoral thesis at the University of Nottingham where I had the privilege to be supervised by Patrick Twomey. I have received invaluable guidance from him. He has spent long hours reading through and commenting on my many drafts, and discussing my ideas with me. I am extremely grateful for his help. I would also like to thank Ian Forbes for his advice and support. My examiners, Guy Goodwin-Gill, Dino Kritsiotis and Richard Aldrich, gave me very helpful suggestions with regard to the final version of this work.

I am particularly indebted to the University of Nottingham and the Jean Monnet Fund for their generous financing of this project. The Schools of Law and Politics have both funded my trips to national and international conferences where I was able to present and discuss my ideas, as well as a trip to Geneva. In addition, I would like to thank the J. C. Smith Travelling Fund (Nottingham) and the Gilbert Murray Trust (Oxford) for funding the field trip to the former Yugoslavia. I would especially like to thank the University of Newcastle for awarding me an internal research fellowship and the School of Law for granting me a period of research leave to allow for the completion of this book. I would further like to thank Finola O'Sullivan of Cambridge University Press for her enthusiasm and encouragement.

For this book, I have interviewed or spoken with many individuals, mainly in Geneva and the former Yugoslavia, who have taken time to discuss my ideas and/or given me access to invaluable source materials. It is impossible for me to list all their names. Special thanks go to Jane Alexander, Axel Bisschop, Jeff Crisp, Birgit van Delft, Thierry Domin, Jacoba van den Ende, Walpurga Englbrecht, Madeleine Garlick,

Marguerite Garling, Lutz Gauger, Daniel Helle, Guy Hovey, Ayaki Ito, Michael Kingsley, Hans Lunshof, Erin Mooney, Viktor Nylund and Werner Wendt. In addition, I would like to thank for their assistance the library staff at the Refugee Studies Centre Library in Oxford and the UNHCR Library in Geneva.

An early version of the Introduction and Chapter 1 of this book was published as 'Internally Displaced Persons and Refugees: Conceptual Differences and Similarities' (2000) 18 *Netherlands Quarterly of Human Rights* 215, and is reproduced here in its adapted form with the kind permission of the copyright holder. An early version of Chapter 3 appeared in 'Improving the United Nations Reponse to Crises of Internal Displacement' (2002) 13 *International Journal of Refugee Law* 491. This is reproduced here with the kind permission of Oxford University Press, as is part of Chapter 5, which was first published as '"Freely to Return": Reversing Ethnic Cleansing in Bosnia and Herzegovina' (2000) 13 *Journal of Refugee Studies* 165.

I would like to thank my family and friends for their constant support throughout the last few years. In particular, friends and colleagues at the Universities of Nottingham and Newcastle have been a source of invaluable help and support. Gemma Hayton, Joanne Pinnock and Ann Sinclair provided unvaluable assistance to complete the manuscript. Finally, I would like to thank Alistair for his critical comments and constant encouragement. All errors and omissions remain mine alone.

CATHERINE PHUONG
October 2003
The law is stated as at 1 October 2003, although later developments have been incorporated where possible.

Table of cases

Table of treaties and other international documents

Abbreviations

1951 Convention	Convention Relating to the Status of Refugees
1967 Protocol	Protocol Relating to the Status of Refugees
ASIL	American Society of International Law
CFSP	Common Foreign and Security Policy (of the EU)
CHR	Commission on Human Rights
CIS	Commonwealth of Independent States
COHRE	Centre on Housing Rights and Evictions
CRPC	Commission on Real Property Claims of Displaced Persons and Refugees (in Bosnia and Herzegovina)
ECHR	European Convention for the Protection of Human Rights and Fundamental Freedoms
ECOSOC	Economic and Social Council
ECRE	European Council on Refugees and Exiles
EHRR	*European Human Rights Reports*
ERC	Emergency Relief Coordinator
ETS	*European Treaty Series*
EXCOM	Executive Committee (of UNHCR)
FRY	Federal Republic of Yugoslavia
GA	General Assembly
GAOR	*General Assembly Official Records*
HC	Humanitarian Coordinator
HIWG	Humanitarian Issues Working Group
IASC	Inter-Agency Standing Committee
ICC	International Criminal Court
ICCPR	International Covenant on Civil and Political Rights
ICESCR	International Covenant on Economic, Social and Cultural Rights

ICISS	International Commission on Intervention and State Sovereignty
ICJ	International Court of Justice
ICRC	International Committee of the Red Cross
ICTR	International Criminal Tribunal for Rwanda
ICTY	International Criminal Tribunal for the former Yugoslavia
ICVA	International Council of Voluntary Agencies
IDP	internally displaced person
ILM	*International Legal Materials*
IOM	International Organization for Migration
IRO	International Refugee Organization
KLA	Kosovo Liberation Army
NGO	non-governmental organisation
OAU	Organization of African Unity
OCHA	Office for the Coordination of Humanitarian Affairs
OHCHR	Office of the High Commissioner for Human Rights
OHR	Office of the High Representative
OJ	*Official Journal of the European Communities*
OSCE	Organization for Security and Cooperation in Europe
PLIP	Property Law Implementation Plan
SC	Security Council
SCOR	*Security Council Official Records*
SFOR	Stabilization Force (in Bosnia and Herzegovina)
UNAMIR	United Nations Assistance Mission in Rwanda
UNDP	United Nations Development Programme
UNHCR	United Nations High Commissioner for Refugees
UNICEF	United Nations Children's Fund
UNMIBH	United Nations Mission in Bosnia and Herzegovina
UNPA	United Nations Protected Area
UNPROFOR	United Nations Protection Force in the Former Yugoslavia
UNTS	*United Nations Treaty Series*
USCR	United States Committee for Refugees
WFP	World Food Programme
WHO	World Health Organization
WLR	*Weekly Law Reports*

Introduction

Whereas the number of refugees assisted by the Office of the United Nations High Commissioner for Refugees (UNHCR) had fallen to 10.6 million by the end of 2002,[1] the number of internally displaced persons was estimated to be about 20–25 million at the same date.[2] Internally displaced persons not only outnumber, by far, refugees, they also raise some of the most urgent human rights and humanitarian problems of our time and present a serious challenge to prevailing conceptions of sovereignty and intervention. They can be found on all continents, but especially in Sub-Saharan Africa, the Middle East, the former Yugoslavia and in the republics of the former Soviet Union. Some countries are particularly affected, such as Sudan with an estimated 4 million internally displaced. In 2003, other countries such as Colombia, the Democratic Republic of Congo, Iraq and Turkey hosted up to, or even more than, a million internally displaced persons each.[3] The refugee definition contained in the 1951 Refugee Convention,[4] as modified by the 1967 Protocol,[5] indicates that internally displaced persons are not refugees because they are still within their country of origin. They have not crossed a frontier, which is a precondition of refugeehood.

Until the beginning of the 1990s, internally displaced persons were defined negatively: they were people who had fled their homes, but who

---

[1] See UNHCR, *Statistical Yearbook 2002: Trends in Displacement, Protection and Solutions* (Geneva: UNHCR, 2004), Table I.1.

[2] See *Internally Displaced Persons, Report of the Representative of the Secretary-General, Mr Francis M. Deng*, E/CN.4/2002/95, 16 January 2002 (hereinafter *2002 Deng Report*), para. 2.

[3] See figures at http://www.idpproject.org/global_overview.htm.

[4] Convention Relating to the Status of Refugees, 28 July 1951, 189 UNTS 150 (hereinafter the 1951 Convention).

[5] Protocol Relating to the Status of Refugees, 1967, 606 UNTS 267 (hereinafter the 1967 Protocol).

were not refugees (having remained within their country). It is only recently that some efforts have been made to devise a comprehensive definition of internally displaced persons. An important step was taken in 1992 when the UN Secretary-General proposed a working definition.[6] That definition was revised in 1998 and the Guiding Principles on Internal Displacement now define internally displaced persons as:

persons or groups of persons who have been forced or obliged to flee or to leave their homes or places of habitual residence, in particular as a result of or in order to avoid the effects of armed conflict, situations of generalised violence, violations of human rights or natural or human-made disasters, and who have not crossed an internationally recognised state border.[7]

While not defined as refugees, internally displaced persons have been dealt with by refugee structures such as UNHCR which provides protection and assistance to them (mostly in returnee-linked programmes), when they are found in the same areas as refugees, and when it considers that this forms an integral part of a comprehensive solution to the refugee problem.[8] However, some concern has been expressed over such arrangements.[9] Internal displacement is linked with the refugee problem, in so far as it often constitutes a preliminary step towards external displacement, but the phenomenon also has specific characteristics and can raise special problems which cannot be solved by traditional methods of protection used in the refugee context. Internal displacement constitutes a distinct problem which has to be dealt with not only in conjunction with the refugee problem, but also separately as it raises issues of a different nature.[10]

This introduction examines the origins, nature and scope of the problem. Some historical background is then given as to how the UN came to deal with the issue in the 1990s. The overall analysis is placed in the context of containment policies implemented by refugee-receiving states which seek to shift the emphasis away from asylum to in-country protection. This raises the question as to whether the recent focus on internally displaced persons risks undermining the institution of asylum.

---

[6] See *Analytical Report of the Secretary-General on Internally Displaced Persons*, E/CN.4/1992/23, 14 February 1992 (hereinafter the *Analytical Report*), para. 17.

[7] *Guiding Principles on Internal Displacement*, E/CN.4/1998/53/Add.2, 11 February 1998. See Annex 1 below.

[8] See Chapter 3, first section.   [9] See Chapter 3, second section.

[10] See R. Cohen and F. M. Deng, *Masses in Flight: The Global Crisis of Internal Displacement* (Washington DC: Brookings Institution, 1998), 26–9.

Internal displacement and containment policies

Internal displacement has always existed and often takes place prior to external displacement which is seen as the last option. Indeed, in situations of danger, people generally prefer to stay within their own community or at least within their own country, close to their homes, envisaging return. Sometimes, people are not able to leave the country because they have limited means of transportation. Moreover, external displacement may not be an option, because when population movements spill over into neighbouring countries, some countries close their borders, as Turkey did when Iraqi Kurds were fleeing repression in Iraq in 1991.[11] In doing so, such states assert their 'power to admit or exclude aliens [which] is inherent in sovereignty',[12] power which is now curtailed by the principle of *non-refoulement*.[13] Refugee flows are sometimes contained by the state of origin which may not wish to see its citizens fleeing abroad, fearing that an exodus might bring about negative publicity for the government, as well as a loss of skills and resources for the country. Moreover, the existence of opponents to the regime abroad creates the possibility of a threat of activities from the countries where they may find refuge.

Although internal displacement is not a new phenomenon, it reached dramatic dimensions after the Cold War. The attitude amongst Western states towards refugees has changed considerably since the 1980s. Refugees had a more important strategic role to play during the Cold War era: welcoming refugees fleeing countries of the opposite bloc was a political act designed to demonstrate the failures of that political system in protecting its own citizens.[14] Refugees no longer play that strategic role and are now viewed more as a threat rather than as political pawns. This has led to the recent trends of containment of refugee flows within countries of origin and the accompanying shift in language which is critical in the debate on internal displacement.

One also has to point to the effects of the globalisation of transport networks, which presents an opportunity for refugees to reach the territories of developed countries, and has modified the nature of

---

[11] See Turkey's statement in the debate leading to the adoption of SC Res. 588, SCOR, S/PV2982, 5 April 1991, 6.

[12] J. H. Carens, 'Aliens and Citizens: The Case for Open Borders' (1987) 49 *Review of Politics* 251 at 251.

[13] Article 33(1) of the 1951 Convention.

[14] See J. Hathaway, 'A Reconsideration of the Underlying Premise of Refugee Law' (1990) 31 *Harvard International Law Journal* 129 at 148–51.

population movements. This has prompted a change of response from potential refugee-receiving countries. Refugees are not only subject to *refoulement* by neighbouring countries, but also by other potential refugee-receiving countries further afield which seek to deter people from entering their territory by implementing policies such as visa requirements, carrier sanctions and concepts such as safe country of origin and safe third country, and curtailing work possibilities and welfare benefits for those who do manage to arrive. In addition, conflicts around the world often involve the targeting of civilians and thus produce situations of internal displacement and humanitarian crises. All these various factors explain the recent explosion in the numbers of internally displaced persons and the correlative decline in the numbers of refugees mentioned above.

The problem of internal displacement is a sensitive one, because it is linked to the willingness of refugee-receiving states to contain refugee flows within the countries of origin. While asserting humanitarian motives, these states may focus on in-country protection simply to preclude their asylum obligations from being activated. By preventing the border-crossing of the populations necessary to activate the obligations contained in the 1951 Convention, states avoid these obligations.

The potential danger of focusing on in-country protection is that of undermining the right to seek asylum abroad, which represents 'an indispensable instrument for the international protection of refugees'.[15] It has been repeated on several occasions that activities on behalf of internally displaced persons 'must not undermine the institution of asylum'.[16] Protection activities undertaken in favour of internally displaced persons which are aimed at securing in-country protection should not amount to a pre-emptive denial of the possibility to seek asylum abroad.

As a result, the increase in the concern for internally displaced persons can be explained by two reasons of a very different nature, one being humanitarian and the other more political and self-serving, namely to prevent internally displaced persons from becoming refugees. One may conclude that obstacles to population movements are now more political than geographical. Nevertheless, the current interest in internally displaced persons is not solely motivated by the intentions of states trying to prevent cross-border movements into their territory, and the terms of the debate are actually more complex than this.

[15] GA Res. 48/116, 20 December 1993.   [16] GA Res. 50/195, 22 December 1995.

The urgent need for protection is a matter of human rights protection. The link between refugee protection and human rights protection has long been established,[17] and a similar link exists between the protection of internally displaced persons and human rights protection. The challenge is to ensure that attempts to improve the international response to crises of internal displacement do not undermine the established refugee protection system.

Some refugee commentators believe that this cannot be avoided and that there is an 'implicit and dangerous logic' in the IDP concept which only serves to divert attention from the refugee problem.[18] There is clearly some resistance to the emergence of a new displacement regime which extends beyond the confines of the international refugee regime which is characterised by a higher and 'comforting' degree of legal certainty. One must concede that, as Suhrke argues, the new discourse on internally displaced persons may reflect a certain political agenda and that it is crucial that IDP researchers 'unpack the concepts, policies and justifications used by political actors when they define IDPs and develop mechanisms to offer them assistance and protection'.[19] Adelman shares these words of caution.[20] This work will endeavour to carefully uncover any political agenda that may underline the legal and policy debates over internal displacement.

Nevertheless, it is suggested here that attempts made to improve the protection of those who could not or did not wish to leave their country should not necessarily be seen as a negative development. Obviously, there is nothing wrong with the idea of improving protection for persons who have been displaced by armed conflict and human rights violations, and avoiding further displacement and suffering. The important issue is that the option of asylum always remains available to these people and that assistance and protection activities for internally displaced persons are never used as a justification for restricting, or even denying,

---

[17] See for instance *Study on Human Rights and Mass Exoduses*, E/CN.4/1503, 31 December 1981, or J. Hathaway, 'Reconceiving Refugee Law as Human Rights Protection', in K. E. Mahoney and P. Mahoney (eds.), *Human Rights in the Twenty-First Century: A Global Challenge* (Dordrecht: Martinus Nijhoff Publishers, 1993), 659–78.

[18] See M. Barutciski, 'Tension Between the Refugee Concept and the IDP Debate', *Forced Migration Review*, vol. 3, December 1998, 14.

[19] A. Suhrke, 'Reflections on Regime Change', in Norwegian University of Science and Technology, *Researching Internal Displacement: State of the Art*, Conference Report, 7–8 February 2003, Trondheim, Norway, 15.

[20] See H. Adelman, 'What is the Place of IDP Research in Refugee Studies?', in Norwegian University of Science and Technology, *ibid.*, 14.

the right to asylum and/or enforcing the premature application of the right of return of refugees to their country of origin. Fitzpatrick suggested that it is difficult to prevent an adverse impact on refugee law, partly because there is limited UNHCR participation in the Commission on Human Rights and the Security Council which are the main international fora of discussion of IDP rights.[21] Nevertheless, UNHCR should not be seen as the only defender of refugee rights and all those dealing with internally displaced persons should also remain concerned with refugee rights.

The present study attempts to take a more optimistic stance by offering a more in-depth analysis of the phenomenon of internal displacement and the responses to the problem, while also analysing the possible implications for the international refugee regime. The research is based on the assumption that protection of internally displaced persons and protection of refugees are distinct but also related. It also assumes that more IDP protection should not inevitably undermine refugee protection. In many cases, most internally displaced persons do not actually wish to leave their country unless they feel compelled to do so in order to ensure their own safety. Sometimes, they are trapped in conflict zones and are unable to leave the country anyway, in which case the provision of IDP protection cannot amount to containment. As a result, there can often be no contradiction between drawing international attention to the plight of the internally displaced and upholding the international refugee protection regime.

A problem of international concern

One of the first situations of large-scale internal displacement to attract international concern was that of Sudan in the early 1970s. Following the 1972 Addis Ababa Agreement putting an end to a protracted civil war and which provided for the return and resettlement of refugees and internally displaced persons,[22] the Economic and Social Council requested that UNHCR coordinate humanitarian assistance on behalf of these populations: it referred to 'the assistance required for voluntary repatriation, rehabilitation and resettlement of the refugees returning

---

[21] See J. Fitzpatrick, 'Human Rights and Forced Displacement: Converging Standards', in A. F. Bayefsky and J. Fitzpatrick (eds.), *Human Rights and Forced Displacement* (The Hague: Kluwer Law International, 2000), 3–25 at 13.

[22] See F. M. Deng, *Protecting the Dispossessed, a Challenge for the International Community* (Washington DC: Brookings Institution, 1993), 71.

from abroad, *as well as* of persons displaced within the country' (emphasis added).[23] One can note that the expression 'internally displaced persons' was not yet in use in 1972. A few months later, the General Assembly encouraged UNHCR to pursue its efforts on behalf of 'refugees and other displaced persons', referring here to internally displaced persons, in Sudan.[24] Beyond Sudan, what really put the issue on the international agenda was the change of political circumstances at the end of the Cold War as explained above.

The extensive media coverage given to the intervention undertaken by a coalition of states led by the United States with the implicit authorisation of the Security Council[25] to protect Kurds in northern Iraq in the spring of 1991 brought international attention to the plight of the internally displaced.[26] 'Operation Provide Comfort' marked a turning-point because it led to an increase of attention being paid by UN organs to the issue of internal displacement.[27] During the first half of the 1990s, several other humanitarian crises of unprecedented scale and involving significant numbers of internally displaced persons appeared around the world in, for instance, the Great Lakes region (Rwanda, Burundi, Democratic Republic of Congo), the former Yugoslavia and, again, in Sudan. This demonstrated that the Kurdish episode was not an isolated incident. It was considered morally unacceptable to provide protection and assistance to refugees, but not to internally displaced persons who were living alongside the former, and sometimes in the same camps. Moreover, it has been demonstrated that internally displaced persons often find themselves in worse conditions than refugees, due to the fact that they can be out of reach of international aid agencies. As a result, the death rates among internally displaced persons can be higher than those of refugees and certainly much higher than those of non-displaced living in the same country.[28]

---

[23] ECOSOC Res. 1705 (LIII), 27 July 1972.

[24] GA Res. 2958 (XXVII), 12 December 1972.   [25] SC Res. 688, 5 April 1991.

[26] See P. Malanczuk, 'The Kurdish Crisis and Allied Intervention in the Aftermath of the Second Gulf War' (1991) 2 *European Journal of International Law* 114, and H. Adelman, 'Humanitarian Intervention: The Case of the Kurds' (1992) 4 *International Journal of Refugee Law* 4.

[27] See OCHA Internal Displacement Unit, *No Refuge: The Challenge of Internal Displacement* (New York and Geneva: United Nations, 2003), 17.

[28] For a comparison between mortality rates in refugee populations and among internally displaced persons, see M. J. Toole and R. J. Waldman, 'The Public Health Aspects of Complex Emergencies and Refugee Situations' (1997) 18 *Annual Review of Public Health* 283 at 289–91.

Assistance and protection activities have traditionally been seen as distinct, but the UN has been trying to put as much emphasis on the humanitarian aspect of the problem as on its human rights aspect. The advocacy efforts and direct involvement with internally displaced persons of the NGO community (but also of small states such as Austria and Norway)[29] have contributed to raising awareness of the problem of internal displacement at the Commission on Human Rights.[30] Two major international conferences focusing on refugees and displaced persons also examined the issue of internal displacement. The first was the International Conference on the Plight of Refugees, Returnees and Displaced Persons in Southern Africa (SARRED) which took place in Oslo in December 1988. It was followed by the International Conference on Central American Refugees (CIREFCA) in May 1989.[31]

In March 1991, the Commission on Human Rights requested that the Secretary-General prepare a report on internally displaced persons.[32] This important report prompted a much more active involvement of the UN, as a whole, in the issue.[33] It defined the scope of the problem and called for more vigorous action, which resulted in the appointment of a Special Representative on Internally Displaced Persons. Mr Francis Deng has assumed this position since then. The first aspect of his mandate is to analyse the normative framework of protection for internally displaced persons. This resulted in the drafting of the 'Compilation and Analysis of Legal Norms',[34] which led to the formulation of the 'Guiding Principles on Internal Displacement' already mentioned above. The second aspect of the mandate is to review the existing institutional framework and seek means of improving coordination between the various UN agencies. The third and final aspect of his mandate consists of on-site visits. So far, the Special Representative has visited more than twenty countries where large internal movements of population have occurred.[35] These

---

[29] See for instance OCHA Internal Displacement Unit, No Refuge, 20.

[30] See S. Bagshaw, Developing the Guiding Principles on Internal Displacement: The Role of a Global Public Policy Network, case study for the UN vision project on global public policy networks, http://www.gppi.net/cms/public/ 86880753f4f7e096dd8b747195113f6cbagshaw%20gpp%202000.pdf, 5–11.

[31] For more detail on SARRED and CIREFCA, see K. Hakata, La protection internationale des personnes déplacées à l'intérieur de leur propre pays, thèse de doctorat en droit, Université de Genève, February 1998, 20–5.

[32] See CHR Res. 1991/25, 5 March 1991.   [33] See the Analytical Report, note 6 above.

[34] E/CN.4/1996/52/Add.2, 5 December 1995.

[35] See the list in Brookings Institution, International Symposium on the Mandate of the Representative of the UN Secretary-General on Internally Displaced Persons: Taking Stock and Charting the Future, Vienna, Austria, 12–13 December 2002, Annex 5.

visits have documented several situations of internal displacement and are also part of his role in raising awareness of this problem. During each visit, he meets representatives of the government in order to discuss means of improving the situation of the internally displaced. The implementation of his recommendations by governments is now systematically reviewed.[36] However, the governments which are less willing to invite the Special Representative are also those who are implicated in the most problematic situations of internal displacement.[37]

The mandate of the Special Representative on internally displaced persons has now been established for more than ten years and one can safely say that its achievements are far from negligible.[38] Francis Deng has truly acted as a 'catalyst' for drawing international and national attention to the issue of internal displacement, in particular through the drafting and dissemination of the Guiding Principles. Nevertheless, he has had mainly an advocacy role, and the margin of progress in improving protection and assistance to the internally displaced in *operational* terms is still wide.

Analysing the problem of internal displacement within a human rights framework

This book argues that the issue of internal displacement is not merely a humanitarian problem, but needs to be discussed within a wider human rights context. Consequently, an analysis of the UN's response to this problem must draw on a human rights framework. Such an approach is required by the UN Charter and the Secretary-General's commitment to integrate human rights into the UN's work.

In order to support the above statement, several key issues need to be addressed. What distinguishes internally displaced persons from refugees? Why should the internally displaced not benefit from the protection regime established for refugees under the 1951 Convention, but be considered more broadly as victims of human rights abuses? These questions will be dealt with in Chapter 1 which explores the conceptual similarities and differences between refugees and internally displaced

---

[36] See *2002 Deng Report*, note 2 above, para. 88.

[37] CHR Res. 1997/39, 11 April 1997, called upon governments to cooperate with the Special Representative.

[38] See *Internally Displaced Persons, Report of the Representative of the Secretary-General, Mr Francis M. Deng*, E/CN.4/2003/86, 21 January 2003.

persons. Since Chapter 1 concludes that internally displaced persons do not require a specific legal status under international law, Chapter 2 proceeds to analyse the legal framework applicable to situations of internal displacement. Part of that framework draws heavily on international human rights law and international humanitarian law.

As explained above, the increase in the numbers of internally displaced persons following the Cold War, as well as the new emphasis on providing in-country protection, prompted the UN to tackle the issue in the 1990s. Chapter 3 examines the UN's understanding of the IDP issue and, in doing so, explores the implications of a human rights approach to the problem of internal displacement on the nature of institutional responses to that problem. More particularly, how does a human rights approach inform the ongoing debate over institutional responsibilities for the internally displaced within the UN system? The scope of the research is limited to the study of the UN system not only for reasons of space and time, but also because of its primary policy role and the fact that states generally delegate responsibility to the organisation in this area. Nevertheless, non-governmental organisations (NGOs) as well as regional organisations and military organisations such as NATO also play a very active role in providing protection and assistance to the internally displaced.

Whereas Chapter 3 puts the focus on agencies' stated approaches to internal displacement, Chapter 4 examines field activities and the extent to which they reflect some of the flaws in the UN's understanding of the problem of internal displacement. It evaluates the efficiency of measures undertaken to protect internally displaced persons from human rights violations, including forced displacement. Some suggestions are made on how field activities can be pursued within a human rights framework and produce a more effective response to the protection needs of internally displaced persons.

This book does not intend to review all national situations of internal displacement.[39] Nevertheless, Chapter 5 is a case study on internal displacement in Bosnia and Herzegovina which illustrates the limits of field activities that are pursued in isolation from a human rights framework and goals. The case study examines how the issues addressed in previous chapters were dealt with in the specific context of Bosnia and

---

[39] For such a review, see Global IDP Survey, *Internally Displaced People, a Global Survey* (London: Earthscan Publications Ltd, 2002, 2nd ed.).

Herzegovina. It also reviews recent initiatives undertaken to promote the return of refugees and internally displaced persons to their homes and reverse ethnic cleansing, and in particular the human rights implications, if any, of these return strategies.

Chapter 6 looks at the problem of internal displacement within a broader conceptual framework, looking at sovereignty and intervention, and how a human rights approach to the problem of internal displacement requires a reconceptualisation of these two concepts with more emphasis on the notion of responsibility.

Throughout the book, numerous references will be made to the notion of IDP protection. Although this notion will be analysed in more detail in Chapter 4,[40] it may still be appropriate to briefly define it here. Protection itself is a term with various meanings, and can refer to active or passive protection, legal protection, physical protection, and so on. According to the International Committee of the Red Cross (ICRC), protection 'encompasses all activities aimed at obtaining full respect for the rights of the individual in accordance with the letter and the spirit of the relevant bodies of law (i.e. human rights law, international humanitarian law, refugee law)'.[41] This definition clearly gives the notion of protection a legal foundation. Nevertheless, it has also been stated that:

protection is not a theoretical or legal construct, even though its practice is framed by an important set of internationally agreed legal principles and guidelines . . . The protection function is dynamic and action oriented . . . it has overarching goals and . . . it is performed through a wide range of specific activities ranging from intervention and programme implementation, through advice, promotion and training, to capacity building.[42]

The latter statement is especially true in the context of internal displacement. The protection of internally displaced persons goes beyond the notion of legal protection. In many cases, it can only be ensured through concrete measures taken in the field. The analysis of the phenomenon of internal displacement and the responses to this problem

---

[40] See Chapter 4, first section, below.
[41] IASC, 'Protection of Internally Displaced Persons', Inter-Agency Standing Committee policy paper, New York, December 1999, 4.
[42] E. Feller, 'Statement by the Director, UNHCR Department of International Protection, to the 18th Meeting of the UNHCR Standing Committee, 5 July 2000' (2000) 12 *International Journal of Refugee Law* 401 at 402.

must then refer to a wide range of debates within refugee, humanitarian, development/migration and security studies.[43] This is why this book attempts to go beyond the analysis of legal documents and proposes an understanding of internal displacement in all its dimensions, including not only institutional and operational, but also political and sociological where possible. The work thus makes extensive use of UN documents and NGO reports.

---

[43] See C. Dubernet, *The International Containment of Displaced Persons: Humanitarian Spaces Without Exit* (Aldershot: Ashgate, 2001), 8.

1 Internally displaced persons and refugees: conceptual differences and similarities

Refugees and the internally displaced are categories of persons which share many similarities such that people in both categories often find themselves in the same material conditions. For historical, political and legal reasons, it has been judged appropriate not to include internally displaced persons in the refugee definition contained in the 1951 Convention.[1] There has been confusion about the concept of internally displaced persons and it has been argued that the internally displaced should be treated as refugees because they are essentially the same.[2] This chapter seeks to determine whether there is a justification for the exclusion of internally displaced persons from the protection and rights afforded to refugees. It calls for a reconceptualisation of the problem of internal displacement which needs to be discussed in a wider human rights context.

For most people, as evident from the media coverage, the term 'refugee' refers to anyone who has been forced to leave his home. Whether the person has left the country or not is seen as irrelevant. The legal terminology is however more precise, as it requires the refugee to be outside his or her country of origin because of a fear of persecution.[3] Internally displaced persons have also been referred to as 'internal refugees'[4] which is an oxymoron. This creates confusion by blurring the

---

[1] Convention Relating to the Status of Refugees, 28 July 1951, 189 UNTS 150 (hereinafter the 1951 Convention).
[2] See pp. 24–5 below.   [3] See p. 17 below.
[4] For instance, Lance Clark entitled his article 'Internal Refugees: The Hidden Half' in the *World Refugee Survey* 1988. More recently, Richard Holbrooke also expressed his preference for the use of the expression: see R. Holbrooke, *Statement at Cardozo Law School on Refugees and Internally Displaced Persons*, USUN Press Release #44 (00), 28 March 2000.

distinction between refugees and internally displaced persons, which, as the chapter argues, should be maintained.[5]

The expression 'internally displaced persons' is of more recent usage. Until the late 1980s, there was no such standard term. Early references to internally displaced persons were made through the emergence of the expression 'displaced persons': this formula was first employed in the Sudanese context,[6] and was subsequently developed for the purposes of material assistance in cases where it was impossible to assist refugees only and not other populations in need.[7] When the UN High Commissioner for Refugees asked the Executive Committee[8] in 1977 to clarify the distinction between refugees and displaced persons, no clear answer was provided, although there seemed to be an understanding that refugees crossed international borders, whereas displaced persons did not.[9] Adding to the confusion, UNHCR suggested the same year that displaced persons referred to people who crossed borders but did not qualify for refugee status, as well as internally displaced persons.[10] Since the 1970s, the expression has been increasingly used without its meaning being clarified. One must note that it was used only in the context of emergency relief operations and not with a view to providing specific protection to these populations.[11] During the preparations of the successive World Conferences[12] which were organised at the beginning of the 1990s during a period of revival of the UN Organization, the question of terminology was always a source of debate and strong disagreements

---

[5] See S. Ogata, 'Protecting People on the Move', Address by the United Nations High Commissioner for Refugees, sponsored by the Center for the Study of International Organization, New York, 18 July 2000.

[6] See GA Res. 2958 (XXVIII), 12 December 1972.

[7] See P. Hartling, 'The Concept and Definition of "Refugee" – Legal and Humanitarian Aspects' (1979) 48 *Nordisk Tidsskrift for International Ret* 125 at 135.

[8] It was set up in 1975 as an organ of UNHCR to assist states with the interpretation of the provisions of the 1951 Convention.

[9] See G. Goodwin-Gill, *The Refugee in International Law* (Oxford: Clarendon Press, 1996, 2nd ed.), 14.

[10] See N. Geissler, *Der völkerrechtliche Schutz der Internally Displaced Persons: eine Analyse des normativen and institutionellen Schutzes der IDPs im Rahmen innerer Unruhen and night-internationaler Konflikte* (Berlin: Duncker & Humblot, 1999), 37.

[11] See K. Hakata, *La protection internationale des personnes déplacées à l'intérieur de leur propre pays*, thèse de doctorat en droit, Université de Genève, February 1998, 19.

[12] The 1993 World Conference on Human Rights in Vienna, the 1994 International Conference on Population and Development in Cairo, the 1995 World Summit on Social Development in Copenhagen and the 1995 Fourth World Conference on Women in Beijing.

appeared. The terminology used was often inconsistent and confusing.[13] The expression 'displaced persons' is now commonly used in the field to refer to internally displaced persons. The problem with this is that different people give to this expression different meanings: logically, it should include all those displaced, whether internally or externally.

The difficulty in using precise terms in a consistent manner can be attributed to the increasing volatility of refugee situations. The porous frontiers between the different categories of displaced persons make it harder to characterise the various groups of persons. In addition, the definition of these categories is closely related to territorial considerations, as they require the crossing or non-crossing of an international border. Territorial changes can thus modify the status of a person, depending on which side of the border this person finds herself. For instance, in the case of the former Soviet Union, 65 million Russians found themselves outside Russia when the Federation created in 1924 ceased to exist. Some of them started to move back to Russia as they realised they had become foreigners in the place where they had lived for so long. When the Special Representative on Internally Displaced Persons visited Russia in 1992, he discussed the matter with the Head of the Russian Federal Migration Service who said that she considered that persons of Russian nationality, which could be acquired by any citizen of the former Soviet Union, came to Russia as internally displaced persons and not as refugees. According to the Ministry of the Interior, displaced persons qualified as internally displaced persons if they had acquired Russian nationality or as refugees if they came from another Republic. In fact, it seemed that the terms 'internally displaced persons' and 'refugees' were used interchangeably by the Russian authorities.[14]

The first section of this chapter explores the relationship between the two categories of displaced persons, internally displaced persons and refugees, and in particular the distinct conceptual basis which has seen different frameworks of protection applied to the two groups. It

---

[13] See P. Kourula, *Broadening the Edges: Refugee Definition and International Protection Revisited* (The Hague: Martinus Nijhoff Publishers, 1997), 71–85, for an analysis of the various formulas employed in the Conference documents.

[14] See F. M. Deng, *Protecting the Dispossessed: A Challenge for the International Community* (Washington DC: Brookings Institution, 1993), 40–8. See also the situation in East Timor, *Internally Displaced Persons: Report of the Representative of the Secretary-General, Mr Francis M. Deng, Profile in Displacement: East Timor*, E/CN.4/2000/83/Add.3, 4 April 2000, paras. 24–6.

considers why the current refugee definition excludes internally displaced persons from its ambit, and the arguments for situating the two
groups within a single legal status. Having explored the differences, the
emphasis is put on the consequences flowing from such differences (the
border-crossing requirement, state sovereignty, in-country protection).
The second section discusses issues of legal definitions for the internally
displaced. It examines the various elements of the 1992 definition of the
Secretary-General and points to the problems raised by that definition,
explaining the move to a new definition of the internally displaced. It
will be argued that any attempt to define internally displaced persons
must focus on the existence of human rights violations.

Refugees and internally displaced persons

The concept of refugee

In order to understand why internally displaced persons were not
included in the refugee definition, a good starting-point is to analyse
this definition. Before the UNHCR was created and the 1951 definition
adopted, refugee instruments were situation-specific. Between the two
World Wars, attention focused on specific groups or categories, such as
German and Russian refugees, for whom special international arrangements were adopted.[15] The International Refugee Organization (IRO) created in 1947 as a UN agency, took a similar approach, and its mandate
covered very specific groups of displaced persons.[16] The 1951 Convention
was thus the first international legal text not to focus on any particular
group of refugees.

The conceptualisation of the refugee problem upon which the 1951
definition is based is probably rooted in the political situation which
prevailed at the end of the Second World War. The wording of the 1951
Convention may have been influenced by the events which had just
occurred in Europe and resulted in the persecution and killing of millions of people, many of whom were targeted because of some attribute
or aspect of their identity. The 1951 Convention reflects the political concerns of its drafters who were primarily Western European states and

---

[15] See Goodwin-Gill, *The Refugee*, pp. 4–7, and J. Hathaway, *The Law of Refugee Status*
(Toronto: Butterworths, 1991), 2–6.
[16] See excerpts of the Constitution of the IRO, in K. Musalo, J. Moore and R. A. Boswell,
Refugee Law and Policy: Cases and Materials (Durham, NC: Carolina Academic Press, 1997),
29.

the United States. States belonging to the Communist bloc refused to participate in the drafting of the Convention and boycotted the vote.[17] As a result, the definition focuses mainly on civil and political rights, as it establishes that a refugee is a person who:

as a result of events occurring before 1 January 1951 and owing to a well-founded fear of being persecuted for reasons of race, religion, nationality, membership of a particular social group or political opinion, is outside the country of his nationality and is unable or, owing to such fear, is unwilling to avail himself of the protection of that country.[18]

Until 1967, when the Protocol deleted the temporal and geographical limitations,[19] the application of the Convention was restricted to persons fleeing events occurring in Europe before 1 January 1951. The 1951 Convention was a deliberately restrictive instrument, because states wished the granting of refugee status to remain exceptional.[20] It has been argued that the refugee definition was drafted in such a manner so as to address the problem of political dissidents fleeing Communist states.[21] The 1951 Convention was thus applied as a political instrument in order to condemn the repressive policies implemented in those states.

No detailed analysis of the 1951 refugee definition will be undertaken here, others having done it elsewhere.[22] In short, the asylum seeker must demonstrate the existence of a 'well-founded fear of being persecuted for reasons of race, religion, nationality, membership of a particular social group or political opinion' to obtain refugee status. This phrase has been the subject of intense discussion as it is open to very different interpretations. No supervisory body has been set up to ensure a common interpretation of the provisions of the 1951 Convention and this has allowed different interpretations of the definition by states[23] and other

---

[17] See J. Hathaway, 'A Reconsideration of the Underlying Premise of Refugee Law' (1990) 31 *Harvard International Law Journal* 129 at 145.

[18] Art. 1(A)(2) of the 1951 Convention.

[19] Protocol Relating to the Status of Refugees, 1967, 606 UNTS 267.

[20] See A. R. Zolberg, A. Suhrke and S. Aguayo, *Escape from Violence: Conflict and the Refugee Crisis in the Developing World* (New York: Oxford University Press, 1989), 25.

[21] See Hathaway, 'A Reconsideration', 148–51.

[22] For a summary and analysis of the 1951 definition, see Hathaway, *The Law of Refugee Status*, and Goodwill-Gill, *The Refugee*.

[23] See J. Y. Carlier, D. Vanheule, K. Hullmann and C. Pena Galiano (eds.), *Who's a Refugee? A Comparative Case Law Study* (The Hague: Kluwer Law International, 1997), for the various national refugee definitions.

actors.[24] States have often construed it in a narrow manner contrary to the guidelines issued by UNHCR.[25] In any case, the applicant must be able to demonstrate not only that he or she is likely to be persecuted if sent back to his or her country of origin, but also that this persecution would occur on account of one of the Convention reasons.

It can be argued that the current refugee definition is inadequate, because the persecution-based standard is too restrictive. A dissenting view is held by Martin who defends a narrow refugee definition in order to maintain the political support for refugees and to guarantee asylum as an entitlement.[26] In some respects, refugees now constitute a privileged 'caste' among the dispossessed, who can benefit from the advantages granted by their legal status.[27] Many persons who are clearly in need of international protection are not covered by the definition, no matter how generously its elements are interpreted. Until recently, women suffering gender-related persecution were not considered to fall within the refugee definition. First, persecution commonly targeted at them was not traditionally seen as political persecution because it tends to take place in the private realm. Secondly, there have been difficulties in identifying social groups for definitional purposes. Indeed, it may be problematic to characterise a certain group of women as a particular social group.[28] Gender-related violence is now more widely considered to fall within the refugee definition, and UNHCR has issued guidelines on gender-based persecution.[29] Homosexuals who are persecuted because of their sexual orientation sometimes face similar problems when they

---

[24] For an analysis of the interpretations of the refugee definition by various international bodies, in particular UN bodies, see Kourula, *Broadening the Edges*.

[25] UNHCR, *Handbook on Procedures and Criteria for Determining Refugee Status* (Geneva: UNHCR, 1979).

[26] See D. A. Martin, 'The Refugee Concept: On Definitions, Politics, and the Careful Use of a Scarce Resource', in H. Adelman (ed.), *Refugee Policy: Canada and the United States* (North York, Ontario: York Lanes Press Ltd, 1991), 30–51.

[27] See J. Hathaway, 'Reconceiving Refugee Law as Human Rights Protection', in K. E. Mahoney and P. Mahoney (eds.), *Human Rights in the Twenty-First Century: A Global Challenge* (Dordrecht: Martinus Nijhoff Publishers, 1993), 659–78 at 660. See also Zolberg *et al.*, *Escape from Violence*, 3.

[28] For an overall view on the issue of women refugees, see the Special issue of the *International Journal of Refugee Law* on gender-based persecution, January 1998. See also J. Castel, 'Rape, Sexual Assault and the Meaning of Persecution' (1992) 4 *International Journal of Refugee Law* 39, and A. Macklin, 'Refugee Women and the Imperatives of Categories' (1995) 17 *Human Rights Quarterly* 213.

[29] See UNHCR, *Guidelines on International Protection: Gender-Related Persecution Within the Context of Article 1A(2) of the 1951 Convention and/or Its 1967 Protocol Relating to the Status of Refugees*, 7 May 2002, reproduced in (2002) 14 *International Journal of Refugee Law* 457.

apply for asylum.[30] Likewise, people fleeing armed conflicts cannot easily demonstrate that they would face individual persecution if they were to return.

Regional variants of the refugee definition were devised in order to compensate for the deficiencies of the 1951 definition. The construction of an expanded refugee definition was first undertaken by African states in 1969[31] and by Latin American states fifteen years later.[32] The aim was to address the specific problems encountered by African and Latin American states and which the 1951 definition does not cover. Article 1(2) of the 1969 OAU Convention provides that 'the term "refugee" shall also apply to every person who, owing to external aggression, foreign domination or events seriously disturbing public order in either part or the whole of his country of origin or nationality, is compelled to leave his place of habitual residence in order to seek refuge in another place outside his country of origin or nationality'. The 1984 Cartagena Declaration includes in its refugee definition 'persons who have fled their country because their lives, safety or freedom have been threatened by generalized violence, foreign aggression, internal conflicts, massive violation of human rights or other circumstances which have seriously disturbed public order'. The refugee definition was thus expanded in order to cover a wider range of situations in which people are compelled to move across borders. In the two definitions mentioned above, more emphasis is also put on the causes of displacement and the wider political context of the country of origin.

Industrialised countries implicitly acknowledge that the 1951 definition is outdated by allowing some individuals denied refugee status for not meeting the requirements of the refugee definition to remain in the country on humanitarian grounds.[33] To some extent, the development

---

[30] See for instance S. Russell, 'Sexual Orientation and Refugee Claims Based on "Membership of a Particular Social Group" under the 1951 Refugee Convention' in F. Nicholson and P. Twomey (eds.), Current Issues of UK Asylum Law and Policy (Aldershot: Ashgate, 1998), 133–51.

[31] OAU Convention Relating to the Specific Aspects of Refugee Problems in Africa, 1001 UNTS 45 (hereinafter the 1969 OAU Convention). For more detail, see for instance the special issue of the International Journal of Refugee Law, 'Organisation of African Unity/United Nations High Commissioner for Refugees Addis Ababa Symposium on Refugees and the Problems of Forced Population Displacements in Africa, 8–10 September 1994', July 1995.

[32] Cartagena Declaration on Refugees, 22 November 1984, OAS/Ser.L/V/II.66, doc.10, rev.1. 190 (hereinafter the 1984 Cartagena Declaration).

[33] See G. Goodwin-Gill, 'The Individual Refugee, the 1951 Convention and the Treaty of Amsterdam', in E. Guild and C. Harlow (eds.), Implementing Amsterdam: Immigration and Asylum Rights in EC Law (Oxford: Hart Publishing, 2001), 141–63 at 150.

of the concept of temporary protection also shows that they are ready to admit some groups who, even though they do not always qualify for refugee status, are in need of protection. However, persons who are allowed to remain, but are not granted refugee status, cannot benefit from the rights attached to this legal status. In particular, the right to *non-refoulement* is the most important right which is granted to all refugees and originally only to them. Article 33 of the 1951 Convention states that a refugee should not be returned to his or her country if he or she would face any threat to his or her life or liberty. This principle of *non-refoulement* has been considered to be the cornerstone of the international refugee protection system.[34] It has since been developed in the context of human rights more generally.[35] Refugee status also activates other obligations upon states which are listed in the Convention. State parties to the Convention must grant a certain range of employment and welfare rights, and issue identity papers and travel documents to those granted refugee status.

There is no mention of the right to asylum in the 1951 Convention. Some attempts have been made to create legal obligations that go beyond the 1951 Convention and establish such a right of territorial asylum. Following the adoption of the UN Declaration on Territorial Asylum in 1967, the Carnegie Endowment Working Group proposed its first draft Convention on Territorial Asylum in 1972,[36] which led to the United Nations Conference on Territorial Asylum in Geneva in 1977. However, the conference failed to adopt the draft Convention, and no further attempt has since been made to develop a right of territorial asylum.

From a more fundamental perspective, the current refugee definition suffers from an inadequate theoretical basis. The concept of refugee is broader than the legal definition. This is reflected in the disjunction between the legal definition and the common meaning usually given to the word 'refugee'. In daily language, the term refers to anyone who has been compelled to leave his or her home, no matter what the circumstances are or which destination is sought. It is generally

---

[34] See G. Goodwin-Gill, '*Non-Refoulement* and the New Asylum Seekers' (1986) 26 *Virginia Journal of International Law* 897.

[35] See E. Lauterpacht and D. Bethlehem, 'The Scope and Content of the Principle of *Non-Refoulement*: Opinion', in E. Feller, V. Türk and F. Nicholson (eds.), *Refugee Protection in International Law: UNHCR's Global Consultations on International Protection* (Cambridge: Cambridge University Press, 2003), 87–177 at 150–63.

[36] See A. Grahl-Madsen, *Territorial Asylum* (Stockholm: Almqvist & Wiksell International, 1980), 174–6.

assumed that what is most important is that the refugee suffers from a lack of protection from his or her state. The legal definition is based on the basic premise that the bond between the citizen and the state has been severed. However, as argued by Shacknove, it is also based on other assumptions which are questionable. The drafters of the 1951 Convention adopted the view that the only physical manifestations of this severed bond between the citizen and the state are persecution and alienage and that these are 'the necessary and sufficient conditions for determining refugeehood'.[37] The regional definitions mentioned above demonstrate that the citizen/state bond can be severed in many ways other than by persecution. In fact, persecution does not capture the essence of refugeehood, namely the failure of the state to protect the citizen's basic needs.[38] The responsibility to provide protection, which includes not merely the physical security of the individual, is the *raison d'être* of the sovereign state.[39] The notion of basic needs suggests that the state is to protect the individual's political and civil, but also economic and social rights, hence the inadequacy of focusing solely on political persecution. A more appropriate approach may be the human rights one, which does not consider persecution the only 'distinguishing feature of refugeehood'.[40]

Nevertheless, Shacknove admits that a concept of refugeehood which is tied to basic needs is not politically acceptable. He prefers to define a refugee as a 'person whose government fails to protect his basic needs, who has no remaining recourse than to seek international restitution of these needs and who is so situated that international assistance is possible'.[41] This definition has the merit of challenging the current legal definition and attempts to reconstruct a new definition from the first basic premise that a bond exists between the citizen and the state and that this bond has been severed in the case of refugeehood. Several elements of the current definition (the criteria of persecution, importance of border-crossing) are challenged, and this could lead to the inclusion of at least some internally displaced persons in this definition. However, this does not go as far as to acknowledge that all internally displaced

---

[37] A. Shacknove, 'Who is a Refugee?' (1985) 95 *Ethics* 274 at 275.   [38] *Ibid.*, 277.

[39] See for instance Locke, who saw the state's *raison d'être* in 'the protection of individuals' rights as laid down by God's will and as enshrined in law', quoted by D. Held (ed.), *States and Societies* (Oxford: Martin Robertson & Co. Ltd, 1983), 10.

[40] G. Coles, 'Placing the Refugee Issues on the New International Agenda' (unpublished), quoted by Hathaway, 'Reconceiving Refugee Law', 663.

[41] Shacknove, 'Who is a Refugee?', 282.

persons can be considered as refugees as it still presupposes that people are within the reach of international assistance. The principle of sovereignty is thus not completely abandoned, but the formula challenges the existing legal definition.

The importance of the border-crossing element: inherent to the concept of refugeehood or imposed by international law?

The importance of border-crossing in the current legal definition arises from the centrality of the state in the international legal system, but also represents a clear indication that the bond between the citizen and his state has been severed. However, as a consequence of what has been said above, it is conceptually irrelevant to the refugee definition, as refugeehood refers to a political relationship, or rather the end of a political relationship, not a territorial relationship.[42] Why then is the requirement of border-crossing (or alienage, as it is also referred to) so fundamental to the current refugee definition? The answer is that it derives from the principle of state sovereignty which remains the basis of the international legal system. The element of border-crossing certainly reinforces the 'statist' perspective of international refugee law.

It has been argued that border-crossing has not always constituted a crucial requirement in refugee definitions and that this element is not so fundamental to the refugee definition that it cannot be dropped.[43] However, Goodwin-Gill argues that alienage has always been an implicit requirement and therefore no refugee definition has ever included internally displaced persons in its provisions.[44] Long before 1951, the central importance of border-crossing in the refugee definition had been established. In 1938, Simpson even characterised alienage, which results from border-crossing, as the 'essential quality' of the refugee, which recalls that he or she is fundamentally an unprotected alien.[45] Hathaway also believes that alienage constitutes a crucial element of the refugee definition even though he acknowledges that it does not constitute a conceptual requirement.[46] Presence outside the country represents the physical

---

[42] Ibid., 283.
[43] See L. T. Lee, 'Internally Displaced Persons and Refugees: Toward a Legal Synthesis?' (1996) 9 Journal of Refugee Studies 27 at 31.
[44] See Goodwin-Gill, The Refugee, 4.
[45] J. H. Simpson, Refugees: A Preliminary Report of a Survey (London: Royal Institute of International Affairs, 1938), 1.
[46] See Hathaway, The Law of Refugee Status, 29.

manifestation that the bond between the state and the citizen referred to above has been severed.[47]

When discussing the future provisions of the 1951 Convention, some states such as Greece mentioned their problems with internally displaced persons and raised concerns that this question had not been properly addressed. These states did not explicitly call for the inclusion of these groups in a refugee definition, but expressed some hope that they would be covered by the new Convention. Thus, when referring to the persons displaced by the civil war, Greece stressed that 'the problem of legal protection did not arise in their case, for they were in their own country, but their material distress was causing grave anxiety in the Greek Government'.[48] However, states such as France and the United States clearly opposed such attempts to discuss the problem of internal displacement. They argued that internally displaced persons raised problems of a different nature which should not be dealt with within the framework of the 1951 Convention. For instance, Mrs Roosevelt of the United States declared that 'internal refugee situations . . . were separate problems of a different character, in which no question of protection of the persons concerned was involved'.[49] She added that it was the responsibility of the states to deal with these problems which 'should not be confused with the problem before the General Assembly, namely, the provision of protection for those outside their own countries, who lacked the protection of a Government and who required asylum'.[50] Such opposition led to the exclusion of internally displaced persons from the refugee definition. For the drafters of the Convention, the text was only concerned with the protection and assistance of a specific group of persons, i.e. those outside their country of origin. One must also bear in mind that the resources available for dealing with the refuge problem were limited, which was another reason for excluding internally displaced persons from the discussion which was taking place at the time.

Hathaway lists two other reasons for the exclusion of internally displaced persons from the 1951 definition.[51] First, states should not address the problem of internal displacement by extending the refugee definition to seek to include the internally displaced because it remains

---

[47] See P. Tuitt, *False Images: The Law's Reconstruction of the Refugee* (London: Pluto Press, 1996), 11.
[48] GAOR, 4th Sess., Third Committee, Summary Records (1949), 110.
[49] GAOR, 4th Sess., Plenary (1949), 473.   [50] *Ibid.*
[51] See Hathaway, *The Law of Refugee Status*, 30–1.

the primary duty of the state to protect its own population. Secondly, it would constitute a violation of national sovereignty as the problems raised by internally displaced persons are invariably part of the internal affairs of the state. In contrast, the refugee is situated within the reach of the international community. It seems that the historical importance of the border-crossing element is imposed by what remain the cardinal principles of international law, namely state sovereignty, and the closely related principles of territorial integrity and non-intervention.[52] However, although it was demonstrated above that the crossing of a frontier is *conceptually* irrelevant to the notion of refugeehood, I do not downplay its importance and suggest that it is '*merely* an incidence of law constrained by a more powerful norm'.[53] This element is fundamental to the refugee definition which is based upon international law and should therefore reflect its most important principle, i.e. state sovereignty. The border-crossing element establishes a clear legal distinction between refugees and internally displaced persons, a distinction which should be maintained for the reasons given below.

Refugees and internally displaced persons: a legal synthesis?

The idea of a legal synthesis between refugees and internally displaced persons has been advanced by Luke Lee.[54] He proposes to achieve this by deleting the border-crossing element from the refugee definition. The basis of his argument lies in the idea that the requirement of border-crossing has lost its relevance in the post-Cold War era and that it must be dropped in order to give states, international organisations and NGOs the legal capacity to address the problem of internal displacement.

Lee first tries to demonstrate that the element of border-crossing is closely linked to the political situation which prevailed during the Cold War: he believes that it had not been such a crucial criterion in previous refugee definitions and that it became so because of the importance of the Iron Curtain, which was the physical manifestation of the ideological divide between the two blocs. The typical situation envisaged by those who drafted and subsequently developed the 1951 refugee definition was of a political dissident *crossing* the Iron Curtain or the

---

[52] See for instance *Declaration on Principles of International Law Concerning Friendly Relations and Co-operation Among States in Accordance with the Charter of the United Nations*, GA Res. 2625 (XXV), 24 October 1970.

[53] Tuitt, *False Images*, 11 (emphasis added).   [54] Lee, 'Toward a Legal Synthesis'.

Berlin Wall and seeking asylum in the West. Now that the Cold War has ended, Lee does not see any justification for maintaining the element of border-crossing and believes that the refugee definition needs to be revised.[55]

He also emphasises the practical difficulties linked to the requirement of border-crossing. This requirement sometimes makes it difficult to draw clear distinctions between refugees, internally displaced persons and returnees. This problem is exacerbated by the fact that the exact location of a border is closely linked to the diplomatic recognition of the state(s) concerned.[56] However, his main argument for abandoning the requirement of border-crossing relates to human rights: he believes that the maintenance of an artificial distinction between refugees and internally displaced persons creates an unfair difference in the standard of human rights protection between the two groups. A remedy for the existence of such inequality of protection would be to merge the two groups and create a single legal status for both.

However, the requirement of border-crossing is not intended to separate the weak (internally displaced persons) from the strong (those who manage to go abroad).[57] Also, Lee does not foresee the possible implications of his proposition. However similar their plight may be, refugees and internally displaced persons cannot be given the same legal status, because they require protection that is different in nature. Internally displaced persons remain within the jurisdiction of their own state and responsibility to protect and assist them should not be shifted entirely to the international community.[58] The protection given to refugees is a *surrogate* protection for persons who have lost the protection of their country and are outside of its borders. As a result, the international refugee protection regime imposes specific obligations on states to protect persecuted aliens. In the case of internally displaced persons, the protection required must remain a *complementary* protection which exists in parallel with national protection, unless national protection is not available. Therefore, I would contend that a legal synthesis between refugees and internally displaced persons is not advisable, as it could possibly undermine the protection system which already exists for refugees.

---

[55] *Ibid.*, 32–3.   [56] *Ibid.*, 34.   [57] See Tuitt, *False Images*, 11.

[58] See *Internally Displaced Persons: Report of the Representative of the Secretary-General, Mr Francis M. Deng*, E/CN.4/1995/50, 2 February 1995 (hereinafter the *1995 Deng Report*), para. 122.

The problem raised by formulating a legal definition of the internally displaced

The establishment of a separate *legal* definition of the internally displaced does not seem to be advisable either. A formal legal definition would never be comprehensive enough to cover the numerous situations which result in the internal displacement of persons. As will be seen later, the root causes of internal displacement are varied: they include natural disasters, inter-state conflicts, intra-state conflicts, human rights violations, development projects and internal strife, to cite only some of the most common situations producing internal displacement. A similar problem is raised by the 1951 refugee definition which excludes from its scope groups of people who are nevertheless in need of international protection. An unduly restrictive legal definition for internally displaced persons would have the effect of excluding some groups of internally displaced persons from its scope.

More fundamental arguments run against the establishment of a legal definition for internally displaced persons. As illustrated by events in the former Yugoslavia, it is not only practically impossible, but also morally questionable to draw distinctions between refugees and internally displaced persons, or between the displaced and the non-displaced. It appears *in some cases* to be artificial to distinguish different categories of people in need and the same degree of assistance should be available to all of them. The inability to distinguish refugees from internally displaced persons is not always fatal and it is actually preferable not to apply such a distinction in some situations. The danger of a legal definition would be to give priority to a certain group and create different standards of treatment when all groups are in the same material conditions: all should simply be treated as victims of human rights violations.

The International Committee of the Red Cross (ICRC) adopts this position and provides protection and assistance to all, whether they have been displaced or not. According to the Special Representative on Internally Displaced Persons, some problems can be addressed without the need for a precise definition and his position is that assistance should be given, not according to the legal status of the persons concerned, but according to their needs.[59] This approach is shared by UNHCR which

---

[59] See F. M. Deng, 'Dealing with the Displaced: A Challenge to the International Community' (1995) 1 *Global Governance* 45 at 50.

prefers to put the emphasis on particular situations rather than on specific categories of persons. As a result, it has extended its mandate to persons who are not refugees.[60]

Sometimes, those who stay behind actually face greater dangers than those who manage to flee. Commenting on the Draft Declaration of Principles of International Law on Internally Displaced Persons proposed by Lee, Hathaway wonders 'why one ought to effectively privilege the internally displaced persons in comparison to other internal human rights victims'.[61] If a separate legal status is afforded to internally displaced persons, this would constitute a major challenge to the principle of state sovereignty. In any case, even if we are to question this principle, this approach may not be the most appropriate one. Again, Hathaway rightly observes that:

> if we are serious that we are now in a position to enter behind the wall of sovereignty, we ought not to privilege those who are displaced, effectively doing a disservice to those who are trapped in their own homes, and we ought simply to get about the business of enforcing international human rights law internally if we honestly believe that is a possibility.[62]

The previous section referred to the proposal to merge the two categories of refugees and internally displaced persons into a single legal regime and concluded that this was not advisable. Similarly, the creation of a separate legal regime for internally displaced persons is undesirable. The internally displaced remain entitled to human rights protection from their government, in contrast to refugees who decided to give up any claim to that protection by placing themselves under the international regime of protection.

It is therefore important to maintain a clear legal distinction between refugees and internally displaced persons, and to be aware of the potential implications for the refugee protection regime of improving protection strategies for the internally displaced: protection for internally displaced persons must not undermine the institution of asylum. Another important consequence of the analysis developed above is that, because refugee law cannot apply to internally displaced persons, 'the promotion of international human rights law . . . appears to be one way to solve the problem'.[63]

---

[60] See Chapter 3, first section.
[61] *Proceedings of the American Society of Public International Law 1996*, 562.   [62] *Ibid.*, 562.
[63] C. Harvey, *Seeking Asylum in the UK: Problems and Prospects* (London: Butterworths, 2000), 69.

One must draw a distinction between a formal legal definition and an operational one. Each serves different purposes and may have different consequences. A legal definition seeks to establish a legal regime of international protection for internally displaced persons, whereas an operational definition is aimed at facilitating material assistance and protection measures on the ground. The differences which exist between refugees and internally displaced persons demonstrate the need for different approaches and the same strategy cannot be adopted with regard to both. It follows that a legal definition for internally displaced persons cannot create rights and obligations similar to those contained in the 1951 Convention. The following section will therefore discuss the elements of an *operational* definition of internally displaced persons.

Defining internally displaced persons

The transposition of the refugee definition

As a preliminary remark, it must be noted that 'there is no firm agreement . . . on what should be included in the definition [of internally displaced persons]'.[64] This lack of consensus on the elements of a definition has been a source of confusion. When attempting to draw up a definition of internally displaced persons, the refugee definition obviously offers some guidance, but here a humanitarian approach rather than a legalistic one will be adopted. However, Melander's definition of internally displaced persons only refers to the 1951 refugee definition by using the 'well-founded fear of persecution' criterion. His initial approach is that there are two categories of refugees, i.e. human rights refugees and humanitarian law refugees.[65] For him, the first category is covered by the 1951 Convention whereas the second category is offered a lower standard of protection from international humanitarian law. He then extends this reasoning to internally displaced persons and argues that 'there are persons who have left their habitual residence in order to avoid humanitarian law violations, i.e. an internal war, but without having crossed an international border. There are also persons who have left their habitual residence because of a well-founded fear of persecution

---

[64] *1995 Deng Report*, note 58 above, para. 118.

[65] See G. Melander, *The Two Refugee Definitions* (Lund, Sweden: University of Lund, 1988), cited in G. Melander, 'Internally Displaced Persons', in G. Alfredsson and P. Macalister-Smith (eds.), *The Living Law of Nations: Essays on Refugees, Minorities, Indigenous Peoples and the Human Rights of Other Vulnerable Groups in Memory of Atle Grahl-Madsen* (Kehl am Rhein: Engel, 1996), 69–74 at 69.

(human rights violations), but still remain in their country of origin.'[66] One could argue here that Melander confuses persecution with human rights violations and that the two notions do not necessarily overlap. Moreover, such a distinction between two categories of internally displaced persons appears to be unnecessary.

It has been argued that internally displaced persons are persons who would be refugees had they left their country.[67] This has been the approach favoured by UNHCR.[68] It is unduly restrictive and the case can also be made that persons other than those who have a well-founded fear of persecution on one of the Convention grounds should be included in the definition. The mere transposition of the refugee definition to our context would amount to adopting a very narrow approach. Indeed, most internally displaced persons are found in situations of internal armed conflict, communal violence or systematic human rights violations, all of which are generally not covered by the 1951 refugee definition.

References to the 1969 OAU Convention definition or the 1984 Cartagena Declaration may be more appropriate as they both cover the situations mentioned above.[69] These two definitions would probably be 'more useful as a standard of comparison'.[70] So far, most of the definitions proposed emphasise the causes of displacement and this reflects the increased emphasis on the prevention of 'forced' population movements. However, not all agree on what situations should be covered and the question of the inclusion of causes of internal displacement such as natural disasters or development projects has been a matter of controversy.

Situations leading to internal displacement

Some of the causes of internal displacement are specific to these movements and have not been discussed with regard to refugee movements. This is why the increasing attention paid to internally displaced persons also sheds new light on problems such as natural disasters, development projects or forced relocation. The recent willingness of the UN to tackle

---

[66] Ibid., 70.

[67] See Comprehensive Study Prepared by F. Deng, Representative of the Secretary-General on the Human Rights Issues Related to Internally Displaced Persons, E/CN.4/1993/35, para. 50.

[68] See UNHCR, UNHCR's Operational Experience with Internally Displaced Persons (Geneva: UNHCR, 1994), 76.

[69] See 1995 Deng Report, note 58 above, para. 118.

[70] F. M. Deng, 'The International Protection of the Internally Displaced' (1995) 7 International Journal of Refugee Law (special issue) 74 at 77.

the problem of internal displacement has offered the opportunity to address these issues from a new perspective.

Some commentators do not consider people displaced by natural disasters, such as drought, floods or earthquakes, as internally displaced persons. These authors emphasise the element of coercion which characterises forced displacement. They interpret coercion as requiring action either by a government or by an insurgent group. They thus refer only to human rights violations.[71] This position can be justified by the fact that 'in the case of most natural or man-made disasters, states are generally willing to extend available internal resources and receive foreign assistance to help displaced persons'.[72] However, internal movements of population caused by natural disasters can also have human rights implications or causes. The 1992 Analytical Report of the Secretary-General on internally displaced persons mentions, for instance, that the relocation subsequent to the mid-1980s famine in Ethiopia was accompanied by grave violations of human rights.[73] The dividing line between natural and man-made disasters is not always entirely clear. In some cases, the reluctance of the authorities to allow international relief into the country can indirectly trigger internal movements of population and/or aggravate the consequences of a natural disaster. The key issue should be whether assistance and protection are made available by the state's authorities.

Another situation which can be envisaged here is displacement caused by development projects. According to the World Bank, around 10 million people have been displaced by development projects every year since 1990.[74] The two main causes of displacement are dam construction and urban transportation projects. Others include the creation of forest and reserve parks, and the construction of mining and thermal power plants.[75] The level of displacement is usually higher in domestic

---

[71] See *Proceedings of the American Society of Public International Law 1996*, 559. See also Norwegian Refugee Council, *Institutional Arrangements for Internally Displaced Persons: the Ground Level Experience* (Oslo: Norwegian Refugee Council, 1995), 7, and UNHCR, *The State of the World's Refugees, A Humanitarian Agenda* (Geneva: UNHCR, 1997), 99.

[72] C. E. Lewis, 'Dealing with the Problem of Internally Displaced Persons' (1992) 6 *Georgetown Immigration Law Journal* 693 at 694.

[73] See *Analytical Report of the Secretary-General on Internally Displaced Persons*, E/CN.4/1992/23, 14 February 1992 (hereinafter the *Analytical Report*), paras. 34–5.

[74] See W. Courtland Robinson, *Risks and Rights: The Causes, Consequences, and Challenges of Development-Induced Displacement*, Brookings Institution occasional paper, May 2003, 3.

[75] See M. M. Cernea, 'Understanding and Preventing Impoverishment from Displacement: Reflections on the State of Knowledge' (1995) 8 *Journal of Refugee Studies* 245 at 250.

rather than internationally financed projects because the World Bank now grants more importance to the issue of displacement when decisions to finance a project are made.[76] Some large-scale projects can cause the internal displacement of hundreds of thousands of persons. For instance, it is estimated that the Three Gorges Dam on the Yangtze river in China will cause the displacement of about 1.2 million people within the next ten years.[77] Another well-known case of development-induced displacement is that of the Sardar Sarovar project in India on which construction started in 1987. It has been the subject of several years of protests, and the World Bank even withdrew its support for the project in 1993.[78] In most cases, the government helps with the relocation of the populations displaced and even pays financial compensation to them, but this is not always the case.[79] In some cases, projects are not decided in consultation with the local population and/or minority groups suffer disproportionate levels of displacement.[80] Again, the central questions should be whether the government really offers assistance to the populations displaced by these development projects, whether there is discrimination in the decisions to relocate minority groups[81] and, more fundamentally, whether such displacement can be described as 'forced' or voluntary.

Forced relocation represents another case of involuntary internal displacement.[82] For instance, one of the gravest cases of internal displacement is taking place in the south east of Turkey where about one million Kurds are said to be displaced.[83] However, it is only recently that UN bodies have addressed the issue of forced relocation. The

---

[76] See Internally Displaced Persons: Report of the Representative of the Secretary-General, Mr Francis M. Deng, E/CN.4/1998/53, 11 February 1998, para. 13.

[77] See M. Stein, 'The Three Gorges: The Unexamined Toll of Development-Induced Displacement', Forced Migration Review, vol. 1, January–April 1998, 8. See also S. Steil and D. Yuefang, 'Policies and Practices in Three Gorges Resettlement: A Field Account', Forced Migration Review, vol. 12, January 2002.

[78] For more detail, see P. Cullet, 'Human Rights and Displacement: The Indian Supreme Court Decision on Sardar Sarovar in International Perspective' (2001) 50 International and Comparative Law Quarterly 973.

[79] See World Commission on Dams, Dams and Development: A New Framework for Decision-Making (London: Earthscan Publications, 2000), 105–10.

[80] Ibid., 110–12.

[81] See also the 'Comprehensive Human Rights Guidelines Concerning the Practice of Development-Based Displacement' in Expert Seminar on the Practice of Forced Evictions: Report of the Secretary-General, E/CN.4/Sub.2/1997/7, Annex, 2 July 1997.

[82] See the Analytical Report, note 73 above, paras. 25–30.

[83] See Internally Displaced Persons: Report of the Representative of the Secretary-General, Mr Francis M. Deng, Profile in Displacement: Turkey, E/CN.4/2003/86/Add.2, 27 November 2002, para. 8.

Sub-Commission on the Prevention of Discrimination and Protection of Minorities (now renamed the Sub-Commission on the Promotion and Prevention of Human Rights) started to look at the problem of population transfers in 1993.[84] It has condemned forced evictions as 'a gross violation of a broad range of human rights'.[85] Previously, most authors had focused on situations in which people flee spontaneously or voluntarily (the distinction between voluntary and involuntary displacement being controversial). Forced relocation obviously involves a situation of coerced movement and it should be included in any definition of internally displaced persons. If it is the government itself which forcibly relocates some populations, these populations are by definition not protected by their government. Minority groups are especially vulnerable to forced relocation by authoritarian regimes. Such movements of populations do not take place only in times of armed conflict, but also in times of peace. Principle 7 of the Guiding Principles on Internal Displacement[86] provides that legal safeguards must be put in place to ensure that decisions requiring the displacement of persons are not taken arbitrarily: national law should specify the permissible grounds and conditions of displacement, and minimum procedural guarantees must be provided to protect the displaced populations. Finally, forcible transfers of population now constitute a crime against humanity, as recognised in the Statute of the International Criminal Court.[87]

A broad approach is also required with regard to returnees who return to their state, but are unable to return to their former homes and find themselves internally displaced. For instance, some returnees in the former Yugoslavia have discovered that the area where they used to live is now dominated by a different ethnic group which does not welcome their return. Also, they often find out that their house is now occupied by another family.[88] These people are sometimes referred to as the 'returned displaced'.[89]

The Analytical Report of the Secretary-General referred to all the scenarios described above, except development projects. What is important in the case of displacement caused by natural disasters and development-induced displacement is that they can involve human

---

[84] See *Human Rights and Population Transfers: Final Report of the Special Rapporteur*, E/CN.4/Sub.2/1997/23, Annex II, 27 June 1997.

[85] Sub-Comm. Res. 1998/9, 20 August 1998.

[86] E/CN.4/1998/53/Add.2, 11 February 1998. See Annex 1.

[87] Art. 7 of the Rome Statute of the International Criminal Court (1998) 37 ILM 999.

[88] See Chapter 5, fourth section.   [89] *1995 Deng Report*, note 58 above, para. 120.

rights violations and these two situations should therefore be examined as well.

Attempts at a definition

Views vary as to who should be considered to be internally displaced; which situations require international action; and what form it should take. As in the case of refugees, the issue of protection remains central, and the challenge is to find a precise, but flexible, definition which would cover all those who are internally displaced and in need of international protection.[90] A first attempt at a definition was made by then UN Secretary-General Boutros-Ghali in his Analytical Report in 1992, which defined internally displaced persons as:

Persons who have been forced to flee their homes suddenly or unexpectedly in large numbers, as a result of armed conflict, internal strife, systematic violations of human rights or natural or man-made disasters; and who are within the territory of their own country.[91]

Since then, in-depth research has been undertaken in order to achieve a better understanding of the phenomenon of internal displacement. As a result, some elements of this definition have been partially modified or abandoned, because deeper knowledge of past and contemporary internal movements of populations have demonstrated that some elements of the Secretary-General's 1992 definition are not always characteristic of such movements. For instance, the 1992 definition described internally displaced persons as fleeing 'suddenly and unexpectedly in large numbers'. However, the two adverbs do not characterise all cases of internal displacement. Moreover, the 1992 definition included the element 'in large numbers' because it wanted to focus on situations of mass displacement and it was considered that other situations involved problems of a different nature which did not fall within the scope of the Analytical Report.[92] If the definition's purpose is to list the conditions which are to be met in order to trigger international action (in the form of relief operations), then this element might prove relevant. However, is it really necessary that internally displaced persons should be fleeing *en masse*? The definition should not be a quantitative one and should not focus solely on situations which involve sudden mass displacement of populations in war-like conditions. The most dramatic internal movements

---

[90] See Recommendation 40 of UNHCR/ICVA, *Oslo Declaration and Plan of Action*, UNHCR, Geneva, 1995.
[91] See the *Analytical Report*, note 73 above, para. 17.   [92] *Ibid.*

of persons which hit the news headlines often shift the focus of attention away from other, protracted, situations of internal displacement
which are not given extensive media coverage. Finally, the requirement
of 'large numbers' has proved 'less useful as a criterion for determining the eligibility of individuals for forms of protection such as travel
documents'.[93]

Research on current situations of internal displacement has demonstrated that internally displaced persons do not always flee in large
numbers. An example documented by the Special Representative on
Internally Displaced Persons is that of Colombia.[94] More than a million
people have been internally displaced (*desplazados*) as a result of protracted guerrilla and other paramilitary activities in the country. It has
been found that a great majority of the people do not flee 'unexpectedly
or suddenly', but that a different pattern of displacement exists. People
may first flee to a nearby town or village in search of security and still
go back to their farms during the day to pursue their normal economic
activities. If the degree of violence reaches a higher level, people then
consider going further and leaving their property for a longer period.
Moreover, people tend to flee in small groups in order not to attract
attention.[95] From this brief description, it appears that the Colombian
case does not fall within the ambit of the Secretary-General's definition
although it constitutes one of the most worrying situations of internal
displacement.[96] It is now widely accepted that there is no unique pattern of displacement, but that internal displacement can take various
forms: the definition should be flexible enough to cover a broad spec-
trum of situations. Most of the definitions proposed in the mid-1990s
take into account the case studies and no longer include the quantitative element.[97]

The part of the 1992 definition which reads 'who are within the territory of their own country' has also been modified to read 'who have

---

[93] R. Plender, 'The Legal Basis of International Jurisdiction to Act with Regard to the
Internally Displaced' (1994) 6 *International Journal of Refugee Law* 345 at 357.

[94] See *Internally Displaced Persons: Report of the Representative of the Secretary-General, Mr
Francis M. Deng, Profiles of Displacement: Colombia*, E/CN.4/1995/50/Add.1, 3 October 1994
(hereinafter *First Colombia Report*); and *Internally Displaced Persons: Report of the
Representative of the Secretary-General, Mr Francis M. Deng, Follow-Up Mission to Colombia*,
E/CN.4/2000/83/Add.1, 11 January 2000.

[95] See *First Colombia Report*, note 94 above, para. 13.

[96] For more detail, see L. Obregón and M. Stavropoulou, 'In Search of Hope: The Plight of
Displaced Colombians', in R. Cohen and F. M. Deng (eds.), *The Forsaken People: Case
Studies of the Internally Displaced* (Washington DC: Brookings Institution, 1998), 399–453.

[97] See for instance UNHCR, *UNHCR's Operational Experience*, 99 or *Proceedings of the American
Society of Public International Law 1996*, 555.

not crossed an internationally recognised state border'. Such modification by the Special Representative was made necessary by the problems raised by the dissolution of states such as the former Soviet Union and the former Yugoslavia at the beginning of the 1990s, i.e. at the time when the Secretary-General's definition was devised. As explained above, the dissolution of such states blurred the distinction between refugees and internally displaced persons. People who moved from one former republic of the federation to another had an unclear status due to the difficulties related to the recognition of the newly constituted states. The exact date when a state came into existence was not always easy to substantiate. It is interesting to note that the wording 'internationally recognised border' is preferred to 'international border', introducing the element of state recognition.[98]

The challenge here is to devise a definition which is neither too broad nor too narrow in order to obtain a text which can cover a large range of situations in which people are internally displaced and in need of international protection, but which is also a workable definition. Differences in approaches reflect the various purposes which are given to such a definition: is it aimed simply at designating to whom assistance and protection would be available, or does it have a more specific purpose which is to determine the situations which call for international intervention on behalf of internally displaced persons? Various definitions put the emphasis either on the causes or the types of situations, but it would seem to be more appropriate to focus both on the causes of displacement and the needs of the people rather than on a description of the situations (people fleeing suddenly and *en masse*) as in the 1992 definition.

The more recent definition offered in the Guiding Principles on Internal Displacement is now widely used. The Guiding Principles define the internally displaced as:

persons or groups of persons who have been forced to flee or obliged to flee or to leave their homes or places of habitual residence, in particular as a result of, or in order to avoid the effects of armed conflict, situations of generalised violence, violations of human rights or natural or human-made disasters, and who have not crossed an internationally recognised state border.[99]

---

[98] On state recognition, see I. Brownlie, 'Recognition in Theory and Practice' (1982) 53 *British Yearbook of International Law* 197; and R. Rich, 'Recognition of States: The Collapse of Yugoslavia and the Soviet Union' (1993) 4 *European Journal of International Law* 36.

[99] See para. 2 of the Introduction to the Guiding Principles.

It is clearly an improvement on the 1992 definition since it removes all the elements which had proved problematic. According to Cohen, it represents 'the broadest definition in use at the international or regional level'.[100] It has been emphasised that this definition reflects 'the descriptive and non-legal nature of the term "internally displaced persons"'.[101] It must also be noted that the list of causes of displacement is not exhaustive, as highlighted by the words 'in particular'.[102] In contrast to the 1992 Analytical Report, the Guiding Principles explicitly refer to development-induced displacement.[103]

When does internal displacement end?

In the case of refugees, the 1951 Convention contains a list of the situations in which refugee status can be terminated.[104] As refugee status is a legal status, it can have a defined commencement and a cessation date. Internally displaced persons can resettle more easily in another place because they are still within their own country, sometimes within their own community, so return may not always be the preferred option. The most important issue is that they *voluntarily* choose to resettle or to return.

The moment when an internally displaced person ceases to be internally displaced cannot therefore be clearly determined. It could be argued that a person ceases to be internally displaced when he or she has taken the decision to return home or to resettle elsewhere in the country after an assessment of security conditions in the area of return.[105] Even then, the term 'home' has not been clarified,[106] and in some cases it has been interpreted as the *exact* house where an individual and his family used to live before being displaced.[107] In any case, such a decision cannot be easily identified and is influenced by a wide range of factors.[108]

---

[100] R. Cohen, 'The Development of International Standards to Protect Internally Displaced Persons', in A. F. Bayefsky and J. Fitzpatrick (eds.), *Human Rights and Forced Displacement* (The Hague: Kluwer Law International, 2000), 76–85 at 82.

[101] W. Kälin, *Guiding Principles on Internal Displacement: Annotations* (Washington DC: ASIL and the Brookings Institution, 2000), 3.

[102] *Ibid.*, 2.   [103] See Guiding Principle 6(2)(c).

[104] Art. 1(C) of the 1951 Convention.

[105] See Geissler, *Der völkerrechtliche Schutz*, 58.

[106] See C. Dubernet, *The International Containment of Displaced Persons: Humanitarian Spaces Without Exit* (Aldershot: Ashgate, 2001), 11.

[107] See for instance Chapter 5, fourth section.   [108] *Ibid.*

In 2002, the Office for the Coordination of Humanitarian Affairs (OCHA) asked the Special Representative to explore the question of when internal displacement ends.[109] This has prompted a number of studies on this particular topic.[110] The search for criteria and mechanisms to determine when an internally displaced person ceases to be internally displaced may not appear to be very meaningful. Likewise, to determine when a victim of human rights violations ceases to be a victim is not especially helpful. Protection and assistance to the internally displaced should cease when their needs are fulfilled. This can only be determined on an *ad hoc* basis after a general assessment of the political and socio-economic situation, as well as a specific assessment of the situation of a particular IDP group.[111]

Conclusion

This chapter has argued that internally displaced persons and refugees share two characteristics, namely the element of forced displacement and the breach of the bond with the state. Nevertheless, if we look more closely at the situation of internally displaced persons, this bond is not completely severed, because they still remain within the jurisdiction of their state which has a duty of protection towards them. This has important implications for the nature of the protection which can be afforded to them. What must not be forgotten is the essentially statist nature of international refugee law which is evidenced by the paramount importance of the border-crossing requirement in the refugee definition: the refugee is an unprotected alien who does not benefit from any protection, whereas the internally displaced is an unprotected resident who requires protection which is necessarily different in nature. Consequently, a legal synthesis between refugees and the internally displaced is meaningless, and a separate legal status should not be given to the internally displaced in international law.[112]

When seeking to devise an operational definition of the internally displaced, the problem lies in the fact that a wide range of situations can be examined, but it has been argued here that the common

---

[109] See *Internally Displaced Persons: Report of the Representative of the Secretary-General, Mr Francis M. Deng*, E/CN.4/2002/95, 16 January 2002, para. 92.

[110] See for instance the special issue of the *Forced Migration Review*, vol. 17, May 2003.

[111] See G. Bettocchi with R. Freitas, 'A UNHCR Perspective', *Forced Migration Review*, vol. 17, May 2003, 13.

[112] See pp. 26–8 above.

denominator to these displaced populations should be the existence of human rights violations. This shows why the issue of internal displacement needs to be discussed within a wider human rights context which shifts the focus of attention from questions of location and geography to the more pertinent ones of individual/group entitlements and state obligations.

2 The legal protection of internally displaced persons

As demonstrated in the previous chapter, the concept of internal displacement needs to be distinguished from the concept of refugeehood. Refugees are covered by an 'established' regime of protection, but internally displaced persons, because they remain within the borders of their state, cannot benefit from it. Although the expression 'internally displaced persons' is not mentioned in any international legal instrument, this does not mean that the internally displaced do not enjoy any legal protection under existing international law. This chapter identifies the legal framework of protection for the internally displaced and demonstrates how it draws heavily on international human rights law. If work with the internally displaced must be pursued in a human rights framework, it must be based on the relevant provisions of human rights law as restated in the Guiding Principles on Internal Displacement.[1]

The protection of internally displaced persons raises several issues. First, it is not clear what protection for internally displaced persons involves: broad interpretations have been adopted and have included at least protection against displacement and protection for those who are displaced. These two aspects were identified in the Analytical Report on internally displaced persons which concluded with the need for new human rights standards.[2] Secondly, protection of internally displaced persons is a sensitive issue for reasons explained earlier: it has been feared that strengthening protection for internally displaced persons, i.e. in-country protection, would serve as a pretext for denying the possibility of protection abroad, i.e. asylum, hence the reluctance of some

---

[1] *Guiding Principles on Internal Displacement*, E/CN.4/1998/53/Add.2, 11 February 1998 (hereinafter Guiding Principles). See Annex 1.

[2] *Analytical Report of the Secretary-General on Internally Displaced Persons*, E/CN.4/1992/23, 14 February 1992 (hereinafter *Analytical Report*), paras. 74–105.

refugee lawyers to increase the focus on internally displaced persons. The International Committee of the Red Cross (ICRC), for instance, even contended for some time that the protection of internally displaced persons under international law was sufficient and that there was no need to develop the law.[3] It could also be questioned whether approaching the problem of internal displacement through law is a useful strategy.[4] The formulation of Guiding Principles on Internal Displacement which were presented to the Commission on Human Rights in March 1998 could prove that it is.

This chapter first presents an overview of the law applicable to situations of internal displacement. It appears that the protection afforded to internally displaced persons under current international law may not be adequate and this is why Guiding Principles on Internal Displacement were drafted by the Special Representative on Internally Displaced Persons and a team of international legal experts. It will be questioned whether these Guiding Principles constitute a correct restatement of the international legal provisions relevant to situations of internal displacement, and whether they should lead to the adoption of an international legally binding instrument.

An overview of the law applicable to situations of internal displacement

One must first identify the needs of the internally displaced in order to determine how the law responds to these needs. When a person or a family becomes internally displaced, their primary concern is often security, as they will have fled in order to find safety somewhere else. The first priority may thus be the need to ensure that their right to life is not violated and that they are protected against torture and any other form of inhuman, cruel and degrading treatment. Internally displaced persons often need assistance, i.e. food, shelter and health care. Families may need to be reunited. Being on the move also makes everyday activities such as going to school or working much more problematic.[5]

---

[3] See p. 53 below.

[4] See D. Helle, 'Enhancing the Protection of Internally Displaced Persons', in Norwegian Refugee Council, *Rights Have No Borders: Worldwide Internal Displacement* (Oxford: Norwegian Refugee Council/Global IDP Survey, 1998), 31–51 at 40.

[5] See R. Cohen, 'The Development of International Standards to Protect Internally Displaced Persons', in A. F. Bayefsky and J. Fitzpatrick (eds.), *Human Rights and Forced Displacement* (The Hague: Kluwer Law International, 2000), 76–85 at 79.

When the internally displaced want to return, they sometimes find that during their absence they have been deprived of their property. This is obviously a major obstacle to return. One can already see that the needs of the internally displaced cover a wide range of areas.

This section does not engage in a detailed compilation and analysis of the legal norms applicable to situations of internal displacement. This has been done elsewhere. Before 1992, the Friends World Committee for Consultation (Quakers) were already advocating the appointment of a Special Rapporteur or a Working Group to prepare draft principles for the protection of internally displaced persons.[6] The Refugee Policy Group also suggested that a compilation of legal norms be made by NGOs, the UN or the academic community.[7] The Commission on Human Rights requested the Special Representative on Internally Displaced Persons to prepare such a study as a first step towards the formulation of Guiding Principles on Internal Displacement.[8] The 200-page report was submitted to the Commission on Human Rights in 1996.[9] Frequent references will be made to this study. Due to constraints of space, regional instruments such as the European Convention on Human Rights,[10] the African Charter on Human and Peoples' Rights[11] and the American Convention on Human Rights[12] will not be examined here.

Effective legal protection requires the existence of legal norms and their application. A gap in protection has been identified with regard to internally displaced persons, and in order to bridge that gap, one must identify some norms of conduct and ensure their observance.[13] Most internally displaced persons are found in situations of armed conflict, hence the importance of international humanitarian law which

---

[6] See *Analytical Report*, note 2 above, para. 83.

[7] See Refugee Policy Group, *Human Rights Protection for Internally Displaced Persons: An International Conference, June 24–25, 1991* (Washington DC: Refugee Policy Group, 1991), 19.

[8] See CHR Res. 1993/95, 11 March 1993.

[9] *Internally Displaced Persons: Compilation and Analysis of Legal Norms*, E/CN.4/1996/52/Add.2, 5 December 1995 (hereinafter the Compilation). It was published by the Office of the United Nations High Commissioner for Human Rights (OHCHR) as *Internally Displaced Persons: Compilation and Analysis of Legal Norms* (New York and Geneva: United Nations, 1998). This compilation was transformed into a handbook to be used in the field: UNHCR, *International Legal Standards Applicable to the Protection of Internally Displaced Persons: A Reference Manual for UNHCR Staff* (Geneva: UNHCR, 1996). See also R. Cohen and F. M. Deng, *Masses in Flight: The Global Crisis of Internal Displacement* (Washington DC: Brookings Institution, 1998), Chapter 3 on the legal framework.

[10] However, on occasion, certain regional institutions will be mentioned below.

[11] 17 June 1981, 21 ILM 58.   [12] 22 November 1969, 9 ILM 673.

[13] See S. Sumit, *International Law of Internally Displaced Persons: The Role of UNHCR*, MPhil dissertation, Jawaharlal Nehru University, New Delhi, 1995, 132.

regulates the conduct of hostilities. Internal displacement also occurs in times of peace (e.g. natural disasters) or internal strife during which humanitarian law is not applicable, whereas human rights norms remain applicable in almost all situations. Therefore, applicable norms depend on the situation envisaged, i.e. situations of tensions and disturbances, disasters, non-international armed conflicts and international armed conflicts. This is the classification used by the Special Representative on Internally Displaced Persons in his reports. The Compilation and Analysis of legal norms applicable to internally displaced persons shows the complementarity of the two bodies of law, human rights law and humanitarian law: each alone does not provide sufficient protection for internally displaced persons but, together, they have the potential to do so.

Protection of internally displaced persons under human rights law

International human rights law developed at a very fast rate in the second half of the twentieth century. A wide range of conventional and customary norms has emerged. The main human rights instruments which are referred to here are the Universal Declaration of Human Rights,[14] the International Covenant on Civil and Political Rights,[15] the International Covenant on Economic, Social and Cultural Rights,[16] the Convention Against Torture and Other Cruel, Inhuman or Degrading Treatment or Punishment,[17] the Convention on the Prevention and Punishment of the Crime of Genocide,[18] the International Convention on the Elimination of All Forms of Racial Discrimination,[19] the Convention on the Elimination of Discrimination Against Women[20] and the Convention on the Rights of the Child.[21] Many organs, both international and regional, have been set up to implement human rights standards.

Human rights law applies to internally displaced persons since it applies to all individuals without distinction and in almost all circumstances. When humanitarian law is not applicable, human rights law becomes the only source of legal protection and ensures that the human rights of internally displaced persons are respected. Internal displacement often occurs in situations of internal disturbance or civil unrest.

---

[14] GA Res. 217 A (III), 10 December 1948 (hereinafter Universal Declaration).
[15] 16 December 1966, 999 UNTS 171 (hereinafter ICCPR).
[16] 16 December 1966, 993 UNTS 3 (hereinafter ICESCR).
[17] 10 December 1984, 23 ILM 1027 and 24 ILM 535.   [18] 9 December 1948, 78 UNTS 277.
[19] 21 December 1965, 660 UNTS 195.   [20] 18 December 1979, 19 ILM 33.
[21] 20 November 1989, 28 ILM 1448.

In such situations which cannot be qualified as armed conflict (internal strife), humanitarian law cannot apply and some human rights can be restricted, sometimes even derogated from: Article 4(1) of the ICCPR provides that, in times of public emergency, some of its provisions can be derogated from. According to Article 4(3), states must nevertheless report to the UN any declaration of a state of emergency.[22] However, the core human rights, such as the right to life, the prohibition of cruel, inhuman and degrading treatment or punishment, the prohibition of slavery and the prohibition of the retroactive application of penal law, are not derogable under any circumstances.[23] This is of crucial importance to internally displaced persons.

Although forced displacement has never been a focus in the development of human rights instruments, these instruments contain provisions which are of particular relevance to internally displaced persons. The Compilation mentioned above identifies their needs and the corresponding legal provisions which can be used to cover such needs. It appears from the Compilation that the needs identified are very similar, if not identical, to those of refugees. Nine areas are listed in the Compilation, namely equality and non-discrimination, life and personal security, personal liberty, subsistence needs, movement-related needs, the need for personal identification, documentation and registration, property-related needs, the need to maintain family and community values, and, finally, the need to build self-reliance. The emphasis is put not only on protection needs, but also on assistance to the internally displaced. Refugees have similar needs, and the 1951 Convention covers most of these issues as far as they are concerned. It was deemed necessary to analyse in depth the law in the relevant areas with a focus on internally displaced persons, because their protection needs are not as clearly covered by a specific international legal instrument.

When individuals are on the move, it is more difficult to ensure that their human rights are protected. Refugees whose specific human rights are no longer protected by their government are covered by a special regime of protection established by the 1951 Convention. In theory, there is a 'continuum of norms protecting the rights of the human person

---

[22] On states of emergency, see J. Fitzpatrick, *Human Rights in Crisis: The International System for Protecting Human Rights During States of Emergency* (Philadelphia: University of Pennsylvania Press, 1994) and J. Oraa, *Human Rights in States of Emergency in International Law* (Oxford: Clarendon Press, 1992).

[23] See Article 4(2) of the ICCPR.

in all situations',[24] but in practice internally displaced persons are not adequately covered. As internally displaced persons are on the move, the protection of their human rights is reduced, but, on the other hand, they cannot benefit from the special regime of protection created for refugees. This is why one can only use refugee law as a point of reference and one has to adopt a creative interpretation of existing norms of human rights law and humanitarian law in order to provide legal protection to internally displaced persons.

The purpose of human rights instruments is to protect individuals from abuses from the state: states cannot treat their population as they wish with impunity. In analysing the legal provisions of human rights law which apply to internally displaced persons, one seeks to demonstrate that states have duties towards these populations, negative obligations (not to displace them, not to inflict inhuman treatment upon them, etc.), as well as positive obligations (to provide sufficient food for them or health services for instance, but also to prevent *others* displacing them). Reaffirming human rights protection for internally displaced persons thus amounts to reminding the state of the fact that internally displaced persons should still benefit from the same protection as anyone else in the country. Not only should the state treat the internally displaced like the rest of the civilian population, but it should also provide extra protection for these vulnerable populations.

Protection under humanitarian law

Humanitarian law contains rules regulating the means and methods of warfare. The main provisions of humanitarian law can be found in the four Geneva Conventions of 1949 and their two additional Protocols of 1977. It is mainly the ICRC which promotes and monitors the application of humanitarian law. As armed conflict constitutes the main cause of forced displacement, including internal displacement, humanitarian law inevitably plays a crucial role as a source of protection for the internally displaced.[25] Humanitarian law seeks to provide means of protection which are adapted to exceptional circumstances.[26] For our purpose, only the provisions relating to the protection of civilians contained in

---

[24] Sumit, *The Role of UNHCR*, 125–6.

[25] See J. P. Lavoyer, 'Forced Displacement: The Relevance of International Humanitarian Law', in A. F. Bayefsky and J. Fitzpatrick (eds.), *Human Rights and Forced Displacement* (The Hague: Kluwer Law International, 2000), 50–65.

[26] See D. Plattner, 'The Protection of Displaced Persons in Non-International Armed Conflicts' (1993) 291 *International Review of the Red Cross* 567 at 569.

the Fourth Geneva Convention Relative to the Protection of Civilian Persons in Time of War[27] and the two Protocols[28] are of relevance. Internally displaced persons benefit from the same protection provided for all civilians in times of armed conflict. The question here is to determine which provisions are especially relevant to the internally displaced.

The Compilation distinguishes between the norms applicable in international armed conflicts and those applicable in non-international armed conflicts, as different provisions apply in each situation. Humanitarian law provides a more comprehensive protection during international armed conflicts to which the Fourth Geneva Convention and Protocol I apply, whereas the law regulating non-international armed conflicts is less elaborate. However, it is during internal conflicts that the highest numbers of internally displaced persons are often produced and the need for specific protection against the government or other warring parties arises. Moreover, most conflicts around the world are now internal conflicts and the regulation of such conflicts has thus gained added importance.

The only provisions of humanitarian law which are applicable during non-international armed conflicts are Article 3 common to the Geneva Conventions (common Article 3) and Protocol II. One must note that the threshold for the application of Protocol II is relatively high: Article 1 of Protocol II stipulates that the Protocol only applies to armed conflicts between the armed forces of a state party and 'dissident armed forces or other organised armed groups which, under responsible command, exercise such control over a part of its territory as to enable them to carry out sustained and concerted military operation'. Common Article 3 is especially important since it contains some fundamental principles which are of customary nature, and has been said to enshrine 'elementary considerations of humanity'.[29] It provides that civilians shall be treated humanely and without discrimination. To this end, it gives a short list of prohibited acts. Its wording remains quite general, whereas the provisions of Protocol II are more specific.

---

[27] 12 August 1949, 75 UNTS 287 (hereinafter the Fourth Geneva Convention).

[28] Protocol Additional to the Geneva Conventions of 12 August 1949 and Relating to the Protection of Victims of International Armed Conflicts, 8 June 1977, 1125 UNTS 3 (hereinafter Protocol I); Protocol Additional to the Geneva Conventions of 12 August 1949 and Relating to the Protection of Victims of Non-International Armed Conflicts, 8 June 1977, 1125 UNTS 609 (hereinafter Protocol II).

[29] *Military and Paramilitary Activities in and against Nicaragua (Nicaragua v. United States)* (Merits) (1986) *ICJ Reports* 14, para. 218.

Humanitarian law is especially useful because it contains provisions on issues of special relevance to the internally displaced such as humanitarian access.[30] Whereas human rights provisions are usually worded in a general sense because they are meant to be universally applied, those of humanitarian law are meant to cover more specific needs arising in armed conflicts. The provisions concerning the protection of civilians during armed conflict provide protection during displacement and cover a wide range of issues. However, some of these provisions cannot be applied to the internally displaced because they only provide protection to non-nationals in international armed conflicts.[31] The protection of internally displaced persons under humanitarian law can be problematic when the provisions dealing with the protection of civilians only cover those who fall into the hands of another state and are defined as 'protected persons'. Under Article 4 of the Fourth Geneva Convention, protected persons are 'those who, at a given moment and in any manner whatsoever, find themselves, in case of a conflict or occupation, in the hands of a Party to the conflict or Occupying Power of which they are not nationals'. International humanitarian law is thus less concerned with the way civilians are treated by their own state during international armed conflicts. This is however precisely the type of protection which the internally displaced may need during such conflicts.

Finally, humanitarian law also contains some specific provisions prohibiting transfers of population.[32] Article 17 of Protocol II which expressly prohibits such transfers is of special importance to the internally displaced. It reads:

1. The displacement of the civilian population shall not be ordered for reasons related to the conflict unless the security of the civilians involved or imperative military reasons so demand. Should such displacements have to be carried out, all possible measures shall be taken in order that the civilian population may be received under satisfactory conditions of shelter, hygiene, health, safety and nutrition.
2. Civilians shall not be compelled to leave their own territory for reasons connected with the conflict.

---

[30] See the Compilation, paras. 359–81.   [31] See p. 49 below.

[32] See C. Meindersma, 'Legal Issues Surrounding Population Transfers in Conflict Situations' (1994) 41 *Netherlands International Law Review* 31. See also *Compilation and Analysis of Legal Norms, Part II: Legal Aspects Relating to the Protection Against Arbitrary Displacement*, E/CN.4/1998/53/Add.1, 11 February 1998 (hereinafter Compilation, Part II), paras. 53–69.

Article 49 of the Fourth Geneva Convention which applies to international armed conflicts also prohibits population transfers from occupied territories. Nevertheless, humanitarian law focuses on forced relocation and does not address comprehensively the problem of forced displacement during armed conflict: as human rights law, humanitarian law, on its own, does not provide a complete normative framework to cover all situations of internal displacement.

Refugee law as a point of comparison

The fact that refugee law does not apply to internally displaced persons does not mean that this body of law is completely irrelevant to them. As problems encountered by internally displaced persons are very similar to those of refugees, refugee law can serve as a point of comparison and 'might also inspire standard-setting for internally displaced persons'.[33] Just to take one example, the provision contained in the 1951 Convention on *non-refoulement* (Article 33) can serve as a reference for internally displaced persons: like refugees, they should not be returned to places where their life or freedom would be threatened. Other principles such as safe and voluntary return could also be applied to internally displaced persons. Finally, the UNHCR guidelines on refugee women and children offer useful guidance for the standards of treatment of internally displaced women and children.[34]

Although refugee law can serve as a point of comparison, it must also be noted that the articulation of certain rights in the IDP context may raise tensions with refugee law. For instance, some states regularly return asylum seekers to their country of origin on the basis that they have an internal flight alternative and can seek safety elsewhere in their state.[35] According to Fitzpatrick, 'refugee law may appear to condone the return of persons who will join the ranks of the internally displaced'.[36]

What came out of the Compilation and Analysis of legal norms applicable to situations of internal displacement was a patchwork of various provisions drawn from several bodies of law, which demonstrates their

---

[33] Compilation, para. 25.   [34] See Chapter 4, pp. 143–7 below.

[35] See J. C. Hathaway and M. Forster, 'Internal Protection/Relocation/Flight Alternative as an Aspect of Refugee Status Determination', in E. Feller, V. Türk and F. Nicholson (eds.), *Refugee Protection in International Law: UNHCR's Global Consultations on International Protection* (Cambridge: Cambridge University Press, 2003), 357–417.

[36] J. Fitzpatrick, 'Human Rights and Forced Displacement: Converging Standards', in A. F. Bayefsky and J. Fitzpatrick (eds.), *Human Rights and Forced Displacement* (The Hague: Kluwer Law International, 2000), 3–25 at 12.

'considerable complementarity'.[37] These provisions do not apply in all circumstances and some only apply to specific groups of persons. It is therefore difficult to determine in each case what applies when, and to whom. Despite the abundance of applicable norms, the protection is not complete. As the Analytical Report had predicted,[38] there are some gaps in the legal protection of internally displaced persons under existing international law.

Since the end of the Second World War, three bodies of law, international human rights law, international refugee law and international humanitarian law, have developed along separate paths, with distinct normative and institutional frameworks. Fitzpatrick has argued that forced displacement is an important 'site of convergence' of the three bodies of law since 'human rights violations associated with armed conflict are a, indeed *the*, major cause of forced displacement'.[39] The drafting of the Guiding Principles on Internal Displacement clearly illustrates recent efforts to synthesise the three bodies of law and has been seen as a breakthrough in the recognition of the synergies between them.[40] Although such an undertaking may appear at first very attractive, one must also identify the possible dangers of this trend towards convergence. These three bodies of law may all seek to protect human dignity, but still have a different conceptual basis and impose distinct legal obligations.

Towards the Guiding Principles on Internal Displacement

Gaps in the normative framework of protection

Some of the norms identified above are not applicable in all circumstances or apply only to segments of the population, which undermines their utility to internally displaced persons. First, norms of humanitarian law are applicable only during armed conflict. In situations of generalised violence which fall below the threshold required for the application of common Article 3 or Protocol II, humanitarian law does not apply. However, some prolonged situations of low-intensity conflict produce substantial numbers of internally displaced persons, as in Colombia

---

[37] J. P. Lavoyer, 'Protection under International Humanitarian Law', in ICRC, *Internally Displaced Persons, Symposium, Geneva, 23–25 October 1995* (Geneva: ICRC, 1996), 26–36 at 26.
[38] *Analytical Report*, paras. 103–4.   [39] Fitzpatrick, 'Converging Standards', 3.
[40] See R. Brett and E. Lester, 'Refugee Law and International Humanitarian Law: Parallels, Lessons and Looking Ahead' (2001) 843 *International Review of the Red Cross* 713 at 714.

for instance.[41] These situations are not characterised as armed conflict, but allow states to impose restrictions on certain human rights. In order to regulate these potentially dangerous situations, attempts have been made to develop minimum humanitarian standards (now fundamental standards of humanity) which would apply at all times. The proposed Turku/Åbo declaration on minimum humanitarian standards addresses the issue of internal displacement by prohibiting population transfers (Article 7).[42]

Secondly, some provisions of humanitarian law are only applicable to specific categories of persons which may not necessarily include internally displaced persons. Part III of the Fourth Geneva Convention, which contains many substantial provisions which could have been of interest to the internally displaced, is only applicable to 'protected persons'. Section III of Part IV of Protocol I relating to the treatment of persons in the power of a party to the conflict is not applicable to the internally displaced either. Other instruments are also of limited application: for instance, the International Labour Organization (ILO) Convention No. 169, which is the only international instrument which explicitly provides protection against arbitrary displacement,[43] concerns specific groups of individuals, namely indigenous and tribal peoples.

Finally, where relevant legal norms do exist, they may be binding only on certain actors. This may be simply because the instrument in which these norms are contained are not ratified by the party or parties concerned (ratification gaps). The Geneva Conventions are amongst the most widely ratified international instruments and have reached almost universal acceptance. However, the same cannot be said of the two Protocols. Protocol II for instance has been by ratified by only 148 states.[44] The problem of non-ratification can only be eluded if the provisions in question have attained customary status, in which case they

---

[41] See L. Obregón and M. Stavropoulou, 'In Search of Hope: The Plight of Displaced Colombians', in R. Cohen and F. M. Deng (eds.), *The Forsaken People: Case Studies of the Internally Displaced* (Washington DC: Brookings Institution, 1998), 399–453.

[42] See A. Eide, A. Rosas and T. Meron, 'Combating Lawlessness in Grey Zone Conflicts Through Minimum Humanitarian Standards' (1995) 89 *American Journal of International Law* 215, and D. Petrasek, 'Moving Forward on the Development of Minimum Humanitarian Standards' (1998) 92 *American Journal of International Law* 557.

[43] Article 16(1) of the Convention Concerning Indigenous and Tribal Peoples in Independent Countries, ILO Convention No. 169 (1989), available from the ILO website, http://www.ilo.org.

[44] See A. Roberts and R. Guelff, *Documents on the Laws of War* (Oxford: Oxford University Press, 2000, 3rd ed.), 498.

are binding on all states, regardless of the ratification status of the relevant instrument. However, not all of the provisions of the two Protocols have reached such status.[45] Human rights law also fails to provide comprehensive protection because some key human rights instruments, such as the two Covenants, have likewise not been ratified by all states. Moreover, human rights treaties are binding on states only, and not on non-state entities. Only states can be held accountable for human rights violations under the various international and regional treaties. Nevertheless, with the development of positive obligations, states have to ensure that individuals do not violate other individuals' human rights and this ensures that individuals are indirectly bound by human rights obligations.

Besides applicability gaps, the Compilation also refers to 'consensus gaps' which exist because there is no consensus on how a general norm can be applied to the internally displaced.[46] The Compilation argues that 'many aspects relating to the right to life, the prohibition of torture, the prohibition of hostage-taking, the prohibition of contemporary forms of slavery, subsistence rights and many aspects of religious rights'[47] are addressed in international law instruments, but that other areas are not because of a lack of explicit norms. A general norm may exist, but no corollary and more specific right is formulated. It is thus sometimes unclear how the general norm can apply in the specific situation of internally displaced persons, as will be demonstrated below. The Compilation refers to the areas mentioned above as 'grey areas' because, although a legal norm exists, it is not clear how this norm should be applied to the internally displaced.

The Compilation identifies seventeen grey areas[48] in which it is considered necessary to clarify the law in order to strengthen the protection for the internally displaced. They include aspects relating to the protection of life (especially during internal armed conflicts), gender-specific violence, free movement and access to international assistance. The focus will be here on movement-related rights and more

---

[45] See T. Meron, *Human Rights and Humanitarian Norms as Customary Law* (Oxford: Clarendon Press, 1989) and C. Greenwood, 'Customary law status of the 1977 Geneva Protocols', in A. J. M. Delissen and G. J. Tanja (eds.), *Humanitarian Law of Armed Conflict: Challenges Ahead: Essays in Honour of Frits Karlshoven* (Dordrecht: Martinus Nijhoff, 1991), 93–114.

[46] See Cohen and Deng, *Masses in Flight*, 123.   [47] Compilation, para. 414.

[48] *Ibid.*, para. 415.

particularly on the right not to be arbitrarily displaced. This issue is not dealt with in the Compilation, but constitutes the object of a separate study.[49]

This study demonstrates that, although the right not to be arbitrarily displaced is not explicitly formulated in any general human rights instrument, it can nonetheless be inferred from a number of provisions. As mentioned above, the only explicit prohibition of forcible displacement is contained in ILO Convention No. 169 on indigenous and tribal peoples. However, the study shows that protection against arbitrary displacement can be inferred from the general provisions contained in human rights treaties concerning the freedom of movement and the right to choose one's residence (Article 13 of the Universal Declaration and Article 12(1) of the ICCPR).[50] The prohibition against forced displacement also encompasses protection from interference with one's home, the right to housing, the prohibition of forced movement in emergencies including situations of armed conflict, the prohibition of religious and racial discrimination and the prohibition of genocide. The study concludes that, although express prohibition of arbitrary displacement can be found in humanitarian law and the law relating to indigenous peoples, prohibition is implicit in general human rights law.[51] This finding was confirmed by the Human Rights Committee which stated in 1999 that the freedom to choose one's residence (Article 12(1) of the ICCPR) 'includes protection against all forms of forced internal displacement'.[52] However, Article 12(1) can be derogated from and can also be subject to some restrictions (Article 12(3)).

The difficulty stems from the fact that the provisions identified do not seem to explicitly address the problems of the internally displaced, and it is only when interpreted in a certain way that these provisions may be directly applicable to them. The example of protection against arbitrary displacement, analysed above, is a good illustration. The rights of freedom of movement and to choose one's residence are of general

---

[49] See Compilation, Part II. This study finds its origin in M. Stavropoulou, 'The Right Not to Be Displaced' (1994) 9 *American University Journal of International Law and Policy* 689.

[50] On the right of freedom of movement within states generally, see C. Benyani, *Human Rights Standards and the Free Movement of People Within States* (Oxford: Oxford University Press, 2000).

[51] Compilation, Part II, para. 84.

[52] Human Rights Committee, *Freedom of Movement (Art. 12)* CCPR/C/21/Rev.1/Add.9, CCPR General Comment 27, 2 November 1999.

application, but they can include protection against arbitrary displacement.

In addition to gaps in application and consensus, normative gaps have also been identified. Such gaps appear where 'no explicit norms exist to address identifiable needs of the displaced'.[53] These normative gaps are identified in the Compilation: they refer to disappearances, the missing and the dead, the use of landmines,[54] detention, the need for personal identification, documentation and registration, property-related needs, relief workers and organisations.[55] These gaps concern important problems for the internally displaced.

Strengthening legal protection for the internally displaced

Given the identified weaknesses of the law applicable to situations of internal displacement, the question arises as to the remedies for these weaknesses. The discussion is related to the comments in the previous chapter on the legal status of the internally displaced and the comparison with the refugee status.[56]

Three key approaches to the problem of legal protection of internally displaced persons can be identified. The first one has been adopted by those who consider that the protection provided by existing international law to internally displaced persons is sufficient and that it is only a matter of implementation of the law. This position can be explained by the fact that its proponents fear that the development of a legal framework of protection specifically tailored to the needs of the internally displaced would actually weaken existing provisions. They are especially opposed to the creation of a new instrument on internally displaced persons which could lead to the erosion of the existing refugee protection system. It has been contended that 'any new instrument concentrating solely on displaced persons might lead to a reaffirmation of state sovereignty, and that it would be difficult to reach a consensus on the definition of the term "displaced persons" since the result would be the lowest common denominator and thus would constitute a backward step in relation to the existing law'.[57]

---

[53] Compilation, para. 411.
[54] See however S. Maselen, 'The Implications of the 1996 Land-Mines Protocol for Refugees and the Internally Displaced' (1996) 8 *International Journal of Refugee Law* 383.
[55] Compilation, para. 416.
[56] See also UNHCR, *The State of World's Refugees: A Humanitarian Agenda* (Geneva: UNHCR, 1997), 124–8.
[57] ICRC, *Internally Displaced Persons*, 44. On definitional issues and legal status, see Chapter 1.

This position was widely held before the conclusion of the Compilation, with the ICRC being one of its main proponents. As it is responsible for the implementation of international humanitarian law, it reaffirmed the application of this body of law to all civilians without distinction[58] and refused to envisage the creation of a new legal instrument which would restate the provisions of humanitarian law with a focus on the internally displaced. It must be noted that the 1991 Working Paper on internally displaced persons of the ICRC only mentioned the possibility of a Code of Conduct on minimum humanitarian standards applicable to all.[59] Since then, the ICRC has modified its position and contributed to the drafting of the Guiding Principles. At the same time, it has reaffirmed its belief that international humanitarian law 'remains fully adequate to address most problems of internal displacement associated with situations of armed conflict'.[60] Even after the drafting of the Guiding Principles, some ICRC staff have continued to express fear that 'the increasingly frequent recourse to principles that are specifically designed to deal with internally displaced persons and are not binding on States and non-State players will ultimately narrow the scope of the protection granted by international humanitarian law to the entire civilian population'.[61]

The Compilation marked a turning-point in confirming that the protection afforded by international law to internally displaced persons is not complete. As a result, those who had previously opposed the creation of a new instrument dealing with internally displaced persons, came to admit that the existence of such a protection gap nevertheless required some action and that a way of improving the implementation of existing law may be to restate some general provisions in order to facilitate their application to the internally displaced.

The second approach rejects both inaction and the need for a new instrument focusing on the needs of internally displaced persons. It is favoured by those who oppose the adoption of a new legal instrument

---

[58] See J. P. Lavoyer, 'Refugees and Internally Displaced Persons: International Humanitarian Law and the Role of the ICRC' (1995) 305 *International Review of the Red Cross* 162. See also ICRC, *Persons Displaced Within Their Own Countries as a Result of Armed Conflict or Disturbances*, working document prepared by the ICRC, Geneva, 1991, 12.

[59] See ICRC, *Persons Displaced*, 12.

[60] ICRC, 'Internally Displaced Persons: The Mandate and Role of the International Committee of the Red Cross' (2000) 838 *International Review of the Red Cross* 491.

[61] M. Contat Hickel, 'Protection of Internally Displaced Persons Affected by Armed Conflict: Concept and Challenges' (2001) 83 *International Review of the Red Cross* 699 at 709.

for reasons explained above, but who nonetheless want to improve the implementation of existing law. It is also favoured by the proponents of a new legal instrument who realise that such a move is not feasible in the current political context and that a 'soft law' or 'incremental approach to developing new human rights standards'[62] is more realistic. It is also remembered that 'several attempts to develop new standards . . . had failed or resulted in diluted or restrictive language'.[63] According to the Analytical Report, this option seems to have been favoured by the UN.[64] After the completion of the Compilation, the Commission on Human Rights encouraged the Special Representative to further develop an '*appropriate* framework' (emphasis added) for the protection of internally displaced persons[65] and 'carefully avoided the term "legal" framework in making its request'.[66] The use of such language by the Commission on Human Rights suggested that it did not favour the adoption of a new legal instrument.

The third approach consists of adopting a comprehensive approach to displacement in order to address the problem of forced migration as a whole. Its justification lies in the fact that refugees and internally displaced persons are two aspects of the same problem, i.e. forced displacement, which should be dealt with within a single instrument. Therefore, having separate standards for both groups can prove counterproductive, and a comprehensive approach to the problem of forced displacement, whether internal or external, should be adopted instead.

As a result, the creation of separate standards for internally displaced persons may not be justified. What is not always very clear in this position is whether guidelines on internal displacement should also be avoided. According to Petrasek,[67] who has argued for a comprehensive approach and seemed to have found some support within UNHCR,[68] internally displaced persons face the same problems as refugees, and large populations of both refugees and internally displaced persons are

---

[62] Refugee Policy Group, *Human Rights Protection*, 12.

[63] *Ibid.*, 12. See for instance Chapter 1, p. 20 above, on past attempts to draft a Convention on Territorial Asylum.

[64] *Analytical Report*, paras. 103–4.   [65] CHR Res. 1996/52, 19 April 1996, para. 9.

[66] Cohen, 'The Development of International Standards', 78.

[67] See D. Petrasek, 'New Standards for the Protection of Internally Displaced Persons: A Proposal for a Comprehensive Approach' (1995) 14 *Refugee Survey Quarterly* 285.

[68] See UNHCR, *A Humanitarian Agenda*, 128. See also D. McNamara, 'UNHCR's Perspective', in ICRC, *Internally Displaced Persons, Symposium, Geneva, 23–25 October 1995* (Geneva: ICRC, 1996), 59–67 at 65–6.

to be found in the same areas. He also emphasises the negative impact that the development of new standards for the protection of internally displaced persons would have on the institution of asylum. Furthermore, he criticises the UN Secretary-General's analysis of the problem of internal displacement as being too simplistic because he had suggested that refugees are a privileged category compared to the internally displaced. Petrasek then makes suggestions as to what should be included in an instrument dealing with forced displacement[69] and evaluates the advantages and disadvantages of such an approach. For him, the main advantage in addressing external and internal displacement within the same instrument would be to reduce the threat to the principle of asylum. Refugees and internally displaced persons would be covered by the same instrument, but would still constitute separate legal categories.

A comprehensive approach to displacement would be welcomed and needed in certain areas, such as return, but it will not be feasible in a legal instrument as long as separate legal categories are maintained.[70] One could also question the relationship of such an instrument with the 1951 Convention. A document aiming at a comprehensive treatment of the problem of forced displacement may lead to the institutionalisation of separate legal categories of forced migrants, when some of them, such as the internally displaced, should simply be treated as human rights victims. A text proposed to cover all aspects of forced displacement would have to address categories of persons in widely differing situations, and this would reduce 'the clarity and readability of the document'.[71] The result might lead to increased confusion.

After the Compilation was completed, the Special Representative and his team decided that not only was a new binding instrument focusing on the rights of the internally displaced neither feasible nor desirable, but also that dealing with the problem within a comprehensive approach to displacement may not be appropriate. A decision was thus made upon the drafting of Guiding Principles on Internal Displacement which appeared to be the only viable option.[72]

---

[69] Petrasek, 'New Standards', 288.   [70] See Chapter 1, pp. 24–5 above.
[71] Helle, 'Enhancing the Protection', 48.
[72] On the drafting process of the Guiding Principles, see S. Bagshaw, *Developing the Guiding Principles on Internal Displacement: The Role of a Global Public Policy Network*, case study for the UN vision project on global public policy networks, http://www.gppi.net/cms/public/86880753f4f7e096dd8b747195113f6cbagshaw%20gpp%202000.pdf.

Legal analysis of the Guiding Principles on Internal Displacement

Following the conclusions of the Compilation and the second study on the protection against arbitrary displacement, thirty Guiding Principles on Internal Displacement were drafted and submitted to the Commission on Human Rights in March 1998.[73] This section analyses these Guiding Principles and argues that they represent an important step towards the improvement of the legal protection of the internally displaced.

A comprehensive approach to internal displacement

The Guiding Principles take a very broad approach to internal displacement based on a general understanding of the meaning of protection for the internally displaced. First, they address all the types of situations described in the Compilation and do not focus only on situations of armed conflict. Whereas the application of the provisions identified in the Compilation depended on the nature of the situation encountered, the Guiding Principles seek to provide guidance at all times.

The document covers a broad range of rights which correspond to the needs of the internally displaced. All phases of displacement are considered, so that the Guiding Principles offer protection against as well as during and after internal displacement. After outlining some general principles such as the protection of the right to asylum, the primary responsibility of states in providing protection to the internally displaced and the principle of non-discrimination, the second part deals with protection against displacement (Principles 5 to 9). For the first time in a UN document, a general right not to be arbitrarily displaced is explicitly formulated (Principle 6). The following part contains the main body of principles which offer protection during displacement (Principles 10 to 23). Here, a very wide range of human rights are addressed, such as education and personal identification. The issue of humanitarian assistance is also dealt with (Principles 24 to 27), as well as problems related to return, resettlement and reintegration (Principles 28 to 30).

The Guiding Principles represent an ambitious document which seeks to provide protection to all internally displaced persons. It deals not only with the consequences of displacement, which has been the general approach adopted so far, but also with the causes of displacement

---

[73] See S. Bagshaw, 'Internally Displaced Persons at the Fifty-Fourth Session of the United Nations Commission on Human Rights, 16 March–24 April 1998' (1998) 10 *International Journal of Refugee Law* 548.

which have usually been seen as political and thus beyond the realm of international law. The Guiding Principles also constitute an innovation insofar as they incorporate elements of international humanitarian law, human rights law and refugee law, and demonstrate the high degree of complementarity between these three bodies of law.[74]

One can immediately observe that the Guiding Principles contain no definition of the term 'internally displaced persons'. This is deliberate. The purpose of this document is not to create a new legal category to which rights and obligations would be attached, but to improve the legal protection for the internally displaced, protection which already exists in international law. The introduction to the Guiding Principles offers only a 'descriptive identification',[75] not a legal definition of internally displaced persons (para. 2).

The emphasis is put on the protection of special groups, notably women and children, who represent the great majority of internally displaced persons.[76] The Commission on Human Rights had asked that special attention be given to these vulnerable groups[77] and this is reflected in the document. The recognition of their special needs is contained in Principle 4(2). Moreover, specific provisions were made to address the issues of gender-specific violence (Principle 11(2)(a)), forcible recruitment of children (Principle 13(1)), women's participation in the distribution of supplies (Principle 18(3)), special health and education needs of women (Principles 19(2) and 23(4)) and equal access to documentation (Principle 20(3)).

In sum, the drafters of the Guiding Principles took an ambitious approach to the issue of protection for the internally displaced by trying to cover all of its aspects. As a result, even persons who are not yet displaced are covered by the provisions relating to protection from displacement. In addition, persons who are no longer displaced are covered by the final provisions. Protection for internally displaced persons has been interpreted as involving protection from displacement, during displacement and after displacement, which is very broad by comparison with what is usually meant by refugee protection. In contrast with the myriad of provisions which were identified in the Compilation and

---

[74] See J. P. Lavoyer, 'Guiding Principles on Internal Displacement: A Few Comments on the Contribution of International Humanitarian Law' (1998) 324 *International Review of the Red Cross* 467.

[75] W. Kälin, 'The Guiding Principles on Internal Displacement – Introduction' (1998) 10 *International Journal of Refugee Law* 557 at 560.

[76] See Chapter 4, pp. 143–7 below.   [77] CHR Res. 1995/57, 3 March 1995.

which only apply in specific circumstances, sometimes only to certain segments of the population, the Guiding Principles would apply at all times and to all internally displaced. They provide guidance not only to states, but also to all 'authorities, groups and persons',[78] which shows that the drafters have sought 'the widest possible scope of observance' for the instrument.[79]

A reformulation of existing law

The first paragraph of each Guiding Principle restates the general norm which is applicable in the relevant area, whereas the second paragraph formulates the specific application of this norm to internally displaced persons. The method used here is to build upon the existing provisions identified by the Compilation in order to facilitate their application to internally displaced persons. The general norm is reformulated with a specific focus on the internally displaced. The implicit guarantees contained in existing law are thus made explicit. In principle, the law is not modified, only clarified and simplified.[80] As mentioned above, it was deemed necessary to have a short list of provisions applicable in all circumstances and to all internally displaced persons, in place of the multitude of provisions identified in the Compilation, which are not.

To illustrate how general human rights provisions are reformulated to facilitate their application to the internally displaced, several Guiding Principles are analysed. The first paragraph of Principle 17 states for instance that '*every human being* has the right to respect of his or her family life' (emphasis added). This formulation stresses that internally displaced persons benefit from the same human rights as every other human being. The second paragraph spells out how this right to family life is applied in the specific context of internal displacement: the emphasis is put on family unity as families become separated during phases of internal displacement. Principles 10 (right to life), 11 (right to dignity and integrity), 12 (right to liberty), 20 (right to recognition everywhere as a person before the law), 21 (right to property) and 23 (right to education), in particular, are all similarly worded.

It may seem superfluous to restate general human rights provisions which apply to all, and one could argue that the Guiding Principles

---

[78] See Principle 2(1).
[79] W. Kälin, *Guiding Principles on Internal Displacement: Annotations* (Washington DC: ASIL and the Brookings Institution, 2000), 9.
[80] See Principle 2(2).

constitute a restatement of the obvious. However, a restatement of the law can be justified by the fact that vulnerable groups whose basic human rights are constantly violated may need special protection. Children, as well as women, have the same human rights as anyone else, but specific instruments have been adopted in order to enhance their protection by stating how the general human rights guarantees should be applied in their particular case.[81] One wonders whether there is an increasing trend to categorise various groups in order to enhance their protection in international law. The side-effect of this is the proliferation of human rights norms which apply to a specific group in each case (women, children, minorities, migrant workers, etc.). It is regrettable that there should be such a need to reformulate general human rights guarantees for a special group, as it suggests that these rights are still widely violated.

The wording of some Guiding Principles shows that they are firmly based on existing law. The formulation is directly inspired by existing provisions contained in human rights and humanitarian law instruments. Several examples of this can be given here. The wording of Principle 6(2)(b) relating to the prohibition of displacement in times of armed conflict is taken from Article 49(2) of the Fourth Geneva Convention. The phrase 'unless the security of the civilians involved or imperative military reasons so demand' is almost identical to the latter provision. Walter Kälin, one of the drafters of the Guiding Principles, acknowledged that this provision was used as a reference for the formulation of this principle.[82] His annotations of the Guiding Principles show how the wording of several Principles carefully follows existing human rights and humanitarian law provisions.[83]

Although the completion of the Compilation delayed the drafting of the Guiding Principles, it gave the latter a relatively strong legal basis. In contrast, no such comprehensive study was undertaken to highlight the deficiencies of the law applicable to population transfers. The 'draft Declaration on Population Transfers and the Implantation of Settlers'[84] received a muted response from the Sub-Commission on the Elimination

---

[81] See Cohen, 'The Development of International Standards', 79.

[82] Walter Kälin speaking at the seminar on internally displaced persons at the Overseas Development Institute, London, 20 July 1998.

[83] See Kälin, *Annotations*. See also R. K. Goldman, 'Codification of International Rules on Internally Displaced Persons' (1998) 324 *International Review of the Red Cross* 463.

[84] *Human Rights and Population Transfers: Final Report of the Special Rapporteur*, E/CN.4/Sub.2/1997/23, Annex II, 27 June 1997.

of Discrimination and Protection of Minorities,[85] perhaps because the Sub-Commission was not convinced that the adoption of such an instrument was justified. One could also add that 'there is little enthusiasm at present within the UN system for any new human rights standard-setting initiatives'[86] and it is therefore quite an achievement that the Guiding Principles were endorsed by the Commission on Human Rights.

The borderline between the restatement of existing law and the creation of new law

As demonstrated above, the Guiding Principles appear to be firmly based on existing law. The methodology followed is clear: the Guiding Principles are based solely on the Compilation and their formulation is inspired by existing provisions of human rights and humanitarian law. Paragraph 3 of the introduction to the Guiding Principles even states that 'these principles reflect and are consistent with international human rights law and humanitarian law'. The drafters claim that they were careful 'to not go beyond what can be based on existing international law'.[87] Where they identified a specific need of internally displaced persons, but no authoritative legal provisions upon which a corresponding guiding principle could be based, they decided not to include the issue in the text. For instance, internally displaced women are sometimes forced to undergo female genital mutilation when they move to an area where it is widely practised, and it had been suggested that the Guiding Principles should address this problem. However, it was concluded that the legal basis for the inclusion of such a provision in the text was not strong enough.[88]

In other cases, the Guiding Principles certainly 'try to progressively develop certain general principles of human rights law where the existing treaties and conventions may contain some gaps'.[89] Certain provisions go beyond existing law, which would amount to the creation of new law. The borderline between the restatement of existing law and the progressive development of new law is not always easy to draw. With regard to human rights instruments on women's and children's

---

[85] See Sub-Comm. Res. 1997/29, 28 August 1997.   [86] Petrasek, 'Moving Forward', 557.

[87] W. Kälin, 'Guiding Principles on Internal Displacement', paper presented at the Overseas Development Institute, London, 20 July 1998, 7.

[88] Interview with Erin Mooney, Office of the High Commissioner for Human Rights, Geneva, 9 February 1999.

[89] Kälin, 'Introduction', 561.

rights, one would not consider that they have created new rights, but rather developed existing law.

In restating existing law to improve its application to a particular situation, the drafters are not supposed to go beyond what is contained in this law and create new law. Nevertheless, in some cases, they do, as in the case of *non-refoulement*. No provision in international law prohibits the return of internally displaced persons to dangerous areas, as the prohibition of *non-refoulement* currently only applies to cross-border movements,[90] but such a prohibition was included in the Guiding Principles. The provisions on humanitarian assistance may also be considered to go beyond those contained in the Geneva Conventions which are limited to humanitarian *access*: Articles 59 to 61 of the Fourth Geneva Convention refer to occupied territories only. Other relevant provisions are Articles 68 to 71 of Protocol I and Article 18 of Protocol II. In contrast, the wording of Principle 25(2) is stronger since it states that 'consent . . . shall not be *arbitrarily* withheld' (emphasis added). Another example of a Guiding Principle that may go beyond the existing legal position is analysed in more detail below.

This bold and extensive interpretation of the law by the drafters of the Guiding Principles fills some of the gaps which exist in the current legal framework. The creation of new law relating to internal displacement is impossible because it raises problems of legal definition of the internally displaced, and because there is currently little political will to move in this direction. Nevertheless, there was a need to clarify the law on internal displacement, which the drafters claim they did. One may wonder whether they intentionally made it look like a restatement of the law and insisted on the fact that there was nothing in the Guiding Principles which did not already exist in international law, but, at the same time, surreptitiously introduced new provisions derived from existing ones. The following example demonstrates how a broad and creative interpretation of existing norms was adopted when drafting the Guiding Principles.

An example: the right of restitution of property in international law

As a result of being displaced, internally displaced persons often lose their property. When they attempt to return to their homes, they may discover that their property has been destroyed or is now occupied by

---

[90] See Article 33 of the 1951 Convention and the jurisprudence of the European Court of Human Rights, in particular *Soering* v. *United Kingdom et al.* (1989) 11 EHRR 439.

other families who may have lived there for several years. In order to facilitate the return of internally displaced persons to their homes, their property should be returned to them. Where restitution is not possible, compensation should be granted to them instead. Principle 29(2) deals with the issue of restitution of property. The question for our purposes is whether such a provision is based on existing international law.

The Universal Declaration of Human Rights, which is not legally binding, recognises a right to own property (Article 17(1)) and to be protected against arbitrary deprivation of property (Article 17(2)). The two Covenants do not contain similar provisions. The right to property is mainly guaranteed under regional instruments.[91] For instance, Article 1 of Protocol No. 1 to the European Convention on Human Rights states that 'every natural or legal person is entitled to the peaceful enjoyment of his possessions'.[92] However, it is, in any case, not an absolute right. Only Article 21(2) of the American Convention on Human Rights mentions the issue of compensation. In cases of loss of property resulting from development-induced displacement, compensation may be easier to obtain. For instance, the World Bank has developed a policy providing for compensation for losses suffered by persons displaced involuntarily as a result of development projects which give rise to severe economic, social and environmental problems.[93] However, restitution or compensation is much more difficult to obtain in situations of armed conflict and/or forcible displacement: the authorities are obviously reluctant to compensate for the loss of property caused by their deliberate action to drive people out of their homes.

There is an increasing trend in international law to award compensation for loss of property resulting from displacement.[94] In the *Miskito* case, the Inter-American Commission on Human Rights recognised that compensation should be awarded to returning internally displaced persons for loss of property.[95] Since 1998, the European Court of Human Rights has awarded compensation for destruction of property by state

---

[91] See the Compilation, para. 273.

[92] First Protocol to the European Convention on Human Rights, 20 March 1952, 213 UNTS 262.

[93] See Operational Policy 4.12 on Involuntary Resettlement, World Bank Operational Manual, December 2001.

[94] See COHRE, *Housing and Property Restitution for Refugees and Internally Displaced Persons: International, Regional and National Legal Resources* (Geneva: COHRE, 2001).

[95] *Report on the Situation of Human Rights of a Segment of the Nicaraguan Population of Miskito Origin*, OEA/Ser.L/V/II.62, Doc. 10, rev.3, 29 November 1983.

security forces which has often led to internal displacement. In *Akdivar*, the Court declared that the burning of houses by Turkish security forces amounted to violations of Article 8 of the Convention[96] (right to respect for private and family life, home and correspondence) and of Article 1 of Protocol No. 1 to the Convention.[97] It subsequently ordered Turkey to compensate the applicants for loss of their houses, cultivated and arable land, household property, livestock and feed, and cost of alternative accommodation.[98] This decision was taken on the basis of Article 50 (now Article 41) of the Convention which allows the Court to award damages to the injured party. Compensation for loss of property has been awarded mainly in cases arising from the eviction of Kurds from their villages in south-east Turkey such as *Selcuk and Asker*,[99] *Mentes*,[100] *Bilgin*[101] and *Yöyler*.[102] In *Loizidou*, compensation was also awarded to a woman who was denied access to her property situated in the northern part of Cyprus which had been invaded by Turkey.[103] Finally, in *Cyprus v. Turkey*,[104] the Court found a continuing violation of Article 1 of Protocol No. 1 by Turkey which denied Greek-Cypriot owners of property in northern Cyprus access to their property as well as compensation for such interference with their property rights.

Restitution of property is often more difficult to achieve than compensation (especially if the property is occupied by third parties), but it is much more likely to lead to the return of refugees and internally displaced persons to their homes. It has been argued that 'conditions of safe and dignified return will not and cannot be met without adequate safeguards designed to protect the rights to housing and property restitution of returnees'.[105] According to its Rules of Procedure and Evidence, the International Criminal Tribunal for the Former Yugoslavia has the power to order the restitution of property in conjunction with

---

[96] European Convention for the Protection of Human Rights and Fundamental Freedoms, 4 November 1950, 213 UNTS 221 (hereinafter the European Convention on Human Rights).

[97] *Akdivar and others v. Turkey* (1997) 23 EHRR 143.

[98] *Akdivar and others v. Turkey* (Article 50), 1 April 1998, Reports, 1998-II, 711.

[99] *Selcuk and Asker v. Turkey* (1998) 26 EHRR 477.

[100] *Mentes and others v. Turkey* (Article 50), 24 July 1998, Reports, 1998-IV, 1686.

[101] *Bilgin v. Turkey* (2003) 36 EHRR 879.

[102] *Yöyler v. Turkey*, Application No. 26973/9524, decision of 24 July 2003.

[103] *Loizidou v. Turkey* (Article 50), 28 July 1998, Reports 1998-IV, 1807.

[104] *Cyprus v. Turkey* (2002) 35 EHRR 30.

[105] S. Leckie, 'Housing and Property Issues for Refugees and Internally Displaced Persons in the Context of Return: Key Considerations for UNHCR Policy and Practice' (2000) 19:3 *Refugee Survey Quarterly* 5 at 7.

a judgment of conviction.[106] This issue has not come up in any of the cases so far decided by the Tribunal. Finally, several peace agreements provide for the restitution of property lost as a result of displacement, or for compensation for that loss. For instance, the Dayton Peace Agreement established the Commission on Real Property Claims of Displaced Persons and Refugees to facilitate the restitution of property.[107]

As mentioned above, no explicit provision guaranteeing the right of restitution of property has been formulated in the main human rights instruments (ICCPR, ICESCR, Universal Declaration, etc.). A principle of compensation for loss of property resulting from forced eviction has been developed mainly by the European Court of Human Rights and the Inter-American Commission on Human Rights. It would therefore appear that Principle 29 anticipated the development of the law, since, at the time of drafting, 'the question as to whether nationals are generally entitled to compensation for losses of their property . . . probably [had] to be answered in the negative'.[108] It may still be too early today to conclude that a right to restitution of property lost as a result of displacement or compensation for such a loss has been firmly established in international law.[109] Nevertheless, the Guiding Principles may contribute to the development of the law in the area,[110] and increasing international attention is now being paid to the issue of housing and property restitution in the context of the return of refugees and internally displaced persons: the Sub-Commission on the Promotion and Protection of Human Rights has recently appointed a Special Rapporteur to examine the problem.[111]

Some provisions contained in the Guiding Principles result from a creative interpretation of existing norms. Sometimes, one may wonder whether the line between the restatement of existing law and the creation of new law has been crossed. The Guiding Principles seek to push

---

[106] See rule 105 of the Rules of Procedure and Evidence, adopted 11 February 1994 by the International Tribunal for the Prosecution of Persons Responsible for Serious Violations of Humanitarian Law Committed in the Territory of the Former Yugoslavia Since 1991, IT/32/Rev.26.

[107] See Chapter 5, pp. 191–3 below. See also the jurisprudence of the Human Rights Chamber for Bosnia and Herzegovina; see Kälin, *Annotations*, 73–4.

[108] R. Hofmann, 'International Humanitarian Law and the Law of Refugees and Internally Displaced Persons', in European Commission, *Law in Humanitarian Crisis* (Brussels: European Commission, 1995), vol. 1, 249–309 at 297.

[109] For a dissenting view, see Leckie, 'Housing and Property Issues', 38–9.   [110] *Ibid.* 39–40.

[111] *Economic, Social and Cultural Rights: Housing and Property Restitution in the Context of the Return of Refugees and Internally Displaced Persons, Preliminary Report of the Special Rapporteur, Paulo Sérgio Pinheiro* E/CN.4/Sub.2/2003/11, 16 June 2003.

the law to its outer limits in order to provide the most complete protection for internally displaced persons, and maybe contribute to the emergence of new norms.

The weaknesses

Although the Guiding Principles address most aspects of the problem of internal displacement, some issues are mentioned too briefly or not at all. Minorities are often the first targets of persecution and, as a result, the first populations to be internally displaced. Cases of forcible relocation of minority groups are too numerous to be cited here. However, minorities are only mentioned once in the whole document, in Principle 9, where they are referred to together with peasants and pastoralists. Another provision contained in Principle 6(2)(a) prohibiting 'ethnic cleansing' indirectly addresses the issue, but more specific and stronger provisions could have been included. The prohibition of forcible relocation is insufficient to prevent the displacement of minorities. Only full respect for minority rights can guarantee protection against displacement.[112]

The issue of safe areas is not mentioned at all in the Guiding Principles. Consequently, the implications of their establishment on the freedom of movement within the country and on the right to asylum are not explored. The Compilation has not addressed the issue, but one may wonder whether safe areas could provide protection to the internally displaced if they are established according to agreed rules. This possibility is not envisaged in the Guiding Principles, but nor is it excluded.[113]

As argued above, the Guiding Principles constitute an ambitious attempt to provide a comprehensive normative framework of protection for the internally displaced. Such an endeavour may be too ambitious. Indeed, it covers such a broad range of issues that 'coherence may be elusive in a document that canvasses a variety of different concerns [which] pose distinct challenges'.[114] To some extent, one may argue that the original objective of the Guiding Principles was to provide a first comprehensive overview of the problems encountered by the internally

---

[112] See the 1995 Framework Convention for the Protection of National Minorities, ETS No. 157, which represents the first legally binding multilateral instrument relating to the protection of national minorities.

[113] On the use of safe areas to provide protection to internally displaced persons, see Chapter 4, pp. 136–40 below.

[114] See Fitzpatrick, 'Converging Standards', 11.

displaced and that coherence may not be so crucial in a non-legally binding instrument.

Be that as it may, the most significant weakness of the Guiding Principles could still be that it is a non-binding instrument. However useful the Guiding Principles may be, states as well as other actors, or even international organisations, are not legally bound to respect them and cannot be held liable for violating them. The obvious danger is that they could become a dead letter, as there is no mechanism to ensure their proper implementation. On the other hand, had they been a legally binding instrument, the Guiding Principles may not have been so comprehensive, and this may actually be seen as a strength. Nevertheless, one must also remember that, although the Guiding Principles are not a legally binding instrument, they contain rules 'that form part of treaty law and that are therefore legally binding'.[115]

Beyond the Guiding Principles?

A practical document intended for the field

The Guiding Principles constitute an innovative attempt to deal with the problem of internal displacement. When compared with the 1951 Refugee Convention, it is clear that they are based upon a radically different approach. The 1951 Convention does not attempt to address such a broad range of issues: it does not deal with the root causes of displacement, with humanitarian assistance to refugees, nor with the restitution of property to facilitate their return. The 1951 Convention is only concerned with the protection of refugees while they are refugees, whereas the Guiding Principles have a more ambitious objective. The two instruments differ in their aims: the 1951 Convention is concerned with rights which individuals acquire when they obtain refugee status, and seeks to achieve equality of treatment between them and the nationals of the country of asylum. The purpose of the Guiding Principles is not to create a legal status to which rights and obligations are attached. They are based upon a humanitarian approach rather than a legalistic one. The differences pertain not only to the nature of the two categories of persons involved,[116] but also to the nature of the instrument. One is a legally binding instrument, whereas the other is a set of non-legally binding guidelines.

---

[115] Lavoyer, 'Guiding Principles'.   [116] See Chapter 1, first section, above.

The Guiding Principles should prove especially useful in situations falling short of armed conflict (internal disturbance) or when issues are not sufficiently covered by current international law, as in the case, for instance, of property-related issues. In areas which are well covered by international humanitarian law, it is expected that ICRC delegates will still continue to rely on the Geneva Conventions and the Additional Protocols,[117] but turn to the Guiding Principles when international humanitarian law is silent on issues that need to be dealt with.[118]

The Guiding Principles not only remind states of their legal obligations towards internally displaced persons, they are also to be used by all those who work with them. The idea was to devise a practical document to be used in the field. The Guiding Principles differ from the approach adopted by the International Law Association (ILA) Committee on Internally Displaced Persons. The provisions of the London Declaration on International Law Principles on Internally Displaced Persons[119] are much more abstract and offer little guidance on how they should be applied in practice. For instance, they merely refer to the main human rights and humanitarian law instruments without further precision (Article 2). One of the drafters stated that, whereas 'the Guiding Principles . . . are intended as a guide to the treatment of IDPs from the perspective of their needs, the Declaration focuses on the status of IDPs under international law'.[120] The scope of the Declaration is not as well defined as that of the Guiding Principles. For instance, the Declaration even deals with cooperation of all actors involved with the Security Council (Article 16). Most of its provisions are drafted in the traditional vocabulary of international law (they refer to GA Res. 2625 in Article 10, for instance)[121] and stress the importance of territorial sovereignty. Overall, the provisions of the Declaration are too vague to be of any practical relevance for those working with the internally displaced.

---

[117] See Contat Hickel, 'Protection of Internally Displaced Persons', 707.

[118] See Lavoyer, 'Guiding Principles'. See also interview with ICRC staff, Geneva, 12 February 1999.

[119] See L. T. Lee, 'The London Declaration of International Law Principles on Internally Displaced Persons' (2001) 95 *American Journal of International Law* 454. For the text of the Declaration, see L. T. Lee, 'The London Declaration of International Law Principles on Internally Displaced Persons: Its Significance and Implications' (2001) 14 *Journal of Refugee Studies* 70.

[120] *Ibid.*, 70.

[121] Declaration on Principles of International Law Concerning Friendly Relations and Co-operation Among States in Accordance with the Charter of the United Nations, GA Res. 2625 (XXV), 24 October 1970.

In contrast, the Guiding Principles seek to provide practical guidance to all those dealing with internally displaced persons.[122] They provide field workers with a legal basis when engaging in assistance and protection activities. They can now confidently rely on a document which is comprehensible to non-lawyers and which they know is firmly based on existing law.[123] For this reason, most NGOs supported the drafting of legal principles.[124] Most UN agencies have also welcomed the drafting of such a set of principles which should facilitate their work.[125] The Office for the Coordination of Humanitarian Affairs (OCHA) has endorsed them as well.[126] In addition, the Guiding Principles can be used as benchmarks to evaluate the situation of the internally displaced in a specific case. The Inter-American Commission on Human Rights has already used them to evaluate the treatment of internally displaced persons by the Colombian government.[127] The Special Representative on Internally Displaced Persons has also used them, for instance, in Azerbaijan to urge the authorities to adopt measures in accordance with the Guiding Principles.[128] Moreover, the existence of Guiding Principles can also serve to raise awareness of the plight of internally displaced populations. In sum, the Guiding Principles are very much seen not only as a 'legal' instrument, but also as an advocacy tool for NGOs.[129]

One last possible use of the Guiding Principles which is not generally discussed, because it could prove highly problematic, relates to the issue

---

[122] See introduction to the Guiding Principles, para. 3.

[123] Interview with Erin Mooney, Office of the High Commissioner for Human Rights, Geneva, 9 February 1999.

[124] See C. W. Lambrecht, *NGO Response Patterns to the Assistance, Protection and Development Needs of the Internally Displaced*, Norwegian Refugee Council, Geneva, July 1996, 28. See also Caritas Internationalis and Friends World Committee for Consultation (Quakers), *Internally Displaced Persons; Joint Oral Statement to the Commission on Human Rights*, 9 April 1998.

[125] See for instance UNHCR Standing Committee, *Progress Report on Informal Consultation on the Provision of International Protection to All Who Need It*, EC/48/SC/CRP.32, 25 May 1998, para. 6.

[126] Kälin, 'Introduction', 562.

[127] See Inter-American Commission on Human Rights, *Third Report on the Situation of Human Rights in Colombia 1999*, Chapter VI, 'Internal Displacement', http://www.cidh.oas.org/countryrep/Colom99en/chapter-6.htm.

[128] See R. Cohen, 'The Guiding Principles on Internal Displacement: A New Instrument for International Organisations and NGOs', *Forced Migration Review*, vol. 2, August 1998, 33.

[129] See M. Vincent and B. R. Sørensen, *Caught Between Borders: Response Strategies of the Internally Displaced* (London: Pluto Press in association with Norwegian Refugee Council, 2001), 9.

of humanitarian intervention. One could argue that the Guiding Principles provide a set of criteria for humanitarian intervention on behalf of the internally displaced: gross violations of the Guiding Principles could trigger humanitarian intervention. In decisions to undertake humanitarian intervention, the widespread and systematic violation of the rights mentioned in the Guiding Principles can be taken into account.[130] However, some states have already expressed their concern over such possible use of the Guiding Principles.[131]

Application of the Guiding Principles

The General Assembly has encouraged 'the further dissemination and application of the Guiding Principles.'[132] Since they are not legally binding, one must first ask what their 'application' involves. Hakata emphasises the pedagogical aspect of the document and suggests that the term 'enhancement' may be more appropriate in this context.[133] This may involve dissemination of the document, training and, possibly, implementation at the national level.

The Guiding Principles are being widely disseminated, not only in UN agencies and NGOs, but also among all those involved with internally displaced persons (international and regional organisations, governments, insurgent groups and internally displaced persons themselves).[134] Although the Commission on Human Rights did not specifically call for dissemination when the Guiding Principles were presented to it,[135] the Inter-Agency Standing Committee (composed of the heads of all UN humanitarian agencies) took the decision in March 1998 to disseminate the document widely, following the strongly positive response of UN agencies.[136] The Guiding Principles have already been translated into the six official languages of the UN, but, more importantly, they

---

[130] See Chapter 6, pp. 223–4 below.
[131] See Brookings Institution, *Summary Report of the International Colloquy on the Guiding Principles on Internal Displacement, Vienna, Austria, September 2000,*
http://www.brook.edu/fp/projects/idp/conferences/vienna20009/summary.htm.
[132] GA Res. 54/167, 17 December 1999, para. 8.
[133] See K. Hakata, 'Vers une protection plus effective des "personnes déplacées à l'intérieur de leur propre pays"' (2002) *Revue Générale de Droit International Public,* No. 3, 619–44 at 630.
[134] See *Internally Displaced Persons; Report of the Representative of the Secretary-General, Mr Francis M. Deng,* E/CN.4/2003/86, 21 January 2003 (hereinafter *2003 Deng Report*), paras. 22–43.
[135] See CHR Res. 1998/50, 17 April 1998.
[136] See *Internally Displaced Persons: Report of the Representative of the Secretary-General, Mr Francis M. Deng,* E/CN.4/2001/5, 17 January 2001 (hereinafter *2001 Deng Report*), para. 9.

should be translated into the languages of the countries where internal displacement occurs, so that not only government officials but also the internally displaced themselves are able to read and use them. For instance, they were translated into Azerbaijani for the visit of the Special Representative, and widely distributed to government officials, local NGOs and the internally displaced themselves.[137]

A handbook has been produced to explain in non-legal terms the content of the Guiding Principles and to suggest strategies to field staff on how to implement them.[138] Special training modules focusing on the Guiding Principles have been developed by the Norwegian Refugee Council,[139] while existing training modules in the ICRC already include a presentation of the document.[140] It has been noted that the staff of some humanitarian agencies are still reluctant to use the Guiding Principles for fear that the host government might react in a hostile way.[141] To counter this, it is important that the OCHA IDP Unit continues to promote greater understanding and use of the Guiding Principles through its training workshops.[142]

No monitoring system exists to ensure the implementation of the Guiding Principles. There have been proposals to establish a 'panel of experts' composed of NGOs, academics, representatives of displaced communities and UN agencies to monitor and promote the implementation of the Guiding Principles.[143] It has also been suggested that a regional approach to monitoring the Guiding Principles may be the most appropriate.[144] Regional organisations could play an important role in disseminating and promoting the Guiding Principles, but also in monitoring their use. For instance, a workshop was convened to explore ways in

---

[137] See *Internally Displaced Persons: Report of the Representative of the Secretary-General, Mr Francis M. Deng, Profile of Displacement: Azerbaijan*, E/CN.4/1999/79/Add.1, 25 January 1999, para. 8.

[138] OCHA, *Handbook for Applying the Guiding Principles on Internal Displacement*, 1999.

[139] See http://www.idpproject.org/idp_guided_tour.htm.

[140] Interview with ICRC staff, Geneva, 12 February 1999.

[141] See Brookings Institution, *International Symposium on the Mandate of the Representative of the UN Secretary-General on Internally Displaced Persons: Taking Stock and Charting the Future*, Vienna, Austria, 12–13 December 2002, 10.

[142] See http://www.reliefweb.int/idp/docs/reports.htm.

[143] See Brookings Institution, *Summary Report of the International Colloquy on the Guiding Principles on Internal Displacement*, Vienna, Austria, September 2000, http://www.brook.edu/fp/projects/idp/conferences/vienna20009/ summary.htm.

[144] See Brookings Institution, *Summary Report of the Regional Workshop on Internal Displacement in the South Caucasus, Tbilisi, Georgia, 10–12 May 2000*, http://www.brookings.edu/fp/projects/idp/conferences/georgia200005/summary.htm.

which the Organisation of African Unity (now the African Union) could participate in the dissemination and implementation of the Guiding Principles.[145] At the national level, some governments have enacted legislation based on the Guiding Principles, or reformed existing legislation to comply with them.[146]

State concerns about the Guiding Principles

When examining the drafting history of the Guiding Principles, it appears that it was mainly the Special Representative and his team of legal experts, and some NGOs, that were the main actors in the process. The only states that really participated in the development of the Guiding Principles were Norway and Austria, which sponsored several meetings of legal experts. There had never been a specific debate on the Guiding Principles in the Commission on Human Rights, which instead simply took note of them in a resolution adopted without a vote.[147]

Certain developing countries became nervous about the growing prominence given to the issue of internal displacement, especially since the formulation of the Guiding Principles. Such concerns were first expressed in the 2000 session of the Economic and Social Council (ECOSOC),[148] and then on the occasion of the adoption of the annual resolution on UNHCR by the General Assembly (Third Committee). In the draft resolution, the General Assembly underlined 'the continuing relevance of the Guiding Principles'.[149] Although these words may appear rather innocuous, several countries took this as an opportunity to express their unease. Egypt, in particular, 'found it difficult to agree to language which emphasised the Guiding Principles on internal displacement',[150] and called for a vote on the relevant paragraph of the draft resolution on UNHCR. This was an unprecedented step. India explicitly stated that the Guiding Principles 'did not enjoy government approval and were not binding'.[151] Consequently, India considered that 'the

[145] See UNHCR/Brookings Institution/OAU, *Internal Displacement in Africa: Report of a Workshop Held in Addis Ababa, Ethiopia, 19–20 October 1998* (1998). See also Brookings Institution, *Report of the Conference on Internal Displacement in Asia, Bangkok, Thailand, 22–24 February 2000*, http://www.brookings.edu/fp/projects/idp/ conferences/contents.htm.

[146] See *2003 Deng Report*, note 134 above, paras. 23–4.

[147] CHR Res. 1998/50, 17 April 1998, para. 1.

[148] See F. M. Deng, 'The Global Challenge of Internal Displacement' (2001) 5 *Washington University Journal of Law and Policy* 141 at 149.

[149] Doc. A/C.3/55/l.67, para. 20.   [150] Press Release, GA/SHC/3624, 10 November 2000.

[151] *Ibid.*

language was out of place, and the resolution sought to confer on those principles a profile they did not deserve'.[152] At the end of the debate, a large majority of states voted in favour of paragraph 20, but thirty states abstained.[153] The initial draft was thus adopted,[154] but, for the first time, serious criticisms had been expressed about the Guiding Principles. This led Rudge to ask whether this constituted 'a serious reverse or merely a temporary interruption to the process of appreciating the situation and needs of IDPs'.[155] So far, it can be noted that such criticisms of the Guiding Principles have prompted some aid agencies to be more cautious when formulating IDP policies.[156]

It appears that the controversy around the Guiding Principles may not be over yet. In 2001, while the Third Committee of the General Assembly discussed a draft resolution on the protection of and assistance to internally displaced persons, Egypt, once again, recalled that the Guiding Principles had not been negotiated on or agreed upon in any intergovernmental forum. It also called for the Special Representative to consult with states when drafting future reports. More worryingly, Egypt threatened that 'until that was done, the question of the Guiding Principles would overshadow the work of the Committee every year'.[157] Syria made similar comments and called for the Guiding Principles to be submitted to an intergovernmental body.[158] At the end of the day, the resolution was nevertheless adopted by consensus.[159] Since then, there has not been any further opportunity to discuss the Guiding Principles, since the UNHCR resolution adopted by the General Assembly in 2002 did not refer to them[160] and there was no resolution on internally displaced persons.

In order to alleviate some state concerns, the Special Representative has held meetings with those governments which were uneasy about the ways in which the Guiding Principles had been developed and were being used.[161] The recent controversy about the Guiding Principles indicates that they are not perceived by all states as a mere restatement of existing international standards that had already been accepted by

---

[152] *Ibid.*   [153] *Ibid.*   [154] GA Res. 55/74, 4 December 2000.

[155] P. Rudge, *The Need for a More Focused Response: European Donor Policies Toward Internally Displaced Persons*, Brookings Institution, Norwegian Refugee Council and US Committee for Refugees, January 2002, 13.

[156] See for instance Chapter 3, pp. 96–7 below.

[157] Press Release, GA/SHC/3676, 29 November 2001.   [158] *Ibid.*

[159] GA Res. 56/164, 19 December 2001.   [160] GA Res. 57/187, 18 December 2002.

[161] *2003 Deng Report*, note 134 above, para. 21.

them (either through treaty or customary international law). Although this controversy does not seem to have undermined in any significant manner the authority gained by the Guiding Principles in the last few years, it may have a more important impact on any further development of the normative framework of protection of the internally displaced.

Towards a legally binding instrument?

The legal status of the Guiding Principles is confusing. On the one hand, it is clearly a non-legally binding instrument to which state consent to be bound has never been expressed.[162] On the other hand, and as analysed above, the Guiding Principles are a restatement of binding norms contained in existing international treaties and/or customary international law. According to Kälin, the Guiding Principles are soft law and 'do not even constitute typical soft law',[163] i.e. declarations made by states not intended to be legally binding upon them. In this case, the Guiding Principles were drafted by legal experts and presented to the Commission on Human Rights which did not formally adopt them. Kälin then argues that we must look at their actual acceptance and use, rather than their legal form.[164] He then ends with the mysterious statement that, if the Guiding Principles are actually accepted and used in practice, 'they become hard standards even if they are *still* not hard law' (emphasis added).[165] The use of legal terminology is slightly unfortunate here and one may be confused by the distinction which is made between 'hard standards' and 'hard law': the two expressions are not clearly defined.

One way to put an end to this confusion may be to call for the adoption of a legally binding instrument. Some NGOs such as Pax International still share this view.[166] However, despite the growing use and acceptance of the Guiding Principles, these cannot and should not be seen as a first step towards a legally binding instrument on internal displacement. A new treaty covering this issue is not feasible, mainly because of the current difficulties affecting treaty-making in the area of human rights.[167]

---

[162] Article 11 of the Vienna Convention on the Law of Treaties (1969) 9 ILM 679.

[163] W. Kälin, 'How Hard Is Soft Law? The Guiding Principles on Internal Displacement and the Need for a Normative Framework', presentation at Roundtable Meeting, Ralph Bunche Institute for International Studies, City University of New York Graduate Center, 19 December 2002, 6.

[164] *Ibid.*, 8.   [165] *Ibid.*

[166] See Pax International, *Internally Displaced Persons – A Discussion Paper*, Washington DC, March 2002, http://www.paxinternational.org/discuss.

[167] Kälin, 'How Hard Is Soft Law?', 2–5.

It is also not desirable because the internally displaced should not constitute a distinct legal category, as refugees do.[168] The development of the Guiding Principles already represents an important achievement, especially in such a short period of time, but it is also the most that can be achieved to improve the legal protection of internally displaced persons.

Although a new treaty or convention on internal displacement is neither feasible nor desirable, the profile of the Guiding Principles could be enhanced by their adoption by the General Assembly. In 1993, the problem of violence against women was given increased international attention when the General Assembly adopted the Declaration on the Elimination of Violence Against Women.[169] A General Assembly resolution adopting the Guiding Principles could constitute another important step in highlighting the problem of internal displacement, and a formal presentation of the document to the General Assembly would provide an opportunity for a debate about the Principles among states.

Conclusion

This chapter has demonstrated the importance of human rights law and humanitarian law in providing a legal framework of protection for the internally displaced. The formulation of the Guiding Principles confirms that work with the internally displaced can and must be based on legal provisions drawn from human rights and humanitarian law instruments.

When the Special Representative on Internally Displaced Persons was appointed by the Secretary-General in July 1992, one of his tasks was to analyse the legal norms applicable in situations of internal displacement, and the possibility of drafting Guiding Principles was already envisaged.[170] The Compilation and Analysis of legal norms was completed in 1996 and the Special Representative was called upon to develop an appropriate framework for the protection of internally displaced persons on the basis of this document. It was not until six years after the Special Representative took up his position that the Guiding Principles were finally completed. The difficulties arising from the drafting of this new international document have suggested that 'the effort to

---

[168] See Chapter 1, first section, above.
[169] UN Doc. A/48/629, reprinted in (1994) 33 ILM 1050.
[170] See CHR Res. 1993/95, 11 March 1993.

explicate the rights of the internally displaced is plagued by conceptual and practical pitfalls'.[171]

The Guiding Principles have stimulated further interest in the problem of internal displacement and, as such, constitute a very important step in raising awareness of this issue. The dissemination phase has been very successful to the extent that all UN agencies as well as a number of NGOs have endorsed them and started to use them in the field. The focus is now on training and implementation. At its fiftieth session, the Commission on Human Rights did not mention any further progress in the development of a legal framework of protection,[172] and the Special Representative also considers that he has fulfilled the legal part of his mandate.[173]

It remains to be seen whether the Guiding Principles will favour the development of customary rules (on restitution of property, for instance), and they have already started to gain authority among international and regional organisations, NGOs and some governments. They should now be implemented as widely as possible. Whereas the General Assembly has merely 'noted' the Guiding Principles,[174] a General Assembly resolution adopting them could be passed in order to strengthen their moral authority. The document should also be referred to in Security Council resolutions when dealing with situations of internal displacement.[175]

---

[171] Fitzpatrick, 'Converging Standards', 10.

[172] See CHR Res. 1998/50, 17 April 1998.

[173] Interview with Erin Mooney, Office of the High Commissioner for Human Rights, Geneva, 9 February 1999.

[174] See GA Res. 54/167, 17 December 1999, para. 6. See also GA Res. 56/164, 20 February 2002, paras. 6–7.

[175] See for instance SC Res. 1286, 19 January 2000, on the situation in Burundi.

3   The institutional framework of protection for the internally displaced

The study of internal displacement cannot be separated from a study of mechanisms, and this chapter therefore evaluates how UN actors approach the IDP issue. It explores the implications of a human rights approach to the problem of internal displacement on the nature of the institutional response to that problem. Indeed, while the analysis concentrates on humanitarian actors, internally displaced persons are victims of human rights violations. Examining UN actors' policies on internal displacement should therefore reflect how these actors are integrating human rights concerns within their respective mandates.

Although a multitude of actors are involved with internally displaced persons, this chapter deals mainly with agencies within the UN system, with the exception of International Committee of the Red Cross (ICRC), the International Organization for Migration (IOM) and the World Health Organization (WHO). Most agencies have been involved with internally displaced persons for more than ten years, but it is only recently that they have explicitly asserted an IDP role and attempted to formulate a specific policy response to the problem of internal displacement. The first two sections below concentrate on UNHCR, while the third section reviews the roles of other agencies. With so many actors having a mandate covering IDP issues, issues of inter-agency cooperation are crucial to ensure that their needs are fully covered: the fourth section below reviews existing coordination mechanisms with regard to internally displaced persons and recent initiatives to improve such mechanisms and ensure that human rights issues are adequately addressed. The focus here is therefore on agencies' stated approaches to internal displacement, rather than on field activities, which will be examined in the following chapter and the case study.

The role of UNHCR with regard to internally displaced persons

UNHCR's mandate

UNHCR's mandate has evolved considerably since the agency was created in 1951. In order to understand how this mandate came to include the internally displaced, one must go back as far as 1946. During its first session, the General Assembly of the United Nations expressed its willingness to consider the refugee problem as one of the priorities of the newly founded organisation.[1] This resulted in the creation four years later of the Office of the United Nations High Commissioner for Refugees (UNHCR)[2] as a subsidiary organ of the General Assembly. It was created under Article 22 of the United Nations Charter which provides: 'The General Assembly may establish such subsidiary organs as it deems necessary for the performance of its functions.' As a result, the High Commissioner has to submit annual reports of the activities of his or her office to the General Assembly, through the Economic and Social Council (ECOSOC). The Office was initially created for three years, and its mandate had to be renewed every five years until recently. For the first time, the mandate of the refugee agency was not restricted to specific national groups, but based upon a general international legal instrument, the 1951 Refugee Convention.[3] The two main functions of the agency are to provide international protection and to promote the search for permanent solutions to the problem of refugees.[4]

UNHCR was not initially supposed to be an operational agency, unlike its predecessor, the International Refugee Organization (IRO).[5] Consequently, UNHCR only had an administrative budget.[6] However, this situation was modified as early as 1952, when UNHCR was authorised to appeal for funds for emergency operations.[7] UNHCR now has a

---

[1] See GA Res. 8 (I), 12 February 1946.

[2] See GA Res. 319 (IV), 3 December 1949 and GA Res. 428 (V), 14 December 1950. The Statute of UNHCR is in the Annex to the second resolution.

[3] Convention Relating to the Status of Refugees, 28 July 1951, 189 UNTS 150 (hereinafter the 1951 Convention).

[4] Article 1 of the UNHCR's Statute.

[5] See G. Goodwin-Gill, *The Refugee in International Law* (Oxford: Clarendon Press, 2nd ed., 1996), 6.

[6] Article 20 of the UNHCR Statute.

[7] See GA Res. 538 (VI), 2 February 1952. See also M. Moussalli, 'The Evolving Functions of the Office of the High Commissioner for Refugees', in V. Gowlland and K. Samson (eds.), *Problems and Prospects of Refugee Law* (Geneva: Graduate Institute of International Studies, 1991), 81–103 at 89.

substantial fund devoted to the promotion of permanent solutions, and assistance programmes represent a major part of its activities. The Executive Committee of UNHCR (EXCOM), originally the Advisory Committee on Refugees, was created in 1957 under Article 4 of the Statute of the UNHCR[8] and is now composed of sixty-four states.[9] It assists the High Commissioner in his or her activities. A sub-committee of the whole on international protection was created in 1975 to help EXCOM examine more technical aspects of refugee protection.

UNHCR's competence is defined in Article 6 of the Statute: the mandate covers persons who qualify for refugee status under the definition in the 1951 Convention. It is therefore a narrow mandate which reflects the close links between UNHCR's Statute and the 1951 Convention. Article 6 defines what is commonly referred to as the statutory mandate, as opposed to the extended mandate.[10] Extension of the mandate was already foreseen by the drafters of the Statute. Nevertheless, according to Article 9, any extension of the mandate is subject to two conditions, i.e. the approval of the General Assembly and the availability of funds for the conduct of the operations.

In the first few years of existence of UNHCR, the mandate as defined in the Statute proved impractical. Individual screening of those fleeing their country was impossible in some circumstances, and UNHCR could provide protection to some populations only by taking the position that these were *prima facie* refugees. There has been a gap between the definitional assumption of individual processing and the reality of refugee movements.[11] Individual screening of internally displaced persons is even less practical, which is another argument militating against the drafting of a precise IDP definition focusing on each individual's personal circumstances.[12]

The concept of 'good offices' was first used with reference to mainland Chinese refugees in Hong Kong. The High Commissioner was requested to use his good offices to assist 'refugees who do not come within the competence of the UN'.[13] One must note that this new development took place only a few years after the creation of UNHCR. The use

---

[8] GA Res. 1166 (XII), 26 November 1957.   [9] GA Res. 57/185, 18 December 2002.

[10] Distinction used by P. Kourula, *Broadening the Edges: Refugee Definition and International Protection Revisited* (The Hague: Martinus Nijhoff Publishers, 1997), 174–83.

[11] See C. Harvey, *Seeking Asylum in the UK: Problems and Prospects* (London: Butterworths, 2000), 142.

[12] See Chapter 1, pp. 26–8 above.   [13] See GA Res. 1388 (XIV), 20 November 1959.

of the concept of 'good offices' was confirmed in subsequent General Assembly resolutions,[14] and was progressively linked to the notion of 'displaced persons'. To some extent, one could argue that 'the "displaced persons" category, with its foundations in humanitarian necessity, was the natural successor to the "good offices" approach'.[15] UNHCR's mandate was extended to this undefined category of persons who were not refugees under the 1951 Convention, but who nonetheless required international assistance.[16]

There was initial resistance to extending assistance to internally displaced persons. Sadruddin, who was the High Commissioner for Refugees in the late 1960s, turned down a request for assistance to internally displaced persons in South Vietnam precisely because they were internally displaced. Loescher considers that 'the Office took a legalistic position, arguing that these situations were not a matter within the competence of the High Commissioner and were not a matter of direct concern to the UNHCR for "constitutional" and legal considerations'.[17] Similar arguments are being made today by commentators such as Goodwin-Gill to criticise UNHCR's activities on behalf of the internally displaced.[18]

Nevertheless, in 1972 the General Assembly authorised UNHCR to provide assistance to 'refugees and other displaced persons', which referred here to internally displaced persons, in the Sudan.[19] On the basis of its particular expertise and experience,[20] the High Commissioner has been increasingly called upon to provide protection and assistance to displaced (and also non-displaced, as in the case of the former Yugoslavia) populations in need of international protection. In most cases, the main criterion for assisting and protecting these populations is simply the lack of protection. These populations are regrouped under the denomination of 'other populations of concern' in UNHCR statistics.[21]

---

[14] See, for instance, GA Res. 1673 (XVI), 8 December 1961.

[15] Goodwin-Gill, *The Refugee*, 12.

[16] For a discussion on the concept of displaced persons, see Chapter 1, pp. 14–15 above.

[17] G. Loescher, *The UNHCR and World Politics: A Perilous Path* (Oxford: Oxford University Press, 2001), 144–5.

[18] See p. 88 below.   [19] GA Res. 2958 (XXVII), 12 December 1972.

[20] This justification was explicitly mentioned for instance in GA Res. 2956 (XXVII), 12 December 1972, para. 2 and GA Res. 31/35, 30 November 1976.

[21] See UNHCR, *Statistical Yearbook 2002: Trends in Displacement, Protection and Solutions* (Geneva: UNHCR, 2004), Table I.1.

UNHCR's mandate now covers not only 1951 Convention refugees, but also refugees as defined in the OAU Convention and the Cartagena Declaration,[22] returnees and stateless persons.[23] This extension of the mandate[24] has not proved problematic, as long as resources were available. Since 1972, the mandate has been further extended to internally displaced persons. UNHCR's mandate has proved very flexible, but the question is to determine how far the agency can and should go in including all internally displaced persons in its mandate.

Increasing involvement with internally displaced persons

The initial involvement of UNHCR with the internally displaced proved inevitable. Where UNHCR engaged in activities for refugees or returnees who lived alongside internally displaced persons, it was very often impractical not to extend these activities to the latter populations. Involvement of the agency with the internally displaced was justified by the fact that it was 'operationally untenable'[25] not to extend assistance and protection to the internally displaced in some situations. As recalled above, General Assembly Resolution 2956 provided the legal basis for UNHCR's involvement with the internally displaced in southern Sudan. Subsequently, UNHCR was again requested to undertake activities outside its mandate on the basis of its 'particular expertise and experience'.

Between 1971 and 1991, UNHCR provided aid, but also engaged in protection activities for the internally displaced in more than a dozen operations.[26] Emergency relief was delivered to them, and, in some cases, specific protection activities were undertaken to protect their human rights. Most of the operations were 'returnee-linked': internally displaced persons just happened to be in areas where UNHCR was involved in assistance and protection activities for refugees returning to their country.

---

[22] Convention Governing the Specific Aspects of Refugee Problems in Africa, 1001 UNTS 45 (hereinafter the 1969 OAU Convention), and Cartagena Declaration on Refugees, 22 November 1984, OAS/Ser.L/V/II.66, doc.10, rev.1. 190 (hereinafter the 1984 Cartagena Declaration).

[23] See the 1954 Convention Relating to the Status of Stateless Persons, 360 UNTS 117.

[24] On UNHCR's current mandate, see V. Türk, 'The Role of UNHCR in the Development of International Refugee Law', in F. Nicholson and P. Twomey (eds.), Refugee Rights and Realities: Evolving Concepts and Regimes (Cambridge: Cambridge University Press, 1999), 153–74 at 154–9.

[25] Leonardo Franco, former Director of International Protection, UNHCR, in UNHCR, UNHCR's Operational Experience with Internally Displaced Persons (Geneva: UNHCR, 1994), foreword.

[26] For a description of these operations, see UNHCR, UNHCR's Operational Experience, 3–15.

During that period, UNHCR also conducted special operations not linked to returnee programs as in Cyprus and Lebanon.

As mentioned earlier, the intervention in northern Iraq in 1991 marked a turning-point in the international approach to the problem of internal displacement.[27] It was also a turning-point in the history of UNHCR's involvement with the internally displaced. Ogata had just become the new High Commissioner for Refugees at the time and her decision to engage UNHCR as the lead agency in Iraq was controversial. The Director of International Protection had argued that she should have stood up to Turkey's refusal to keep its borders open to Iraqi Kurds, but Ogata ignored that advice.[28] This created the uneasy impression that UNHCR's involvement with internally displaced persons constituted an implied recognition of the failure to uphold the right of asylum.

Since 1991, UNHCR has become involved with internally displaced persons in an increasing number of operations. Between 1991 and 1994, programmes were undertaken in favour of the internally displaced in twenty countries.[29] Since then, UNHCR has also started some programmes in other countries, such as Colombia in 1998.[30] This increased involvement of UNHCR has come under question because the agency does not have the capacity, nor the resources, to assume responsibility for all internally displaced persons. Its current activities may also prove incompatible with its core mandate, i.e. the international protection of refugees.

UNHCR engages in both assistance and protection activities in favour of internally displaced persons. Patterns of involvement vary from one crisis to another. Once a conflict breaks out, UNHCR sometimes intervenes to prevent displacement or more displacement. However, it tends to concentrate its efforts on the return phase at the end of the conflict. This type of intervention can sometimes take place only after the hostilities have ceased for reasons of staff security.[31]

UNHCR's involvement with internally displaced persons has increased, but remains limited in terms of the numbers of people covered. In 2001, five million internally displaced persons were 'of concern' to UNHCR, which assisted and protected almost 20 million persons in total.[32] The

---

[27] See pp. 6–9 above.   [28] See Loescher, *The UNHCR and Global Politics*, 288.

[29] For a description of these operations, see UNHCR, *UNHCR's Operational Experience*, 16–67.

[30] See *Internally Displaced Persons: Report of the Representative of the Secretary-General, Mr Francis M. Deng: Follow-Up Mission to Colombia*, E/CN.4/2000/83/Add.1, 11 January 2000, para. 58.

[31] See UNHCR, *UNHCR's Operational Experience*, 19–20 and 81.

[32] UNHCR, *Statistical Yearbook 2002*, Table I.1.

internally displaced thus represent one-quarter of the beneficiaries of UNHCR's programmes. However, only a minority of the 20–25 million internally displaced persons in the world are assisted by the agency. Moreover, UNHCR is not present in some countries that have a problem of internal displacement. UNHCR does not have activities targeted at internally displaced persons in countries such as Turkey or Myanmar (Burma) which host large populations of them. Nevertheless, one must not evaluate UNHCR's involvement only in terms of the numbers of persons assisted, or of countries where the agency is present.

Criteria for involvement

Since the beginning of the 1990s, UNHCR has attempted to develop criteria for involvement in order to select the situations of internal displacement which should be prioritised. The 1992 Note on International Protection issued by EXCOM recognised that 'certain responsibilities have to be assumed on behalf' of the internally displaced.[33] EXCOM has supported UNHCR's involvement with internally displaced persons provided that there are a specific request, the consent of the parties involved, the availability of funds, the possibility of full access, security of the staff, political support, and depending on whether other UN agencies are already operating in the country.[34] In 1992, the General Assembly explicitly recognised the extension of UNHCR's mandate to internally displaced persons, and also emphasised the crucial importance of the existence of a special request from the Secretary-General, or the competent principal organs of the UN, and the consent of the state concerned.[35]

The criteria for involvement have been refined over the years. In 1993, UNHCR issued internal guidelines which reiterated the general criteria identified earlier,[36] but also emphasised that there must be a clear link with UNHCR's mandate. This will be the case when

(1) returnees are returning or will return to areas where internally displaced persons are present;
(2) both internal displacement and a refugee flow have the same root causes, e.g. the same conflict; and

---

[33] See Note on International Protection, A/AC.96/799, 25 July 1992, para. 33.
[34] See also EXCOM Conclusion No. 68 (XLII) – 1992, General Conclusion on International Protection.
[35] See GA Res. 47/105, 16 December 1992.
[36] UNHCR's Role with Internally Displaced Persons, IOM/33/93-FOM/33/93, 28 April 1993, para. 7.

(3)   the internal displacement threatens to be transformed into external displacement (potential for cross-border movement).[37]

The 'link criterion' was endorsed by EXCOM later that year,[38] and more importantly by the General Assembly.[39] At the time, it was considered that the General Assembly resolution provided a firm legal basis for UNHCR's involvement.[40] The resolution implicitly accepted the 'link criterion' by supporting UNHCR's involvement with internally displaced persons 'where such efforts could contribute to the prevention or solution of refugee problems'.[41] In fact, this demonstrated that UNHCR would only get involved if it has an *interest* to do so, i.e. when such involvement with internally displaced persons is related to its central mandate (the search for solutions to refugee problems).

The criteria for involvement were further refined in an EXCOM document of 1994.[42] EXCOM stated that UNHCR may also get involved where refugees and internally displaced persons live alongside each other in the same area in the *country of asylum*[43] (and not just in the country of origin). This was the case in eastern Zaire where both Rwandan refugees and Zairian internally displaced found refuge. Moreover, the document specified that, where there is no direct link with UNHCR's mandate, the agency may still get involved in situations involving a 'life-threatening emergency' although there was no further explanation of what that meant in precise terms.[44]

The last time the General Assembly confirmed the criteria for UNHCR's involvement with internally displaced persons was in 1998. General Assembly Resolution 53/125 supported UNHCR's activities on behalf of the internally displaced undertaken on the basis of specific requests from the Secretary-General or other competent UN organs, with the consent of the state concerned, and 'taking into account the complementarities of the mandates and expertise of other relevant organisations'.[45] The General Assembly also emphasised that these activities must not undermine the institution of asylum.[46]

---

[37] *Ibid.*, para. 8.
[38] See *Note on International Protection*, A/AC.96/815, 31 August 1993, para. 46.
[39] See GA Res. 48/116, 20 December 1993.
[40] See *EXCOM Conclusion No. 75 (XLV) – 1994, Internally Displaced Persons*, para. (j).
[41] GA Res. 48/116, 20 December 1993, para. 12.
[42] *Protection Aspects of UNHCR Activities on Behalf of Internally Displaced Persons*, EC/SCP/87, 17 August 1994.
[43] *Ibid.*, para. 15.   [44] *Ibid.*, para. 16.
[45] GA Res. 53/125, 9 December 1998, para.16.   [46] *Ibid.*

An extended role for UNHCR?

UNHCR's ambivalence toward internally displaced persons

It has been repeated on many occasions in UNHCR official documents that the agency 'does not have a general competence for internally displaced persons'.[47] One cannot predict the involvement of UNHCR,[48] since the criteria for involvement are 'purposely broad and flexible'.[49] Even where the criteria are fulfilled, this does not automatically lead to UNHCR's involvement.[50] For instance, the previous High Commissioner Ogata turned down requests for UNHCR to intervene in Cambodia and Zaire in 1992.[51] Loescher believes that the criteria for involvement were worded in such a way as to avoid a formal commitment to the internally displaced, while allowing for the flexibility to get involved in IDP emergencies which are considered to be politically important to address.[52] As a result, the criteria were not really meant to 'clarify the scale, scope, or duration of the UNHCR's operational involvement'.[53]

Moreover, it is not always up to the agency to decide to engage in activities in favour of the internally displaced, as there must be a request from the Secretary-General or the General Assembly according to Article 9 of the Statute.[54] However, Goodwin-Gill disagrees with such an interpretation of Article 9 and considers that the provision does not allow any extension of the mandate beyond the refugee context.[55] Nevertheless, the General Assembly has consistently supported UNHCR's work with internally displaced persons throughout the 1990s.[56]

---

[47] *UNHCR's Role with Internally Displaced Persons*, IOM/33/93-FOM/33/93, 28 April 1993, para. 3. See also *Protection Aspects of UNHCR Activities on Behalf of Internally Displaced Persons*, EC/SCP/87, 17 August 1994, para. 9.

[48] See for instance T. G. Weiss and A. Pasic, 'Dealing with the Displacement and Suffering Caused by Yugoslavia's Wars', in R. Cohen and F. M. Deng (eds.), *The Forsaken People* (Washington DC: Brookings Institution, 1998), 175–231 at 221.

[49] See Loescher, *The UNHCR and Global Politics*, 294.

[50] *Protection Aspects of UNHCR Activities on Behalf of Internally Displaced Persons*, EC/SCP/87, 17 August 1994, para. 17.

[51] See Loescher, *The UNHCR and Global politics*, 294.

[52] *Ibid.*, 294.   [53] *Ibid.*, 295.

[54] See UNHCR, *Internally Displaced Persons: The Role of the United Nations High Commissioner for Refugees*, EC/50/SC/INF.2, 20 July 2000.

[55] See G. Goodwin-Gill, 'UNHCR and Internal Displacement: Stepping into Legal and Political Minefield', *World Refugee Survey 2000*, http://www.refugees.org/world/articles/wrs00_unhcr.htm.

[56] See for instance GA Res. 55/74, 4 December 2000, para. 20. However, in the last three sessions, no mention was made of internally displaced persons in the annual

UNHCR has invoked several reasons to justify decisions not to get involved in particular situations. One of them has been the absence of a 'link' with the mandate, as in Peru for instance where UNHCR found no 'serious risk of cross-border spilling'.[57] Other factors mentioned are related to the lack of donor interest,[58] operational constraints (access and security), the presence of other UN agencies (as in Mozambique and Sudan) and the risk of a threat to the institution of asylum.[59] The last consideration constitutes the most problematic issue for UNHCR which does not wish its in-country activities to be incompatible with its core mandate.

UNHCR has been willing to become involved with internally displaced persons when such involvement contributes to the search for solutions to refugee problems. However, this involvement is now sometimes perceived by commentators as producing the opposite effect. This was especially true with regard to the former Yugoslavia,[60] and prompted the High Commissioner to emphasise the role of the UN *as a whole* in situations of internal displacement and the importance of a 'comprehensive and integrated approach'.[61]

Proposals to improve the UN response to crises of internal displacement

Although the creation of a new agency for the internally displaced was proposed at the beginning of the 1990s,[62] this option is now seen as being neither feasible nor desirable.[63] There are neither funds nor the

resolutions on UNHCR: see GA Res. 56/137, 19 December 2001, GA Res. 57/187, 18 December 2002 and GA Res. 58/151, 22 December 2003.

[57] UNHCR, *UNHCR's Operational Experience*, 34.

[58] See A. Feldmann, 'Rational Ambivalence: The UNHCR Responses to Internal Displacement Emergencies', unpublished paper presented at the International Studies Association Convention, Los Angeles, 15–18 March 2000.

[59] See UNHCR, *UNHCR's Operational Experience*, 75–6.

[60] See Chapter 5, second section, below.

[61] See the Address by the High Commissioner, reproduced in Norwegian Refugee Council and Refugee Policy Group, *Norwegian Government Roundtable Discussion on United Nations Human Rights Protection for Internally Displaced Persons, Nyon, Switzerland, February 1993* (Washington DC: Refugee Policy Group, 1993), 81–7.

[62] See *Comprehensive Study Prepared by Mr Francis M. Deng, Representative of the Secretary-General, on the Human Rights Issues Related to Internally Displaced Persons*, E/CN.4/1993/35, 21 January 1993, para. 285.

[63] See for instance *Internally Displaced Persons: Report of the Representative of the Secretary-General, Mr Francis M. Deng*, E/CN.4/1996/52, 22 February 1996 (hereinafter the *1996 Deng Report*), para. 16.

political will to create such an agency.[64] A review of the capacities of the various agencies demonstrates that they have already developed some expertise in the field of internal displacement and, consequently, there is no need for the creation of a new agency. Mention should also be made here of the two-agency proposal to assign assistance activities to the Department of Humanitarian Affairs (now Office for the Coordination of Humanitarian Affairs (OCHA)) and protection activities to the High Commissioner for Human Rights.[65] It has been argued that protection issues should be dealt with by an organisation other than the organisation in charge of distributing aid and that a new organ should take on such a mandate.[66] Since OCHA is not an operational unit, such a proposal cannot be acted upon. Moreover, separating assistance and protection activities is an artificial distinction which should be avoided.

Instead of creating a new agency specifically dealing with the internally displaced, the Netherlands proposed in 1993 that the agency take overall responsibility for the internally displaced.[67] This proposal was based on three arguments: the agency's long-standing experience in working with uprooted populations; the protection aspect of its activities; and the link with its current mandate, as most internally displaced are potential refugees. Ogata was reluctant to accept this proposal and declared that 'the needs of the internally displaced . . . remain to be addressed largely . . . through *ad hoc* operational measures and mechanisms'.[68] Some states saw this proposal as a potential interference in their internal affairs and opposed the extension of UNHCR's mandate to

---

[64] See L. M. E. Sheridan, 'Institutional Arrangements for the Coordination of Humanitarian Assistance in Complex Emergencies of Forced Migration' (2000) 14 *Georgetown Immigration Law Journal* 941 at 953.

[65] See R. Cohen and J. Cuénod, *Improving Institutional Arrangements for the Internally Displaced* (Washington DC: Brookings Institution and Refugee Policy Group, 1995), 80–1, and *Internally Displaced Persons: Report of the Representative of the Secretary-General, Mr Francis M. Deng*, E/CN.4/1995/50, 2 February 1995 (hereinafter the *1995 Deng Report*), para. 201.

[66] See G. Melander, 'Internally Displaced Persons', in G. Alfredsson and P. Macalister-Smith (eds.), *The Living Law of Nations: Essays on Refugees, Minorities, Indigenous Peoples and the Human Rights of Other Vulnerable Groups in Memory of Atle Grahl-Madsen* (Kehl am Rhein, Strasbourg, Arlington: Engel, 1996), 69–74 at 72–4.

[67] See R. Cohen and F. M. Deng, *Masses in Flight: The Global Crisis of Internal Displacement* (Washington DC: Brookings Institution, 1998), 170.

[68] Address by the High Commissioner, reproduced in Norwegian Refugee Council and Refugee Policy Group, *Norwegian Government Roundtable Discussion*.

the internally displaced.[69] Moreover, it was recognised that no agency can cover the needs of the internally displaced on its own.[70]

The debate was revived in March 2000 by a more high-profile proposal to give UNHCR full responsibility for the internally displaced. Richard Holbrooke, then president of the Security Council, suggested that 'the mandate for internal refugees should be given to a single agency, presumably the UNHCR'.[71] This proposal was based on the opinion that 'there is no real difference between a refugee and an internally displaced person'.[72] Holbrooke also believed that coordination between UN agencies was inefficient, and concluded that responsibility for the internally displaced should therefore be given to a single agency in order to ensure that the UN response to crises of internal displacement is comprehensive and predictable. Faced with criticisms, he retreated from his earlier position and announced that the lead agency model could also resolve the institutional gap.

Reactions

Holbrooke's proposal produced various reactions. The High Commissioner for Refugees Ogata reiterated her reservations to the suggestion that UNHCR take the lead on internal displacement. She defended UNHCR's record with internally displaced persons against the allegation that it was not doing enough, but also emphasised the importance of inter-agency collaboration. She added that the distinction between refugees and internally displaced persons should not be blurred,[73] because refugees benefit from an established regime of protection and internally displaced persons do not. On this particular point, one should agree with her that the distinction between refugees and internally displaced persons should be maintained.[74] UNHCR reacted to the

---

[69] See for instance *Internally Displaced Persons: Report of the Representative of the Secretary-General, Mr Francis M. Deng, Profiles in Displacement: Colombia*, E/CN.4/1995/50/Add.1, 3 October 1994, para. 103.

[70] See *1995 Deng Report*, note 65 above, para. 199.

[71] R. Holbrooke, *Statement at Cardozo Law School on Refugees and Internally Displaced Persons*, USUN press release #44 (00), 28 March 2000. See also R. Holbrooke, 'A Borderline Difference', *Washington Post*, 8 May 2000.

[72] Holbrooke, *Statement at Cardozo Law School*.

[73] See S. Ogata, 'Protecting People on the Move', Address by the United Nations High Commissioner for Refugees, sponsored by the Center for the Study of International Organization, New York, 18 July 2000.

[74] See Chapter 1, pp. 24–5 above.

proposal by issuing a 'new' policy paper which in fact just reiterated the agency's previous position.[75] The agency attempted to appear less cautious and more willing to make a positive contribution to improve UN efforts on behalf of the internally displaced. Nevertheless, the agency carefully reasserted its commitment to full cooperation with other UN agencies which may be hostile to Holbrooke's proposal. The Inter-Agency Standing Committee, composed of all the heads of the UN's humanitarian agencies, reacted to the proposal by launching new initiatives to strengthen inter-agency coordination both at the field level and at the headquarters level (guidelines to field coordinators, and the creation of the Senior Inter-Agency Network).[76]

The debate over whether UNHCR should assert a more formal role on behalf of the internally displaced is part of the ongoing debate about the future role of the agency. It has been argued that increased involvement in situations of internal displacement would compromise the traditional mandate of the UNHCR, which is to provide protection to refugees, and would also lead to the further politicisation of its work. Goodwin-Gill, for instance, is opposed to any extended involvement of the agency with the internally displaced.[77] He argues that by responding to the Secretary-General's requests, UNHCR threatens its own independence, and runs the risk of being used as a substitute for political action.[78] In response to Holbrooke's proposal, Goodwin-Gill has reaffirmed his strong belief that UNHCR's involvement with the internally displaced should remain 'functional at most, [and] incidental to programs for its primary constituency, refugees'.[79] More fundamentally, he argues that such involvement diverts UNHCR from its original mandate, which is to provide international protection to refugees. Likewise, the EU 'does not support the idea that UNHCR should be given an expanded mandate'.[80] Other countries oppose the creation of a new agency or the formal extension of UNHCR's mandate to cover the internally displaced for different

---

[75] See UNHCR, *Internally Displaced Persons: The Role of the High Commissioner.*

[76] See pp. 105–10 below.

[77] See G. Goodwin-Gill, 'Refugee Identity and Protection's Fading Prospect', in Nicholson and Twomey (eds.), *Refugee Rights and Realities*, 220–49 at 246.

[78] Goodwin-Gill, 'Refugee Identity', 227–8. See also S. A. Cunliffe and M. Pugh, 'UNHCR as Leader in Humanitarian Assistance: A Triumph of Politics over Law?', in Nicholson and Twomey (eds.), *Refugee Rights and Realities*, 175–99.

[79] Goodwin-Gill, 'UNHCR and Internal Displacement'.

[80] P. Rudge, *The Need for a More Focused Response: European Donor Policies Toward Internally Displaced Persons*, Brookings Institution, Norwegian Refugee Council and US Committee for Refugees, January 2002, 19.

reasons: to them, internal displacement is primarily the responsibility of states.[81]

Using similar arguments based on an analysis of UNHCR's experience in the former Yugoslavia, Barutciski has argued that UNHCR's in-country involvement with the internally displaced was explained by donor states' concern to contain refugee flows within the countries of origin.[82] He also refers to UNHCR's experience with internally displaced persons in Kosovo to demonstrate that it 'left the agency ill-prepared for its core and primary asylum protection duties when NATO's bombing campaign started'.[83] One cannot deny that UNHCR's in-country presence could be used as an excuse by some states to close their borders, arguing that protection is already available inside the country. When accused of containing refugee flows, the agency has responded by suppressing any reference to the 'prevention of refugee flows', which was used as a basis for UNHCR's involvement with the internally displaced, especially in 1993–4.[84] The focus is now on protection, and the discourse of the agency has thus been modified so as to avoid any misinterpretation.

On the other hand, IDP advocates have argued that there is no contradiction between in-country activities and the provision of asylum. If protection can be effectively provided to internally displaced persons, they will not feel compelled to move further and leave the country. The problem is that potential asylum states interpret in-country activities as a ground for restricting asylum. UNHCR should put more emphasis on advocacy to ensure that states abide by their commitments to the institution of asylum: its presence within the country of origin does not mean that some people are not still at risk of persecution. In-country activities undertaken on behalf of the internally displaced should not be seen as undermining UNHCR's traditional activities, but as complementary to them.[85]

The funding of these activities is not always linked to a desire of containment of refugee flows because, in some cases, internally displaced

---

[81] See for instance the comments of the Russian Federation's delegate to EXCOM, in A/AC.96/SR.562, 9 October 2002.

[82] See M. Barutciski, 'The Reinforcement of Non-Admission Policies and the Subversion of UNHCR: Displacement and Internal Assistance in Bosnia-Herzegovina, 1992–1994' (1996) 8 *International Journal of Refugee Law* 49 at 58.

[83] M. Barutciski, 'A Critical View on UNHCR's Mandate Dilemmas' (2002) 14 *International Journal of Refugee Law* 365 at 368.

[84] Interview with UNHCR staff, Geneva, 8 February 1999.

[85] See for instance E. D. Mooney, 'In-Country Protection: Out of Bounds for UNHCR?', in Nicholson and Twomey (eds.), *Refugee Rights and Realities*, 200–19.

persons do not have the possibility to leave their country anyway. UNHCR's present involvement with internally displaced persons can also be seen as 'merely the culmination of a decades-long process of evolution of its intentionally dynamic mandate'.[86] In this respect, Cohen has been a strong advocate for an increased UNHCR role with the internally displaced.[87] The Special Representative also stated once that UNHCR was still developing strategies for providing in-country protection to internally displaced persons and was just delaying its 'decision to take on a general responsibility for [them]'.[88] He is now resigned to the fact that this will not happen in the near future.[89]

Risks of politicisation and operational problems

It has been argued, especially in relation to its operation in the former Yugoslavia, that UNHCR's involvement with the internally displaced and its role as lead agency have led to its politicisation.[90] In 1991, the UN Secretary-General requested the agency to assist displaced persons in Croatia and Bosnia and Herzegovina. As a result, UNHCR became involved in one of the most difficult operations in its history.[91] UNHCR's involvement with internally displaced persons has thus led the agency into new and uncertain areas. Refugee protection consists mainly of legal activities undertaken in the countries of asylum and, where needed, assistance and protection activities for refugee populations.[92] In contrast, activities on behalf of internally displaced persons often take place in the midst of active internal armed conflicts, where UNHCR faces very different challenges, i.e. logistical problems, negotiating access to the targeted populations, staff security, cooperating with the military, evacuations, etc. In such an environment, UNHCR runs the risk of being manipulated both by external powers as a substitute for political action and by the warring parties which seek to divert humanitarian aid to feed the combatants or 'their' civilian population.

Involvement with the internally displaced during armed conflict has inevitably led UNHCR to pay more attention to protection issues and thus

---

[86] Ibid., 205.
[87] See for instance R. Cohen, 'Internally Displaced Persons: An Extended Role for UNHCR', discussion paper for UNHCR, International Conference 'People of Concern', 21–24 November 1996.
[88] Cohen and Deng, Masses in Flight, 171.
[89] See 'Interview with Francis Deng', Refugees magazine, issue 117 (1999).
[90] See for instance S. A. Cunliffe and M. Pugh, 'The Politicisation of UNHCR in the Former Yugoslavia' (1997) 10 Journal of Refugee Studies 134.
[91] See Chapter 5, second section, below.   [92] See Article 8 of the UNHCR Statute.

to rethink its mandate in human rights terms.[93] One must also consider UNHCR's activities for the internally displaced in the context of its role as lead agency, as crises in which it assumes such a role always involve large populations of internally displaced. However, when UNHCR is the lead humanitarian agency, there is a risk that IDP protection issues may be overlooked, because too much energy is already being invested in coordinating the international humanitarian effort within the country in question. The relationship between these two roles thus needs to be re-examined.[94] More recently, UNHCR has shared the 'lead agency' role with OCHA.

Giving UNHCR full responsibility for the internally displaced would create serious operational problems. These were already experienced in the former Yugoslavia where UNHCR provided assistance to the internally displaced as well as a certain number of non-displaced persons. Where such large numbers of civilians are affected by civil war, as was the case in Angola for instance, it was noted that 'the protection needs of the targeted IDPs were vast, and were not essentially different from those faced by the Angolan population at large'.[95] Assigning responsibility to UNHCR for all internally displaced persons may lead UNHCR to become in fact the agency for populations in need. If the IDP problem is to be addressed within a broader human rights context, it is beyond the remit of one single agency and therefore beyond the remit of UNHCR alone.

Nevertheless, this does not mean that UNHCR should retreat from its current involvement with the internally displaced. The agency can formulate a clearer policy position on the issue of internal displacement and this policy position should focus on its protection role. When UNHCR's Evaluation and Policy Analysis Unit (EPAU) reviewed the agency's programmes for internally displaced persons, it has consistently found that the agency had a comparative advantage in protection (physical protection, personal documentation, legal aid, etc.).[96] It is in this difficult area, rather than in the delivery of material

---

[93] See Chapter 4, pp. 130–4 below.

[94] On UNHCR's role as lead agency, see Cunliffe and Pugh, 'The Politicisation of UNHCR'.

[95] UNHCR, *UNHCR's Programme for Internally Displaced People in Angola: A Joint Danida/ UNHCR Review*, EPAU/2001/04, May 2001, para. 75.

[96] See for instance UNHCR, *UNHCR's Programme for Internally Displaced People in Angola*, paras. 94–8, and UNHCR, *UNHCR's Programme For Internally Displaced Persons in Sri Lanka: Report of a Joint Appraisal Mission by the UK Department for International Development and UNHCR*, EPAU/2002/04, May 2002, paras. 21–5.

assistance, that UNHCR can make a specific contribution to the improvement of the situation of the internally displaced.[97] While the ICRC has more experience and expertise in interventions in conflict areas,[98] UNHCR could concentrate its interventions on the post-conflict situations.[99] In recent years, the agency has focused increasingly on these situations, especially 'where there are clear linkages with refugee repatriation'.[100]

Formulating coherent IDP policies in other international agencies

In the last decade, UN agencies, in addition to UNHCR, have all started to express an interest in the issue of internal displacement. Before dealing with the mandates of the main agencies, mention must be made of other actors such as peacekeeping forces or the World Bank which are no less concerned by the problem of internal displacement. The role of peacekeeping forces with regard to internally displaced persons will be looked at in the next chapter.[101] As for the World Bank,[102] mention should be made of its recently issued guidelines for the funding of projects which may lead to the displacement of populations. Borrowers are now required to ensure that the project concerned creates minimum disruption for the local population, to prepare a resettlement plan, as well as to provide for compensation.[103]

Most UN agencies, as well as the ICRC, the IOM and the WHO, have become involved with internally displaced persons either because they were already intervening in situations producing internal displacement, or because their expertise and operational capacity, e.g. food delivery for

---

[97] See for instance UNHCR, *Evaluation of UNHCR's Programme for Internally Displaced Persons in Colombia*, EPAU/2003/03, May 2003, para. 19.

[98] See pp. 93–6 below.

[99] See UNHCR, *Evaluation of UNHCR's Programme for Internally Displaced Persons in Colombia*, para. 21.

[100] *Report by the High Commissioner to the General Assembly on Strengthening the Capacity of the Office of the High Commissioner for Refugees to Carry Out Its Mandate*, A/AC.96/980, 20 August 2003, para. 27.

[101] See Chapter 4, second section, below.

[102] For more information, see http://www.worldbank.org.

[103] See *Internally Displaced Persons: Report of the Representative of the Secretary-General, Mr Francis M. Deng*, E/CN.4/1998/53, 11 February 1998 (hereinafter the *1998 Deng Report*), para. 13, and *Operational Policy 4.12 on Involuntary Resettlement*, World Bank Operational Manual, December 2001.

the World Food Programme, directly relates to a specific IDP need that calls for their involvement. In most situations, as was previously the case with UNHCR, these international agencies saw their programmes with internally displaced persons as a 'natural' extension of their traditional mandates. They initially did not endeavour to formulate any specific IDP policy. Nevertheless, as there was growing awareness that the international response to the problem of internal displacement was *ad hoc* and uncoordinated, there has been more pressure to clarify each agency's role with regard to the internally displaced.

Intervening in situations of armed conflict: the International Committee of the Red Cross[104]

The ICRC has a mandate to operate in armed conflicts, and is responsible for the promotion and respect of humanitarian law. As armed conflict is the most common cause of internal displacement, the ICRC has an especially important role to play with the internally displaced. It is also present in some situations which fall below the threshold in that they are not considered as armed conflict, but as 'civil unrest'. As a result, the ICRC is present in most situations of internal displacement.[105] The organisation engages in a broad range of activities (promotion of humanitarian law, evacuation of civilians, provision of relief aid, etc.),[106] and, in some countries, the ICRC is the only organisation present in insurgent-held areas, either because other organisations are not permitted to operate there, or because they have withdrawn, due to security concerns.

Although it was previously reluctant to take up the issue of internal displacement, the ICRC no longer avoids using the term. On the contrary, it is trying to sensitise its staff to protection issues related to internally displaced persons, and has recently been more explicit in defining its IDP role. In 2000, the ICRC produced its first policy document reviewing (briefly) its activities undertaken on behalf of the internally displaced.[107] The ICRC remains pragmatic in its approach. It acknowledges that there is a wide range of contexts in which internal displacement takes place

---

[104] For more information, see http://www.icrc.org.
[105] See Norwegian Refugee Council, *Institutional Arrangements for Internally Displaced Persons: The Ground Level Experience* (Oslo: Norwegian Refugee Council, 1995), 10.
[106] See Cohen and Deng, *Masses in Flight*, 132. See also ICRC, *Internally Displaced Persons: The Mandate and Role of the ICRC*, March 2000.
[107] See ICRC, *The Mandate and Role of the ICRC*.

and that it cannot adopt a single strategy. The ICRC has always been reluctant to operate a distinction between local residents and the internally displaced, because the latter 'do not fall into a separate category under humanitarian law'.[108] Moreover, it may not always be relevant to single out the internally displaced for operational purposes and the ICRC 'seeks to strike a balance between cases where the internally displaced are best helped through *targeted activities* and those where they are assisted through *more general efforts* aimed at broader segments of the population'.[109]

The organisation puts strong emphasis on its neutrality, which allows it to gain access to all groups. In addition, ICRC staff are more prepared than UN or NGO staff to operate in armed conflict situations, and it is often the first organisation to arrive in the field, as was the case in the former Yugoslavia in 1991.[110] One main feature of the ICRC's interventions lies in the fact that it does not draw any distinction between assistance and protection.[111] Its advocacy role with regard to IDP rights has to be exercised differently, as the ICRC, in order to retain access to all parties, has a strict policy of confidentiality and is reluctant to publicly denounce human rights abuses.[112] Nevertheless, if the ICRC is committed to the defence of the human rights of the internally displaced, it may find it difficult to maintain its current stance on confidentiality.[113] More fundamentally, the ICRC's traditional role in the monitoring of international humanitarian law differs from its more recent commitment to the defence of human rights. Although there is a trend towards the convergence of humanitarian law and human rights law,[114] the two bodies of law are still distinct and rely on different institutional frameworks. The ICRC may find itself moving towards a new type of relationship with the parties to a conflict: when providing protection for internally displaced persons, it may have to be more outspoken about human rights abuses.

---

[108] See J. de Courten, 'The ICRC's Focus: Access to Victims of Armed Conflict and Internal Disturbances', in ICRC, *Internally Displaced Persons, Symposium, Geneva, 23–25 October 1995* (Geneva: ICRC, 1996), 84–7 at 86. See also J. P. Lavoyer, 'Guiding Principles on Internal Displacement: A Few Comments on the Contribution of International Humanitarian Law' (1998) 324 *International Review of the Red Cross* 467.

[109] *Ibid.*   [110] Norwegian Refugee Council, *Institutional Arrangements*, 11.

[111] See de Courten, 'The ICRC's Focus', 85.

[112] *Ibid.* See also Cohen and Deng, *Masses in Flight*, 132.

[113] See Chapter 5, p. 176 below.   [114] See Chapter 2, pp. 47–8 above.

While UNHCR has become increasingly involved in in-country activities, there has been a need to clarify the ICRC and UNHCR's respective responsibilities towards refugees and, more problematically, internally displaced persons. In recent years, the ICRC has been much more outspoken in affirming its primary responsibility to those civilians who are internally displaced and affected by armed conflict.[115] It considers that UNHCR is more solution-oriented, and can play a more important role in the post-conflict/return phase which is not part of the ICRC's expertise.[116] When dealing with internally displaced persons, the ICRC believes that it has several comparative advantages over UNHCR. The most important one is probably that it 'bases its work for internally displaced persons on binding treaties, unlike UNHCR, whose work for them is essentially based on the Guiding Principles on Internal Displacement'.[117] The argument is that the law determines each agency's mandate in clear terms: UNHCR has primary responsibility for refugees under the 1951 Convention, while the ICRC can deal with displaced civilians in armed conflicts under international humanitarian law. The ICRC also argues that it can intervene (more) quickly because it does not need the UN Secretary-General or General Assembly's authorisation to do so.[118] Goodwin-Gill supports this division of labour between UNHCR and the ICRC when stating that 'in principle, the protection of the internally displaced, while still the responsibility of the territorial state, should be entrusted, as is now often the case, to the International Committee of the Red Cross, complemented as appropriate by the distinctive role of the United Nations High Commissioner for Human Rights, and/or by a competent regional organisation'.[119]

Encouraging the ICRC to assume primary responsibility for the internally displaced appears to be an attractive proposition. There is a clear legal basis for operations undertaken on their behalf. Secondly, the ICRC has extensive experience and expertise in field operations conducted in the midst of armed conflict. Thirdly, the ICRC is independent of states which cannot manipulate the organisation into acting according to their desires to contain refugee flows. Finally, the ICRC does not have the same protection dilemmas as UNHCR in terms of the tension between focusing

---

[115] See F. Krill, 'The ICRC's Policy on Refugees and Internally Displaced Civilians' (2001) 843 *International Review of the Red Cross* 607 at 621.

[116] Interview with ICRC staff, Legal Division, Geneva, 12 February 1999.

[117] Krill, 'The ICRC's Policy', 623. See also Chapter 2 above.

[118] Krill, 'The ICRC's Policy', 624.   [119] Goodwin-Gill, 'UNHCR and Internal Displacement'.

on refugees and internally displaced persons. All of these points suggest that the ICRC is the ideal candidate and should continue to assert a more active role with the internally displaced.

Responding to specific IDP needs: the World Food Programme,[120] *the International Organization for Migration*[121] *and the World Health Organization*[122]

The WFP's activities concentrate on food distribution, rehabilitation, recovery and development programmes. Although priority was previously given to development assistance, emergency relief now accounts for 70 per cent of the work of the agency.[123] As the WFP is the single largest provider of food aid to the internally displaced, it plays a crucial role in relation to this group. In 1998, the WFP provided assistance to 19 million internally displaced persons,[124] who have become the largest category of beneficiaries in terms of numbers.[125]

The WFP has conducted an extensive review of its activities of providing food aid to the internally displaced.[126] On the basis of this review, the agency has attempted to define a 'WFP policy and strategy framework for situations of displacement and internally displaced persons'.[127] An IDP action framework has been proposed to the WFP's Executive Board. The suggested framework stated that the internally displaced do not constitute a target group for food assistance, except where appropriate (e.g. when in IDP camps).[128] Despite recent efforts to formulate a specific IDP policy within the WFP, the Executive Board of the agency has still not adopted a policy paper because of the recent debates on the Guiding Principles taking place in ECOSOC and the General Assembly.[129] This indicates that some state comments may have prompted the

---

[120] For more information, see http://www.wfp.org.

[121] For more information, see http://www.iom.int.

[122] For more information, see http://www.who.int/en/.

[123] See Cohen and Deng, *Masses in Flight*, 137.

[124] See WFP, *WFP's IDP Review: WFP – Reaching People in Situations of Displacement*, discussion paper, version II, April 2000, 4.

[125] See Cohen and Deng, *Masses in Flight*, 135.   [126] See WFP, *WFP 's IDP Review*.

[127] WFP, *Chairperson's Summary of the Second Consultation on Humanitarian Issues – Situations of Internal Displacement: Issues and Experiences*, WFP/EB.3/2000/3-C, 28 September 2000, 3. See also WFP, *Looking Forward: Humanitarian Policy Concerns for WFP*, WFP/EB.3/99/9-B, 16 September 1999, paras. 23–4.

[128] See WFP, *Reaching People in Situations of Displacement: Framework for Action*, WFP/EB.A/2001/4-C, 17 April 2001, para. 28.

[129] See WFP, *Consolidated Framework of WFP Policies – An Updated Version*, May 2003, 8.

WFP to be more cautious in its approach to the problem of internal displacement.[130]

Since the WFP's primary mandate is the alleviation of hunger, the agency had not focused on the protection aspects of its programmes. It has readily admitted that 'even though WFP's role in relation to protection has not been uniform, awareness of protection issues and responsibilities is growing'.[131] It is now crucial that this increased awareness for protection issues is translated into concrete measures. For instance, WFP has started monitoring the distribution of food, which is often used by the men in charge of the distribution as a means of obtaining sexual favours from refugee and internally displaced women.[132] The WFP intends to strengthen its advocacy of IDP rights, 'including entitlements and property rights, especially for women'.[133] Unfortunately, whereas the IDP review emphasised the need for stronger linkages between assistance and protection, the 2001 framework for action does not put sufficient emphasis on IDP protection issues, although it does mention (physical) security.[134]

Although it is often associated with UN agencies, the IOM is not part of the UN system: it is an intergovernmental organisation, whose objective is the orderly migration of persons in need of migration assistance.[135] Up to 1996, the IOM had become involved with internally displaced persons in more than a dozen countries.[136] In its policy documents, the IOM emphasises the fact that it is the only organisation with a specific mandate with regard to internally displaced persons. Its Constitution explicitly mentions activities in favour of displaced persons, which includes the internally displaced.[137]

The IOM has been particularly active in providing temporary shelter for the internally displaced, as well as transportation for those who want to return home and need assistance because of the breakdown of transport associated with situations of armed conflict. It has thus played an important role in the return and reintegration phase and is now a major implementing partner of UNHCR in returning the internally

---

[130] See Chapter 2, pp. 71–3 above.

[131] WFP, *WFP's IDP Review*, 10.

[132] See R. Cohen, 'Protecting Internally Displaced Women and Children', in Norwegian Refugee Council, *Rights Have No Borders: Worldwide Internal Displacement* (Oxford: Norwegian Refugee Council/Global IDP Survey, 1998), 63–74 at 69.

[133] See WFP, *Reaching People in Situations of Displacement*, para. 42.   [134] *Ibid.*, paras. 43–6.

[135] See IOM, *Internally Displaced Persons: IOM Policy and Programmes* (Geneva: IOM, 1997), 4.

[136] For a description of the IOM's programmes in these countries, see *ibid.*, 11–27.

[137] *Ibid.*, 9.

displaced to their original place of residence.[138] The IOM has initiated special programmes for the reintegration of demobilised soldiers when they are internally displaced. These programmes were especially successful in Mozambique and Angola. The IOM also provides assistance to states and helps them strengthen their capacities to respond to crises of internal displacement.[139] In response to the accusation of complicity in forced relocations, the IOM tries to ensure that transportation is offered only to persons who *voluntarily* return to their homes.[140] Despite increased involvement with the internally displaced, it appears from IOM documents that the organisation does not really have a specific approach to IDP issues, but only responds to certain needs where required.

In addition to food, shelter and transportation needs, the internally displaced also have vital health needs, since displacement increases the risk of illness and death. Their access to health care is often restricted, or even excluded, by the parties to a conflict. The WHO therefore plays a crucial role with regard to the internally displaced, but it has been particularly slow in recognising such a role. It was only on the occasion of the IDP debate at the Humanitarian Affairs segment of ECOSOC in 2000 that the agency explicitly formulated for the first time some principles for action on behalf of the internally displaced.[141] This gave the impression that the WHO felt compelled to engage with the issue of internal displacement simply because every other aid agency was already involved in the debate.

The WHO paper which was presented to ECOSOC restates that the agency's main role in emergency situations is to make rapid health assessments and provide guidelines and advice on how to respond to specific health needs.[142] One of the limits of the WHO's action on behalf of the internally displaced is that its mandate is mainly 'to assist its primary constituent, the member state'.[143] However, governments are often unable and/or unwilling to provide health care to the internally displaced. Further involvement with the internally displaced may lead the WHO to undertake more work with NGOs and UN aid agencies.

---

[138] Norwegian Refugee Council, *Institutional Arrangements*, 10. See also IOM, *The Reintegration of Internally Displaced Vulnerable Groups in the IOM's Assistance Programme* (Geneva: IOM, 1993).

[139] IOM, *Internally Displaced Persons*, contribution of the IOM to the 3 February 1993 meeting of the IASC, Geneva, February 1993, para. 15.

[140] IOM, *Statement by IOM to the Commission on Human Rights*, Geneva, April 1998.

[141] See WHO, *Internally Displaced Persons, Health and WHO*, paper presented to the Humanitarian Affairs Segment of ECOSOC, New York, 19–20 July 2000.

[142] *Ibid.*, 9.   [143] *Ibid.*, 7.

Dealing with vulnerable groups: the United Nations Children's Fund[144]

More than half of the internally displaced around the world are children.[145] They are covered by UNICEF's mandate. UNICEF is a development agency, but has been increasingly involved in emergency work which now represents a quarter of its overall activities.[146] These activities include the provision of basic health care, nutrition, water and sanitation, but also basic education programmes.

When internal displacement became an issue of international concern, UNICEF was rather reluctant to recognise its importance. Like the ICRC, UNICEF took the position that internally displaced persons should not constitute a special category of persons in need, because this would create discrimination against those not displaced.[147] This position has since been modified, and UNICEF has now developed a number of policies and programmes for the internally displaced.[148] As it used to be criticised for focusing on assistance activities and overlooking protection issues,[149] UNICEF has reacted by shifting the emphasis from assistance to advocacy using the Convention on the Rights of the Child,[150] e.g. direct intervention with governments, regular reporting on situations of internal displacement, making representations to donors.[151] More emphasis has also been put on protection activities which are defined as protecting children from physical and psycho-social violence, preserving their cultural identity and responding to their basic needs.[152] More recently, UNICEF has been at the forefront of human rights issues by developing 'a rights-based approach to programming'.[153]

A number of initiatives have been undertaken by UNICEF to raise awareness of IDP issues within the agency and to define its own IDP

---

[144] For more information, see http://www.unicef.org.

[145] See J. Kunder, *The Needs of Internally Displaced Women and Children: Guiding Principles and Considerations*, UNICEF, Office of Emergency Programmes, New York, Working Paper Series, September 1998, 1.

[146] Cohen and Deng, *Masses in Flight*, 137.   [147] *Ibid.*, 138.

[148] For a description of these policies and programmes, see UNICEF, *Internally Displaced Children: The Role of UNICEF*, discussion paper on issues related to internally displaced persons (New York: UNICEF, date of publication unknown) and Kunder, *The Needs of Internally Displaced Women and Children*.

[149] Cohen and Deng, *Masses in Flight*, 138.

[150] Convention on the Rights of the Child, 20 November 1989, 28 ILM 1448. See UNICEF, *Enhanced Monitoring and Reporting: UNICEF's Observations and Recommendations*, Panel discussion on monitoring and reporting, CRS Conference on Human Rights and Forced Displacement, York University, Toronto, 7–9 May 1998, 1–4.

[151] See Kunder, *The Needs of Internally Displaced Women and Children*, 11.

[152] *Ibid.*, 19–21.   [153] See http://www.unicef.org/programme/rights/mainmenu.html.

policy. These include notably the project examining field practices in internal displacement. Since 1998, field visits have been undertaken in Sri Lanka, Colombia, Sudan and Sierra Leone in order to collect information on protection activities undertaken in the field on behalf of the internally displaced.[154] Drawing from these missions, but also from other agencies' experiences (though only when these agencies are actually willing to cooperate with UNICEF in the process),[155] UNICEF has helped in the drafting of the Manual on Field Practice in Internal Displacement.[156] Other important initiatives have been undertaken to study the gender dimension of internal displacement.[157]

UNICEF has thus now become one of the most active agencies in the field of internal displacement. In the late 1990s, UNICEF may have decided to take the lead in this area to fill a gap left by UNHCR. The agency considers that, in contrast with UNHCR, involvement with these populations is an integral part of its mandate, and such involvement is also perceived as less controversial than for UNHCR.[158] In addition, UNICEF is engaged in both emergency and development work, which could contribute to ensuring a continuum between these two phases. However, it clearly does not have the mandate to assume overall responsibility for all internally displaced persons, but only for internally displaced women and children.[159]

Bridging the gap between emergency relief and development: the United Nations Development Programme[160]

The organisations considered above all concentrate most of their efforts during the displacement phase, as well as the return phase. By contrast,

---

[154] See UNICEF, *Mission to Sri Lanka with a View to Develop Best Practices to Internal Displacement*, New York, Office of Emergency Programmes, Working Paper Series, August 1998; and UNICEF, *Mission to Colombia with a View to Develop Best Practices to Internal Displacement*, New York, Office of Emergency Programmes, Working Paper Series, December 1999.

[155] Interview with UNICEF staff, Geneva, 12 February 1999.

[156] See OCHA, *Manual on Field Practice on Internal Displacement: Examples from UN Agencies and Partner Organisations of Field-Based Initiatives Supporting Internally Displaced Persons*, Inter-Agency Standing Committee Policy Paper Series No. 1, 1999.

[157] See UNICEF, *The Gender Dimension of Internal Displacement: Concept Paper and Annotated Bibliography*, New York, Office of Emergency Programmes, Working Paper Series, September 1998 and UNICEF, *Expert Meeting on Gender Dimension of Internal Displacement*, New York, 14–15 June 1999. See also Chapter 4, pp. 143–5 below.

[158] Interview with UNICEF staff, Geneva, 12 February 1999.

[159] *The Impact of Armed Conflict on Children: Report of the Expert of the Secretary-General, Ms Graca Machel*, A/51/306, 26 August 1996, para. 90(d).

[160] For more information, see http://www.undp.org.

when the UNDP intervenes, it usually does so once the crisis is over and people have returned to their communities or settled down among other communities. As a development agency, it focuses on reintegration programmes, and tries to build a continuum between relief and development which is often lacking. As the UNDP has a continued field presence in many countries, it can also have a role into early-warning. Indeed, since its activities have a direct influence on the formation of the root causes of displacement, i.e. issues of governance, development, human rights awareness and so on, the agency can contribute to the prevention of displacement.[161]

As far as the UNDP is concerned, internally displaced persons do not constitute a special category of beneficiaries because it has been considered that the reintegration needs of war-affected populations are best addressed 'through area-based approaches at the community level and not at the target-group level'.[162] The UNDP has thus supported the development of the communities which the internally displaced have joined.[163] For instance, it has together with UNHCR launched a joint programme in Somalia to promote the reintegration of returning refugees and internally displaced persons by providing basic social services and supporting the creation of social and economic opportunities for the returnees and their communities.[164] The UNDP has also engaged in programmes specifically targeted at the reintegration of demobilised soldiers who were internally displaced, one example being Mozambique where it worked in close cooperation with the IOM.

The UNDP plays a special role with regard to the internally displaced, as its resident representatives are mandated to coordinate assistance programmes to them. This issue will be examined later in the chapter.[165] Finally, it must be noted that the UNDP has been very reluctant to become involved in protection issues, considering that this would be incompatible with its development activities which require close cooperation with governments.[166] The UNDP has been heavily criticised on this matter.[167] This issue will be examined in detail in the next

---

[161] See Chapter 4, pp. 122–5 below, on preventive protection.

[162] UNDP, *Sharing New Ground in Post-Conflict Situations: The Role of UNDP in Support of Reintegration Programmes*, DP/2000/14, 9 February 2000, 3.

[163] UNDP, *UNDP and Internally Displaced Persons*, draft of 7 May 1997, Geneva, 3–4.

[164] See UNDP, *UNDP Somalia Launches Three Major New Programs to Help Somalis Rebuild Their Lives*, news release, 6 July 2001. UNHCR phases out its participation at the end of 2003.

[165] See pp. 111–12 below.   [166] Cohen and Deng, *Masses in Flight*, 134.

[167] See for instance Human Rights Watch/Africa, *Failing the Internally Displaced: The UNDP Displaced Persons Program in Kenya* (New York: Human Rights Watch/Africa, 1997).

chapter.[168] The UNDP recently revised this policy, and declared a strong commitment to link its development work with human rights issues.[169] Such a commitment should also be reflected in its work with the internally displaced.

Human rights mechanisms

Although all humanitarian agencies are obliged to pay attention to human rights issues,[170] the lead agency is the Office of the High Commissioner on Human Rights (OHCHR).[171] Its role will be examined in more detail in the next chapter.[172] The Office has endeavoured to raise awareness of IDP issues within the UN system by actively supporting the work of the Special Representative on Internally Displaced Persons (whose mandate and functions have already been analysed).[173] A variety of human rights issues arise in the context of internal displacement and are subject to the Office's attention.

From this brief review of the IDP policies of UN agencies, the ICRC and the IOM, it appears that these agencies are still in the process of defining a coherent approach to the problem of internal displacement. Most of them have undertaken reviews of their own programmes for internally displaced persons, but have not always managed to formulate concrete policies as a result of these reviews. As argued in this book, each agency's approach must be based on a human rights framework and goals. The IDP policy process is pursued mainly within each separate agency and is closely linked to the ongoing difficulties of integrating human rights in their activities. Agencies must endeavour to coordinate not only their activities for the internally displaced, but also their policy approaches to the problem.

Improving the UN response to crises of internal displacement

Since no single UN agency can provide leadership on the issue of internal displacement, one must look at how this issue is dealt with within

---

[168] See Chapter 4, p. 127 below.

[169] See UNDP, *Integrating Human Rights with Sustainable Development: A UNDP Policy Document*, New York, January 1998, available at http://magnet.undp.org.

[170] See Chapter 4, pp. 125–9 below.

[171] See E. D. Mooney, *Internally Displaced Persons: The Role of OHCHR*, paper presented at the informal meeting of experts on measures to ensure international protection to all who need it, Geneva, 11 May 1998.

[172] See Chapter 4, pp. 151–2 below.   [173] See Introduction, pp. 8–9 above.

the framework of inter-agency coordination. This section will not deal with inter-agency coordination issues in general. Instead, the analysis will focus on inter-agency coordination in the area of IDP activities. The coordination of UN efforts on behalf of the internally displaced should have two distinct objectives: first, to ensure a rapid allocation of responsibilities in each situation; and, secondly, to promote a common understanding of the IDP problem. The analysis will be restricted to inter-agency coordination within the UN system. In order to protect its independence, the ICRC has refrained from participating in predetermined coordination arrangements.[174]

The role of OCHA

At the beginning of the 1990s, with the rise in the number of complex emergencies which required the involvement of the UN, an urgent need appeared to strengthen the coordination of humanitarian assistance. To respond to this need, the post of Emergency Relief Coordinator (ERC) was created in 1992.[175] The ERC chairs the Inter-Agency Standing Committee (IASC) and is the head of the Office for the Coordination of Humanitarian Affairs (OCHA) which serves as the Secretariat for the IASC. Prior to 1998, the OCHA was called the Department of Humanitarian Affairs (DHA). The IASC is composed of the executive heads of all UN humanitarian agencies, the High Commissioner for Human Rights and the Special Representative on Internally Displaced Persons. The latter two persons were invited to participate in some of the meetings of the IASC at the end of 1994. From 1997, they were invited to attend all IASC meetings.[176]

The UN also needs to coordinate its activities with other organisations, and, as a result, the IOM, the ICRC, the International Federation of the Red Cross and Red Crescent Societies (IFRCS) and three international NGO consortia (InterAction, the International Council of Voluntary Agencies, and the Steering Committee for Humanitarian Response) were also invited to participate in IASC meetings. In these meetings, heads of agencies are consulted on humanitarian matters, and make common decisions to ensure that the UN's response to humanitarian crises is as coherent and comprehensive as possible. The main advantage of this mechanism is that decisions are taken by heads of agencies themselves.

---

[174] See ICRC, *The Mandate and Role of the ICRC*.
[175] In accordance with GA Res. 46/182, 12 December 1991.
[176] See *1998 Deng Report*, note 103 above, para. 31.

The ERC has had difficulties in fulfilling his coordination role,[177] mainly because he does not have any authority over the heads of the other agencies. He does not outrank them, because each member of the IASC is accountable to the board of his or her agency and not to the ERC.[178] As a result, he cannot direct the operations himself. More fundamentally, some UN agencies are reluctant to accept his authority.[179] It must be noted, for instance, that UNHCR has a strong culture of independence, and initial tensions appeared when working with the DHA (now the OCHA).[180]

One of the *raisons d'être* of the IASC and the OCHA is to ensure that sufficient attention is being paid to internally displaced persons and other vulnerable populations who are not the central focus of any agency. In 1993, the IASC created a Task Force on internally displaced persons. The original mandate of the Task Force was to propose institutional reforms aimed at improving the UN's response to crises of internal displacement. The Task Force made some recommendations to the IASC at the end of 1994.[181] It suggested that the ERC should become the reference point in the UN system to receive information on situations of internal displacement and requests for assistance and protection for the internally displaced. In his Programme for Reform, the Secretary-General took up the suggestion and designated the ERC as the focal point for IDP issues.[182] The IASC had suggested that this role involve advocacy on behalf of the internally displaced, resource mobilisation and the identification of gaps in the international response, the assignment of responsibilities among agencies, information management and support to field operations.[183] In addition, the Task Force recommended that the Special Representative on Internally Displaced Persons and the High Commissioner for Human Rights be invited to meetings of the IASC in order to ensure

---

[177] See for instance S. Lautze, B. D. Jones and M. Duffield, *Strategic Humanitarian Coordination in the Great Lakes Region 1996–1997: An Independent Study for the Inter-Agency Standing Committee*, New York, March 1998, paras. 173–8.

[178] *Ibid.*, para. 167.   [179] See Sheridan, 'Institutional Arrangements', 971–3.

[180] See for instance UNHCR, *Evaluation of UNHCR's Programme for Internally Displaced Persons in Colombia*, para. 46, and UNHCR, *UNHCR's Programme for Internally Displaced People in Angola*, para. 41.

[181] Inter-Agency Task Force on Internally Displaced Persons, *Internally Displaced Persons: Report of the Inter-Agency Task Force on Internally Displaced Persons to the Inter-Agency Standing Committee*, November 1994, cited in T. Wichert, *Internally Displaced Persons – Discussion Paper*, Quaker United Nations Office, Geneva, April 1995, 4.

[182] 'Renewing the United Nations: A Programme for Reform', para. 186.

[183] See *1998 Deng Report*, note 103 above, para. 28.

that protection issues were not overlooked.[184] In 1995, the Task Force was re-established, but with the much broader mandate to review current situations of internal displacement, identify the assistance and protection needs of the internally displaced in each situation, examine the capacities to respond to them, both at the national and international levels, recommend measures to prevent internal displacement, review generic problems, and develop a workplan for the IASC each year.[185]

It has been suggested that the Task Force was asked to pursue too many objectives and as a result did not appear to have achieved much in the end. The Task Force was finally abolished in 1997.[186] The Special Representative on Internally Displaced Persons has always emphasised that strong leadership was needed from the IASC in order to ensure that IDP issues were properly addressed within the UN. However, it had appeared that the Task Force had been rather cautious in its approach.[187] Most UN agencies had hoped that the IASC and the OCHA would provide more leadership on issues regarding internal displacement and facilitate the allocation of tasks when a crisis arose. The IASC has attempted to define a common approach to some IDP issues. In particular, it has adopted a document which seeks to reflect a shared understanding of the notion of protection in the context of internal displacement.[188] This important document will be analysed in more detail later.[189] Further analysis of the operational challenges posed by internal displacement is now undertaken by yet another body, the OCHA Internal Displacement Unit.[190]

Mechanisms for initiating and coordinating UN action for the internally displaced

In order to improve the current response to crises of internal displacement, the UN system must first improve its system of collection of information on potential and actual situations of internal displacement. In this regard, the Global IDP Database has been established by the Norwegian Refugee Council to provide comprehensive information on

---

[184] See P. Brandrup, 'The Task Force of the Inter-Agency Standing Committee: Stride for a Coherent Response', in ICRC, *Internally Displaced Persons*, 68–72 at 69–70.

[185] *Ibid.*, 70–1.   [186] See Cohen and Deng, *Masses in Flight*, 148.

[187] *Internally Displaced Persons: Report of the Representative of the Secretary-General, Mr Francis M. Deng*, E/CN.4/1996/52, 22 February 1996 (hereinafter the *1996 Deng Report*), para. 25.

[188] See IASC, 'Protection of Internally Displaced Persons', Inter-Agency Standing Committee policy paper, New York, December 1999.

[189] Chapter 4, pp. 119–20 below.   [190] See pp. 110–11 below.

countries with an existing problem of internal displacement.[191] One must note that, with regard to refugees, UNHCR is responsible for collecting data and other information, but that no similar arrangement existed for internally displaced persons. Such collection of information is absolutely crucial to the establishment of an effective early-warning system.[192] Refugee flows are generally very visible because they involve the crossing of an international frontier, whereas internal movements of populations are not always so easy to identify, especially when there is little or no international presence within the country to report on such movements. Therefore, use must be made of a wide range of information sources, and in particular the NGO network.

The availability of information is a prerequisite for a more rapid mobilisation of the UN system in any given crisis of internal displacement. This should be accompanied by the development of an inter-agency mechanism to rapidly assign responsibilities to the agencies in each situation. The OCHA is the appropriate forum to decide such assignments of responsibilities. When a crisis is impending and the ERC receives a request from the state concerned for assistance, he should be able to convene an IASC emergency meeting and assign responsibilities to each agency, so that action can be taken quickly in the field. Alternatively, the ERC can designate a lead agency to coordinate complex emergencies.[193] The current High Commissioner for Refugees supports the principle that the ERC should be in charge of the inter-agency mechanism to allocate responsibilities in each IDP crisis. He added that the ERC should be able to activate this mechanism 'at his own initiative, or on the recommendation of one of the humanitarian agencies'.[194] In order to facilitate the ERC's work in coordinating UN efforts on behalf of the internally displaced and improve the predictability of UNHCR's involvement, UNHCR has started to provide an annual notification of its current and anticipated IDP operations.[195] It would be quite useful if other UN agencies did the same.

[191] For more information, see http://www.idpproject.org.

[192] See J. Borgen, *The Protection of Internally Displaced Persons by NRC: Platforms, Concepts and Strategies* (Oslo: Norwegian Refugee Council, 1994), 14–15.

[193] See 'Renewing the United Nations: A Programme for Reform', action 13.

[194] See Letter from the High Commissioner for Refugees to the Emergency Relief Coordinator, 20 March 2001.

[195] See *Report by the High Commissioner to the General Assembly on Strengthening the Capacity of the Office of the High Commissioner for Refugees to Carry Out Its Mandate*, A/AC.96/980, 20 August 2003, para. 29.

There are many ways in which the coordination of assistance and protection activities for the internally displaced could be improved.[196] In particular, a rapid assignment of responsibilities in each situation would be greatly facilitated by the prior identification of each agency's areas of expertise. Memoranda of understanding could prove useful in this regard. The last few years have seen the multiplication of memoranda of understanding signed between UN agencies to delineate their respective areas of responsibility. The purposes of these memoranda of understanding are to avoid duplication and minimise overlap, to ensure that there are no gaps in the intervention of the humanitarian agencies of the UN system, and to clarify the responsibilities of agencies 'on the basis of recognition of a comparative advantage'.[197] The focus is here on the memoranda of understanding signed by UNHCR with other agencies, as they are the most relevant to internally displaced persons.

These bilateral agreements do not focus on the coordination of assistance and protection activities in favour of the internally displaced as such, but they are especially useful to determine the respective responsibilities of the agencies with regard to this category of persons. Internally displaced persons are mentioned in all the memoranda of understanding signed by UNHCR. However, these agreements only cover the internally displaced who are 'of concern' to the agency. Whereas the memoranda of understanding signed at the end of the 1980s and the first half of the 1990s tended to be fairly general, laying down some principles upon which coordination between the two agencies is to be based, more recent agreements are much more operational. A good example is the memorandum of understanding signed between UNHCR and the WFP in 1997 and revised in 2002, which contains provisions directly applicable in the field.[198] Other memoranda of understanding remain on the level of general principles, and must be implemented through country-specific agreements or field-level letters of understanding.[199]

---

[196] See Cohen and Deng, *Masses in Flight*, 172–84. See also International Council of Voluntary Agencies (ICVA), *A Discussion Paper on Future Options for an Institutional Response to Internally Displaced Persons*, Geneva, 30 January 2001, and International Council of Voluntary Agencies (ICVA), *Some NGO Views on an Institutional Response to Internally Displaced Persons*, Geneva, 26 March 2001.

[197] *Memoranda of Understanding*, EC/47/SC/CRP.51, 15 August 1997.

[198] See *Memorandum of Understanding Between UNHCR and WFP*, 9 July 2002.

[199] See *Framework for Operational Cooperation Between UNHCR and UNDP*, 10 April 1997.

Nevertheless, not all UN aid workers agree on the level of detail that is required in a memorandum of understanding.[200]

The relatively defensive approach of UNHCR in the various agreements with regard to cooperation relating to internally displaced persons must be noted. For instance, the memorandum of understanding signed with UNICEF[201] states explicitly that UNICEF has responsibility for unaccompanied children within the country of origin, including internally displaced children, whereas UNHCR will assume responsibility for refugee children. More revealing is the provision inserted in most memoranda of understanding, which provides that 'the intervention of both agencies in favour of internally displaced persons are usually part of a broader UN coordinated plan of action'.[202] This clause may serve as a reminder that UNHCR considers that the problem of internal displacement is not the concern of humanitarian agencies alone, but also requires political action.

Memoranda of understanding have also been concluded with agencies outside the UN system, for instance the IOM.[203] One potential problem arises from the different IDP definitions used by the two agencies. For example, in the memorandum of understanding signed with the IOM, the IOM considers that persons displaced by natural disasters are internally displaced persons, whereas UNHCR considers that people displaced by natural disasters do not come under its mandate.[204] The memorandum notes that 'UNHCR's involvement is selective, applying to persons displaced internally for reasons that would make them of concern to UNHCR had they crossed an international boundary'.[205]

Memoranda of understanding could prove a very efficient tool of coordination if properly implemented in the field. There is now a series of memoranda of understanding concluded between UN agencies which could contribute to filling the gaps in the assistance and protection of internally displaced persons. It is acknowledged that UN agencies have begun 'to clearly define respective areas of responsibility through

---

[200] See N. Reindorp and P. Wiles, *Humanitarian Coordination: Lessons from Recent Field Experience*, study commissioned by the Office for the Coordination of Humanitarian Affairs and the Overseas Development Institute, London, June 2001, 38.

[201] See *Memorandum of Understanding Between UNHCR and UNICEF*, 14 March 1996.

[202] *Ibid.*, para. 11, and *Memorandum of Understanding Between UNHCR and WHO*, March 1997, para. 3.7.

[203] See *Memorandum of Understanding Between UNHCR and IOM*, 15 May 1997.

[204] See Chapter 1, pp. 29–33 above.

[205] See *Memorandum of Understanding Between UNHCR and IOM*, para. 17.

the exchange of memoranda of understanding'.[206] Memoranda of understanding concluded before a situation develops into a full humanitarian crisis could contribute to the rapid assignment of responsibilities to each agency. Another way of ensuring that the issue of internal displacement receives appropriate attention in each crisis is to include relevant data and analysis, as well as specific projects in UN consolidated inter-agency appeals.[207] One must nevertheless note that, in 2002, less than half of the countries experiencing internal displacement were covered by these appeals.[208]

In order to reinforce the operational response to crises of internal displacement, the IASC has created an inter-agency network composed of *senior* IDP focal points from each agency/organisation which is an IASC member.[209] The Senior Inter-Agency Network is mandated to conduct country reviews and to make long-term recommendations for an improved response to the needs of the internally displaced.[210] Following each mission, the Network makes some recommendations for action on how to improve the situation in the field, e.g. strengthen inter-agency coordination, improve dialogue with all armed actors, respond to the protection needs of internally displaced persons by encouraging all agencies to engage the government and non-state actors on the issue and incorporate human rights concerns into their work.[211] In April 2001, the Special Coordinator, who chairs the Network, made a series of proposals for an improved international response to the problem of internal displacement. His most interesting proposal was the creation of a small, non-operational, Office for IDP Coordination within the OCHA in order to strengthen headquarters support capacity.[212] Following

[206] *1998 Deng Report*, note 103 above, para. 35.
[207] See F. M. Deng and J. Kunder, *The Consolidated Appeals and IDPs: The Degree to Which UN Consolidated Inter-Agency Appeals for the Year 2000 Support Internally Displaced Populations*, Brookings Institution and UNICEF, August 2000, http://www.brook.edu/views/papers/deng/200008CAP.htm.
[208] See Global IDP Survey, *Internally Displaced People: A Global Survey* (London: Earthscan Publications Ltd, 2002, 2nd ed.), 11.
[209] See IASC, *Senior Inter-Agency Network to Reinforce the Operational Response to Situations of Internal Displacement*, New York, 15 September 2000.
[210] See D. McNamara, *Information Note by the UN Special Coordinator of the Senior Inter-Agency Network on Internal Displacement*, 13 September 2000.
[211] See for instance Senior Inter-Agency Network on Internal Displacement, *Mission to Ethiopia and Eritrea, 16–21 October 2000, Findings and Recommendations*, and Senior Inter-Agency Network on Internal Displacement, *Mission to Burundi, 18–22 December 2000, Findings and Recommendations*.
[212] See D. McNamara, *Interim Report from the Special Co-ordinator of the Network on Internal Displacement*, 9 April 2001.

this proposal, the OCHA Internal Displacement Unit was established in 2002.

Promoting a common understanding of the IDP problem: the OCHA Internal Displacement Unit[213]

Coordination of UN activities for internally displaced persons should go beyond the prevention of duplication and overlap, and seek to promote a common understanding of the IDP problem. The Internal Displacement Unit is a fairly small administrative structure based in the OCHA. Its mandate includes monitoring situations of internal displacement, undertaking systematic reviews of selected countries, identifying operational gaps and making suggestions on how to address them, providing training on IDP-related issues, mobilising resources, and further developing inter-agency policies on IDP issues.[214] The final aspect of the mandate may constitute the most important contribution of the Unit. Indeed, agencies have so far been unable to develop and adopt a single, comprehensive policy response to internally displaced persons, but such a policy response can only be based on a common understanding of the problem of internal displacement. The Unit could play a crucial role in promoting inter-agency dialogue on a range of IDP issues, which may lead to the adoption of a common strategy. For instance, the Unit has undertaken a 'protection survey' in order to identify current protection approaches/arrangements and to suggest possible improvements of protection strategies for the internally displaced.[215]

There is a concern that the OCHA Internal Displacement Unit has created just another layer of bureaucracy. There are three specific mechanisms which are now solely devoted to the issue of internal displacement, i.e. the Special Representative, the Senior Inter-Agency Network and the OCHA Internal Displacement Unit. It is somewhat ironic that these three entities had to sign agreements to delimit their respective responsibilities.[216] It remains to be seen whether the creation of the Unit

---

[213] For more detail, see http://www.reliefweb.int/idp/index.htm.
[214] See Terms of Reference for an IDP Unit within OCHA,
    http://www.reliefweb.int/idp/docs/references/IDPUnitTORFinal.pdf.
[215] See OCHA Internal Displacement Unit and the Brookings Institution-SAIS Project on Internal Displacement, *The Protection Survey*,
    http://www.reliefweb.int/idp/docs/references/ProtSurvProp.pdf.
[216] See for instance *Memorandum of Understanding Between the IDP Unit and the Representative of the Secretary-General on Internally Displaced Persons*, 17 April 2002,
    http://www.reliefweb.int/idp/docs/references/MoUDengpressrel.html.

'will simply perpetuate the coordination difficulties already observed'[217] or whether it will in fact strengthen the OCHA's capacity to coordinate UN activities on behalf of the internally displaced.

It was noted above that UN agencies' responses to the problem of internal displacement were largely *ad hoc* and that the UN system-wide response has reflected this. Over the years, there have been many discussion groups, task forces, working groups, networks and so on, focusing on internal displacement,[218] but the establishment of specific mechanisms has not always led to the formulation of coherent policies. Faced with the increased media exposure of the problem of internal displacement (especially since Holbrooke's comments),[219] the UN has reacted by creating new structures, i.e. the Senior Inter-Agency Network and then the OCHA Internal Displacement Unit, in order to demonstrate that the issue was being finally and properly addressed. As usual, the test is whether the establishment of these new institutional mechanisms will be translated into increased and more effective coordination in the field.

Coordination in the field

As mentioned above, several mechanisms at the highest level within the OCHA are designed to ensure inter-agency coordination. However, there is resistance to coordination which seems to come from the top, and is perceived as imposed by bureaucrats based in New York or Geneva who seem unaware of the conditions in the field. At field level, the general rule is that the UNDP Resident Coordinators in the country are designated Humanitarian Coordinators for the whole UN system, and are responsible for coordinating assistance to the internally displaced.[220] The UNDP was chosen to fulfil this role because it has an extensive network of field offices. Resident Coordinators are presumed to have an in-depth understanding of the local situation and a network of contacts in the country. A person other than the Resident Coordinator may be designated Humanitarian Coordinator, although this occurs

---

[217] M. Contat Hickel, 'Protection of Internally Displaced Persons Affected by Armed Conflict: Concept and Challenges' (2001) 843 *International Review of the Red Cross* 699 at 708.

[218] See OCHA Internal Displacement Unit, *No Refuge: The Challenge of Internal Displacement* (New York and Geneva: United Nations, 2003), 33.

[219] See p. 87 above.   [220] See GA Res. 44/136, 15 December 1989, para. 7.

infrequently.[221] In some cases, as in the former Yugoslavia in the 1990s, a lead agency is nominated to coordinate UN activities in a designated country.

With respect to the internally displaced, the mandate of the Resident/ Humanitarian Coordinator (RC/HC) involves responsibility for ensuring that their needs are adequately met, advocacy on rights issues, recommending to the ERC a division of operational responsibilities among the agencies, and, in some situations, recommending to him that a lead agency be designated to assume operational responsibilities for the internally displaced.

Where the RC/HC has competence and experience only in development work, as is often the case, he or she has encountered problems in the coordination of some emergency programmes.[222] In order to help UNDP Resident Coordinators to work in complex emergencies, specific training modules are being created.[223] In some countries, the RC/HCs have been cautious in their advocacy role for the internally displaced, because, in the function of coordinator, they must maintain good relations with the government, which has led to protection problems in some cases.[224] Another difficulty when combining the two roles of UNDP Resident Coordinator and Humanitarian Coordinator is that, in the exercise of the first function, the RC/HC is to report to the UNDP, whereas, in the exercise of the second, he reports to the ERC. It has been argued that the RC/HC model is better suited to situations where a single authority existed, whereas in countries divided by several warring groups, a person other than the Resident Coordinator and who would be perceived as more neutral, should be designated Humanitarian Coordinator.[225]

In some countries, specific mechanisms have been set up to ensure that IDP issues are not overlooked, as in Somalia and Sri Lanka where IDP task forces were created in 1995.[226] Such an initiative would be especially welcomed in countries where UNHCR serves as the lead agency for the UN system. The lead agency model can have important implications for the internally displaced. Where UNHCR served as the lead agency, protection activities for refugees and internally displaced persons were given a lower priority. It may therefore be useful to designate a 'focal point in each crisis to assume primary operational responsibility for the

---

[221] See Reindorp and Wiles, *Humanitarian Coordination*, 20.
[222] *Ibid.*   [223] *Ibid.*
[224] See for instance Human Rights Watch/Africa, *Failing the Internally Displaced*.
[225] See Lautze *et al.*, *Strategic Humanitarian Coordination*, para. 160.
[226] See Cohen and Deng, *Masses in Flight*, 149.

internally displaced',[227] primary not meaning exclusive responsibility. There is a danger, though, of coordination activities being splintered by dealing with separate groups, and coordination should only be in relation to specific needs.

Problems may arise from the multiplication of formal coordination mechanisms. In some crises, the Secretary-General has designated a Special Representative to undertake political initiatives to resolve the conflict, e.g. to act as a mediator between the warring parties. Although this person has a political role and is not mandated to coordinate assistance programmes, he nevertheless shapes the overall strategy of the UN in a particular country, and his action needs to be coordinated with the activities of humanitarian agencies. For the first time in the Great Lakes region in 1996, a Regional Humanitarian Coordinator (RHC) was designated to coordinate the provision of relief aid in the region.[228] When the same humanitarian crisis affects several countries in the same region, it makes sense to have an RHC. In such situations where a Special Representative of the Secretary-General and/or an RHC is or are appointed for a designated country, the problem of 'coordination of the coordinators' may arise.[229]

An example of ineffective coordination is the situation in Rwanda (1994–6). The Rwandan genocide and its aftermath are well documented,[230] and the focus here is therefore on issues of inter-agency coordination.[231] One must first note that more than one coordination office was set up: the Office of the RHC based in Kigali, later in Nairobi; the Office of the RH/HC; and the DHA Office/UN Rwanda Emergency Office (UNREO).[232] More specifically on internally displaced persons, an Integrated Operation Centre (IOC) was formed to coordinate activities on their behalf. The IOC was composed of members of all international agencies and NGOs, as well as ministries of the Rwandan government.

[227] *1998 Deng Report*, note 103 above, para. 36.
[228] See Lautze *et al.*, *Strategic Humanitarian Coordination*, para. 174.
[229] See Reindorp and Wiles, *Humanitarian Coordination*, 40.
[230] See for instance *Report of the Independent Inquiry into the Actions of the United Nations During the 1994 Genocide in Rwanda*, S/1999/1257, 16 December 1999.
[231] For more detail on the internally displaced in Rwanda, see S. T. E. Kleine-Ahlbrandt, *The Protection Gap in the International Protection of Internally Displaced Persons: The Case of Rwanda* (Geneva: Institut Universitaire des Hautes Etudes Internationales, 1996), and L. Minear and R. C. Kent, 'Rwanda's Internally Displaced: A Conundrum Within a Conundrum', in Cohen and Deng (eds.), *The Forsaken People*, 57–95.
[232] Lautze *et al.*, *Strategic Humanitarian Coordination*, para. 187.

However, most agencies showed little interest in attending the meetings.[233]

Although UNREO did fulfil most of its coordinating functions, it encountered substantial problems as far as IDP protection issues were concerned. It had little political weight or expertise to put pressure on the government whose objective was to close (by force if necessary) IDP camps as well as refugee camps situated across the border in the Democratic Republic of Congo (DRC).[234] There were also coordination problems between the peacekeeping force (UNAMIR) and humanitarian agencies, which partly resulted from a lack of clarification over the respective mandates of the Special Representative and the Humanitarian Coordinator.[235] Overall, there was a lack of coherence in the UN field structure and 'little evidence of medium- to long-term thinking, analysis of the changing political situation, or development of humanitarian strategy'.[236] One must also add that the resources available for coordination functions were largely inadequate.

As demonstrated above, there is no shortage of formal coordination *mechanisms*. However, they do not form 'a coherent *system* for strategic coordination'.[237] Very often, effective coordination in the field depends on the personality of the person performing as RC/HC. The IASC has issued guidelines as to how RC/HCs can ensure that gaps in the response to a crisis of internal displacement in a particular country are systematically addressed.[238] Recent country missions by the Special Representative have revealed 'considerable improvement in the official policy on the issue of internal displacement, contrasted with a continuing passivity, even reluctance, on the part of the United Nations country teams to become meaningfully engaged in addressing the assistance and especially protection needs of the internally displaced, presumably building on the old policy climate'.[239] Despite the IASC guidelines, there is therefore still a long way to go before IDP protection issues are fully mainstreamed within UN field activities.

---

[233] See Kleine-Ahlbrandt, *The Protection Gap*, 68.   [234] *Ibid.*, 73.

[235] See Minear and Kent, 'Rwanda's Internally Displaced', 71.

[236] See Lautze *et al.*, *Strategic Humanitarian Coordination*, para. 213.   [237] *Ibid.*, para. 153.

[238] See IASC, *Supplementary Guidance to Humanitarian/Resident Co-ordinators on Their Responsibilities in Relation to IDPs*, 29 March 2000.

[239] *Internally Displaced Persons: Report of the Representative of the Secretary-General, Mr Francis M. Deng*, E/CN.4/2003/86, 21 January 2003, para. 72.

Conclusion

At the end of the 1980s, no agency, apart from UNHCR, really talked about internally displaced persons in explicit terms. In fact, most agencies refused to distinguish the internally displaced from other beneficiaries, and the term 'internally displaced persons' was nowhere to be found in their policy documents. In recent years, most UN agencies have become increasingly active in the field of internal displacement. One could question the reasons for their sudden interest in IDP issues, and it may just be that there is increased funding for IDP activities, which reflects the changing priorities of donor states. One would nevertheless not regret such a competition between agencies if it contributes to mainstream IDP issues, although a risk of duplication may arise. Despite recent improvements, it appears that 'the response to specific situations of internal displacement nonetheless remains *ad hoc* and still largely focused on assistance'.[240]

Problems arise from the fact that none of the agencies has a clear policy approach to the IDP issue. UN actors, the ICRC and the IOM must reconceptualise the IDP issue in human rights terms, and this in turn must influence the IDP policy process. For the reasons explained above, UNHCR should not be given overall responsibility for the internally displaced, but it still needs to develop a coherent policy on internal displacement in collaboration with the OCHA and other agencies. UNHCR's increased involvement with the internally displaced has been part of the evolution of the agency's humanitarian activities covering a wider population of persons in need. It is also part of the move towards the integration of human rights in UNHCR's activities and there is now an awareness that 'growing involvement with the internally displaced has also led [the agency] further into human rights monitoring and promotion'.[241]

In light of the analysis of UNHCR and other agencies' activities, it can be argued that UNHCR should continue activities relating to internally displaced persons, but needs to focus on those protection activities for which it has experience and expertise, e.g. legal assistance for return-related problems. This would leave more scope for increased ICRC

---

[240] *Internally Displaced Persons: Report of the Representative of the Secretary-General, Mr Francis M. Deng*, E/CN.4/2002/95, 16 January 2002, para. 55.

[241] I. Martin, 'A New Frontier: The Early Experience and Future of International Human Rights Field Operations' (1998) 16 *Netherlands Quarterly of Human Rights* 121 at 125.

involvement, which may be more appropriate for the reasons explained above. UNHCR could also have more influence on the UN's understanding of IDP protection,[242] and ensure that the possibility of asylum always remains available. Stronger leadership on the IDP issue should be provided by the OCHA Internal Displacement Unit to promote collaboration between agencies at headquarters and field levels, and to ensure that work with the internally displaced is based on human rights protection goals.

---

[242] See UNHCR, *Protection and Solutions in Situations of Internal Displacement: Learning from UNHCR's Operational Experience*, EPAU/2002/10, August 2002, 4.

4 Protection strategies for the internally displaced

Internal displacement has been recognised as one of today's major humanitarian problems, but the key issue of protection has not always received appropriate attention, in spite of the view that 'the main problem is not assistance but rather protection for internally displaced persons'.[1] The Vienna Declaration and Programme of Action adopted at the end of the World Conference on Human Rights held in 1993 mentioned the case of the internally displaced as a human rights matter.[2] Internally displaced persons are indeed often among not only the most destitute, but also the most vulnerable to human rights abuses. They face problems of physical safety, lack of food and water, access to health and other social services, and are often separated from their family.

Whereas the previous chapter put the focus on UN agencies' stated approaches to internal displacement, the present chapter examines field activities and the extent to which they reflect some of the flaws in the UN's understanding of the problem of internal displacement. It examines protection strategies implemented on the ground by a variety of international actors such as humanitarian agencies, peacekeeping forces and human rights field monitors. Such strategies assume that an international presence has already been established in the country concerned with or without the consent of the government.[3] The chapter evaluates the efficiency of measures undertaken to protect internally displaced persons from human rights violations, including forced displacement.

---

[1] T. G. Weiss, 'Whither International Efforts for Internally Displaced Persons?' (1999) 36 *Peace Research* 363 at 369.

[2] See *Vienna Declaration and Programme of Action*, A/CONF.157/23, 12 July 1993, para. 23.

[3] On issues of intervention on behalf of the internally displaced, see Chapter 6 below.

Although Chapter 1 argued that natural disasters and development projects can lead to displacement involving human rights violations, this chapter concentrates mainly on protection strategies for the internally displaced in armed conflicts.

Refugee protection consists mainly in the defence of the legal rights of refugees as defined in the 1951 Convention.[4] In contrast, IDP protection is less legalistic and frequently depends on non-legal skills and initiatives, hence the need for a chapter on protection strategies separate from the chapter on the legal framework of protection (Chapter 2). The first section attempts to define in more detail what protection for internally displaced persons entails. As noted by UNHCR, 'it is not so clear what type of protection is required to be exercised by the international community'[5] in the case of the internally displaced. The following section looks at protection strategies ranging from mere international presence to evacuations. The third section focuses on the specific protection problems faced by vulnerable groups of internally displaced persons such as women, children, the elderly and the handicapped. Some suggestions are made on how field activities should be pursued within a human rights framework to produce a more effective response to the protection needs of internally displaced persons. The discussion is placed in the wider context of the mainstreaming of human rights in the UN and recent initiatives to improve the protection of civilians in armed conflict. These initiatives are directly relevant to the internally displaced since the overwhelming majority of them are civilians in situations of armed conflict.

Defining protection for internally displaced persons

Focusing on human rights protection

Part of the initial problem encountered when dealing with internal displacement was the 'lack of conceptual clarity as to the meaning of "protection"'.[6] A good starting point when trying to formulate an understanding of the concept of IDP protection is the concept of refugee protection. Indeed, the latter has been developed over the last half-century

---

[4] Convention Relating to the Status of Refugees, 28 July 1951, 189 UNTS 150 (hereinafter the 1951 Convention).

[5] UNHCR, *UNHCR's Operational Experience with Internally Displaced Persons* (Geneva: UNHCR, 1994), 78.

[6] *Internally Displaced Persons: Report of the Representative of the Secretary-General, Mr Francis M. Deng*, E/CN.4/2002/95, 16 January 2002, para. 58.

into a sophisticated framework of protection from which elements can be used by analogy for our purpose. Nowhere in the 1951 Convention is the expression 'refugee protection' mentioned, but it has become the underlying principle of the instrument, upon which the work of UNHCR is based. Article 8 of the UNHCR Statute[7] details the activities to be undertaken to promote the protection of refugees. In comparison, no international legal instrument defines what IDP protection involves, though the Guiding Principles on Internal Displacement[8] give an indication of what it entails. Principle 1 provides that 'internally displaced persons shall enjoy full equality, the same rights and freedoms under international and domestic law as do other persons in their country'. Principle 1 also contains a non-discrimination clause. Unlike refugees, the internally displaced do not have a specific legal status which grants them special rights. Because they are still under the jurisdiction of their own country, they are entitled to its protection. As previously explained, IDP protection involves both the reinforcement of national protection by the state, and an element of international protection.[9]

Although Principle 1 suggests what IDP protection ultimately aims at, it does not give any brief definition of what IDP protection is. Instead, the Guiding Principles seek to articulate standards of protection for each phase of displacement. They take a very broad approach to the idea of IDP protection, as they deal with protection against, during and after displacement.[10] The Guiding Principles put great emphasis on the protection of human rights, not only civil and political rights, but also economic, social and cultural rights.[11] It was argued earlier that IDP protection cannot be based on a specific legal instrument as refugee protection is,[12] and consequently it can only be rooted within the broader human rights framework. At the same time, specific protection strategies need to be devised for the internally displaced as they form a special category of human rights victims who encounter specific problems.

On the basis of the Guiding Principles, the Inter-Agency Standing Committee (IASC) composed of UN agencies and international NGOs has drafted a policy paper on the protection of internally displaced

---

[7] Annex to GA Res. 428 (V), 14 December 1950.
[8] *Guiding Principles on Internal Displacement*, E/CN.4/1998/53/Add.2, 11 February 1998. See Annex 1 below.
[9] See Chapter 1, p. 27 above.   [10] See Chapter 2, pp. 56–8 above.
[11] See, for instance, Principles 18, 19 and 23.   [12] See Chapter 1 above.

persons.[13] The paper borrows its definition of protection from the ICRC: a conception of protection which 'encompass[es] all activities aimed at obtaining full respect for the rights of the individual in accordance with the letter and the spirit of the relevant bodies of law (i.e. human rights law, international humanitarian law, refugee law)'.[14] The paper insists on the importance of the Guiding Principles on Internal Displacement as a protection tool, and the need to integrate protection concerns into assistance programmes. It constitutes the first UN document to articulate in any detail what IDP protection entails and how to translate it into effective protection in practice. Fourteen strategic areas of protection are identified and grouped under three categories, i.e. environment building, responsive action and remedial action.[15] Emphasis is put on the preparedness of the UN system to respond to IDP protection problems: the paper mentions training, vulnerability assessment and coordinated programming of assistance. It also notes the need for the UN system to improve its knowledge of IDP protection issues and of specific situations, and for individual agencies to be prepared to work together on protection. Overall, the IASC policy paper remains at the level of general strategies and does not give a clear overview of the range of activities which can be undertaken to provide effective protection to the internally displaced. One could argue that the paper constitutes only a first attempt at analysing the concept of IDP protection. Examples of field practice have subsequently been examined,[16] and the OCHA Internal Displacement Unit is still working on improving the understanding of IDP protection.[17]

Two elements seem to come up in any discussion of IDP protection: physical safety and the protection of human rights. This is the view at least of UNHCR.[18] IDP protection should indeed involve all activities aimed at defending the rights of the internally displaced as defined in human rights law, including activities aimed at securing their physical safety. Human Rights Watch also defines IDP protection in terms of

---

[13] See IASC, 'Protection of Internally Displaced Persons', Inter-Agency Standing Committee policy paper, New York, December 1999.

[14] *Ibid.*, 4.   [15] *Ibid.*, 6.

[16] See OCHA, *Manual on Field Practice in Internal Displacement: Examples from UN Agencies and Partner Organisations of Field-Based Initiatives Supporting Internally Displaced Persons*, Inter-Agency Standing Committee Policy Paper Series No. 1, 1999.

[17] See OCHA Internal Displacement Unit and the Brookings Institution-SAIS Project on Internal Displacement, *The Protection Survey*, http://www.reliefweb.int/idp/docs/references/ProtSurvProp.pdf.

[18] See *Protection Aspects of UNHCR Activities on Behalf of Internally Displaced Persons*, EC/SCP/87, 17 August 1994, para. 28.

physical safety and the defence of human rights,[19] but goes further when specifying that 'protection encompasses both security of persons *and property*, as well as guarantees of legal protection and redress for rights abuses' (emphasis added).[20] The protection of property has become an increasingly important issue, especially in the context of the return of refugees and internally displaced persons.[21] The Special Representative on Internally Displaced Persons also refers to respect for human rights and physical safety when attempting to define IDP protection, but he mentions in addition respect for dignity and specifies that one must go beyond assistance to provide protection to the internally displaced.[22] The primary need of internally displaced persons is often physical safety as they find themselves caught in the midst of armed conflict and/or subject to direct physical attack or threat thereof.[23] Consequently, it is justified that physical safety should be the priority of all those actors concerned with protecting the internally displaced.

The Special Representative on Internally Displaced Persons has repeated on several occasions that assistance falls within the meaning of protection.[24] The provision of emergency relief certainly reinforces the protection of the persons assisted, but food may not always be the first priority for persons whose physical safety is not ensured.[25] Assistance and protection certainly complement each other, although it may not be desirable to amalgamate the two. The concern is that by stating that assistance also contributes to improving the protection of the populations concerned, this shifts the focus away from more difficult protection activities. Assistance alone does not necessarily equal protection and the IASC paper mentioned above insists on the integration of protection in assistance programmes and the protection role (monitoring and reporting) of humanitarian agencies.[26]

---

[19] See Human Rights Watch/Africa, *Failing the Internally Displaced: The UNDP Displaced Persons Program in Kenya* (New York: Human Rights Watch/Africa, 1997), 29.

[20] *Ibid.*, 2.   [21] See Chapter 2, pp. 61–5 above.

[22] See R. Cohen and F. M. Deng, *Masses in Flight: The Global Crisis of Internal Displacement* (Washington DC: Brookings Institution, 1998), 257.

[23] See USGAO, *Internally Displaced Persons Lack Effective Protection*, Report to the Chairman and the Ranking Minority Member, Committee on Foreign Relations, US Senate, Washington DC, August 2001, 10–11.

[24] See *Internally Displaced Persons: Report of the Representative of the Secretary-General, Mr Francis M. Deng, Profiles of Displacement: Azerbaijan*, E/CN.4/1999/79/Add.1, 25 January 1999 (hereinafter the *Azerbaijan Report*), para. 59.

[25] See B. Frelick, 'Assistance Without Protection: Feed the Hungry, Clothe the Naked, and Watch Them Die', *World Refugee Survey 1997*, 24.

[26] See IASC, 'Protection of Internally Displaced Persons', 8–10.

Defining preventive protection

The notion of preventive protection finds its origins in the shift of focus from redress towards pre-emption of human rights abuses. In this context, the idea of protection from displacement suggests that special protection should be afforded to populations which are likely to be displaced. The argument is simple: it is preferable to act before people feel compelled to leave their homes, rather than intervening *ex post* when displacement has already taken place. Effective preventive protection requires an early and active involvement in a potential crisis, including efficient early-warning systems.[27] During the 1980s, initiatives were undertaken to develop such systems.[28] At the time, UNHCR was rather reluctant to participate in initiatives aimed at dealing with the causes of displacement for fear of compromising its non-political mandate.[29] However, it changed its attitude at the beginning of the 1990s following a shift of attention by states to the root causes of displacement.

The notion of protection from displacement has been translated in the context of internal displacement into a so-called 'right to remain' or a 'right not to be arbitrarily displaced'. In 1997, the Special Representative on Internally Displaced Persons commissioned a study on the legal protection against arbitrary displacement,[30] which led to the drafting of several Guiding Principles on protection from displacement. These provisions seek to define the conditions in which organised transfers of population can take place, and to identify some procedural safeguards setting conditions to ensure that the displacement is not arbitrary.[31] Nevertheless, protection from arbitrary displacement is one thing, and protection from displacement, which is primarily a matter of human rights protection and conflict-prevention, another. People are forced to flee when they face widespread human rights violations and/or armed conflict. The only way to protect people from displacement is to act on the potential root causes of displacement, and prevent a full crisis

---

[27] See UNHCR, *The State of World's Refugees: The Challenge of Protection* (Geneva: UNHCR, 1993), 127.

[28] See B. G. Ramcharan, 'Early-Warning at the United Nations: The First Experiment' (1989) 1 *International Journal of Refugee Law* 379.

[29] See G. Goodwin-Gill, *The Refugee in International Law* (Oxford: Clarendon Press, 2nd ed., 1996), 286.

[30] See *Internally Displaced Persons: Compilation and Analysis of Legal Norms, Part II: Legal Aspects Relating to the Protection Against Arbitrary Displacement*, E/CN.4/1998/53/Add.1, 11 February 1998. See also, by the author of the study, M. Stavropoulou, 'The Right Not to Be Displaced' (1994) 9 *American University Journal of International Law and Policy* 689.

[31] See Guiding Principles 5 to 8.

from developing. In theory, preventive protection can cover many activities, ranging from human rights monitoring and conflict prevention to development. Anything which can prevent the causes of displacement can potentially be seen as preventive protection activities.[32]

When UNHCR first became involved in countries of origin, rather than in countries of asylum, the basis for such involvement was the need to prevent refugee flows. It defined prevention as 'the elimination of causes of departure, rather than the erection of barriers which leave causes intact, but make departure impossible'.[33] It was later emphasised that prevention sought to 'attenuate the causes of departure and to reduce or contain cross-border movements or internal displacements', but that it was not 'a substitute for asylum'.[34] Activities aimed at preventing refugee flows have taken UNHCR into new areas of activities, and have led the agency to pay more attention to human rights. Among the list of activities to be undertaken in relation to prevention are:

- reinforcing national protection capacities;
- addressing the problem of statelessness;
- protecting internally displaced people;
- consolidating solutions in war-torn societies;
- organising mass information campaigns to address broader problems of migration; and
- alerting the international community to the causes of forced displacement.[35]

Protection of internally displaced persons was considered by UNHCR an important aspect of the prevention of refugee flows.[36] The focus is now on the prevention not only of refugee flows but also of internal movements of populations, with a recent emphasis on the so-called 'right not to be arbitrarily displaced'. Again, it may be more appropriate to concentrate on human rights protection for the civilian population at large. In this respect, it is fundamental that such efforts be linked with political efforts to resolve the conflict where it is the cause of displacement. Activities aimed at preventing the internal displacement of civilians include the monitoring of the treatment of minorities and active intervention in the political conflict. The objective is to deliver

[32] See Goodwin-Gill, *The Refugee*, p. 293.

[33] *Note on International Protection*, A/AC.96/777, 9 September 1991, para. 43.

[34] *Note on International Protection*, A/AC.96/799, 25 July 1992, para. 26.

[35] See *Follow-Up to ECOSOC Resolution 1995/56: UNHCR Activities in Relation to Prevention*, EC/46/SC/CRP.33, 28 May 1996.

[36] See also *Note on International Protection*, A/AC.96/777, 9 September 1991, para. 46.

the conditions so that people do not feel compelled to flee. However, equally important is the fact that people should not feel compelled to stay as a result of these activities. The populations targeted should not be forced to stay in dangerous areas, or be given the illusion of safety by international presence.

It appears to have been difficult to translate such principles into practice. There is always a fine line between prevention of refugee flows and containment. Prevention seeks to address the root causes of displacement so that people do not feel compelled to flee. Containment only seeks to prevent people who need protection elsewhere from leaving the country by erecting barriers. One simple way of evaluating the success of preventive protection activities is to look at whether the populations targeted end up being 'worse off, in the sense of remaining exposed to danger or risk to life and limb, while also losing the possibility of flight to refuge and asylum'[37] as a result of the *in situ* focus. It is difficult to give concrete examples of preventive protection activities, because, in fact, all human rights activities are preventive protection activities. It has been argued that preventive protection activities are simply protection activities carried out in a preventive context.[38] One must note that activities aimed at preventing internal displacement are usually aimed at the whole population and amount to monitoring to prevent human rights abuses in general. One example that can be given of successful international intervention to prevent displacement was UNHCR's activities undertaken in response to an imminent danger of displacement in a fishing village in Sri Lanka. UNHCR engaged in a range of focused activities including mediation between armed forces and the villagers, monitoring the behaviour of patrols in the area and implementing micro-projects to stabilise the village.[39] These activities sought to specifically address all the circumstances that may have led to displacement.

As mentioned earlier, the focus on protection from displacement for 'potential internally displaced persons' results from recent efforts to prevent refugee flows, and must be analysed in this context. The development of the concept of preventive protection at the beginning of the 1990s can be explained by two factors: first, a renewed emphasis on

[37] Goodwin-Gill, *The Refugee*, p. 283.

[38] See P. Kourula, *Broadening the Edges: Refugee Definition and International Protection Revisited* (The Hague: Martinus Nijhoff Publishers, 1997), 214.

[39] See IASC, *Growing the Sheltering Tree: Protecting Rights Through Humanitarian Action* (New York: UNICEF, 2002), 169.

human rights within the UN; and, secondly, the emergence of restrictive asylum policies in developed states. Following events in Bosnia and Herzegovina,[40] the term 'preventive protection' has gradually disappeared from the discourse of UNHCR, whereas it used to be a central feature of the agency's strategy in the search for solutions to refugee problems between 1990 and 1993–4. Recent official UNHCR documents no longer mention preventive protection.

Means of protection for internally displaced persons

The purpose of the present section is to analyse various protection strategies after displacement has occurred. These strategies are often combined and there is certainly some overlap between them. The choice of strategies depends on the characteristics of the crisis, as well as the availability of resources. IDP protection is not provided through international mechanisms alone and one must acknowledge the capacity of internally displaced communities to develop their own coping mechanisms, but since the focus of this book is the UN capacity to protect the internally displaced, community-based protection will not be examined here.[41]

Protection through humanitarian assistance

Protection activities often have to be undertaken in situations where access to the internally displaced is difficult, if not denied by governmental authorities or insurgent groups in control of the areas concerned. If the internally displaced are associated with insurgent groups, the central authorities are more reluctant to allow access to them. In contrast, where the internally displaced belong for instance to the same ethnic group as those in power or are not considered a political threat, the central authorities may welcome or even ask for international assistance. In Georgia, for instance, the authorities have allowed international assistance to be provided to the internally displaced who are ethnic Georgians and were displaced from Abkhazia by ethnic Armenians.[42] The

[40] See Chapter 5, pp. 165–7 below.
[41] For more detail, see M. Vincent and B. R. Sørensen, *Caught Between Borders: Response Strategies of the Internally Displaced* (London: Pluto Press in association with the Norwegian Refugee Council, 2001).
[42] See E. Mooney, 'Internal Displacement and the Conflict in Abkhazia: International Responses and Their Protective Effect' (1996) 3 *International Journal on Group Rights* 197.

same behaviour can be witnessed on the part of the central authorities in Azerbaijan which allowed international aid to be provided to ethnic Azeris displaced from Nagorno-Karabakh. In contrast, the authorities denied access to Nagorno-Karabakh itself and therefore access to internally displaced Armenians who were displaced to that part of the country. They argued that they wanted to prevent any international involvement in their domestic affairs which would contribute to conferring some recognition of the territories occupied by rebel forces.[43]

Internal armed conflicts do raise a further challenge for securing humanitarian access because there is often no structured dialogue between humanitarian actors and non-state actors.[44] It is of course difficult to generalise but, all too often, physical access to the internally displaced is hindered by domestic political considerations. The first step when attempting to provide protection to the internally displaced is thus to negotiate access to them.[45] The Security Council has emphasised the 'importance of safe and unhindered access of humanitarian personnel to civilians in armed conflict, including refugees and internally displaced persons'.[46] It even went as far as declaring that the denial of humanitarian access to civilian populations may constitute a threat to international peace and security within the meaning of Article 39 of the UN Charter.[47]

Humanitarian assistance in the midst of armed conflict raises very serious problems of staff security which, in Bosnia and Herzegovina for instance, led many aid agencies to request military protection from peacekeeping forces. Militarisation of humanitarian aid was originally resisted,[48] but UNHCR then hired security consultants, and staff members were required to wear flak-jackets and travel in armoured personnel carriers (APCs).[49] UNPROFOR was requested to directly involve itself in the delivery of aid by airdrops and in the airlift to Sarajevo, and UNHCR

---

[43] See *Azerbaijan Report*, para. 53.

[44] See *Report of the Secretary-General to the Security Council on the Protection of Civilians in Armed Conflict*, S/2002/1300, 26 November 2002, para. 25.

[45] See *Report of the Secretary-General to the Security Council on the Protection of Civilians in Armed conflict*, S/2001/331, 30 March 2001, para. 22.

[46] SC Res. 1265, 17 September 1999, para. 7.   [47] See Chapter 6, pp. 219–23 below.

[48] See S. A. Cunliffe and M. Pugh, 'The Politicization of UNHCR in the Former Yugoslavia' (1997) 10 *Journal of Refugee Studies* 134 at 144.

[49] See L. Minear, J. Clark, R. Cohen, D. Gallagher, I. Guest and T. G. Weiss, *Humanitarian Action in the Former Yugoslavia: The UN's Role 1991–1993*, Occasional Paper No. 18 (Providence, RI: Thomas J. Watson Jr Institute for International Studies and Refugee Policy Group, 1994), 76.

convoys were escorted into dangerous areas by its units. UNHCR staff have generally welcomed the collaboration with UNPROFOR, whereas some outside commentators have been more ambivalent about such a collaboration.[50] There was indeed a concern that any association with the military would compromise the impartiality of humanitarian assistance.

Although international presence may have a deterrent effect, humanitarian assistance alone can only provide limited protection if more direct protection of the aid recipients is not offered. Some humanitarian actors have been reluctant to condemn human rights violations or to engage in proactive protection of the civilian populations, including internally displaced persons.[51] They may feel that this would politicise their work[52] and fear that, by being outspoken, they could lose access to the internally displaced or that staff security could be jeopardised.[53] This is a particular concern for the ICRC which has a strict policy of confidentiality.[54] Some agencies have openly acknowledged their 'incapacity' or unwillingness to engage in issues such as advocacy on behalf of the internally displaced. For instance, in response to a Human Rights Watch report criticising the UNDP's programme for internally displaced persons in Kenya, the UNDP defended itself by invoking 'its limitations to engaging in "sovereign" issues for which it has no mandate'.[55] Because the UNDP has since committed itself to the integration of human rights within its development activities, one would hope that it now takes a different stance on such issues.[56]

One is confronted here with the issue of state sovereignty and the reluctance of UN agencies to intervene in the internal affairs of the state. As a result, agencies are often 'more willing to provide IDPs with humanitarian assistance than with protection, since protection questions a "sovereign" government's ability to govern its own territory',[57] or

---

[50] See K. Newland and D. Waller Meyers, 'Peacekeeping and Refugee Relief' (1999) 5 *International Peacekeeping* 15 at 29.

[51] See USGAO, *Internally Displaced Persons Lack Effective Protection*, 10.

[52] See Commission on Human Security, *Human Security Now*, New York, 2003, 28.

[53] See A. Mawson, R. Dodd and J. Hilary, *War Brought Us Here: Protecting Children Displaced Within Their Own Countries by Conflict* (London: Save the Children, 2000), 22.

[54] See Chapter 3, p. 94 above.

[55] See Human Rights Watch/Africa, *Failing the Internally Displaced*, 35.

[56] See Chapter 3, pp. 100–2 above.

[57] See S. T. E. Kleine-Ahlbrandt, *The Protection Gap in the International Protection of Internally Displaced Persons: The Case of Rwanda* (Geneva: Institut Universitaire des Hautes Etudes Internationales, 1996), 98–9.

at least is so perceived. It is however counterproductive to provide assistance without ensuring the protection of the populations concerned, and there is an increasing need to engage more actively with protection issues. Humanitarian activities should not operate in a vacuum: they must be complemented by protection activities, but also by serious political efforts to address the root causes of the conflict.

The delivery of humanitarian assistance may also prove counterproductive to the extent that it directly or indirectly prolongs the conflict which produces the displacement. One extreme example was the provision of assistance to Rwandan refugees in eastern Zaire (now the Democratic Republic of Congo) between 1994 and 1996. It was clear that among the refugees were some individuals who were responsible for planning and conducting the genocide in Rwanda and the delivery of aid to the refugee camps was strengthening their position.[58] The delivery of aid can thus run counter to other protection strategies to the extent that it allows human rights abusers to go unpunished and even be strengthened. As a result, the guilty were able to continue to wage attacks inside Rwanda. Providing aid in such a context can lead to an endless cycle of feeding and clothing people without other human rights issues being addressed. This explains why some aid programmes have actually been suspended because part of the aid was diverted to feed the combatants.[59] For instance, some NGOs withdrew from the refugee camps in eastern Zaire at the end of 1994,[60] despite the international pressure not to suspend the aid. It is therefore crucial that civilians and armed elements be separated in order to guarantee that assistance is only provided to the former, but also to ensure their protection.[61] So far, attention has been given to the issue of separation between civilians and armed elements mainly in the context of refugee movements, but this issue should also be considered in situations of internal displacement.[62] Separation between civilians and armed elements can be established by

---

[58] See M. Frohart, D. Paul and L. Minear, *Protecting Human Rights: The Challenge to Humanitarian Organisations*, Occasional Paper No. 35 (Providence, RI: Thomas J. Watson Jr Institute for International Studies, 1999), 67–8.

[59] UNHCR/Brookings Institution/OAU, *Internal Displacement in Africa: Report of a Workshop Held in Addis Ababa, Ethiopia, 19–20 October 1998* (Geneva: UNHCR/Brookings Institution/OAU, 1998), para. 8.

[60] See Frelick, 'Assistance Without Protection', 30. See also B. Barber, 'Feeding Refugees, or War? The Dilemma of Humanitarian Aid' (1997) 76:4 *Foreign Affairs* 8 at 13.

[61] See *2002 Report on the Protection of Civilians in Armed Conflict*, paras. 31–40.

[62] See UNHCR, *Protection and Solutions in Situations of Internal Displacement: Learning from UNHCR's Operational Experience*, EPAU/2002/10, August 2002, 6.

the presence of peacekeepers early in the movement of internally displaced persons[63] and/or by the deployment of international military observers in IDP camps where the infiltration of armed elements is suspected.[64]

In order to ensure that protection concerns are addressed by UN aid agencies, efforts have been made to develop an integrated approach to humanitarian assistance and protection.[65] Such an approach follows from the Secretary-General's call to fully integrate human rights into all UN activities.[66] It has been noted that so far, UN agencies have adopted an 'add-on' approach whereby they have merely increased collaboration with human rights specialists such as the Office of the High Commissioner for Human Rights (OHCHR), whereas they should adopt a 'transformative' approach, i.e. reconceptualise their current activities to integrate human rights goals.[67]

In order to encourage humanitarian agencies to fully integrate human rights in their activities and, more specifically, to engage in protection activities for the internally displaced, the OCHA initiated in 1998 a project on best practices on internal displacement. UNICEF was requested to compile for each country faced with an important problem of internal displacement a list of programmes which had had an impact on the protection of the internally displaced. It is quite a useful exercise of lesson-learning which could inspire UN agencies to undertake similar activities in other countries. Most UN agencies, apart from UNHCR, do not currently have enough expertise and experience in protection activities. The project has resulted in the publication of a 'Manual on Field Practice in Internal Displacement'.[68] The Manual gives a brief description of activities undertaken to support internally displaced persons and which could be replicated in other situations. Most of these initiatives illustrate the importance of integrating human rights in all programmes for internally displaced persons in all phases of displacement. Nevertheless, the human rights focus could have been more explicitly articulated in the Manual.

---

[63] See *Report of the Secretary-General to the Security Council on the Protection of Civilians in Armed Conflict*, S/1999/957, 8 September 1999, recommendation 33.

[64] *Ibid.*, recommendation 35.   [65] See IASC, *Growing the Sheltering Tree*.

[66] See 'Renewing the United Nations: A Programme for Reform', Secretary-General's Report, 14 July 1997, A/51/950, paras. 78–9.

[67] See K. Kenny, *When Needs Are Rights: An Overview of UN Efforts to Integrate Human Rights in Humanitarian Action*, Occasional Paper No. 38 (Providence, RI: Thomas J. Watson Jr Institute for International Studies, 2000).

[68] See OCHA, *Manual on Field Practice on Internal Displacement*.

Engaging in more proactive protection strategies

International presence alone has sometimes been sufficient to prevent violence against the internally displaced. For instance, the continuing presence of volunteers residing with threatened individuals or communities in Colombia has deterred attacks by combatants.[69] Similarly, UNHCR's full-time presence in the Open Relief Centre in Madhu (Sri Lanka) temporarily ensured the security of the internally displaced residing there.[70] Nevertheless, events in Croatia and Bosnia and Herzegovina in the early 1990s demonstrated that an international presence does not automatically lead to protection.[71] Likewise, a very strong international presence in Rwanda in 1995 did not prevent the closure of the Kibeho camp and the killing of several thousand internally displaced persons.[72] Consequently, as mentioned in the previous section, humanitarian agencies are now trying to be 'actively' present by acting as human rights monitors and advocates. Advocacy includes reporting on the conditions of the internally displaced and engaging with national and local authorities when problems arise. Humanitarian agencies also sometimes need to speak out in public to stop or prevent human rights abuses.[73]

Human rights monitoring has traditionally been undertaken by the Commission on Human Rights, monitoring bodies established under international human rights treaties and specialised human rights NGOs. The IASC has encouraged UN agencies to engage in operational monitoring and reporting. This involves field monitoring to allow 'regular needs assessment and the identification of groups that are particularly at risk'.[74] Where required, field officers relay the information to the Emergency Relief Coordinator (ERC), the Office of the High Commissioner for Human Rights (OHCHR) or the Special Representative on Internally Displaced Persons to ensure an early and appropriate response to the situation. Operational monitoring and reporting can thus play an important function in terms of early-warning. Among UN agencies, UNHCR

---

[69] *Ibid.*, 29.   [70] *Ibid.*, 40.

[71] See Lawyers Committee for Human Rights, *Protection by Presence? The Limits of United Nations Safekeeping Activities in Croatia*, Discussion Paper, New York, September 1993; and E. D. Mooney, 'Presence, Ergo Protection? UNPROFOR, UNHCR and the ICRC in Croatia and Bosnia and Herzegovina' (1995) 7 *International Journal of Refugee Law* 407.

[72] See S. Kleine-Ahlbrandt, 'The Kibeho Crisis: Towards a More Effective System of International Protection of IDPs', *Forced Migration Review*, vol. 2, August 1998.

[73] See IASC, *Growing the Sheltering Tree*, 16.

[74] See IASC, 'Protection of Internally Displaced Persons', 10.

is the most experienced UN agency and its protection activities for the internally displaced are 'adapted from the refugee experience'.[75] While some agencies have been more reluctant to go beyond a mere presence and engage in protection activities,[76] UNICEF has developed expertise in dealing with the protection problems of women and children, and has sought to integrate human rights monitoring and reporting into its traditional activities.[77]

For aid agencies whose work has not traditionally focused on protection issues, engaging more actively in these issues has not been perceived as being in the interest of the agency itself, nor of the aid recipients. Sometimes, involvement in human rights, and thus political, matters is even considered as being incompatible with the principle of neutrality which should be guiding humanitarian action. Agencies fear that by condemning the actions of one side, they are perceived as favouring the other. However, this attitude is based on a misinterpretation of the principle of neutrality. Agencies such as UNHCR and some NGOs have shown that taking sides in favour of refugees and internally displaced persons is not a violation of the principle of neutrality.[78] Advocacy is not likely to be accepted by all parties, as acknowledged by UNICEF which stated that 'when displacement is associated with membership in an identifiable religious, ethnic or political group that is party to a conflict, advocacy . . . may engender opposition, including from host government colleagues and other program partners'.[79] Indeed, humanitarian agencies have feared that engaging in protection issues and criticising the government may mean that their relationship with the national authorities would be damaged. This is especially true of agencies engaged in development work which depends heavily on the cooperation of the government concerned. As mentioned earlier, the UNDP has for instance been reluctant to take on a protection role. Agencies often seek to balance their protection efforts with the 'potential long-term costs . . . of undermining development programs'.[80] Finally, there is a fear that access to the victims will be withdrawn. NGOs face the same

---

[75] Cohen and Deng, *Masses in Flight*, 256.   [76] See Chapter 3, third section, above.

[77] See Chapter 3, pp. 99–100 above.

[78] See Cohen and Deng, *Masses in Flight*, 269. See also D. Forsythe, 'UNHCR's Mandate: The Politics of Being Non-Political', UNHCR Working Paper No. 33, March 2001.

[79] J. Kunder, *The Needs of Internally Displaced Women and Children: Guiding Principles and Considerations*, UNICEF, Office of Emergency Programmes, New York, Working Paper Series, September 1998, 11.

[80] Kunder, *The Needs of Internally Displaced Women and Children*, 11.

dilemmas and some have adopted a 'pragmatic low-profile notion of protection'.[81]

UNHCR has tried to focus on human rights monitoring of the situation of the internally displaced, especially when they belong to a vulnerable group (whether a minority or majority group). It has also engaged in the reporting of human rights violations and, where required, has intervened with the relevant authorities. In addition, the agency has been involved in the evacuation of civilians from situations of danger, the defence of the freedom of movement and the creation of safe conditions for return.[82] In some countries, UNHCR has engaged in activities such as investigating and reporting cases of human rights violations, protecting the physical safety of specific individuals (by parking a UNHCR vehicle in front of their house for instance) or assisting the authorities to provide personal documentation.[83]

UNHCR's involvement in Tajikistan from 1993 to 1996 is a good example of how proper emphasis on protection issues contributes to ensuring the success of a return operation. In 1992, the conflict in Tajikistan displaced 600,000 people to the south-east of the country. The ICRC started its operations there the same year and was joined by UNHCR at the beginning of 1993. After the conflict ended in 1993, UNHCR organised the return of internally displaced persons and engaged in active monitoring in areas of return. Field officers endeavoured to assist the returnees who were facing problems with the authorities. They systematically investigated cases of human rights violations and urged prosecutors to take these cases up. They also intervened with the relevant authorities, urging them not to remain passive.[84] By mid-1995, most internally displaced persons had returned to their homes. UNHCR's role in Tajikistan amounted

---

[81] U. von Buchwald, *Response Systems of Non-Governmental Organisations to Assistance and Protection Needs of the Internally Displaced Persons*, draft report, Norwegian Refugee Council, Geneva, March 1996, 10.

[82] See *UNHCR's Protection Role in Countries of Origin*, EC/46/SC/CRP.17, 18 March 1996, para. 8.

[83] See *Protection Aspects of UNHCR Activities on Behalf of Internally Displaced Persons*, EC/SCP/87, 17 August 1994, para. 29.

[84] See *Internally Displaced Persons: Report of the Representative of the Secretary-General, Mr Francis M. Deng, Profiles of Displacement: Tajikistan*, A/51/483/Add.1, 24 October 1996, paras. 44–6. See also J. McLean and T. Greene, 'Turmoil in Tajikistan: Addressing the Crisis of Internal Displacement', in R. Cohen and F. M. Deng (eds.), *The Forsaken People: Case Studies of the Internally Displaced* (Washington DC: Brookings Institution, 1998), 313–58, especially 342–4.

in effect to that of a human rights field operation,[85] which raises a potential problem of overlap between the mandates of UNHCR and OHCHR.[86] UNHCR managed to establish an active international presence which contributed to restoring confidence in the authorities. Protection activities were subsequently taken over by the Organisation for Security and Cooperation in Europe (OSCE) in 1995 only because 'no one else, not even UN human rights bodies, stepped forward'.[87]

In some countries, human rights field operations are specifically established to monitor, report on and investigate human rights violations. They have sometimes facilitated the return of internally displaced persons. Such operations can be undertaken under the aegis of OHCHR. Previous human rights field operations were established as part of military peacekeeping operations by the Department of Peacekeeping Operations or by the Department of Political Affairs. The first human rights field operation to be deployed by a UN human rights body was created in 1992 in the former Yugoslavia.[88]

The human rights field operation in Rwanda (HRFOR, 1994–8) involved a much greater number of field officers and was the first operation to be entirely managed by OHCHR. It had a specific mandate to facilitate the return of refugees and displaced persons,[89] which included creating conditions of safety for return, ensuring that return was entirely voluntary and solving property disputes. However, the operation was hampered by a serious lack of financial and other resources, and the staff had not always been properly trained.[90] Moreover, tensions appeared between HRFOR and UN agencies operating in the country, especially the UNDP.[91] There is a potential overlap between human rights field operations' peace-building efforts and the UNDP's governance programme, because both are aimed at reconstructing for instance the country's

---

[85] On UNHCR's role in Tajikistan, see UNHCR, *The State of World's Refugees: Fifty Years of Humanitarian Action* (Geneva: UNHCR, 2000), 196–7.

[86] See I. Martin, 'A New Frontier: The Early Experience and Future of International Human Rights Field Operations' (1998) 16 *Netherlands Quarterly of Human Rights* 121 at 126.

[87] McLean and Greene, 'Turmoil in Tajikistan', 343.

[88] See K. E. Kenny, 'Formal and Informal Innovations in the United Nations Protection of Human Rights: The Special Rapporteur on the Former Yugoslavia' (1995) 48 *Austrian Journal of Public International Law* 19 at 50–62.

[89] See T. Howland, 'Mirage, Magic, or Mixed Bag? The United Nations High Commissioner for Human Rights' Field Operation in Rwanda' (1999) 21 *Human Rights Quarterly* 1 at 17.

[90] *Ibid.*, 18–21.   [91] *Ibid.*, 48–9.

judicial system. In contrast, there was close cooperation between HRFOR and UNHCR, which was based on a rather detailed note which provided for the sharing of information and which established a division of labour between the two.[92]

As far as internally displaced persons were concerned, it seems that no sufficient attention was given to their protection. The first Chief of Mission of HRFOR himself acknowledged that 'the extent to which internally displaced persons were at some critical times left without protection is the most controversial single issue'.[93] He noted for instance that no international protection was given to those fleeing Kibeho in April 1995. Consequently, it has been suggested that each operation nominate an official as an IDP focal point who is familiar with the Guiding Principles on Internal Displacement and who can ensure that IDP issues are not overlooked.[94] For instance, there is an IDP focal point for the human rights field operation in Colombia.[95]

In situations of internal displacement, human rights field officers can make a difference by establishing a visible and active presence, notably in camps and areas of return. They can advocate more vigorously the rights of the internally displaced. There is currently a severe lack of funding and staff for human rights field operations, but some improvements may nevertheless be made within current resources. A major constraint is the issue of staff security: it is difficult for field officers to operate during armed conflicts, and very often they can intervene only in the post-conflict period when displacement has already taken place. There is still wide scope for progress in terms of training, lesson-learning, and dialogue with the host society.[96]

Due to the limited capacity of OHCHR to establish a field presence, human rights field operations deployed under its aegis have remained exceptional. In comparison, peacekeeping operations are deployed in a much greater number of countries faced with problems of internal displacement. Some of these have included a human rights component,

---

[92] *Note on Cooperation Between United Nations High Commissioner for Refugees (UNHCR) and the United Nations Human Rights Field Operation in Rwanda (HRFOR): Respective Functions for UNHCR and HRFOR*, 29 September 1995.

[93] W. Clarance, 'Field Strategy for the Protection of Human Rights' (1997) 9 *International Journal of Refugee Law* 229 at 248.

[94] UNHCR/Brookings Institution/OAU, *Internal Displacement in Africa*, para. 39.

[95] See *Internally Displaced Persons: Report of the Representative of the Secretary-General, Mr Francis M. Deng, Follow-Up Mission to Colombia*, E/CN.4/2000/83/Add.1, 11 January 2000, para. 57.

[96] See for instance K. Kenny, 'Introducing the Sustainability Principle to Human Rights Operations' (1997) 4 *International Peacekeeping* 61.

such as the human rights division of the United Nations Observer Mission in El Salvador (ONUSAL), or the human rights component of the UN Transitional Authority in Cambodia (UNTAC).[97] Peacekeepers have not always paid sufficient attention to the protection problems of the internally displaced and to human rights issues in general,[98] even though in some cases they had a specific mandate to ensure the safe return of all displaced persons. This was the case of the UN Assistance Mission in Rwanda (UNAMIR).[99] Some peacekeeping forces such as the UN Protection Force in the former Yugoslavia (UNPROFOR) were criticised for interpreting their mandate too narrowly as only requiring the protection of the delivery of humanitarian aid. Indeed, the Special Rapporteur on the former Yugoslavia complained about the reluctance of UNPROFOR to report information on human rights violations.[100] In the last fifteen years, peacekeepers have been called to play a role which goes well beyond their traditional role of monitoring cease-fires. In the context of the mainstreaming of human rights within the UN, peacekeeping forces are required to give proper attention to protection problems, especially when they have been mandated to protect civilians and assist the return of internally displaced populations. Training peacekeepers to be more sensitive to IDP protection issues may help. For instance, peacekeepers in Angola were given a pamphlet to sensitise them to the issue of internal displacement.[101] Although giving documentation does not constitute adequate training, it is a first step towards raising awareness of IDP issues among peacekeepers.

The Brahimi Report on peacekeeping has recommended that OHCHR be much more closely involved in the planning and organisation of the human rights components of peacekeeping operations.[102] This would constitute a welcome development which will require a significant increase of the resources of OHCHR.[103] The Report also pointed out

---

[97] See A. H. Henkin (ed.), *Honoring Human Rights and Keeping the Peace: Lessons from El Salvador, Cambodia and Haiti* (Washington DC: Alpen Institute, 1995).

[98] See for instance Human Rights Watch, *The Lost Agenda: Human Rights and UN Field Operations* (New York: Human Rights Watch, 1993).

[99] See SC Res. 918, 17 May 1994.

[100] *Situation des droits de l'homme dans le territoire de l'ex-Yougoslavie, sixième rapport périodique soumis par M. Tadeusz Mazowiecki, Rapporteur spécial de la Commission des droits de l'homme*, E/CN.4/1994/110, 21 February 1994, para. 339.

[101] See OCHA, *Manual on Field Practice on Internal Displacement*, 39.

[102] See *Report of the Panel on United Nations Peace Operations*, A/55/305-S/2000/809, 21 August 2000, para. 244.

[103] See pp. 151–2 below.

that 'peacekeepers who witness violence against civilians should be presumed to be authorised to stop it, within their means'.[104] It is true that, while UN agencies, human rights field officers and peacekeepers can and should all be involved in the monitoring and reporting of human rights abuses, those actors who are able to go further and intervene to stop these abuses should do so. This is expected by the civilians who are subject to such abuses: the establishment of an international presence in a conflict area often creates very high expectations of protection among civilian populations.[105] Resources must be made available to peacekeeping operations in order for them to meet these expectations.[106]

A particular protection strategy: providing protection in safe areas

Access to safety is often the primary concern of internally displaced persons. One obvious way of providing physical protection during armed conflict is to move them away from dangerous areas. The creation of safe areas represents one of the most controversial strategies used so far to afford protection to internally displaced populations in war zones. Safe areas have also been referred to as safe havens, safety zones, or security zones. The idea is not new as it finds its origin in international humanitarian law. Article 23 of the First Geneva Convention[107] envisages the creation of hospital zones and localities for the sick and wounded in armed forces. This provision is extended to the civilian sick and wounded by Article 14 of the Fourth Geneva Convention.[108] Article 15 of the same Convention allows for the creation of neutralised zones which would be open to all civilians, whether wounded or not. Additional Protocol I[109] also contains provisions allowing for the creation of non-defended localities (Article 59) and demilitarised zones (Article 60). These provisions have been rarely used in practice,[110] and the safe areas

---

[104] *Report of the Panel on United Nations Peace Operations*, para. 62.

[105] See for instance *Report of the Independent Inquiry into the Actions of the United Nations During the 1994 Genocide in Rwanda*, S/1999/1257, 16 December 1999, 51.

[106] See *Report of the Panel on United Nations Peace Operations*, para. 63.

[107] Geneva Convention for the Amelioration of the Condition of the Wounded and Sick in Armed Forces in the Field, 12 August 1949, 75 UNTS 3.

[108] Geneva Convention Relative to the Protection of Civilian Persons in Time of War, 12 August 1949, 75 UNTS 287.

[109] Protocol Additional to the Geneva Convention of 12 August 1949 and Relating to the Protection of Victims of International Armed Conflicts, 8 June 1977, 1125 UNTS 3 (hereinafter Additional Protocol I).

[110] See Y. Sandoz, 'The Establishment of Safety Zones for Persons Displaced Within Their Country of Origin', in N. Al-Naumi and R. Meese (eds.), *International Legal Issues Arising*

created in Iraq in 1991, Bosnia and Herzegovina in 1993 or Rwanda in 1994, although inspired by the provisions of international humanitarian law, were different from those envisaged by the Geneva Conventions.[111]

Chimni defines a safety zone as a 'clearly demarcated space in which individuals fleeing danger can seek safety within their own country'.[112] The creation of safe areas thus seeks to protect the civilians who are already living in these areas, but also to provide a destination for those in search of temporary refuge in a location where protection is supposedly guaranteed. Nevertheless, the creation of safe areas may have another less explicit objective, which is to divert potential cross-border movements into other countries towards the safe areas. The move to establish a safe haven in northern Iraq to protect the Kurds fleeing persecution from the Iraqi regime was a direct response to the decision of Turkey to close its border to the Kurds, and has been criticised for legitimising that decision.[113] It has been argued that the safe areas created in the 1990s find their conceptual origin in the then emerging humanitarian discourse on 'preventive protection' and the 'right to remain'.[114] One cannot deny that a more interventionist agenda has emerged in the aftermath of the Cold War and has reflected the trend towards the containment of refugee flows.[115] Although the stated objective of the establishment of safe areas is the protection of internally displaced persons, actual practice raises the question of whether such a measure is protecting states' interests rather than the physical safety of the internally displaced.[116]

The safe areas established so far differed from those envisaged by international humanitarian law. The main difference is that safe areas were often established *without the consent* of the warring parties. Moreover, they were not properly demilitarised, as envisaged in Articles 59 and 60

---

from the United Nations Decade of International Law (The Hague: Martinus Nijhoff, 1995), 899–927 at 926.

[111] See K. Landgren, 'Safety Zones and International Protection: A Dark Grey Area' (1995) 7 *International Journal of Refugee Law* 436 at 441; and Sandoz, 'The Establishment of Safety Zones', 924.

[112] B. S. Chimni, 'The Incarceration of Victims: Deconstructing Safety Zones', in Al-Naumi and Meese (eds.), *International Legal Issues*, 823–54 at 825.

[113] *Ibid.*, 837.

[114] See P. Hyndman, 'Preventive, Palliative, or Punitive? Safe Spaces in Bosnia-Herzegovina, Somalia, and Sri Lanka' (2003) 16 *Journal of Refugee Studies* 167 at 168.

[115] See A. C. Helton, *The Price of Indifference – Refugees and Humanitarian Action in the New Century* (Oxford: Oxford University Press, 2002), 172.

[116] See Hyndman, 'Preventive, Palliative, or Punitive?', 182.

of Additional Protocol I. They thus lacked the legitimacy that they would have enjoyed if established under international humanitarian law. The experience from the 1990s has raised a number of questions to which answers will determine whether the practice of establishing safe areas in war zones is to be confirmed in the future. These questions include:

whether the idea of establishing a protected area based on consent is realistic, whether the establishment of a protected area using international force can be effective, whether the creation of such areas might contribute (unwittingly) to ethnic cleansing, to what extent the creation of a protected area undermines the right to asylum, to what extent might the creation of such an area permanently influence international borders, and to what extent does the construction of such an area affect the treatment of civilians outside the area.[117]

The possible answers to these questions will be examined in more detail when analysing the experience in Bosnia and Herzegovina.[118]

The Open Relief Centres (ORCs) established in Sri Lanka in 1990 are closer to the model envisaged by international humanitarian law and were relatively successful in providing both assistance and protection to the internally displaced.[119] They benefited from the implicit, and later explicit, consent of all parties to the conflict and retained a civilian character: no weapons nor any military presence (including peacekeeping forces) were allowed on site.[120] The consent of the parties, the exclusive civilian character of the safe areas, and the safeguarding of the right of asylum appear to be the main principles to be followed when establishing safe areas in war zones. Other principles have been identified, such as the clear delimitation of the area (as in Articles 59(5) and 60(2) of Additional Protocol I), and the definition of a more precise mandate of the force in charge of the defence of such areas. In addition, Hyndman argues that the establishment of safe areas is most likely to work when they have 'local connotations of sanctuary or safety',[121] i.e. where the designated area has traditionally been considered as a place of refuge.

The implications of the establishment of safe areas on IDP protection issues still need to be assessed. In Iraq and perhaps in Bosnia and Herzegovina, safe areas were established as a response to the refusal of

---

[117] OCHA, Report on the Inter-Agency Expert Consultation on Protected Areas, April 1999, cited in Hyndman, 'Preventive, Palliative, or Punitive?', 170.

[118] See Chapter 5, pp. 171–4 below.

[119] For more detail, see W. D. Clarance, 'Open Relief Centres: A Pragmatic Approach to Emergency Relief and Monitoring During Conflict in a Country of Origin' (1991) 3 *International Journal of Refugee Law* 320.

[120] See Hyndman, 'Preventive, Palliative, or Punitive?', 179.   [121] *Ibid.*, 168 and 180.

neighbouring and other states to offer asylum to internally displaced persons. This statement must be mitigated by the fact that it was not physically possible for the people of for instance Srebrenica to get to a frontier. Nevertheless, the creation of safe areas has probably been used in some cases to justify the 'rejection' of asylum claims. Hathaway and Neve argue that France, for instance, 'blocked' some asylum applications on the basis of its efforts to protect Rwandans in the safe area established within Rwanda.[122] The focus has thus shifted away from the right to asylum, to the idea of a right to remain, or a right not to be displaced which may just be a rhetorical tool to justify policies of containment.

Despite the mixed experience of the 1990s, and in particular the critical failure to protect the internally displaced at Srebrenica in 1995, the Security Council has nevertheless expressed the willingness to 'consider the appropriateness and feasibility of temporary security zones and safe corridors for the protection of civilians and the delivery of assistance in situations characterised by the threat of genocide, crimes against humanity and war crimes against the civilian population'.[123] In times of internal armed conflict, it may be useful, as a measure of last resort, to direct movements of populations to safe areas, provided that protection is effectively guaranteed there by the availability of 'sufficient and credible force'.[124] The requirement of a credible military force to defend a safe area is especially important when the safe area has been established without the consent of the warring parties.[125] Part of the problem in Bosnia and Herzegovina and Rwanda was that although the Security Council authorised the use of force, the authorisation was 'broad and unspecific, with no guidance as to how much force could be used and what principles of law applied to the use thereof'.[126] When the Security Council decides to establish safe areas, it is therefore crucial that, where required, it also provides a credible military force with a clear mandate to defend the area.

The creation of safe areas should not exonerate international aid agencies and peacekeepers from responsibility for providing protection to

---

[122] See J. Hathaway and R. A. Neve, 'Making International Refugee Law Relevant Again: A Proposal for Collectivised and Solution-Oriented Protection' (1997) 10 *Harvard Human Rights Journal* 115 at 136–7.

[123] SC Res. 1296, 19 April 2000, para. 15.

[124] See *1999 Report on the Protection of Civilians in Armed Conflict*, recommendation 39.

[125] See B. M. Oswald, 'The Creation and Control of Places of Protection During United Nations Peace Operations' (2001) 844 *International Review of the Red Cross* 1013 at 1027.

[126] *Ibid.*, 1026.

internally displaced persons outside those areas or upholding their right to asylum. Although it has been suggested that 'a smoothly functioning safe haven system could render the normal refugee protection system . . . obsolete in situations of mass influx',[127] one should insist that the creation of safe areas remains exceptional and not be institutionalised as an alternative for the international refugee protection regime nor for states' obligations to people within their territory.

Protection through evacuation

When the lives of the internally displaced and other civilians are directly threatened, evacuation may need to be considered by humanitarian agencies and/or peacekeeping forces present in the field. It has been feared that measures of evacuation would amount to cooperation with the policies of ethnic cleansing. In Bosnia and Herzegovina, evacuations from besieged areas falling into the hands of another warring party had first been ruled out and were the subject of intense debate among agencies.[128] The question is whether agencies should still attempt to provide protection *in situ*, or acknowledge that people are no longer safe despite the international presence and that they can only find safety elsewhere.

The evacuation of Georgians from Abkhazia did not prompt such a debate.[129] However, it must be noted that the political situation in Georgia was very different from the complex situation prevailing in Bosnia and Herzegovina. Indeed, Georgian authorities were not opposed to such evacuation, whereas Bosnian Muslim authorities did not have the same attitude and were more reluctant to allow the evacuations of Muslim populations from areas they wanted to retain control over. When all other means of protection have failed, evacuation may be the only form of protection left. Evacuation should not always be perceived as a negative thing if people find safety elsewhere, do not find themselves in a cycle of displacement which leads people to be displaced several times, and if such a measure is linked to efforts to ensure that it is temporary.

However, even where evacuations are decided, the priority for international agencies should still be to put pressure on neighbouring countries

---

[127] See A. T. Arulanantham, 'Restructured Safe Havens: A Proposal for Reform of the Refugee Protection System' (2000) 22 *Human Rights Quarterly* 1 at 56.

[128] See Chapter 5, pp. 169–71 below.

[129] See Mooney, 'Internal Displacement and the Conflict in Abkhazia', 224–5.

to ensure that borders remain open, in case the internally displaced want to seek refuge there. The presence of international relief agencies in the country of origin should not disqualify internally displaced persons from seeking asylum. International agencies, especially UNHCR, must insist that neighbouring countries leave their borders open.[130]

Protection upon return, resettlement and reintegration

Programmes promoting the return or resettlement of the internally displaced should go beyond the reconstruction of houses and the provision of transport to areas of origin. Protection concerns need to be integrated into such programmes for them to be successful.[131] It is indeed crucial to ensure that such return or resettlement is voluntary and informed,[132] and that the security of the people concerned is guaranteed. International protection upon return and reintegration is especially problematic in countries where displacement resulted from ethnic conflict. In such situations, the return of the internally displaced can be violently opposed, and international presence and protection activities are needed in areas of return to prevent human rights violations.

In order to avoid return to unsafe areas, assessment visits can be facilitated by international organisations: the internally displaced themselves can assess conditions in areas of return and decide whether they want to return now or later. Such visits have been organised by UNHCR which established special bus lines in Bosnia and Herzegovina and in Sri Lanka.[133] In some cases, an international presence (including sometimes a military presence) can also be established in areas of return to monitor the human rights situation. Such measures are part of confidence-building and can encourage the internally displaced to overcome their reluctance to return home. Protection upon return includes protection against attacks and protection against all forms of discrimination against returnees. In many cases, return is not envisaged by the internally displaced if they know they will be denied employment opportunities or access to public services. Such problems have been

---

[130] See for instance OCHA, *Manual on Field Practice on Internal Displacement*, 40–1.
[131] See IASC, 'Protection of Internally Displaced Persons', 10.
[132] See UNHCR, *Protection and Solutions in Situations of Internal Displacement*, 13.
[133] See UNICEF, *Mission to Sri Lanka with a View to Develop Best Practices to Internal Displacement*, New York, Office of Emergency Programmes, Working Paper Series, August 1998, 11.

encountered for instance by people attempting to return to their homes in Bosnia and Herzegovina.[134]

One issue which often distinguishes internally displaced persons from other victims of armed conflict is the problem of restitution of land and property rights. The internally displaced may not be able to return home if their former houses are now occupied by other people who themselves may also be displaced, and international assistance can be provided to assist them in recovering their property. This involves the provision of legal advice to the claimants, and, where needed, assistance to the authorities in drafting property laws. UNHCR has engaged in such activities in Georgia for instance, where it offered advice to the government on the resolution of property disputes.[135] Where resources are available, a specific institution which is independent of the national judicial system can also be created to deal with the property problems of refugees and internally displaced persons. The first of such institutions was established in Bosnia and Herzegovina.[136]

Special protection strategies for vulnerable groups of internally displaced persons

More than 70 per cent of internally displaced persons are either women and/or children, who are particularly vulnerable to abuse.[137] This can be explained by their inability to make the long journey to neighbouring countries because women have to take their children with them, but also because they often lack the financial means to go abroad. Some specific human rights issues arise for women and children in the wake of displacement, including their presence in camps. The Commission on Human Rights and the General Assembly have therefore encouraged the Special Representative on Internally Displaced Persons to focus more on gender and children issues.[138] More recently, attention has also been paid to other vulnerable groups of internally displaced persons, such as older people and the handicapped who are often unable to leave the country.

---

[134] See Chapter 5, pp. 184–90 below.
[135] See OCHA, *Manual on Field Practice on Internal Displacement*, 74.
[136] See Chapter 5, pp. 191–3 below.
[137] R. Cohen, 'Protecting Internally Displaced Women and Children', in Norwegian Refugee Council, *Rights Have No Borders: Worldwide Internal Displacement* (Oxford: Norwegian Refugee Council/Global IDP Survey, 1998), 63–74 at 63.
[138] See CHR Res. 1994/68, 9 March 1994, and GA Res. 50/195, 22 December 1995.

Internally displaced women

The increased attention paid to the specific protection problems of internally displaced women is part of the ongoing process of mainstreaming gender issues at the UN. The Fourth World Conference on Women, in Beijing in 1995, contributed to raising awareness of the protection problems faced by internally displaced women.[139]

According to a special report by UNICEF on internally displaced women, the main problems faced by them include having to cope with new gender roles as a result of displacement (female head of household), gender violence, break-up of families, and loss of social and cultural ties.[140] Gender violence probably represents the gravest problem for internally displaced women. As families are separated, unaccompanied women are more vulnerable to gender violence. This can take the form of rape, sexual slavery, forced female genital mutilation, or forced sale into marriage.[141] Forced female genital mutilation for instance can happen when internally displaced women move to an area where the practice is widespread and imposed on the female members of the community, including new ones. For instance, over 1,000 young internally displaced girls were forcibly circumcised in a mass ceremony in Sierra Leone in December 1996.[142]

Refugee women may be exposed to similar dangers, but internally displaced women can be said to be more vulnerable to abuses as there is usually less international presence in IDP situations. During the genocide in Rwanda and the conflict in Bosnia and Herzegovina, rape and other forms of sexual abuse were used in a systematic way against the women of a particular ethnic group. Rape was intentionally used as a weapon of war. As an important step, the two international criminal courts established to prosecute the crimes perpetrated in the former Yugoslavia and in Rwanda have examined cases of sexual abuse.[143] The International Criminal Tribunal for Rwanda has recognised 'sexual violence as an integral part of the genocide in Rwanda' and rape as a crime

---

[139] See *Report of the Fourth World Conference on Women* (Beijing, 4–15 September 1995), A/CONF.177/20, 17 October 1995, para. 147.

[140] See UNICEF, *The Gender Dimension of Internal Displacement: Concept Paper and Annotated Bibliography*, Office of Emergency Programmes, Working Paper Series, New York, September 1998, 13–16.

[141] See Guiding Principle 11(2).

[142] See UNICEF, *The Gender Dimension of Internal Displacement*, 3.

[143] See K. D. Askin, 'Sexual Violence in Decisions and Indictments of the Yugoslav and Rwandan Tribunals: Current Status' (1999) 93 *American Journal of International Law* 97 at 107.

against humanity.[144] The International Criminal Tribunal for the former Yugoslavia (ICTY) has delivered its first conviction for rape as a crime against humanity.[145]

Other problems specific to displaced women may be mentioned here. First, increased attention is now being paid to issues of reproductive health, an area often neglected.[146] For instance, diseases such as HIV/AIDS are likely to spread more rapidly among refugee and internally displaced populations.[147] Secondly, some women face many problems when trying to reclaim their property or inherit property from a deceased husband:[148] in Burundi for instance, widows cannot inherit land from their husbands.[149] This has important consequences on their ability to return home, and impedes their reintegration in their former community. Finally, it has been observed that internally displaced women did not really have the opportunity to participate in the organisation of IDP camps,[150] and this can have crucial implications in terms of the protection afforded to them.

When widespread abuses against women are reported, it is advisable to send a UN mission to monitor the situation and, where possible, deter further abuses. This was for instance the case in Liberia where a UN fact-finding mission was sent in 1993.[151] Another mission was sent to Bosnia and Herzegovina in January 1993 to investigate allegations of mass rape and to collect specific data such as rates of pregnancy and sexually transmitted diseases.[152]

There is a range of strategies which can be employed to prevent gender-related violence, and some have already been used for refugee women. They start with simple measures such as providing lighting in camps, or modifying the layout of camps to ensure that women have separate quarters or at least separate washing facilities. Escorts could also be provided to women who for instance have to collect fuel. Health services

---

[144] See *Prosecutor* v. *Akayesu*, Case No. ICTR-96-4-T, Judgment, 2 September 1998.

[145] See *Prosecutor* v. *Kunarac, Kovac and Vukovic*, Case Nos. IT-96-23 and IT-96-23/1, Judgment, 22 February 2001.

[146] See UNICEF, *Expert Meeting on Gender Dimension of Internal Displacement*, New York, 14–15 June 1999, 13.

[147] See M. J. Toole and R. J. Waldman, 'The Public Health Aspects of Complex Emergencies and Refugee Situations' (1997) 18 *Annual Review of Public Health* 283 at 296.

[148] See *Internally Displaced Persons: Report of the Representative of the Secretary-General, Mr Francis M. Deng*, E/CN.4/1996/52, 22 February 1996, para. 50.

[149] See L. Farha, 'Women's Rights to Land, Property and Housing', *Forced Migration Review*, vol. 7, April 2000, 23.

[150] See Cohen, 'Protecting Internally Displaced Women and Children', 69.

[151] See Cohen and Deng, *Masses in Flight*, 272.

[152] See Kenny, 'Formal and Informal Innovations', 67–8.

should take into account the special needs of women.[153] As some men running refugee and IDP camps use their position to obtain sexual favours from women, the World Food Programme (WFP) ought to pay more attention to the monitoring of food distribution in camps.[154] For instance, in Uganda, the WFP decided to distribute food only through women.[155] More generally, internally displaced women should be given more opportunities to participate in the organisation of camp life and the planning of assistance programmes.[156] UNHCR has developed considerable expertise in the area with regard to the protection of refugee women and adopted policies to ensure that they receive 'adequate and equitable access to food, shelter, health care and education as well as to employment opportunities and legal protection'.[157] In the 1990s, UNHCR adopted guidelines on refugee women.[158] These guidelines have recently been revised and their scope extended to cover returnees and internally displaced persons.[159]

A range of options are already available to improve the protection of internally displaced women, and ways are being explored to incorporate gender concerns into IDP protection measures.[160] The UNDP has for instance deployed a small team of gender specialists, though they are not specialised in IDP issues.[161] However, the protection of internally displaced women should not remain the preserve of gender specialists and one must ensure that gender concerns are taken into account by all actors which are present in situations of internal displacement.

Internally displaced children

Internally displaced children form a group with special needs.[162] They are especially vulnerable to abuse when unaccompanied, hence the

---

[153] See Guiding Principle 19(2).   [154] See Chapter 3, p. 97 above.
[155] See for instance Global IDP Survey, *Internally Displaced People: A Global Survey* (London: Earthscan Publications Ltd, 1998), 75.
[156] See Guiding Principle 18(3). See also UNICEF, *The Gender Dimension of Internal Displacement*, 23–4.
[157] See Cohen, 'Protecting Internally Displaced Women and Children', 64.
[158] See UNHCR, *Guidelines on the Protection of Refugee Women*, EC/SCP/67, 22 July 1991, and UNHCR, *Sexual Violence Against Refugees: Guidelines on Prevention and Response*, Geneva, 1995.
[159] See UNHCR, *Sexual and Gender-Based Violence Against Refugees, Returnees and Internally Displaced Persons: Guidelines for Prevention and Response*, May 2003.
[160] See UNICEF, *Expert Meeting on Gender Dimension*.
[161] See UNICEF, *The Gender Dimension of Internal Displacement*, 27.
[162] See Guiding Principle 4(2).

emphasis on family unity being preserved during displacement. When separated from their families, internally displaced children are at greater risk of exploitative labour, sexual abuse and forced recruitment by armed forces.[163] In order to reduce exposure to such abuses, and in accordance with international humanitarian law,[164] efforts should be made to reunite separated families as soon as possible.[165] In addition, the education of internally displaced children is interrupted as a result of displacement, which may impact heavily on their future prospects. One should also note that the effects of malnutrition and psycho-social trauma are far greater in the case of children.

According to Save the Children, in a detailed report on internally displaced children, 'it is still rare to find consistent, analytical understanding across agencies for [their] specific protection needs'.[166] UNICEF, being the main agency responsible for the defence of children's rights, should continue to encourage other agencies to pay more attention to the protection needs of internally displaced children.[167] UNICEF has interpreted the protection of internally displaced children as encompassing protection against physical and psycho-social harm, preserving their 'identity and cultural, linguistic, and inheritance rights', and responding to their basic needs.[168] In the search for solutions for internally displaced children, special emphasis should be put on family unity and mental health support for children who suffer from severe trauma.[169]

Forced recruitment of internally displaced children and other vulnerable children has been a subject of increasing concern in recent years.[170] An Optional Protocol to the Convention on the Rights of the Child on the involvement of children in armed conflicts has been adopted to address this problem.[171] Unlike refugee children, internally displaced children are often still present in active conflict zones. They represent an easy target for the warring parties in search of cheap and obedient recruits. Some children may be easily impressed and led to believe that they

---

[163] See UNHCR/Brookings Institution/OAU, *Internal Displacement in Africa*, para. 45.
[164] See Article 4(3)(b) of Protocol Additional to the Geneva Conventions of 12 August 1949 and Relating to the Protection of Victims of Non-International Armed Conflicts, 8 June 1977 1125 UNTS 609.
[165] See Guiding Principle 17(3).   [166] See Mawson *et al.*, *War Brought Us Here*, 23.
[167] See UNICEF, *Mission to Sri Lanka*, 7.
[168] See Kunder, *The Needs of Internally Displaced Women and Children*, 19.
[169] See UNHCR/Brookings Institution/OAU, *Internal Displacement in Africa*, paras. 46–7.
[170] See for instance I. Cohn and G. Goodwin-Gill, *Child Soldiers: The Role of Children in Armed Conflict* (Oxford: Oxford University Press, 1994).
[171] GA Res. 54/263, 25 May 2000.

would be safer by putting themselves under the protection of a local warlord. The practice of forced recruitment of children is widespread in many war-torn countries, and internally displaced children are more likely to be forcibly recruited when they lose the protection of their family during displacement.[172]

Innovative programmes have been undertaken in some countries in response to the needs of internally displaced and other children affected by armed conflict. For instance, in Sri Lanka, where a protracted conflict prevented children from living a normal life, UNICEF negotiated 'days of tranquillity' during which all parties agreed to interrupt the fighting in order to allow immunisation campaigns to take place.[173] User-friendly mine awareness training has also been provided to internally displaced children, who often play in unfamiliar surroundings with little knowledge of where the mines are likely to be placed.[174] Such initiatives could be replicated in other situations of internal displacement. Again, certain provisions of the UNHCR guidelines on refugee children such as those on culture, psycho-social well-being, health and nutrition, education, and unaccompanied children could be applied to internally displaced children.[175]

Other vulnerable groups of internally displaced persons: older persons and the handicapped

Older and/or handicapped persons are much more likely to be internally displaced persons than refugees since they often cannot travel long distances. The Guiding Principles recognise that these groups should be given particular attention (Principle 4). It is estimated that older persons may constitute up to 30 per cent of the internally displaced.[176] They have specific mental and physical needs which are often overlooked.[177] For instance, it has been noted that few aid agencies have developed protection guidelines and policies for older persons.[178] UNHCR has formulated a policy on older refugees,[179] but, although older internally displaced are mentioned once (para. 4), it is not clear whether this policy applies to them. This should be stated more explicitly.

---

[172] See Guiding Principle 13.   [173] See UNICEF, *Mission to Sri Lanka*, 5.

[174] *Ibid.*   [175] See UNHCR, *Refugee Children: Guidelines on Protection and Care*, Geneva, 1994.

[176] See F. MacDonald, 'Legal Protection of the Vulnerable: The Case of Older IDPs', *Forced Migration Review*, vol. 14, July 2002, 8.

[177] See *Abuse of Older Persons: Recognising and Responding to Abuse of Older Persons in a Global Context*, E/CN.5/2002/PC/2, 9 January 2002, para. 15.

[178] See Commission on Human Security, *Human Security Now*, 26.

[179] See UNHCR, *Policy on Older Refugees*, EC/50/SC/CRP.8, Annex I, 7 February 2000.

Some internally displaced persons may have been handicapped prior to displacement or as a result of displacement. It is not uncommon for internally displaced persons to step on anti-personel mines and/or to get caught up in cross-fire as they travel through war zones. Mine-awareness programmes are one way to protect internally displaced persons from becoming handicapped during displacement. Those who have been handicapped as a result of wounding during armed conflict will obviously be protected by the provisions on international humanitarian law covering the civilian wounded. Aid agencies should ensure that the special needs of handicapped internally displaced are addressed by, for instance, providing access to prosthetic services. A new international human rights convention may be developed to address the rights of disabled persons[180] but the focus appears to be mainly on equal opportunities and the advancement of disabled persons, and there is no mention of the specific protection needs of handicapped internally displaced.

New initiatives

Mainstreaming IDP protection issues within the UN

UNHCR has a specific mandate to provide refugees with assistance and protection, whereas it falls on every single UN agency to pay attention to IDP protection issues when implementing their own programmes. As demonstrated in the previous chapter, UN aid agencies were initially reluctant to engage in IDP issues, but all of them are now more willing to address the problem within their own mandates. Peacekeeping forces and human rights field officers also have a role to play in providing protection to both refugees and internally displaced persons. All sections of the UN are thus now involved with IDP issues and must understand the importance of protection issues, which has so far been the main weakness of UN interventions in favour of the internally displaced.

Protection measures should be coordinated among agencies to reflect a coherent and consistent *strategy* in each crisis. Crises should also be reviewed to learn how to prevent and respond to other crises. The appointment of IDP focal points in each agency and/or in each crisis

---

[180] See *Comprehensive and Integral International Convention on Protection and Promotion of the Rights and Dignity of Persons with Disabilities*, A/58/118, 3 July 2003, para. 20.

can contribute to ensuring that IDP protection issues are properly addressed. It was mentioned earlier that, at the highest level, the Inter-Agency Standing Committee (IASC) has produced a paper on IDP protection which defines a common policy for all UN agencies. The presence of the Special Representative on Internally Displaced Persons at IASC meetings should ensure that IDP protection issues receive sufficient attention, and internal displacement has become the only standing item on the agenda of IASC meetings. Such developments demonstrate that the humanitarian arm of the UN is paying increasing attention to IDP protection issues. Nevertheless, it remains to be seen how these concerns will be reflected in the field, and whether agencies will be less reluctant than previously to engage more directly in protection issues. It has been suggested that an inter-agency Protection Working Group composed of members of aid agencies be formed to develop ideas for protection strategies and to disseminate them to the field.[181] This suggestion has been taken up by the OCHA Internal Displacement Unit which has established a 'protection coalition' to explore new directions for improving IDP protection strategies.[182] In order to implement such strategies more effectively and according to each particular situation, protection working groups can be set up at the local level: such groups have for instance been established in some areas of Angola to promote dialogue on protection among the internally displaced and all those concerned with them.[183]

In order to sensitise staff to IDP protection issues, efforts are currently being made to disseminate both the Guiding Principles on Internal Displacement and a handbook to facilitate their application in the field.[184] For some time, training modules on the international protection of refugees have been organised by UNHCR. With regard to internal displacement, similar modules have now been developed by the Norwegian Refugee Council.[185] On the basis of these modules, the IASC has

---

[181] See D. Paul, *An Integrated, Strategic Approach to the Protection of Internally Displaced Persons*, 14 November 2000, http://www.lchr.org/conference/MEMOPaul.htm.

[182] See OCHA Internal Displacement Unit, 'Protection Coalition on Internal Displacement – Terms of Reference', http://www.reliefweb.int/idp/docs/references/ToRProtCoalition240702.pdf.

[183] See OCHA Internal Displacement Unit, *No Refuge: The Challenge of Internal Displacement* (New York and Geneva: United Nations, 2003), 92.

[184] See Chapter 2, pp. 66–9 above.

[185] Five modules can be downloaded at http://www.idpproject.org/idp_guided_tour.htm.

set up a training course on internal displacement.[186] Efforts are thus being made to ensure that UN staff have more precise knowledge about IDP issues, and, in particular, protection issues. Although specific policies on internal displacement have been defined only recently, UN agencies have been dealing with internally displaced persons in the field for much longer and have therefore developed some field practice. Examples of field practice have been compiled at the inter-agency level so that successful initiatives can be replicated or adapted for use in other situations.[187]

As for the human rights mechanisms of the UN, the Commission on Human Rights, which took the lead by calling for the appointment of a Special Representative on Internally Displaced Persons,[188] has called on all human rights mechanisms to address the issue of internal displacement in their work[189] and to monitor the plight of the internally displaced.[190] As a result, some Special Rapporteurs, whether thematic or country-specific, have included in their reports information about internally displaced persons when relevant to their own mandate. They have formulated some recommendations to governments on how to handle the problem. The Special Rapporteur on Violence Against Women has addressed the problems faced by internally displaced women in one of her reports.[191] Similarly, the Expert of the Secretary-General on Children in Armed Conflict has dealt with the issue of internally displaced children in her report.[192] Country rapporteurs, such as those on Sudan, the Democratic Republic of Congo and Burma, have also included in their reports some recommendations on how to address the problem of internal displacement.[193] The former Special Rapporteur on the former Yugoslavia created a precedent by inviting the Special Representative on Internally Displaced Persons to accompany him during his second field visit.[194] Finally, human rights treaty monitoring bodies which examine state reports regularly make references to the situation of

---

[186] See http://www.idpproject.org/training/IASC_modules/IASC_ modules.htm.

[187] See OCHA, *Manual on Field Practice on Internal Displacement*.

[188] See Introduction, p. 8 above.   [189] CHR Res. 1994/68, 9 March 1994.

[190] See P. Alston, 'The Downside of Post-Cold-War Complexity: Comments on Hathaway' (1995) 8 *Journal of Refugee Studies* 302 at 304.

[191] See *Report of the Special Rapporteur on Violence Against Women, Its Causes and Consequences,* Ms Radhika Coomaraswamy, E/CN.4/1998/54, 26 January 1998.

[192] See *The Impact of Armed Conflict on Children: Report of the Expert of the Secretary-General, Ms Graça Machel,* A/51/306, 26 August 1996, especially paras. 81–3.

[193] See Cohen and Deng, *Masses in flight,* 152.   [194] See Chapter 5, p. 177 below.

internally displaced persons in their concluding observations.[195] These recent developments demonstrate that the call by the Commission on Human Rights has been heard by most UN human rights mechanisms, but it remains to be seen whether states will take into account the comments to improve the national protection of internally displaced persons.

An extended role for the Office of the High Commissioner for Human Rights

OHCHR is 'uniquely placed to help draw the attention of all sectors of UN activity to problems of internal displacement and to ensure that a protection perspective is integrated into the responses to them'.[196] The position of the High Commissioner for Human Rights was created in 1994 to take the lead in all human rights matters in the UN. The former Centre for Human Rights was renamed the Office of the High Commissioner for Human Rights (OHCHR). Although the Office plays a role as important as any of the humanitarian agencies, it is extremely small in comparison.[197] Until very recently, the Office was not operational, and still does not have an emergency unit. With the establishment of a growing number of field offices, the Office is strengthening its field presence, but it remains very limited compared with the numbers of offices established by humanitarian agencies around the world. Its main activities consist of advisory services and technical assistance to countries which want to strengthen their national institutions and laws in order to improve the protection of human rights.

With regard to internally displaced persons, the Office plays several roles. It provides administrative support to the mandate of the Special Representative on Internally Displaced Persons. The Office also has to ensure that all human rights organs pay attention to IDP issues. In addition, when it manages human rights field operations, it intervenes directly in the country concerned to provide protection to the internally displaced. One of its main contributions lies in its advisory services and technical assistance programme which has devised specific projects targeted at internally displaced persons. For instance, a project was initiated

---

[195] These references have been compiled at http://66.36.242.93/bytheme.php/id/1020.
[196] E. D. Mooney, 'Internally Displaced Persons: The Role of OHCHR', Informal Meeting of Experts on Measures to Ensure International Protection to All Who Need It, Geneva, 11 May 1998, para. 16.
[197] See Cohen and Deng, Masses in Flight, 154.

in Rwanda to address property issues in order to facilitate the return of the internally displaced.[198]

There is scope for OHCHR to increase activities in countries of origin. There needs to be more cooperation between UNHCR and OHCHR in countries where UNHCR is providing in-country protection. The Office must be granted more funds, so that it can truly become operational. If the Office had the material means to provide more support at the country level, for instance by sending human rights field officers who are experienced and properly trained to address situations of internal displacement, this would complement the work of humanitarian agencies. In his recent proposals for further UN reform, the Secretary-General has suggested that OHCHR's management be strengthened to provide better human rights support at the country level.[199]

The operationalisation of the Office is a potential key to overcoming the protection problems faced by internally displaced persons. As UNHCR may be reluctant to extend further its operations on behalf of the internally displaced and other aid agencies may not be able to engage so fully in protection issues, there is an opportunity for the Office to take the lead in this area. Nevertheless, protection activities for the internally displaced should not become the responsibility of the Office alone, but, on the contrary, in the context of the mainstreaming of human rights at the UN, IDP protection should be the concern of every UN actor. The protection mandates of UN agencies need to be coordinated to ensure that all IDP protection needs are covered. The previous identification of each agency's expertise in the field of IDP protection can contribute to facilitating the assignment of responsibilities in each crisis. Such exercise has been undertaken and should help define the most appropriate institutional arrangements in any given situation.[200]

Conclusion

This chapter has argued that field activities for internally displaced persons must be pursued within a human rights framework in order to

---

[198] See Mooney, 'Internally Displaced Persons: The Role of OHCHR', para. 14.

[199] See 'Strengthening of the United Nations: An Agenda for Further Change', Secretary-General's Report, 9 September 2002, A/57/387, action 2.

[200] See IASC, 'Protection of Internally Displaced Persons', Inter-Agency Standing Committee policy paper, New York, December 1999, Annex: Outline of the Capacities of Different Organisations with Regard to the Protection of Internally Displaced Persons.

produce effective, prompt and durable solutions to their plight. Indeed, field activities have so far been premised on the flawed assumption that assistance and protection should be distinguished from each other, when human rights should in fact be fully integrated into all activities for the internally displaced. The chapter argued further that special attention should be paid to the protection of the human rights of vulnerable groups of internally displaced persons. It finally suggested that OHCHR be given a more extended role in promoting IDP protection within the UN system.

The close relationship between IDP protection and human rights has been emphasised. IDP protection encompasses the protection of the human rights of the internally displaced and is thus about delivering on human rights guarantees. It was argued here that the provision of aid in the midst of internal armed conflict poses new challenges as to how humanitarian action should be conducted.[201] When faced with complex emergencies, humanitarian agencies have had to broaden their range of activities and perform new functions. It is increasingly acknowledged that human rights play a crucial part in humanitarian action: where the delivery of aid is pursued in isolation from a human rights framework, assistance programmes do not have the desired impact. In any case, all UN agencies have a duty under Article 55 of the UN Charter to promote 'universal respect for, and observance of, human rights and fundamental freedoms'. When looking at the activities of humanitarian agencies, it seems that increased involvement in IDP protection issues has led them to address human rights concerns more generally. IDP protection has thus provided a strong link between humanitarian assistance and human rights.

The most serious protection problems often occur far from the eyes of external observers. Where a government is persecuting a group of persons within its borders, it is unlikely that it will grant access to international observers and aid agencies. Therefore the gravest situations involve 'countries that either do not acknowledge or do not permit international involvement with displacement within their borders'.[202] One should finally note that the protection strategies examined in this chapter can only provide short-term protection to internally displaced

---

[201] See for instance L. Minear and T. G. Weiss, *Mercy under Fire: War and the Global Humanitarian Community* (Boulder: Westview, 1995).

[202] *Internally Displaced Persons: Report of the Representative of the Secretary-General, Mr Francis M. Deng*, E/CN.4/1999/79, 25 January 1999, para. 93.

persons whose human rights are at risk. As illustrated by the case study presented in the next chapter, one should not forget that 'protection strategies and programs, no matter how innovative or courageous, are not a substitute for the international political will necessary to deter the intentional harming of civilian populations'.[203]

[203] Frohart *et al.*, *Protecting Human Rights*, 32.

5 Case study: internal displacement in Bosnia and Herzegovina

The present chapter provides, based on field and other research, a case study on internal displacement in Bosnia and Herzegovina which examines how the issues addressed in previous chapters were dealt with in the specific context of Bosnia and Herzegovina. It illustrates the limits of field activities pursued in isolation from a human rights framework and goals. It also reviews initiatives undertaken to promote the return of refugees and internally displaced persons to their homes and to reverse ethnic cleansing in order to examine the human rights implications of these return strategies.

The situation in Bosnia and Herzegovina has been chosen as the case study for the following reasons. First, it is the only situation of internal displacement where virtually all the protection strategies discussed in the previous chapter were applied. Attempts to provide international protection to the internally displaced have taken place in the prevention phase, during displacement and upon return, whereas, in other crises, international efforts have not focused on each phase of displacement. The case study thus serves as an illustration of how protection strategies were implemented in a concrete case and the limits of such strategies. Secondly, Bosnia and Herzegovina is also one of the rare situations in which most UN human rights and humanitarian bodies have been involved, and therefore provides an opportunity to analyse coordination mechanisms. Peacekeeping forces and humanitarian organisations were present in the country, as well as a small human rights monitoring team. Thirdly, the crisis of internal displacement took place at a crucial time when UNHCR was rethinking its role in the post-Cold War period, and Western European states were endeavouring to coordinate their asylum and immigration policies at the EU level. The Bosnian crisis provided an opportunity to develop temporary protection schemes, whose impact on internally displaced persons and the refugee protection regime must be evaluated. As a result, Bosnia and Herzegovina constitutes one of the most complex situations of internal displacement, and raises many problematic questions as to how to respond to such crises. There is no typical situation of internal displacement, and in many respects the situation in Bosnia and Herzegovina had some unconventional features. Nevertheless, analysing the problems encountered as well as the impact of the solutions proposed by the United Nations may provide some lessons for the future.

The conflicts in the former Yugoslavia have been the subject of numerous studies covering some or all of the issues covered here.[1] This chapter focuses on the international responses to the crisis of internal displacement and their human rights implications. The focus of the case study is not confined to Bosnia and Herzegovina. As there was a strong link between internal and external movements of populations, the crisis of internal displacement in Bosnia and Herzegovina must be analysed within its regional context, and some reference will be made to Croatia in particular. In the context of the dissolution of the former Yugoslavia, many people displaced from one former republic to another were left with an unclear status.[2]

This case study is based on the analysis of a range of sources including UN documents, especially UNHCR documents dealing with the crisis in the former Yugoslavia, NGO reports and secondary literature. It is also based on interviews conducted with officials of the international organisations involved with internally displaced persons in Bosnia and Herzegovina and representatives of the relevant NGOs. These interviews took place in Geneva (February 1999) and in Bosnia and Herzegovina (September 1999). Interviewees were selected from a wide range of organisations operating in Bosnia and Herzegovina in order to collect various opinions about international responses to the problem of internal displacement in the country. These organisations include UN organisations such as UNHCR and the Office of the High Representative (OHR), other intergovernmental organisations (OSCE), and military organisations (SFOR).

---

[1] See for instance X. Bougarel, *Bosnie: anatomie d'un conflit* (Paris: La Découverte, 1996); S. L. Burg and P. S. Shoup, *The War in Bosnia-Herzegovina: Ethnic Conflict and International Intervention* (Armonk, NY: M. E. Sharpe, 2000); M. Glenny, *The Fall of Yugoslavia* (London: Penguin Books, 1993); L. Silber and A. Little, *Yugoslavia: Death of a Nation* (New York: Penguin Books, 1997); and S. Woodward, *Balkan Tragedy: Chaos and Dissolution after the Cold War* (Washington DC: Brookings Institution, 1995).

[2] See Chapter 1, p. 15 above.

Interviews were also conducted with officials in international NGOs to find out how the overall UN strategy was perceived by them.

Background to the crisis

Overview of displacement (1991–1996)

Explanations of the origins of the Yugoslav crisis, and a description of the conflicts which broke out in the region between 1991 and 1995, are beyond the scope of this book. Nevertheless, in order to analyse the international response to the crisis of internal displacement in Bosnia and Herzegovina, it is essential to understand the dynamics of displacement in the region. When Croatia declared its independence on 25 June 1991, Croatian Serbs living in Krajina and eastern Slavonia declared their own secession from Croatia. As a result, about 300,000 Croats and members of other minorities were expelled from Serb-controlled areas, while 134,000 Croatian Serbs also fled the fighting and took refuge in Serbia.[3] The United Nations Protection Force (UNPROFOR) was deployed in the United Nations Protection Areas (UNPAs)[4] which covered the Serb areas within Croatia. Despite the presence of UNPROFOR, expulsions of Croats from the UNPAs continued unabated.[5]

Conflict then broke out in Bosnia and Herzegovina which was the most ethnically mixed republic in the former Yugoslavia. The first important wave of displacement took place at the beginning of the conflict. From April 1992, Bosnian Serb paramilitary forces were expelling Muslim populations from eastern Bosnia and an estimated 100,000 men were taken to camps.[6] Once the people had vacated their houses, Serb forces would destroy them, or give them to Serbs displaced from elsewhere, to ensure that the people expelled would not be able to return in the future. Such a strategy of forced evictions, also referred to as ethnic cleansing, was adopted by the other warring parties throughout the conflict.

Most internally displaced persons had no choice but to seek refuge in urban centres under the control of their own ethnic group. Such cities saw their populations increase dramatically during the war.[7] Some

[3] See Médecins sans frontières, *Populations in Danger 1995: A Médecins sans frontières Report* (London: MSF/UK, 1995), 146.
[4] SC Res. 743, 21 February 1992.
[5] See Lawyers Committee for Human Rights, *Protection by Presence? The Limits of United Nations Safekeeping Activities in Croatia*, Discussion Paper, New York, September 1993.
[6] See Médecins sans frontières, *Populations in Danger 1995*, 147.
[7] See S. Albert, *Les réfugiés bosniaques en Europe* (Paris: Montchrestien, 1995), 37.

internally displaced persons were able to stay with other families, others could only find temporary accommodation in collective centres, i.e. schools and other public buildings converted to host displaced families. In the space of a few months in 1992, 2.6 million Bosnians out of a total pre-war population of 4.4 million were thus uprooted.[8] Out of those, around 1.3 million were internally displaced, 500,000 were refugees in neighbouring countries and 700,000 had fled to Western Europe.[9] The burden was especially heavy on what remained of the Federal Republic of Yugoslavia (FRY, composed of Serbia and Montenegro) which did not receive any humanitarian aid because economic sanctions had been imposed on that state.[10] Large movements of population still took place in the first six months of 1993, creating an unprecedented humanitarian crisis. As the conflict reached a stalemate, relatively few population movements occurred throughout 1994 compared with the two previous years, which contributed to the crystallisation of the results obtained through the policies of ethnic cleansing.

Each side launched important military campaigns in 1995 to make decisive territorial gains. Following the Croat offensive in Krajina, up to 200,000 Croatian Serb refugees fled and found refuge in Serbia or in northern Bosnia. Only 5,000 Serbs remained in Krajina.[11] Most of the Croatian Serb refugees who fled to Serbia were subsequently resettled in Vojvodina or in Kosovo.[12] The expulsions of the last non-Serbs from the Banja Luka area[13] and the arrival of tens of thousands of Serbs from Croatia completed the 'ethnic cleansing' of northern Bosnia. Bosnian Serb populations were driven out of their homes in western Bosnia by

---

[8] See K. Young, 'UNHCR and ICRC in the Former Yugoslavia: Bosnia-Herzegovina' (2001) 843 *International Review of the Red Cross* 781 at 782.

[9] *Ibid.*, 783.

[10] SC Res. 757, 30 May 1992. On the impact of such sanctions on humanitarian aid to refugees, see US Committee for Refugees (USCR), *East of Bosnia: Refugees in Serbia and Montenegro* (Washington DC: USCR, 1993).

[11] See V. Grecic, 'Refugees and Internally Displaced Persons in the Former Yugoslavia in the Light of Dayton and Paris Agreements', *Refuge*, vol. 16, No. 5, November 1997, 31 at 31.

[12] See T. G. Weiss and A. Pasic, 'Dealing with the Displacement and Suffering Caused by Yugoslavia's Wars', in R. Cohen and F. M. Deng (eds.), *The Forsaken People* (Washington DC: Brookings Institution, 1998), 175–231 at 187.

[13] See *Report of the Secretary-General on Violations of International Humanitarian Law in the Areas of Srebrenica, Zepa, Banja Luka and Sanski Most*, S/1995/988, 27 November 1995, para. 42.

the joint offensive of Bosnian Croat and Muslim forces[14] and around 130,000 people fled to eastern Bosnia, or beyond to Serbia.

Events of the summer of 1995 opened the possibility for a peace settlement as each of the two parties (Bosnian Croats and Muslims, and Bosnian Serbs) now controlled half of the territory, and as these territories were more or less contiguous. The map which resulted from the military operations conducted in the summer of 1995 was more 'simple' than previous ones, because some Muslim enclaves had fallen and the Muslim–Croat Federation had regained some territories. Most importantly, the map was now consistent with the peace settlement that had been prepared by the US.[15] Almost 500,000 people were displaced between May and October 1995, mainly Serbs from the UNPAs and western Bosnia, and Muslims from the 'safe areas'.[16]

The General Framework Agreement for Peace in Bosnia and Herzegovina (hereinafter the Dayton Peace Agreement) was signed in Paris on 14 December 1995.[17] It envisaged the creation of two entities, the Muslim–Croat Federation and the Republika Srpska, together forming a single state, Bosnia and Herzegovina. Several transfers of territories between the two parties took place as a result of the agreement,[18] which provoked further movements of populations. The most important transfer of territory took place in Sarajevo in the spring of 1996 when the control of Serb suburbs was transferred to the Muslim–Croat Federation. This transfer occurred amidst important political tensions, and resulted in the exodus of 62,000 Serb residents who represented the great majority of the pre-war Serb population in Sarajevo.[19] In addition, expulsions of ethnic minorities continued throughout 1996, although to a much lower degree than during the war.[20] Most of the people displaced in 1996 were internally displaced, and did not seek refuge abroad.

As of September 1996, according to UNHCR, there were more than a million internally displaced persons in Bosnia and Herzegovina, and around a million people had fled to other countries. Croatia hosted 180,000 refugees from Bosnia and Herzegovina, and the Former Republic

---

[14] See the map in R. Holbrooke, *To End a War* (New York: The Modern Library, 1999), 161.
[15] See pp. 179–82 below.
[16] See Weiss and Pasic, 'Dealing with the Displacement', 186.
[17] (1996) 35 ILM 75.   [18] See the map in Holbrooke, *To End a War*, 84.
[19] See Bosnia and Herzegovina, in US Committee for Refugees (USCR), *World Refugee Survey 1997* (Washington DC: USCR, 1997), 172.
[20] *Ibid.*, 174.

of Yugoslavia 255,000. The remaining Bosnian refugees were scattered all around Europe, especially in Germany which hosted 345,000 of them. In addition, there were 200,000 internally displaced persons in Croatia, and up to 300,000 Croatian Serb refugees in FRY.[21]

The failure of international diplomacy

The international response to the crisis of internal displacement in Bosnia and Herzegovina must be understood within the context of a general lack of political will to address the root causes of displacement. International diplomatic efforts to solve the crisis posed by the dissolution of the former Yugoslavia started in 1991 and were based on a poor understanding of the conflicts. The premature recognition of the independence of Croatia advocated by Germany contributed to the speeding up of events leading to the disintegration of Bosnia and Herzegovina, as Bosnian Serbs were inevitably going to oppose such recognition. More generally, foreign political leaders assumed that ethnic conflicts were recurrent in the region and fuelled by 'ancient feudal hatreds' which no external intervention could stop.[22] However, a closer look at the history of Bosnia and Herzegovina shows that the different ethnic groups were not always at war against each other.[23] Another problem lay in the fact that international mediation efforts were always based on the idea of ethnic partition of Bosnia and Herzegovina.[24]

Earlier diplomatic initiatives were conducted by the European Community, which established the Arbitration Commission to examine applications for EC recognition.[25] In September 1991, the EC Conference on Yugoslavia started under the chairmanship of Lord Owen. The Balkan crisis constituted the first test for the EU's new Common Foreign and Security Policy (CFSP).[26] The United Nations joined its efforts to those of the EU, and the International Conference on the Former Yugoslavia

---

[21] See Humanitarian Issues Working Group, *Implementation of Durable Solutions in Bosnia and Herzegovina, Croatia and the Federal Republic of Yugoslavia During the Peace Consolidation Period*, HIWG/96/6/Corr.1, 12 December 1996.

[22] See for instance Woodward, *Balkan Tragedy*, 307.

[23] See N. Malcolm, *Bosnia: A Short Story* (London: Papermac, 1996, 2nd ed.).

[24] See pp. 179–82 below.

[25] For more detail, see R. Rich, 'Recognition of States: The Collapse of Yugoslavia and the Soviet Union' (1993) 4 *European Journal of International Law* 36.

[26] For more detail on early EC initiatives, see J. Gow, *Triumph of the Lack of Will: International Diplomacy and the Yugoslav War* (New York: Columbia University Press, 1997), chapters 3 and 4.

(ICFY) was established in September 1992. The United States then decided to take on a more active role in the peace negotiations, which led to the signing of the Dayton Peace Agreement in November 1995.

The peace talks suffered from several major problems. First, there were no concerted international efforts, as the main players remained divided on the strategies to be used in Bosnia and Herzegovina. A Contact Group was finally set up in 1994 to coordinate international diplomatic efforts to solve the conflict. Secondly, such diplomatic efforts were not sufficiently backed by a credible threat to use force. The main powers were extremely reluctant to take more vigorous military action to stop the conflict, and only sought to prevent the conflict from spreading in the region. American initiatives may have been ultimately successful because they were backed by NATO air strikes on Bosnian Serb forces, but also because, by the autumn of 1995, the conflict had redrawn the map to the relative satisfaction of the parties. The main powers also sought to contain refugee flows by offering some short-term relief to the civilians. They justified providing assistance within the country by arguing that to do otherwise would entail complicity in ethnic cleansing.[27] The focus on humanitarian assistance thus served as a 'substitute for, and may have actually impeded more creative Western diplomatic pressure'.[28]

EU asylum and immigration policies

The numbers of internally displaced persons within Bosnia and Herzegovina were partly linked to the restrictive immigration and asylum policies adopted by EU member states. If people could not find safety abroad, they had no choice but to seek safety elsewhere within their own country. The human displacement produced by the wars following the disintegration of the former Yugoslavia constituted the first massive displacement crisis in Europe since the Second World War. In 1991, 115,500 persons from the former Yugoslavia, mainly from Croatia, sought asylum in ten European countries.[29] When war broke out in Bosnia and Herzegovina, the refugee crisis worsened and, by 1992, there were 428,200 asylum seekers from the former Yugoslavia in the same

---

[27] Ibid., 111.
[28] See T. G. Weiss, 'UN Responses in the Former Yugoslavia: Moral and Operational Choices' (1994) 8 Ethics and International Affairs 1 at 20.
[29] See UNHCR, The State of World's Refugees: The Challenge of Protection (Geneva: UNHCR, 1993), 158.

ten European countries.[30] This unprecedented influx of asylum seekers in Western Europe took place at a crucial time. Western European states were already adopting increasingly restrictive policies, because they feared an influx of immigrants from Eastern Europe after the fall of the Iron Curtain. Moreover, they were attempting to coordinate their immigration policies, which pushed for alignment on the lowest common denominator. It is in this context that the response to the refugee crisis in Bosnia and Herzegovina must be analysed.

In 1991, refugee-receiving states were fairly generous to asylum seekers from Croatia. It was the beginning of the crisis, and states were still willing to admit people from the former Yugoslavia. It had also been observed that Croats, being Catholics, were perhaps more welcome than Muslim refugees from Bosnia and Herzegovina.[31] As the crisis unfolded in that country, states feared a massive exodus, and visa requirements were imposed by most European countries in 1992–3 on Bosnian nationals wishing to enter their territories.[32] Visas were not easy to obtain, since most European embassies in Sarajevo had closed.[33] It was argued at the time that evacuations to countries outside the region would amount to an implicit support of the policies of ethnic cleansing.[34] Consequently, people were compelled to stay in the region where little protection was afforded to them. The same debate resurfaced later in 1999 with regard to evacuations of Kosovo Albanian refugees to third countries outside the region.[35] It must be noted that even the evacuation of former camp prisoners from Bosnia and Herzegovina to countries outside the region, which the ICRC called for, was painfully slow due to the lack of cooperation of European states.[36]

All exit routes were progressively closed as Croatia restricted entry to its territory, and this was especially true for Bosnian Muslims who were probably most in need of international protection, but could not

---

[30] *Ibid.* For figures in each asylum country, see Albert, *Les réfugiés bosniaques*, 64–72.

[31] See M. Barutciski, 'The Reinforcement of Non-Admission Policies and the Subversion of UNHCR: Displacement and Internal Assistance in Bosnia-Herzegovina, 1992–1994' (1996) 8 *International Journal of Refugee Law* 49 at 74.

[32] See Albert, *Les réfugiés bosniaques*, 137, and J. van Selm-Thorburn, *Refugee Protection in Europe: Lessons of the Yugoslav Crisis* (The Hague: Martinus Nijhoff, 1998), 122.

[33] See van Selm-Thorburn, *Refugee Protection in Europe*, 123.

[34] *Ibid.*, 111.

[35] See UNHCR, *The Kosovo Refugee Crisis: An Independent Evaluation of UNHCR's Emergency Preparedness and Response*, EPAU/2000/001, February 2000, 91–3.

[36] See Albert, *Les réfugiés bosniaques*, 129.

find refuge in either Croatia or Serbia. Bosnian Croats and Serbs were still admitted in those countries respectively. By 1994, Croatia was hosting 139,000 Bosnian Croat refugees, but only 48,000 Bosnian Muslim refugees.[37] Entry to the FRY (Serbia and Montenegro) was restricted for Bosnian Muslims, since that country mainly accepted Bosnian or Croatian Serb refugees.[38] Slovenia was also reluctant to receive refugees from Bosnia and Herzegovina. In contrast, 80 per cent of those from the former Yugoslavia who found refuge outside the region were Muslim.[39] Croatia and Slovenia could have received larger numbers of Bosnian refugees due to their geographical proximity, but were reluctant to do so since they knew that they could not rely on other European countries to share the burden.[40] Western European states were perhaps reluctant to press Croatia and Slovenia to keep their borders open to Bosnian refugees, because they would then probably have had to accept some of them on their own territories. They were thus more interested in other protection measures such as safe areas or temporary protection, which ensured that Bosnian refugees would not be allowed to stay for long periods or even permanently on their territories. It must be noted that some countries such as France, Belgium, Italy and Sweden only granted refugee status to people coming from areas of Bosnia and Herzegovina which were affected by the fighting, and applied the internal flight alternative (IFA) test.[41] Protection had to be sought within the country first, even if that meant the person was thereby internally displaced.

In light of the reluctance of European states to grant asylum to applicants from the former Yugoslavia, the High Commissioner for Refugees felt compelled to ask those states to grant them temporary protection instead. One suspects that she came to accept that these states would not grant refugee status on a group basis to victims of armed conflict or mass violations of human rights,[42] and that temporary protection was

---

[37] See Humanitarian Issues Working Group, *Post-Conflict Solutions: UNHCR Programme in Bosnia and Herzegovina and Other Countries in the Region*, HIWG/96/2, 10 January 1996, para. 29.

[38] See *Bosnia and Herzegovina: Return of Refugees and Displaced Persons*, Report of the Parliamentary Assembly of the Council of Europe, Committee on Migration, Refugees and Demography, Doc. 7973, 23 December 1997, para. 8.

[39] *Ibid.*

[40] See Barutciski, 'The Reinforcement of Non-Admission Policies', 74.

[41] See Albert, *Les réfugiés bosniaques*, 154 and 156.

[42] See P. Kourula, *Broadening the Edges: Refugee Definition and International Protection Revisited* (The Hague: Martinus Nijhoff Publishers, 1997), 110.

a compromise to encourage states to admit more people from Bosnia and Herzegovina. Temporary protection was presented as an element of the comprehensive response to the humanitarian crisis in the former Yugoslavia and 'a flexible and pragmatic means of affording needed protection to large numbers of people fleeing human rights abuses and armed conflict in their country of origin, who might otherwise have overwhelmed asylum procedures'.[43]

The idea of temporary protection is not a new one, and asylum is by its nature temporary. According to the cessation clauses of the 1951 convention,[44] refugee status can be withdrawn when the grounds for asylum cease to exist. These clauses are rarely applied.[45] The Bosnian crisis provided the first opportunity to implement temporary protection schemes in Europe. UNHCR emphasised that temporary protection was used as a 'pragmatic tool' to afford international protection in situations of mass outflows,[46] but it was aware of the problems raised by such a scheme. Indeed, there was uncertainty about what rights would be granted to those benefiting from it, or how it would be terminated.[47] In contrast, relatively precise UNHCR guidelines were issued on minimum standards of treatment in countries participating in the Humanitarian Evacuation Programme (HEP) for Kosovo Albanians in 1999.[48] Back in the early 1990s, temporary protection schemes varied greatly from one country to another,[49] but efforts were subsequently made to harmonise these schemes at the EU level.[50] It must finally be noted that the temporary protection schemes established to deal with persons coming from Bosnia and Herzegovina were applied to some persons who according

---

[43] See *Note on International Protection*, A/AC.96/815, 31 August 1993, para. 25.

[44] Art. 1(C) of the Convention Relating to the Status of Refugees, 28 July 1951, 189 UNTS 150 (hereinafter the 1951 Convention).

[45] See J. Fitzpatrick and R. Bonoan, 'Cessation of Refugee Protection', in E. Feller, V. Türk and F. Nicholson (eds.), *Refugee Protection in International Law: UNHCR's Global Consultations on International Protection* (Cambridge: Cambridge University Press, 2003), 491–544 at 512–13.

[46] See *Note on International Protection*, A/AC.96/830, 7 September 1994, para. 45.

[47] See *Note on International Protection*, A/AC.96/815, 31 August 1993, para. 25.

[48] See UNHCR, *The Kosovo Refugee Crisis*, 93.

[49] See Albert, *Les réfugiés bosniaques*, 158–66, and for a detailed analysis of temporary protection schemes in four European countries, see van Selm-Thorburn, *Refugee Protection in Europe*, 173–238.

[50] See Council Directive 2001/55/EC of 20 July 2001 on minimum standards for giving temporary protection in the event of a mass influx of displaced persons and on measures promoting a balance of efforts between Member States in receiving such persons and bearing the consequences thereof, OJ 2001 L212/12.

to UNHCR might otherwise have obtained refugee status,[51] and would consequently have benefited from a more favourable regime.

International responses to internal displacement

Preventive protection

The idea of preventive protection was promoted by UNHCR at the beginning of the 1990s,[52] and the former Yugoslavia represented the first opportunity to test this strategy on the ground. The main objective was to prevent further displacement out of the UNPAs, and then out of Bosnia and Herzegovina. The Serb offensive in the UNPAs had produced large movements of populations to other areas of Croatia and abroad,[53] and Western European states were concerned at the prospect of further displacement. UNHCR was therefore sent to Croatia to provide preventive protection, with the assistance of UNPROFOR.

It had been suggested at the time that preventive protection encompassed two forms of activities, i.e. 'negotiations to create conditions that would make it possible for people to stay', and assistance.[54] The High Commissioner for Refugees declared that she saw 'an inherent link between international assistance and preventive protection'.[55] UNHCR field staff did not actually understand what preventive protection really meant, nor what it actually involved.[56] It cannot be denied that the aid brought to the civilian population in the region helped some people to remain where they were. Nevertheless, most people did not flee starvation, but violence. Where there was a severe shortage of food in besieged areas such as Sarajevo or Bihac, people no longer had the option to flee. Because of the specific context in which displacement took place, namely amidst an armed conflict which sought to displace populations,

---

[51] See G. Goodwin-Gill, *The Refugee in International Law* (Oxford: Clarendon Press, 1996, 2nd ed.), 200, note 151. See also the European Consultation on Refugees and Exiles (ECRE)'s position in van Selm-Thorburn, *Refugee Protection in Europe*, 124.

[52] See Chapter 4, pp. 122–5 above.

[53] See p. 157 above.

[54] See J. M. Mendiluce, 'War and Disaster in the Former Yugoslavia: The Limits of Humanitarian Action', *World Refugee Survey 1994*, http://www.refugees.org/world/articles/yugoslavia_wrs94.htm.

[55] S. Ogata, *Statement of the United Nations High Commissioner for Refugees to the International Meeting on Humanitarian Aid for Victims of the Conflict in the Former Yugoslavia*, Geneva, 29 July 1992.

[56] See UNHCR, *Working in a War Zone: A Review of UNHCR's Operations in Former Yugoslavia*, EVAL/YUG/14, April 1994, para. 55.

more emphasis could have been put on protection instead, either for instance through negotiation with the warring parties or, where possible, through military interposition between these warring parties and the civilians they were seeking to expel. This required a larger and more active 'peacekeeping' force and a much more credible threat to use force. Incorrect conceptualisation of preventive protection led to the use of inadequate strategies in the former Yugoslavia. This led the former special UNHCR envoy in the region to conclude that such strategies failed to prevent further displacement from the UNPAs and Bosnia and Herzegovina.[57] The experience in Croatia and Bosnia and Herzegovina has had crucial implications for the future of the notion of 'preventive protection'. Not surprisingly, by the end of 1992, the concept of 'preventive protection' had already disappeared from UNHCR's vocabulary.[58]

One of the important lessons to be learnt from the experience in the former Yugoslavia with regard to preventive protection is the risk of manipulation of the notion to justify policies of containment and limit the right to seek asylum. Authors such as Frelick and Barutciski have argued that Western European states, as well as neighbouring states such as Croatia and Slovenia, have interpreted 'preventive protection' as preventing refugee flows by closing their borders to Bosnian refugees.[59] In effect, they prevented people from leaving Bosnia and Herzegovina, but did not address the causes of displacement. Croatia for instance constituted the only possible exit route for many persecuted Bosnian Muslims, but it gradually closed its borders for fear of a massive exodus of refugees. As early as July 1992, at the height of the ethnic cleansing in eastern and western Bosnia, Croatia only allowed Bosnian refugees with 'letters of guarantee' from friends or relatives in Croatia or other European countries to enter its territory. Later, it further restricted the conditions of entry, and people were allowed to enter Croatia provided it was only for transit to another country.[60] Other European states adopted a similar attitude.[61]

UNPROFOR, which was mandated to patrol much of the border between Croatia and Bosnia and Herzegovina, limited the entry of refugees. A UN peacekeeping force should not have been associated with

---

[57] See Mendiluce, 'War and Disaster in the Former Yugoslavia'.

[58] See UNHCR, Working in a War Zone, para. 106.

[59] See B. Frelick, '"Preventive Protection" and the Right to Seek Asylum: A Preliminary Look at Bosnia and Croatia' (1992) 4 International Journal of Refugee Law 439 at 452, and Barutciski, 'The Reinforcement of Non-Admission Policies', 60–1.

[60] See Frelick, 'Preventive Protection', 444–5.   [61] See pp. 161–5 above.

a violation of the principle of *non-refoulement* and was in breach of its obligations under the UN Charter.[62] In contrast, in 1999, UNHCR adopted a stricter policy towards the Former Yugoslav Republic of Macedonia (FYROM) and strongly protested against attempts to close the border to Kosovo Albanians.[63] Frelick raises the question of who is being really protected by the concept of preventive protection, i.e. asylum states from refugee flows or civilians from forced displacement?[64] The implementation of the strategy of 'preventive protection' resulted in the persecuted populations of Bosnia and Herzegovina not being allowed to flee life-threatening situations, and being exposed to further human rights violations.

Delivery of humanitarian assistance

Once the conflict was spreading to Bosnia and Herzegovina and once it was becoming increasingly difficult to prevent the displacement of populations which was one of the prime objectives of the war, efforts were made to limit the effects of the conflict on the civilian population by bringing them humanitarian assistance. Therefore, the main objective of the initial international presence in Bosnia and Herzegovina was to bring emergency relief to civilians. In a letter addressed by the Secretary-General to the High Commissioner for Refugees, UNHCR was designated lead agency to coordinate humanitarian operations in Croatia,[65] and later in Bosnia and Herzegovina. To some extent, UNHCR's lead agency role was limited to coordinating its own activities with those of ICRC and more than a hundred NGOs, because other UN agencies (apart from the World Food Programme) had a more limited involvement in the former Yugoslavia.[66] UNHCR was generally unable to support the work of most NGOs.[67] Regarding cooperation with the ICRC, some tensions appeared because of their different mandates and approaches.[68]

---

[62] See *Report on the Situation of Human Rights in the Territory of the Former Yugoslavia Submitted by Mr Tadeusz Mazowiecki*, E/CN.4/1992/S-1/10, 27 October 1992, para. 13.

[63] See UNHCR, *The Kosovo Refugee Crisis*, 90.

[64] See Frelick, 'Preventive Protection', 452.

[65] See *Report of the Secretary-General Pursuant to Security Council Resolution 721*, S/23280, 11 December 1991, para. 16. The letter is referred to in G. Goodwin-Gill, 'Refugee Identity and Protection's Fading Prospect', in F. Nicholson and P. Twomey (eds.), *Refugee Rights and Realities: Evolving International Concepts and Regimes* (Cambridge: Cambridge University Press, 1999), 220–49 at 226.

[66] See UNHCR, *Working in a War Zone*, paras. 224–5.   [67] *Ibid.*, paras. 218–21.

[68] *Ibid.*, paras. 229–35.

From 1992 onwards, UNHCR deployed the largest humanitarian operation in its history. By the end of 1993, 700 international staff members were operating from twenty-nine offices in the former Yugoslavia,[69] bringing humanitarian aid to a total of 3.6 million people in the region.[70] UNPROFOR's initial mandate only covered the UNPAs, but it was extended to cover the territory of Bosnia and Herzegovina and to include the protection of humanitarian convoys.[71] The force was deployed in Sarajevo and Bihac.[72] By the end of 1992, it was also escorting humanitarian convoys all over the country.[73] As the other specialised agencies (WFP, WHO, UNICEF) only started operating in Bosnia and Herzegovina later,[74] UNHCR became involved in many programmes, and its budget for the former Yugoslavia soon reached US$500 million per year,[75] i.e. almost half of the agency's total budget. This massive humanitarian operation took place in extremely difficult conditions. In this context, humanitarian organisations were rather successful in at least feeding war-affected populations.

Humanitarian aid was aimed at alleviating not only the effects of displacement, but also the effects of the conflict on the general civilian population. Those who were on the move were not always the worst off, whereas those who remained trapped within an area sometimes did not have access to humanitarian aid. The Joint Appeal issued in October 1993 noted that 'the general economic collapse and blockade of commercial traffic has created a situation in which those who are not refugees or displaced are often in as great a need as those internally or externally displaced'.[76] Extending the provision of aid to the non-displaced was a direct consequence of an intervention in a war zone.[77] In March

---

[69] See S. A. Cunliffe and M. Pugh, 'The Politicization of UNHCR in the Former Yugoslavia' (1997) 10 *Journal of Refugee Studies* 134 at 136. See also the map on UNHCR, UNPROFOR and ICRC presence in Bosnia and Herzegovina as of 1 July 1993, in UNHCR, *The Challenge of Protection*, 81.

[70] See UNHCR, *The Challenge of Protection*, 83.   [71] See SC Res. 776, 14 September 1992.

[72] See *Further Report of the Secretary-General Pursuant to Security Council Resolutions 757, 758 and 761*, S/24263, 10 July 1992, para. 17.

[73] See *Report of the Secretary-General*, A/47/747, 3 December 1992, para. 10.

[74] See L. Minear, J. Clark, R. Cohen, D. Gallagher, I. Guest and T. G. Weiss, *Humanitarian Action in the Former Yugoslavia: The UN's Role 1991–1993*, Occasional Paper No. 18 (Providence, RI: Thomas J. Watson Jr Institute for International Studies and Refugee Policy Group, 1994), 28–30.

[75] See Weiss and Pasic, 'Dealing with the Displacement', 200.

[76] Quoted in Minear *et al.*, *Humanitarian Action in the Former Yugoslavia*, 52.

[77] See T. G. Weiss and A. Pasic, 'Reinventing UNHCR: Enterprising Humanitarians in the Former Yugoslavia, 1991–1995' (1997) 3 *Global Governance* 41 at 47–8.

1997, non-displaced persons (referred to as 'war-affected') constituted 11 per cent of the beneficiaries of UNHCR's programmes in the former Yugoslavia.[78] Similar operational problems would be encountered were UNHCR to take on general responsibility for the internally displaced.[79] Aid workers did not apply any distinction between the beneficiaries who were displaced and those who were not, nor between refugees and internally displaced persons. The operation in Bosnia and Herzegovina has undoubtedly taken the agency into new areas of activity. UNHCR was originally mandated to provide legal protection to refugees, and was now involved in a massive humanitarian operation whose target population included mainly internally displaced persons, but also persons who had not been displaced. The agency coordinated a difficult logistical operation involving an airlift to Sarajevo, as well as airdrops of relief items in besieged areas.

Although UNHCR had provided in-country protection to internally displaced persons on numerous occasions before,[80] this was usually during the post-conflict period, as was the case for example in northern Iraq in 1991. In Bosnia and Herzegovina, the intervention took place as the fighting was still going on. As a result, UNHCR had to operate in an unusually complex political and military environment which was radically different from its previous experience of in-country operations.

Protection in situ?

Knowing that the displacement of populations was the objective of the warring parties, it was problematic to respond to requests from civilians to be evacuated from dangerous areas, because it would serve the objectives of those who sought their displacement. On the other hand, refusing assistance to these populations meant putting them at risk of being persecuted, brought to detention camps or even killed. When humanitarian agencies decided to assist evacuations, their efforts were sometimes opposed by Muslim leaders for instance who feared the loss of control over the areas Muslim populations wanted to abandon.[81] The original position of the international agencies operating in Bosnia and Herzegovina was to provide protection as close as possible to the homes

[78] See UNHCR, *The State of World's Refugees: A Humanitarian Agenda* (Geneva: UNHCR, 1997), 103.
[79] See Chapter 3, pp. 90–2 above.   [80] See Chapter 3, first section, above.
[81] See Woodward, *Balkan Tragedy*, 243, and Burg and Shoup, *The War in Bosnia-Herzegovina*, 172.

of origin, and help people remain where they were. In order to thwart efforts to ethnically cleanse areas, emphasis was put on the 'right to remain'.[82] The objective was thus to bring safety to people, rather than people to safety. However, very quickly, it appeared that, in some circumstances, people were not safe, and could only save their lives by leaving their homes. Nevertheless, if international aid agencies helped people to leave, they would be accused of collaborating with the policies of ethnic cleansing, which explains why they were reluctant to assist evacuations. This dilemma was rightly described by the High Commissioner for Refugees, who stated that 'by promoting asylum, we may be encouraging "ethnic cleansing". On the other hand, if we fail to help people reach safety, we may condemn them to persecution, detention and perhaps even death.'[83]

Initially, UNHCR persistently refused to evacuate Bosnian Muslims from the country. As a refugee agency, its mandate is to assist refugees in countries of asylum and not to assist people in *becoming* refugees. However, when faced with such large-scale atrocities, some Bosnian Muslims were transferred by the ICRC from the Banja Luka area to other parts of the country and even to Croatia.[84] In some cases, some minority groups only wanted 'to leave, and to be helped to leave'.[85] In early 1993, a major evacuation exercise took place when between 8,000 and 9,000 Muslims were evacuated from Srebrenica to Tuzla in UN convoys.[86] Medical evacuations were obviously less controversial and regularly took place.[87] Although other types of evacuations were much more controversial, some NGOs acknowledged that they took some civilians out of the country.[88]

---

[82] See for instance S. Ogata, 'UNHCR in the Balkans: Humanitarian Action in the Midst of War', in W. Biermann and M. Vadset (eds.), *UN Peacekeeping in Trouble: Lessons Learned from the Former Yugoslavia* (Aldershot: Ashgate, 1998), 186–99 at 187.

[83] S. Ogata, 'Refugees: Challenge of the 1990s', Statement of the United Nations High Commissioner for Refugees, New School for Social Research, New York, 11 November 1992. See also another quote from January 1993 in M. Mercier, *Crimes Without Punishment: Humanitarian Action in the Former Yugoslavia* (London: Pluto Press, 1995), 123.

[84] See E. D. Mooney, 'Presence, Ergo Protection? UNPROFOR, UNHCR and the ICRC in Croatia and Bosnia and Herzegovina' (1995) 7 *International Journal of Refugee Law* 407 at 428.

[85] Young, 'UNHCR and ICRC in the Former Yugoslavia', 796.

[86] See *Report of the Secretary-General: The Fall of Srebrenica*, A/54/549, 15 November 1999, para. 40.

[87] See for instance Young, 'UNHCR and ICRC in the Former Yugoslavia', 784.

[88] See U. von Buchwald, *Response Systems of Non-Governmental Organisations to Assistance and Protection Needs of the Internally Displaced Persons*, draft report, Norwegian Refugee Council, Geneva, March 1996, 21.

After many heated internal debates, the Special Envoy of UNHCR in the former Yugoslavia decided in early June 1992 that evacuations should be undertaken in some circumstances, because UNHCR 'chose to have more displaced persons or refugees than more bodies'.[89] Assistance for evacuation would be provided when the individuals concerned were in an 'acute, life-threatening situation'.[90] In practice, it was not always very clear what constituted a life-threatening situation.[91] Evacuations were in rare cases 'organised' by international aid agencies themselves. In most cases, aid workers, or even UNPROFOR soldiers, simply escorted convoys of civilians out of besieged areas. In some situations, civilians preferred to be internally displaced rather than stay in their homes where their lives were at risk. As long as the conflict was going on, real safety could only be found by seeking asylum abroad, but this was very often not an option for many persecuted individuals.[92]

With the benefit of hindsight, it has even been suggested that UNHCR could have evacuated more people to safety.[93] Nevertheless, UNHCR's cautious approach to evacuations can be defended on the ground that they were very difficult to organise in practice, but also because they could have major drawbacks. Indeed, in some cases, once evacuations had started, there was increased persecution of those remaining in the hope that they would leave the area or be evacuated.[94] As a result, although evacuations brought some individuals to relative safety, they could also contribute to undermine the position of those who remained.

Creation of safe areas

The creation of safe areas in Bosnia and Herzegovina was a proposal originally made by the ICRC.[95] It was supported by neighbouring countries such as Slovenia and Croatia, as well as by several Western European states,[96] i.e. states which were reluctant to receive more refugees from Bosnia and Herzegovina. This may suggest that safe areas were established as a sort of containment measure to prevent Bosnians from

---

[89] Mendiluce, 'War and Disaster in the Former Yugoslavia'.
[90] See Minear *et al.*, *Humanitarian Action in the Former Yugoslavia*, 67, and also UNHCR, *The Challenge of Protection*, 91.
[91] See Young, 'UNHCR and ICRC in the Former Yugoslavia', 797.
[92] See pp. 161–5 above.   [93] See UNHCR, *Working in a War Zone*, para. 134.
[94] See Young, 'UNHCR and ICRC in the Former Yugoslavia', 798.
[95] See Barutciski, 'The Reinforcement of Non-Admission Policies', 85. See also Mercier, *Crimes Without Punishment*, 66.
[96] See van Selm-Thorburn, *Refugee Protection in Europe*, 110–11.

leaving their country. However, caution must be expressed before making such an assumption, because it was clear at the time that the Muslim populations targeted by this measure were surrounded by Serb lines and thus physically unable to travel to seek asylum abroad. It is therefore unlikely that containment was the motivation for the establishment of the safe areas.

In Srebrenica, the population had swollen from 7,000 to almost 60,000 as inhabitants from surrounding areas came to seek safety in the city.[97] In November 1992, UNHCR managed to bring some humanitarian convoys into the enclave, but triggered a crisis as civilians who were desperate to leave were crushed onto the trucks.[98] As the city was about to fall into Serb hands, the High Commissioner for Refugees wrote to the Secretary-General to alert him to the situation in Srebrenica.[99] The severe humanitarian crisis which had also developed in the other Muslim enclaves in eastern Bosnia in 1993 prompted the Security Council to declare them 'safe areas'. The Security Council first declared Srebrenica a safe area.[100] Subsequently, Bihac, Gorazde, Sarajevo, Tuzla and Zepa were also declared safe areas.[101]

Several problems were already identified at the time. These safe areas were established without the consent of the warring parties (i.e. Bosnian Serb forces). Moreover, not enough troops were sent to defend the safe areas. The Security Council did not specify what protection was to be given to the civilians to ensure that the safe areas were truly safe. It extended the mandate of UNPROFOR, and authorised it 'acting in *self-defence* to take the necessary measures, including the use of force, in reply to bombardments against the safe areas by any of the parties or to armed incursion into them or in the event of any deliberate obstruction in or around those areas to the freedom of movement of UNPROFOR or of protected humanitarian convoys'.[102] The Security Council also envisaged the use of air strikes by member states (i.e. NATO), which were however reluctant to authorise them.[103] The Secretary-General estimated that, in order to fulfil the mandate as defined in Security Council Resolution

---

[97] See *Periodic Report on the Situation of Human Rights in the Territory of the Former Yugoslavia Submitted by Mr Tadeusz Mazowiecki*, E/CN.4/1994/3, 5 May 1993, para. 30.

[98] See UNHCR, *The Challenge of Protection*, 91.

[99] See *Letter from the High Commissioner for Refugees to the Secretary-General on Srebrenica Dated 2 April 1993*, S/25519, 3 April 1993.

[100] SC Res. 819, 16 April 1993.   [101] SC Res. 824, 6 May 1993.

[102] SC Res. 836, 4 June 1993, para. 9.

[103] See *Report of the Secretary-General*, S/1994/555, 9 May 1994, para. 10.

836, 34,000 additional troops were required, but a 'light option' of 7,600 could be considered as a starting point.[104] The Security Council chose the latter option.[105] Even then, those troops took a year to deploy in and around the safe areas.[106]

The main objective of the establishment of the safe areas was to provide immediate protection to the civilian population in the midst of armed conflict. Under those circumstances, this required international military protection of the civilians in the safe areas. One problem with safe areas is that more people living in surrounding villages were attracted to them, as they believed that they would be safer there.[107] One may wonder whether external powers believed that the creation of the safe areas exonerated them from any responsibility towards the civilians living outside those areas. It could be read as a promise to provide protection in the safe areas, but only there. The establishment of the safe areas contributed to create 'micro' IDP situations as it actually '*encouraged* . . . displacement and "ghetto-ization" in the enclaves'.[108]

As the safe areas were neither properly defended, nor precisely delimited,[109] nor demilitarised,[110] their creation had a more harmful than positive impact on the protection of civilians. There was a false assumption that the mere presence of peacekeepers in the safe areas would deter attacks. Since they were situated in contested territories, they inevitably came under attack. One of the main objectives of the conflict was to displace or kill civilians to control ethnically homogenous territories, and the concentration in one location of members of the ethnic group targeted made it easier for the opponents to direct their military operations. Indeed, Hyndman commented that 'the UN unwittingly created a target for aggressors *and* participated in a humanitarian exercise that inadvertently ethnically cleansed large tracts of rural territory now available to these same aggressors'.[111] The rest of the story is well known. Srebrenica fell to Serb attacks in July 1995 and thousands of civilians were either killed or fled to Muslim-occupied

---

[104] See *Report of the Secretary-General*, S/25939, 14 June 1993, para. 5.
[105] See SC Res. 844, 18 June 1993.
[106] See *Report of the Secretary-General*, S/1994/1389, 1 December 1994, para. 54.
[107] See for instance Mooney, 'Presence, Ergo Protection?', 416.   [108] *Ibid.*, 418.
[109] See *Report of the Secretary-General*, S/1994/555, 9 May 1994, para. 13.
[110] See for instance the case of Bihac in *Report of the Secretary-General*, S/1994/1389, 1 December 1994, para. 34–7.
[111] P. Hyndman, 'Preventive, Palliative, or Punitive? Safe Spaces in Bosnia-Herzegovina, Somalia, and Sri Lanka' (2003) 16 *Journal of Refugee Studies* 167 at 175,

territories. These events were documented in several reports,[112] including an official UN report.[113] Another safe area, Zepa, also fell at the end
of July 1995.

International media pressure may have contributed to the impetus to
create safe areas. Western states' motivation was perhaps to promise protection to the internally displaced in fairly restricted areas, and one may
wonder whether they did so to avoid responsibility for the protection
of the people outside those areas. However, they were not even committed to the protection of the residents and internally displaced in the
safe areas. This led Barutciski to write that 'there was never a real commitment to replace external asylum possibilities with genuine internal
protection in the form of local safe havens'.[114]

International responsibility towards the internally displaced

Direct responsibility for the abuses committed during the conflict in
Bosnia and Herzegovina obviously falls on the warring parties themselves. The purpose of this section is not to attribute international
responsibility for the unfolding of the crisis in the Balkans. Rather, it
seeks to show the impact, if any, of international intervention in the
conflict on issues of assistance and protection of refugees and internally displaced persons. Whereas the previous section looked at the assistance and protection strategies used in the field, this section attempts
to explain why such choices of strategies were made by Western powers.
Instead of dealing with the conflict itself, and thus with the root causes
of displacement, international efforts were targeted at the symptoms.
Higgins rightly pointed out that 'we have chosen to respond to major
unlawful violence, not by stopping that violence, but by trying to provide relief to the suffering. But our choice of policy allows the suffering
to continue.'[115]

---

[112] See Human Rights Watch, *Bosnia-Herzegovina: The Fall of Srebrenica and the Failure of UN
Peacekeeping* (Washington DC: Human Rights Watch, 1995), D. Rodhe, *A Safe Area:
Srebrenica: Europe's Worst Massacre Since the Second World War* (New York: Simon and
Schuster, 1997), and *Report of the Secretary-General: The Fall of Srebrenica*, A/54/549, 15
November 1999. See also G. Peress and E. Stover, *The Graves: Forensic Efforts in Srebrenica
and Vukovar* (Zurich: Scalo, 1998).

[113] See *Report of the Secretary-General: The Fall of Srebrenica*, A/54/549, 15 November 1999.

[114] Barutciski, 'The Reinforcement of Non-Admission Policies', 89–90.

[115] R. Higgins, 'The New United Nations and Former Yugoslavia' (1993) 69 *International
Affairs* 465 at 469.

Over-emphasis on assistance to the detriment of protection

The main international response to the crisis was, as described above, the provision of humanitarian aid. Resources were thus focused on humanitarian aid, and especially on the delivery of food which was seen as the 'top priority'.[116] Sarajevo airport was reopened to allow for the airlifting of emergency items, and food was also brought to besieged areas. As a result, few people died of starvation in Bosnia and Herzegovina, and nobody can deny that this was not a success for the humanitarian organisations whose staff took considerable risks to bring food to people.[117] During the war, nowhere in Bosnia and Herzegovina was there a severe food shortage (except in some Muslim enclaves such as Gorazde or Srebrenica).[118] However, the main cause of displacement was not starvation, but attacks on physical security. As a result, the provision of food did not prevent displacement.[119]

Because of the over-emphasis on food and emergency relief in general, protection aspects were sometimes overlooked. Before the end of the war, it was already noted that 'protection suffered from the relative lack of priority it was accorded, particularly as contrasted with assistance efforts'.[120] As a result, few active interventions were undertaken by UNPROFOR or humanitarian agencies to protect people at risk of abuse. UNPROFOR was reluctant to use force against the warring parties because this might jeopardise humanitarian access. This was for instance the concern of the military commander of UNPROFOR in Bosnia and Herzegovina in 1994.[121] Priority was not given to the monitoring and reporting of human rights violations either. Human rights field officers were dispatched to the region to report and investigate allegations of human rights violations, but no permanent presence was established in Bosnia and Herzegovina until the spring of 1994. Even then, that presence remained very limited.[122]

---

[116] See Minear et al., Humanitarian Action in the Former Yugoslavia, 53.
[117] See Burg and Shoup, The War in Bosnia-Herzegovina, 399.
[118] See B. Frelick, 'Assistance Without Protection: Feed the Hungry, Clothe the Naked, and Watch Them Die', World Refugee Survey 1997, 24 at 26.
[119] See Mooney, 'Presence, Ergo Protection?', 430.
[120] See Minear et al., Humanitarian Action in the Former Yugoslavia, 25.
[121] See M. Rose, 'Field Coordination of UN Humanitarian Assistance, Bosnia, 1994', in J. Whitman and D. Pocock (eds.), After Rwanda: The Coordination of UN Humanitarian Assistance (London: Macmillan, 1996), 149–60 at 156.
[122] See Ninth Periodic Report on the Situation of Human Rights in the Territory of the Former Yugoslavia, A/49/641, S/1994/1252, 4 November 1994, para. 3, and Situation of Human Rights in the Territory of the Former Yugoslavia, E/CN.4/1995/57, 16 January 1995, para. 121.

In the situation in which UNPROFOR was unable or unwilling to use force to protect civilians, and the then UN Centre of Human Rights did not have the resources to establish a stronger human rights field presence, the protection task was basically left to UNHCR and other aid agencies. These agencies often had neither the expertise nor the capacity to engage in more direct protection activities. The mere presence of UNHCR in the field had a limited protective impact.[123] Although the presence of international aid agencies was not itself a form of protection, it has been argued that the humanitarian presence still served the important function of bearing witness to the human rights abuses which were taking place.[124] Agencies such as UNHCR and ICRC kept reports of violations of international humanitarian and human rights law.[125] These reports have been used by the International Criminal Tribunal for the former Yugoslavia (ICTY), although, ironically, the ICRC refused to share information with the Tribunal because of its policy of confidentiality. The Trial Chamber of the ICTY decided that the ICRC has a right to non-disclosure of information under customary international law and need not testify before the Tribunal.[126] The same rule will apply with regard to the International Criminal Court.[127] In contrast, and as a departure from its traditional practice, UNHCR developed close relations with the media to get reports of abuses publicly reported.[128]

The humanitarian operation saved many lives, but it also probably prolonged the conflict.[129] In the long term, protection of the civilians could only be truly achieved through a resolution of the conflict. However, part of the humanitarian aid ended up feeding the combatants of all sides. Aid workers were often aware of this phenomenon, as it was they who for instance consciously gave more food to Bosnian Serbs than to the other warring parties in exchange for a right of passage.[130] It is impossible to assess what percentage of the humanitarian aid was

---

[123] See Mooney, 'Presence, Ergo Protection?', 422–3.
[124] See Young, 'UNHCR and ICRC in the Former Yugoslavia', 785.   [125] Ibid., 786.
[126] See Prosecutor v. Simic et al., Case No. IT-95-9, Decision on the prosecution motion under rule 73 for a ruling concerning the testimony of a witness, 27 July 1999 and Decision denying request for assistance in securing documents and witnesses from the International Committee of the Red Cross, 7 June 2000. See also S. Jeannet, 'Recognition of the ICRC's Long-Standing Rule of Confidentiality – An Important Decision by the International Criminal Tribunal for the Former Yugoslavia' (2000) 838 International Review of the Red Cross 403.
[127] See Rules of Procedure and Evidence, ICC-ASP/1/3, sub-rules 73.4 to 73.6.
[128] See Young, 'UNHCR and ICRC in the Former Yugoslavia', 802.
[129] See Burg and Shoup, The War in Bosnia-Herzegovina, 398.
[130] See Frelick, 'Assistance Without Protection', 26.

diverted from the intended beneficiaries. It would be unfair to argue that no humanitarian aid should have been delivered because a certain amount of aid is in any case diverted to supporting the combatants in each emergency crisis.[131] The difference is that such diversion of aid is usually 'inadvertent', while in the present case, it was consciously agreed to. Aid workers were confronted with the dilemma of refusing to negotiate humanitarian access with the risk of losing that access, or negotiating with the knowledge that part of the aid would support the armed forces.[132]

To a certain extent, the over-emphasis on assistance to the detriment of human rights protection was also evidenced by the reaction of the Commission on Human Rights. In response to media reports which showed thousands of men being detained in camps in northern and eastern Bosnia, an emergency session of the Commission on Human Rights was convened on 13–14 August 1992 at the initiative of the United States. The Commission appointed a Special Rapporteur on the former Yugoslavia who was to submit periodic reports 'as the situation warrants'. These reports were made available to the Security Council, but also to the International Conference for the former Yugoslavia.[133] A second emergency session of the Commission was convened in November 1992 at the initiative of Turkey. Although internal displacement was not the focus of the Special Rapporteur's mandate, he showed some concern for IDP protection issues, and the Special Representative on Internally Displaced Persons accompanied him on his second mission to the region in October 1992.[134] However, the Special Rapporteur was never given enough resources to be able to put enough field officers on the ground. Despite limited resources, a team of medical experts was still sent to Bosnia and Herzegovina in January 1993 to collect evidence on allegations of mass rape.[135]

---

[131] See B. Barber, 'Feeding Refugees, or War? The Dilemma of Humanitarian Aid' (1997) 76:4 *Foreign Affairs* 8.

[132] See Minear *et al.*, *Humanitarian Action in the Former Yugoslavia*, 121–5, and M. Cutts, 'The Humanitarian Operation in Bosnia, 1992–95: Dilemmas in Negotiating Humanitarian Access', UNHCR Working Paper No. 8, May 1999, http://www.unhcr.ch/refworld/pub/wpapers/wpno8.htm.

[133] See CHR Res. S-1/1, 14 August 1992.

[134] See K. E. Kenny, 'Formal and Informal Innovations in the United Nations Protection of Human Rights: The Special Rapporteur on the Former Yugoslavia' (1995) 48 *Austrian Journal of Public International Law* 19 at 47.

[135] See *Report of the Team of Experts on Their Mission to Investigate Allegations of Rape in the Territory of the Former Yugoslavia from 12 to 23 January 1993*, E/CN.4/1993/50, Annex II, 10 February 1993.

The mandate of the Special Representative had clear limits, because his intervention could only be *reactive*. He and the field officers were only able to denounce human rights violations, and were not in a position to protect civilians from abuses. The appointment of the Special Representative resulted from the fact that external powers wanted to be seen to be doing something to stop human rights violations in Bosnia and Herzegovina. Such a measure could not in itself have protected civilians. The events in Srebrenica in July 1995 prompted the Special Representative to denounce the lack of commitment to the protection of the safe areas and resign from his position.[136]

Manipulation of UNHCR?

As mentioned earlier, the Secretary-General requested UNHCR to lead the humanitarian effort in the region, and the agency agreed.[137] Goodwin-Gill argues that it should not have done so,[138] because the agency is not directly accountable to the Secretary-General, but to the General Assembly through the Economic and Social Council (ECOSOC).[139] The agency was soon 'pushed into a vacuum where there [was] no overall UN strategy',[140] because Western states preferred to fund emergency relief programmes rather than tackle the problem more directly. The High Commissioner for Refugees repeated on many occasions that the humanitarian effort should not be used as a substitute for a political response to solve the conflict.[141] UNHCR appeared to be manipulated into spearheading the humanitarian effort in Bosnia and Herzegovina so that external powers could be seen to be doing something.[142]

Although humanitarian considerations seemed to prevail over all others, UNHCR concerns were overlooked when the UN defined policies which had a direct impact on its work on the ground. The clearest example concerns the issue of sanctions,[143] upon which UNHCR was not

---

[136] See *Letter Dated 27 July 1995 Addressed by Mr Tadeusz Mazowiecki to the Chairman of the Commission on Human Rights*, E/CN.4/1996/9, Annex 1, 22 August 1995.

[137] See p. 167 above.   [138] See Goodwin-Gill, 'Refugee Identity', 227.

[139] See Article 11 of UNHCR's Statute, Annex to GA Res. 428, 14 December 1950.

[140] Cunliffe and Pugh, 'The Politicization of UNHCR', 138.

[141] See for instance S. Ogata, 'The Interface Between Peacekeeping and Humanitarian Action', Statement by the United Nations High Commissioner for Refugees at the International Colloquium on New Dimensions of Peacekeeping at the Graduate Institute of International Studies, Geneva, 11 March 1994.

[142] See Young, 'UNHCR and ICRC in the Former Yugoslavia', 788.

[143] Imposed by SC Res. 757, 30 May 1992, and confirmed by SC Res. 820, 17 April 1993.

consulted, and which directly affected its work.[144] In addition, UNHCR's efforts were not coordinated with political initiatives to solve the crisis.[145] In some ways, UNHCR was 'trapped in a no-win situation'.[146] Without the prospect of a resolution of the conflict, the agency was to continue its operations for an undefined period. Humanitarian aid could have been used as a point of leverage on the warring parties. Indeed, the threat to suspend aid might have helped to negotiate access to victims or push the warring parties into ceasing attacks on UNHCR staff. In February 1993, the High Commissioner temporarily suspended relief operations to 'protest against the politicisation of aid by all sides'.[147] Such an initiative was thwarted by the Secretary-General, and aid delivery was resumed a few days later.[148]

As UNHCR became overwhelmed by its task of coordinating the humanitarian effort in Bosnia and Herzegovina, little time or resources were left for protection activities. This incompatibility between the two roles has led some commentators to denounce the role of UNHCR as lead agency as inappropriate.[149] Others believe that the lead agency model should be applied in all complex emergencies.[150] UNHCR was left to deal with the crisis on its own, a task which was beyond its capacities. The minimal involvement of the Department of Humanitarian Affairs (DHA), which was supposed to have coordination functions, did not contribute to alleviating the burden on UNHCR.[151]

An implicit acceptance of the partition of Bosnia and Herzegovina

From very early on, the conflict in Bosnia and Herzegovina was interpreted by external powers as an ethnic conflict, which influenced the way they would try to deal with it. Indeed, the various peace plans proposed to the warring parties were not well conceptualised, as there was no clear choice between a unitary and a partitioned Bosnia and

---

[144] See S. A. Cunliffe and M. Pugh, 'UNHCR as Leader in Humanitarian Assistance: A Triumph of Politics over Law?', in Nicholson and Twomey (eds.), *Refugee Rights and Realities*, 175–99 at 196.

[145] See Minear *et al.*, *Humanitarian Action in the Former Yugoslavia*, 72.

[146] Mendiluce, 'War and Disaster in the Former Yugoslavia'.

[147] See Ogata, 'UNHCR in the Balkans', 194.

[148] See Weiss and Pasic, 'Dealing with the Displacement ', 214, and Frelick, 'Assistance Without Protection', 25.

[149] See Cunliffe and Pugh, 'UNHCR as Leader', 197.

[150] See Weiss and Pasic, 'Reinventing UNHCR', 52–3.

[151] See Minear *et al.*, *Humanitarian Action in the Former Yugoslavia*, 109.

Herzegovina. The only point of agreement between the international negotiators was that the country should not be carved up between Serbia and Croatia, as they had already recognised Bosnia and Herzegovina as an independent and sovereign state. External powers were pursuing two contradictory strategies. On the one hand, they strongly condemned policies of ethnic cleansing, but, on the other hand, successive peace plans took into account territorial gains which had been consolidated by such policies. Woodward rightly observes that 'the major powers with soldiers on the ground argued that the territorial gains of ethnic armies were largely irreversible and that ethnic partition (preferably within Bosnia-Herzegovina because they had also recognised its sovereignty and territorial integrity) was inevitable'.[152] She also argues that no representatives other than nationalist politicians were called to participate in the peace negotiations.[153]

The peace plan which came closest to being accepted by all warring parties was the Vance–Owen Plan which was sponsored jointly by the UN and the EU at the beginning of 1993. The plan sought to retain a multi-ethnic Bosnia and Herzegovina by creating ten provinces in which all three ethnic groups would be represented. Each province would have a governor from the majority community, a vice-governor from the second largest group, and the composition of the ten-person government would reflect the ethnic composition of the province according to the 1991 census.[154] The US never supported the Vance–Owen Plan,[155] which was rejected anyway by the Bosnian Serbs in May 1993, because they wanted contiguous ethnically homogeneous territories.[156]

After the demise of the Vance–Owen Plan, the Americans and the Europeans agreed to negotiate some form of partition of Bosnia and Herzegovina.[157] The ethnic logic adopted by the negotiating parties only encouraged each group to continue to seek the internal displacement of populations. The warring parties knew that the repartition of territory resulting from the war (and not the 1991 census) would be taken into account in new peace plans.[158] As a result, it was an incentive for each warring party to make new territorial gains and consolidate recent ones before a new peace proposal was made. Moreover, each new draft peace plan involving territorial shifts seemed to have induced population displacement in the areas concerned.[159]

---

[152] See Woodward, *Balkan Tragedy*, 9.
[153] See Weiss and Pasic, 'Dealing with the Displacement', 212–13.
[154] See Gow, *Triumph of the Lack of Will*, 238–9.   [155] *Ibid.*, 248–53.
[156] See Burg and Shoup, *The War in Bosnia-Herzegovina*, 249.   [157] *Ibid.*, 263.
[158] See for instance *ibid.*, 235.   [159] See Ogata, 'UNHCR in the Balkans', 199, note 12.

The evolution from the Vance–Owen map to the Dayton map, via the Owen–Stoltenberg map (September 1993) and the Contact Group map (July 1994),[160] shows how the idea of internal partition gradually came into being.[161] In retrospect, the Dayton map does look more sustainable to the extent that it provides for contiguous territories (with the exception of Brcko), whereas previous maps might have been unworkable in the short term. If a 51%-49% deal was to be reached in order to achieve a balance of power between Croats and Muslims on the one hand and Serbs on the other, the Americans, now leading the negotiations, had two tasks. The first one was to convince Bosnian Croats and Muslims to form a Federation. Such an alliance was concluded by the Washington Agreement signed in March 1994, but it must be said that cooperation between the two parties has always remained difficult. Secondly, the Federation had to make more territorial gains in order to justify it being given 51 per cent of the territory. The Croats were thus encouraged by the Americans to take some important cities in northern Bosnia.[162]

Large movements of population took place during the Croat offensive in 1995. Perhaps the major powers believed that such 'transfers' of population were the price to be paid for partition and peace in Bosnia and Herzegovina. People internally displaced in the summer of 1995 were thus displaced with the tacit acceptance of major powers, but as long as they remained within their own country, this did not have major consequences for Western countries. These countries could not however accept internal displacement taking place on too large a scale (except for Sarajevo), and thus refused to let Croat forces take Banja Luka which was the second largest Serb city in the country.[163] One may conclude that internally displaced persons became pawns in the race to obtain the map which would lead to the American-sponsored peace settlement. It was considered that no peace deal could be brokered without some further population movements.

At the time when partition was proposed, some commentators already predicted that such a proposal would mean more displacement,[164] and, indeed, further movements of population took place following the signature of the Dayton Peace Agreement. As expected, the two entities, the

---

[160] See the maps in Silber and Little, *Yugoslavia*, 11–14.
[161] See D. Campbell, 'Apartheid Cartography: The Political Anthropology and Spatial Effects of International Diplomacy in Bosnia' (1999) 18 *Political Geography* 395 at 402–16.
[162] See Holbrooke, *To End a War*, 160.   [163] *Ibid.*, 160 and 168.
[164] See Mendiluce, 'War and Disaster in the Former Yugoslavia'.

Muslim–Croat Federation and the Republika Srpska, started to function independently from each other, each having some of the main attributes of a classic state with its own army and government, and using its own currency. Although a convertible Mark (equivalent to one Deutschmark, which was the currency most valued in the country) had been introduced as the national currency, Yugoslav dinars were still in use in parts of the Republika Srpska, as well as the Croatian kuna in Croat-inhabited parts of the Federation. The internal partition of the country also meant that the prospects of return for internally displaced persons were diminished.

Kumar has argued that external powers revived the idea of partition as a response to ethnic conflict, and attempted to promote a new application of this 'principle'. However, she believed that such internal partition could not lead to peace and stability.[165] Waters, by contrast, was of the opinion that ethnic partition was the best guarantee for stability at the time.[166] Nevertheless, one could argue that external powers considered internal partition as the only way to stop the conflict in 1995 because they had followed the ethnic logic imposed by the warring parties.

Recreating the pre-war Bosnia and Herzegovina?

A central aspect of the Dayton Peace Agreement is spelt out in Annex 7, the agreement on refugees and displaced persons, whose first article states that:

All refugees and displaced persons have the right freely to return to their homes of origin. They shall have the right to have restored to them their property of which they were deprived in the course of hostilities since 1991 and to be compensated for any property that cannot be restored to them. The early return of refugees and displaced persons is an important objective of the settlement of the conflict in Bosnia and Herzegovina.

By imposing an annex on the return of refugees and displaced persons in the Dayton Peace Agreement, the major powers made a commitment to reverse the policies of ethnic cleansing carried out during the war. Return and reintegration of refugees and internally displaced persons has recently become an integral part of the peace-building effort within

---

[165] See R. Kumar, *Divide and Fall? Bosnia and the Annals of Partition* (London: Verso, 1997).
[166] See T. W. Waters, 'The Naked Land: The Dayton Accords, Property Disputes, and Bosnia's Real Constitution' (1999) 40 *Harvard International Law Journal* 517 at 592–3.

UN operations.[167] It is worth noting that Annex 7 was the first international agreement to state in specific terms that not only should refugees be able to return to their country of origin, but also that refugees and internally displaced persons should be able to return to their pre-war homes.[168] Traditionally, the work of UNHCR was limited to repatriation to the country of origin, and did not go as far as to assist each refugee to return to his or her own *home*. The promotion of refugee and IDP return is a direct response to the systematic policies of ethnic cleansing, and constitutes the international organisations' main strategy for recreating a multi-ethnic country. One cannot but notice a reversal of strategy pursued by the major powers after the war, and this could have been perceived by people in Bosnia and Herzegovina as an expression of guilt for not having stopped campaigns of ethnic cleansing during the war.

It is somewhat paradoxical that the Agreement institutionalises the ethnic division of the country by creating two entities, and, on the other hand, promotes the return of refugees and displaced persons to recreate a multi-ethnic country.[169] In fact, the second task is crucial for the stability of Bosnia and Herzegovina, to the extent that refugee and IDP return should ensure that the creation of the two entities does not lead to ethnic partition. In this regard, UNHCR has reaffirmed that:

The underlying rationale for this position [Article I of Annex 7] in international law is grounded in the fact that peace-building, peace consolidation and the creation of secure and stable conditions in [Bosnia and Herzegovina] are related to reversing the effects of ethnic cleansing, that is, forced displacement to gain effective control over territory, which was the prime objective of the conflict.[170]

One must therefore place Annex 7 within the overall reconstruction and stabilisation effort in Bosnia and Herzegovina. It is assumed that without the return of refugees and internally displaced persons, peace will never be achieved in the country. This has had important implications for other UN operations, especially in Kosovo. Annex 7 set an

---

[167] See E. Rosand, 'The Right to Return under International Law Following Mass Dislocation: The Bosnia Precedent?' (1998) 19 *Michigan Journal of International Law* 1091 at 1120.

[168] See M. Garlick, 'Protection for Property Rights: A Partial Solution? The Commission for Real Property Claims of Displaced Persons and Refugees (CRPC) in Bosnia and Herzegovina' (2000) 19:3 *Refugee Survey Quarterly* 64 at 68.

[169] See M. Cox, 'The Dayton Agreement in Bosnia and Herzegovina: A Study of Implementation Strategies' (1999) 70 *British Yearbook of International Law* 201 at 204–5.

[170] UNHCR, *Update of UNHCR's Position on Categories of Persons from Bosnia and Herzegovina Who Are in Continued Need of International Protection*, May 1999, Sarajevo, para. 1.4.

extremely ambitious objective – to return more than two million people to their homes. If this objective is not achieved, it is the whole authority of the United Nations which is challenged. Failure to return people to their homes in Bosnia and Herzegovina would have meant that agreements similar to the Dayton Peace Agreement would not be promoted, or at least that future operations might take a different conceptual approach and not attempt to promote return in an ethnically divided country. On the other hand, success would 'establish a strong precedent for [a] broadened right to return under international law'.[171] The analysis of the implementation of Annex 7 in the next section is therefore relevant not only in the context of the international intervention in Bosnia and Herzegovina, but also, and more importantly, for future UN operations in post-conflict situations.

In order to assist people to return, massive financial and human resources have been invested in the country. In the early years following the Dayton Peace Agreement, more than a hundred international organisations were operating there, and virtually all of them were involved in the return process. Most of these organisations clearly put the emphasis on minority returns, which involve persons returning to areas where they would now belong to the minority group. Majority returns, which involve persons returning to areas controlled by their own ethnic group, have been much less problematic.

Reversing ethnic cleansing: strategies for the return of refugees and internally displaced persons

Initial obstacles to minority returns (1996–2000)

Between 1992 and 1996, more than two million persons fled their homes in Bosnia and Herzegovina, which meant that potentially the same number of people may want to return to their pre-war homes. It was therefore crucial to ensure that such returns took place in an organised manner. Return to Bosnia and Herzegovina has been a very complex process requiring the coordination of all the actors involved, i.e. returnees, persons currently occupying their property, local authorities and, if required, international organisations. The political environment in which the return process has taken place has not always been the most conducive to cooperation between all the actors.

---

[171] Rosand, 'The Right to Return', 1095.

After the end of the war, procedures were put in place to deal with applications for return. However, these were not uniform throughout the country, and also varied from one organisation to another. It was only in 1998, when the political environment allowed it, that return procedures were standardised under pressure from, and with the support of, UNHCR. Each entity passed a set of Instructions which are almost identical to each other.[172] A state Instruction was also adopted to facilitate inter-entity returns.[173]

When a person decides to return to his pre-war home, the procedure is as follows. First, an application form for voluntary return must be completed, in which personal data, data about other returning family members and data related to the former home must be provided. On the basis of the information provided, a team of local officials carries out an assessment on the property. This assessment involves checking whether the property is undamaged, damaged or destroyed, evaluating the cost of repairing or reconstructing the house, and checking the occupancy status (i.e. whether someone else is occupying the property). A decision is then reached on the case. The returnee and his family will only be able to return home when all works are carried out on the property and/or the occupants have been evicted.

In the years following the Dayton Peace Agreement, this process was partly functioning in the Muslim–Croat Federation, and barely functioning in the Republika Sprska. Indeed, local authorities often lacked the capacity to carry out the assessments themselves, and it was therefore important to pursue the process of institution-building. The relevant institutions have now been created in each municipality to deal with applications for voluntary return, but there have still been problems in the implementation of the Instructions on return. Some municipalities have obstructed the process by illegally charging returnees fees, or demanding they submit additional documentation.[174] At least, as of 1998, the procedures have been in place, and it has been more a

---

[172] *Instruction on the Method of Organising the Return of Displaced Persons and Repatriates for the Territory of the Federation of Bosnia and Herzegovina*, Bosnia and Herzegovina Official Gazette, No. 6/98. 9 March 1998, and the Republika Srpska, *Instruction on the Method of Organising the Return of Displaced Persons and Repatriates for the Territory of the Republika Srpska*, Republika Srpska Official Gazette, No. 18/98, 8 June 1998.

[173] See *Instruction on the Return of Bosnian Refugees and Displaced Persons to/within the Territory of Bosnia and Herzegovina*, Bosnia and Herzegovina Official Gazette, No. 22/99, 15 December 1999.

[174] Global IDP Database, *Profile of Internal Displacement: Bosnia and Herzegovina*, January 2003, 125–6.

matter of implementing the provisions. In addition, laws dealing with the treatment and return of refugees and internally displaced persons were drafted with the cooperation of UNHCR[175] and adopted in both entities and at the state level.[176]

Despite the existence of procedures and legislation dealing with the return of refugees and internally displaced persons, there were initially very few minority returns taking place. This can be explained by several factors which range from security problems, socio-economic factors, discrimination against returnees and local political obstruction. Return strategies had to go beyond the mere reconstruction or repair of houses and address these protection problems.

One of the first problems to address was the issue of security. There have been numerous incidents against people returning to areas where they belonged to a minority group.[177] These have included physical attacks on returnees and damage to their property. The presence of SFOR units (NATO-led Stabilisation Force) in potential trouble spots for minority returns has often acted as a deterrent.[178] In the case of minority returns which were likely not to be well accepted by the local population, UNHCR has sometimes asked SFOR to patrol the area the day before the planned return and for a few days after to prevent attacks on returnees. In addition, the International Police Task Force (IPTF) has pursued its training of local police forces, and has pushed for the inclusion of minority groups within these forces in areas of minority returns. In 1998, only 1.17 per cent of police officers in the Muslim–Croat Federation police force were Bosnian Serb, while 2.77 per cent of the police officers in the Republika Srpska were Bosnian Croats or Muslims.[179] An increase in the proportion of police officers from minority groups

---

[175] See UNHCR, *Update of UNHCR's Position on Categories of Persons from Bosnia and Herzegovina in Need of International Protection*, August 2000, 6.

[176] See *Law on Displaced-Expelled Persons and Repatriates in the Federation of Bosnia and Herzegovina*, Bosnia and Herzegovina Official Gazette, No. 19/2000, 26 May 2000; *Law on Displaced Persons, Refugees and Returnees in the Republika Srpska*, Republika Srpska Official Gazette, No. 33/99, 26 November 1999; and *Law on Refugees from Bosnia and Herzegovina and Displaced Persons in Bosnia and Herzegovina*, Bosnia and Herzegovina Official Gazette, No. 23/99, 23 December 1999.

[177] See Global IDP Database, *Profile of Internal Displacement*, 29–30.

[178] See A. Ito, 'Politicisation of Minority Return in Bosnia and Herzegovina – The First Five Years Examined' (2001) 13 *International Journal of Refugee Law* 98 at 119.

[179] See *Situation of Human Rights in the Former Yugoslavia: Report of the Special Rapporteur*, E/CN.4/1999/42, 20 January 1999, para. 27.

(10 per cent)[180] has helped to improve the confidence of potential returnees in the local police force, which constitutes an important factor for minority returns.[181] Despite some exceptions, the overall incidence of security problems linked to minority returns has diminished dramatically in recent years.[182] It must finally be noted that the high-profile SFOR arrests of well-known war criminals indicted by the ICTY has encouraged minority returns to places such as the Prijedor area which had witnessed many atrocities during the war.[183]

The problem is not just about whether people return or not to a repaired house, but about the quality of life in the minority area. People do not want to return to places where they have no economic prospects. The Bosnian economy has slowly recovered from the war, but, for a long time, one could argue that it did not even exist, having been integrated into the overall economy of the former Yugoslavia and specialising in heavy industries which were destroyed during the war. In 2000, unemployment was estimated by the Office of the High Representative (OHR) to be above 40 per cent.[184] The economic gap between the two entities may explain why many displaced persons who had fled to the Muslim–Croat Federation had no interest in returning to economically depressed areas in the Republika Srpska.[185] Even within the Federation, there has been quite a difference between the western part whose local economy was almost integrated with the comparatively rich Croatian economy,[186] and other areas of central Bosnia. Some displaced Croats who used to live in central Bosnia and fled to western Bosnia, enjoyed a standard of living which they could not enjoy anywhere else in the country. In a country where economic resources are scarce, this has represented a strong incentive not to return to areas of origin.

Another important factor which explains the lack of return is the traditional opposition between town and country. The war contributed to accelerating the natural phenomenon of migration to urban centres.

---

[180] See International Crisis Group, *The Continuing Challenge of Refugee Return in Bosnia and Herzegovina*, ICG Balkans Report No. 137, Sarajevo/Brussels, 13 December 2002, 17.

[181] See *Report of the Secretary-General on the United Nations Mission in Bosnia and Herzegovina*, S/2002/1314, 2 December 2002, para. 24.

[182] See International Crisis Group, *The Continuing Challenge of Refugee Return in Bosnia and Herzegovina*, 18.

[183] *Ibid.*, 26.

[184] See UNHCR, *Update of UNHCR's Position on Categories of Persons 2000*, 11.

[185] See D. Chandler, *Bosnia: Faking Democracy after Dayton* (London: Pluto Press, 1999), 106.

[186] See Cox, 'The Dayton Agreement', 213.

Bosnia and Herzegovina used to be a mainly rural country. Most displaced persons found refuge in urban areas, and it now appears that some of them, especially the younger generation, do not wish to return to the rural areas, because they have got used to the more 'exciting' urban way of life. Job opportunities are also more numerous in cities. As a result, most of the people who returned to villages in the immediate post-war period were older people who were more attached to their homes.[187] In the longer term, this may raise a problem of availability of labour in the countryside. It is thus crucial that international efforts are also directed at making return sustainable by supporting the local economy in the areas of return. However, as such movements of population take place in all industrialised societies and are not directly linked to the war, they may prove irreversible. Migration to urban centres usually accompanies the transition from a rural economy to an industrialised economy and would therefore have happened in Bosnia and Herzegovina had no war taken place.[188]

The factors mentioned above apply equally to all displaced, but some affect more particularly people wishing to return to areas where they would belong to the minority. Difficult as it is to find employment anywhere in Bosnia and Herzegovina, it is especially so for minority groups. Employment discrimination is a widespread phenomenon in the country, and it is extremely difficult for members of a minority group to find employment in the return area.[189] In response to this problem, labour legislation has now been reformed to include new anti-discrimination clauses.[190] Returnees also face other forms of discrimination. There are numerous stories of people being illegally charged fees to have the electricity or telephone connection restored to their former home. Some returnees have been presented with bills for electricity or gas consumed by war-time occupants.[191] In addition, parents may not want to send their children to the local school which teaches the nationally specific curriculum corresponding to the majority group in the area.[192] Finally,

---

[187] Ibid., 232.

[188] See E. Rosand, 'The Right to Compensation in Bosnia: An Unfulfilled Promise and a Challenge to International Law' (2000) 33 Cornell International Law Journal 113 at 124.

[189] See International Crisis Group, The Continuing Challenge of Refugee Return in Bosnia and Herzegovina, 14–15.

[190] See UNHCR, Update of UNHCR's Position on Categories of Persons from Bosnia and Herzegovina in Need of International Protection, September 2001, 23.

[191] Ibid., 20.

[192] See International Crisis Group, The Continuing Challenge of Refugee Return in Bosnia and Herzegovina, 19–20.

returnees also encounter problems of access to pensions, health care and other social benefits.

The social and economic environment has made minority returns more difficult, but it is political obstruction from local authorities which has constituted the main obstacle to minority returns. The central government in Bosnia and Herzegovina is weak, and power is mainly located at the level of the canton and the municipality which is the basic administrative unit. The return situation in a given municipality has often depended on the attitude of those in charge in that municipality. It has been at this level that political obstruction to minority returns operates, but with the implicit approval and encouragement of higher authorities. It must be noted that most people in power in the country are still the same as those who led the country during the war.[193] These people, who often carried out the policies of ethnic cleansing themselves, have been most reluctant to support minority returns.

Political obstruction has operated on different levels. Several examples have already been mentioned above, i.e. the administration not following the correct procedures, local firms not employing returnees, public services not being made available to them or with hidden charges, and especially eviction orders not being executed. Some local authorities have tried everything in their power to prevent minorities from returning. Political obstruction can also take more subtle forms. Local politicians aware of an imminent return of minorities have used the press to warn the local population of this, and discreetly organised 'spontaneous' riots against the returnees.[194] Following the instructions of the local authorities, the local police has not always intervened to protect the returnees.[195]

Politicians have often argued that they could only accept minority returns if their counterparts accepted the same number of minority returns. This argument cannot be held as valid as most movements of populations were not exchanges of populations between two areas. Such demands for reciprocity were based on self-interest; they were only used to justify a deadlock in minority returns and shift the responsibility for this deadlock to the other side.[196] It has therefore been important

---

[193] See Cox, 'The Dayton Agreement', 205.
[194] See Amnesty International, *Bosnia-Herzegovina: Waiting on the Doorstep: Minority Returns to Eastern Republika Srpska* (London: Amnesty International, 2000), 16.
[195] See International Crisis Group, *Going Nowhere Fast: Refugees and Internally Displaced Persons in Bosnia*, ICG Balkans Report No. 23, Sarajevo, 1 May 1997, 34–6.
[196] See Waters, 'The Naked Land', 573–6.

to break the dependence on reciprocity which was always used as an excuse for not accepting minority returns.[197]

It must finally be mentioned that the displaced persons themselves have been victims of political manipulation. Some local authorities did not actually want them to return to their pre-war homes, as it would result in freeing up space for other minority returns, and also in the loss of votes. Politicians knew that displaced persons are often among the most destitute, and are more responsive to nationalist rhetoric. They have thus represented loyal supporters whom local politicians did not want to lose, because it would have weakened their power base. It has therefore been in the personal interest of such politicians to obstruct the return process. What is at stake is a potential modification of the ethnic balance in a given municipality.[198]

Various strategies have been used to overcome local political opposition to minority returns. One of the most high-profile was the Open Cities initiative launched by UNHCR in 1997. It consisted in granting 'Open City' status to a municipality which had declared (rather than shown) a 'genuine' commitment to accept minority returns.[199] In exchange, this municipality received increased support from international organisations and in particular additional funding. If the municipality did not live up to its commitment of allowing more minority returns, it could be de-recognised by UNHCR. For instance, Vosgosca was de-recognised in October 1998.[200] More than a dozen cities had been recognised as Open Cities, while, as of 15 July 1999, UNHCR had funded numerous projects in those cities totalling more than US$22 million.[201] However, this did not always result in the municipality being more 'open' to minority returns. The International Crisis Group conducted an evaluation of the project, and compared the numbers of minority returns which took place in the municipalities before and after recognition as an 'Open City'. It discovered that, in some Open Cities, the number of minority returns had not increased after recognition, whereas minority returns continued to take place in cities which had not been granted such status.[202]

---

[197] See International Crisis Group, *Minority Return or Mass Relocation?*, ICG Balkans Report No. 33, Sarajevo, 14 May 1998, 10–11.

[198] See International Crisis Group, *Preventing Minority Return in Bosnia and Herzegovina: The Anatomy of Hate and Fear*, ICG Balkans Report No. 73, Sarajevo, 2 August 1999, 3–4.

[199] See International Crisis Group, *Minority Return or Mass Relocation?*, 20.

[200] See UNHCR, *Open Cities Initiative*, Sarajevo, 1 August 1999, 13.

[201] *Ibid.*, 13.   [202] See International Crisis Group, *Minority Return or Mass Relocation?*, 17.

At the heart of the return process: solving property disputes

Very often, return is wholly dependent on whether the person is able to recover his property. During the war, property legislation was adopted by the various entities to allow people to occupy so-called 'abandoned property'.[203] This legislation which had been maintained after the end of the war obviously favoured the rights of the current occupant (who usually belonged to the ethnic majority of the area) over those of the pre-war occupant seeking to return. Under international pressure, new property legislation suspending the application of these laws was adopted in both entities in 1998,[204] but many difficulties were encountered in its implementation.[205]

The resolution of property issues is one of the main requirements for returns to take place. A specific mechanism was set up immediately after the war to deal with such issues. Annex 7 to the Dayton Peace Agreement envisaged the creation of a commission for displaced persons and refugees (chapter two of the Annex). This body was established as the Commission on Real Property Claims of Displaced Persons and Refugees (CRPC).[206] It is not competent to deal with every aspect of the refugee problem, but more specifically with property issues. Property problems are at the heart of the return process because most of those who left their homes between 1992 and 1996 but who did not go abroad ended up occupying flats or houses abandoned by members of other ethnic groups. Those who now wish to return to their homes thus sometimes find their property being occupied by other displaced persons. Large numbers of people were either forced to sign documents transferring their property to municipal ownership or lost legal documents in the course of the war.[207] It is the task of the CRPC to assist refugees and internally displaced persons to reclaim their property by issuing certificates regarding the identity of legitimate property owners.

The mandate of the CRPC is defined in Article XI of Annex 7. It deals only with real property claims and not with personal property lost

---

[203] See Waters, 'The Naked Land', 519.

[204] See *Law on the Cessation of the Application of the Law on Temporarily Abandoned Real Property Owned by Citizens*, and *Law on the Cessation of the Application of the Law on Abandoned Apartments*, Bosnia and Herzegovina Official Gazette, No. 11/98, 3 April 1998; and *Law on the Cessation of the Application of the Law on the Use of Abandoned Property* was also adopted, Republika Srpska Official Gazette, No. 38/1998, 11 December 1998.

[205] See UNHCR, *Update of UNHCR's Position on Categories of Persons 2000*, 3.

[206] For more detail, see Garlick, 'Protection for Property Rights: A Partial Solution?'.

[207] See Amnesty International, *'Who's Living in My House?' Obstacles to the Safe Return of Refugees and Displaced People* (London: Amnesty International, 1997), 3.

during the war. Between 1996 and 2003, the CRPC received and issued decisions on more than 300,000 claims.[208] The claims are received in person in one of the offices of the CRPC since no claim can be received by post. Since the end of 1997, the CRPC has also opened offices in various other countries to receive claims from refugees.[209] The claims are for both private property owned on 1 April 1992, and flats with an occupancy right exercised on 30 April 1991. In the former Yugoslavia, some flats were 'socially owned', i.e. owned by companies, governmental organs or other social organisations, and rented to employees.[210] A certain number of flats were also set aside for members of the Federal Army (JNA flats) and involve complex property law questions.

The decision issued by the CRPC is final and not subject to appeal. The CRPC has been given wide-ranging powers in order to resolve property claims. Its unrestricted access to all property records in the country[211] has allowed it to gather impressive amounts of information, including a cadastral record of properties in all municipalities.[212] It also has authority to declare invalid any property transfer which was made under duress.[213] Refugees and internally displaced persons wishing to recover their property have emphasised the importance of a CRPC decision that represents 'a certification of their interest which local bodies or officials could not contradict, without firm grounds'.[214] To that extent, the CRPC has been perceived by refugees and internally displaced persons as a neutral legal institution whose decisions reinforce the legitimacy of their property claims.

Despite a difficult start, it appears that the CRPC is now fulfilling its mandate. The implementation of its decisions was initially problematic. By 1999, it appeared that, out of the 50,000 certificates issued by the CRPC, only an extremely small minority of them, 3 per cent according to the International Crisis Group,[215] had resulted in the claimant actually recovering his property. In the great majority of cases, the possession of a CRPC certificate had not enabled claimants to recover lost

---

[208] See http://www.crpc.org.ba/new/en/main.htm.

[209] See H. van Houtte, 'Mass Property Claim Resolution in a Post-War Society – The Commission for Real Property Claims in Bosnia and Herzegovina (CRPC)' (1999) 48 *International Comparative Law Quarterly* 625 at 632.

[210] *Ibid.*, 634.   [211] Annex 7, Article XII.1.

[212] See Garlick, 'Protection for Property Rights: A Partial Solution?', 74.

[213] Annex 7, Article XII.3.

[214] See Garlick, 'Protection for Property Rights: A Partial Solution?', 76.

[215] See International Crisis Group, *Is Dayton Failing?: Bosnia Four Years after the Peace Agreement*, ICG Balkans Report No. 80, Sarajevo, 28 October 1999, 35.

property. In order to ensure the implementation of the CRPC's decisions, the High Representative, who oversees the implementation of the Dayton Peace Agreement, required, by a decision of 27 October 1999, the enactment of a specific law on that subject.[216] Such legislation has greatly improved the rate of implementation of the CRPC's decisions. The CRPC is a unique institution, a 'public international institution'[217] created for very special circumstances. It is central to current international efforts to return people to their previous homes. With the support of the High Representative, the CRPC has finally managed to gain some credibility, and such an approach to the settlement of property claims in post-war societies has now been adopted elsewhere.[218]

Property issues have also been dealt with by other institutions. The Human Rights Chamber is a judicial body established under Annex 6 to the Dayton Peace Agreement. It is composed of fourteen members, eight international and six national. The Chamber hears applications based upon alleged violations of the European Convention on Human Rights[219] or alleged discrimination arising in the enjoyment of the rights provided for in the agreements attached to Annex 6. The Human Rights Chamber has been dealing with a very large number of property cases on the basis of Article 8 of the European Convention on Human Rights (right to respect for private and family life, home and correspondence) and Article 1 of Protocol No. 1[220] to the Convention (right to peaceful enjoyment of one's possessions). In 2000, it was estimated that 80 per cent of pending cases were property-related.[221] The Chamber has on several occasions ordered the relevant authorities 'to take immediate steps to reinstate the applicant into his apartment', i.e. to carry out evictions.[222]

Annex 7 to the Dayton Peace Agreement (Article XI) offered the possibility of just compensation in lieu of property. The creation of a Property Fund was envisaged by Article XIII. In reality, funds for compensation

---

[216] *Decision on the Law on Implementation of the Decisions of the Commission for Real Property Claims of Displaced Persons and Refugees*, 27 October 1999.

[217] Van Houtte, 'Mass Property Claim Resolution', 629.

[218] See for instance S. Leckie, 'Resolving Kosovo's Housing Crisis: Challenges for the UN Housing and Property Directorate', *Forced Migration Review*, vol. 7, April 2000.

[219] *European Convention for the Protection of Human Rights and Fundamental Freedoms*, 4 November 1950, 213 *UNTS* 221.

[220] *First Protocol to the European Convention on Human Rights*, 20 March 1952, 213 *UNTS* 262.

[221] See A. C. Helton, *The Price of Indifference – Refugees and Humanitarian Action in the New Century* (Oxford: Oxford University Press, 2002), 44.

[222] See W. Kälin, *Guiding Principles on Internal Displacement: Annotations* (Washington DC: American Society of International Law and the Brookings Institution, 2000), 73–4.

were never made available by international donors, and the provision has remained a dead letter.[223] One wonders whether 'such an unconditional option to choose compensation might induce refugees not to return to their places of origin'.[224] Some commentators have argued for the implementation of the right to compensation for loss of property.[225] However, such an option was perhaps not considered compatible with the overall strategy of trying to reverse the effects of ethnic cleansing by encouraging return to minority areas.[226] This right has thus not been implemented in Bosnia and Herzegovina, maybe because of the context of the policies of ethnic cleansing.

Even though some refugees and internally displaced persons have managed to prove their ownership rights, they have been prevented from repossessing their properties by the refusal to implement decisions on evictions. Indeed, the great majority of such decisions were not carried out by the local police on the instructions of local politicians. The argument put forward to justify such an attitude was that politicians did not want to put the current occupants on the street, especially when they belonged to their own ethnic group. As a result, they claimed that no eviction should be carried out if no alternative accommodation was provided for the people evicted. This could have been considered a valid argument, but it seemed to be used as an excuse not to carry out evictions in general. Cases of double occupancy and even multiple occupancy resulted from families who continued to occupy abandoned housing units while still retaining ownership of their own property. The large number of cases of double occupancy offered the possibility to carry out evictions which, at least in theory, should not have been problematic. Evictees had alternative accommodation to go to and were in illegal occupation of somebody else's property.

By 1999, progress in the implementation of property legislation had been very limited and, consequently, minority returns were not taking place at the expected rate. Several international bodies operating in Bosnia and Herzegovina, including the Organization for Security and

---

[223] See M. Cox, 'The Right to Return Home: International Intervention and Ethnic Cleansing in Bosnia and Herzegovina' (1998) 47 *International and Comparative Law Quarterly* 599 at 611.

[224] E. Popovic, 'The Impact of International Human Rights Law on the Property Law of Bosnia and Herzegovina' in M. O'Flaherty and G. Gisvold (eds.), *Post-War Protection Human Rights in Bosnia and Herzegovina* (The Hague: Martinus Nijhoff Publishers, 1998), 141–56 at 155.

[225] See Rosand, 'The Right to Compensation in Bosnia'.

[226] See Cox, 'The Right to Return Home', 612.

Cooperation in Europe (OSCE), the UN Mission in Bosnia and Herzegovina (UNMIBH), the Office of the High Representative (OHR), UNHCR and the CRPC, adopted a Property Law Implementation Plan (PLIP) which formulates a unified strategy for overcoming resistance to minority returns.[227] The PLIP seeks to coordinate the efforts of the five international bodies at the local level and to monitor the activities of local housing authorities. The overall aim of the PLIP is to resolve all outstanding property claims by applying the same legal and political pressure to all officials and municipalities across the country.[228] A new approach to property issues was adopted in the PLIP. Indeed, there was a conscious decision to attempt to depoliticise the property issue and reconceptualise it in strictly legal terms.[229] In other words, the resolution of property issues were no longer presented as a tool for reversing ethnic cleansing, but as a neutral application of the rule of law. The success of the PLIP has largely contributed to a major increase in minority returns from 2000 onwards.

Return or relocation?

One must remember that, in the years following the Dayton Peace Agreement, the results were far from encouraging. The majority of the two million people who had fled their homes during the war were still in search of durable solutions. The majority of people had returned to areas controlled by their own ethnic group. In fact, in the early years of the peace process, very few minority returns took place. In particular, virtually no non-Serbs returned to the Republika Srpska. In order to avoid ethnic partition, international efforts were concentrated on trying to return Serb displaced persons to the Muslim–Croat Federation, and Muslim and Croat displaced persons to the Republika Srpska. Minority returns also had to take place within the Federation with Muslims returning to western Bosnia and Croats returning to some areas of central Bosnia.

As of 1999, the bulk of majority returns had already taken place, and almost all the remaining persons in search of permanent solutions were persons who would have been in the minority if they returned to their homes. In 1999, an increasing number of areas opened up to allow small numbers of minority returns. They included for instance Stolac,

---

[227] For an overview of the PLIP, see OSCE, UNMIBH, OHR, UNHCR and CRPC, *Property Law Implementation Plan: Inter-Agency Framework Document*, October 2000.
[228] *Ibid.*, 3.   [229] *Ibid.*, 5.

Table 1 *Minority returns to Bosnia and Herzegovina, 1996–2003.*

Year	Minority returns
1996	11,666
1997	33,837
1998	41,191
1999	41,007
2000	67,445
2001	92,061
2002	102,111
2003	44,868

Source: Minority Returns 2003,
http://www.unhcr.ba/return/T5-min12.pdf.

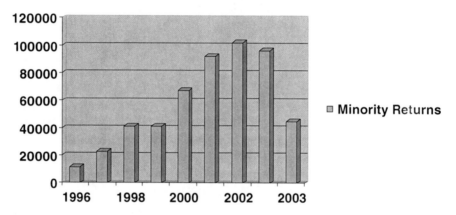

Figure 1 *Minority returns to Bosnia and Herzegovina, 1996–2003*

Drvar, central Bosnia and some areas in the Republika Srpska. Despite the exceptional level of international involvement in the country, the overall progress was still quite slow. Less than 160,000 minority returns had taken place so far, and there were still more than 800,000 internally displaced persons in the country. Moreover, the important breakthrough expected for 1999 did not happen, as the NATO intervention in Kosovo at the end of March (i.e. just when people start returning each year) not only halted the influx of minority returns to the Republika Srpska, but also provoked a substantial transfer of human and financial resources to Kosovo.

The return process was made more difficult with the premature return of refugees from abroad. Although priority had initially been granted to returns of internally displaced persons over refugees, this strategy was soon abandoned. At the end of 1996, Germany which had granted refuge to 345,000 persons from Bosnia and Herzegovina during the war, started to return the majority of these persons,[230] despite pressure from UNHCR not to do so.[231] In 1997, out of the 69,000 refugees returning to Bosnia and Herzegovina, 58,000 of them came from Germany. The phenomenon was accelerated the following year when 90,500 refugees, out of a total return figure of 98,000, were repatriated from Germany.[232] Germany wanted to proceed with the final repatriation of all Bosnian refugees.[233] Such a large-scale return movement from abroad had decisive implications for the return strategies employed in Bosnia and Herzegovina.[234] Most returnees were unable to return to their pre-war homes, and were sent back to situations of internal displacement. In 2001, UNHCR estimated that more than 107,000 out of 379,000 returnees from abroad were unable to return to their pre-war homes and became internally displaced within their country of origin.[235]

Several years into the peace process, it appeared that some people may never be able to return to their homes. This prompted a debate over whether it was actually reasonable for international organisations to insist on people returning to areas where they would now be in the minority. One issue of concern was whether international organisations were not only supporting minority returns, but almost forcing people to return home by not giving them any alternative. Weiner, for instance, questioned international efforts promoting minority returns in an effectively partitioned country.[236] If some displaced persons did not wish to return to areas where they would be ostracised, and face constant

---

[230] See Amnesty International, 'Who's Living in My House?', 13.
[231] See S. Ogata, *Statements by the United Nations High Commissioner for Refugees at the Humanitarian Issues Working Group of the International Conference on Former Yugoslavia*, Geneva, 10 October 1995 and 13 May 1996. See also Humanitarian Issues Working Group, *Background Note, Temporary Protection Following the General Framework Agreement for Peace in Bosnia and Herzegovina*, HIWG/96/2. Annex II, 10 January 1996.
[232] See UNHCR, *Statistical Package*, 1 October 2000.
[233] See Amnesty International, *Waiting on the Doorstep*, 33.
[234] See Cox, 'The Right to Return Home', 622.
[235] See UNHCR, *Update of UNHCR's Position on Categories of Persons 2001*, 1.
[236] See M. Weiner, 'Bad Neighbors, Bad Neighborhoods: An Inquiry into the Causes of Refugee Flows' (1996) 21:1 *International Security* 5 at 38.

harassment, then relocation may be 'the lesser of two evils'.[237] Some displaced persons could not or did not want to return to their pre-war homes, but were still in search of a permanent solution to their plight. In these cases, a possible durable solution could be to help them relocate to areas where they would belong to the majority group. However, 'relocation' was not approved by all international organisations involved in the return process in Bosnia and Herzegovina. Such a strategy was of course highly controversial, because it would have contributed to consolidating the ethnic separation produced by the war. It only differs from the ethnic cleansing referred to earlier in the method used. The result is the same, i.e. people from the same ethnic group are concentrated in the same areas. Until then, the strategy followed by international organisations was to focus on minority returns as the only viable objective of the peace process.

It had appeared though that a certain number of displaced persons did not wish to return to their homes. According to a survey undertaken under the auspices of the CRPC and UNHCR looking at the intentions of refugees and internally displaced persons, in answer to the question 'Would you like to return to your pre-war home?', 64.5 per cent responded yes, 18 per cent no and 17.5 per cent were undecided.[238] Moreover, it also appeared that refugees only returned when they had no other option and could no longer stay in the host country.[239] A curious phenomenon which was relatively widespread, though not widely publicised, was the existence of empty houses which had just been reconstructed or repaired. For instance, in the Central Bosnia Canton alone, around 3,000 repaired houses were reported to be empty in 1999.[240] There were no precise figures. Nevertheless, according to UNHCR, the occupancy rate of property which had been reconstructed was only about 60 per cent.[241] In 2002, there were still about 20 per cent of reconstructed properties which remained empty.[242] Some displaced persons may decide not to move back into their homes, even after expressing the wish to return and signing the contracts with the relevant entities

---

[237] See A. Bayefsky and M. W. Doyle, *Emergency Return: Principles and Guidelines* (Princeton: Center of International Studies, Princeton University, 1999), 31.

[238] See CRPC and UNHCR, *Return, Relocation and Property Rights: A Discussion Paper*, Sarajevo, December 1997, 14.

[239] See International Crisis Group, *Preventing Minority Return*, 11.

[240] See International Crisis Group, *Is Dayton Failing?*, 37.

[241] See Cox, 'The Dayton Agreement', 232.

[242] See International Crisis Group, *The Continuing Challenge of Refugee Return in Bosnia and Herzegovina*, 11.

(canton, municipality, organisation in charge of reconstruction). Some of them resell their properties once they are repaired/repossessed, and do not return to their homes. According to the survey mentioned above, between 45 and 50 per cent of the displaced persons surveyed responded that they would be ready to sell or exchange their properties.[243] Alternatively, some displaced persons have rented out their repossessed properties while waiting to decide whether to return.[244]

Refugees and displaced persons have been strongly encouraged by international organisations to return to their pre-war homes. If they chose to return and requested assistance, they were strongly supported by international organisations, whether in terms of repairing or reconstructing their house and obtaining other means of support, or in applying pressure on the municipality to obtain the eviction of the current occupant. If they chose not to return and instead to start a new life in an area where they belonged to the majority group, they were more likely to receive less support from international organisations. The main reason for this was the emphasis of international organisations on assisting people to return to minority areas. For these organisations, it almost appeared as if minority returns constituted the only indicator of success of the international intervention in Bosnia and Herzegovina. As a result, it was deemed by many international organisations too early to give displaced persons the alternative option of relocation.

In order to justify this position, UNHCR argued that displaced persons were not yet in a position to make a free and informed choice. In fact, if the option of relocation to another area was offered, most people would have chosen to relocate, instead of attempting to return to their pre-war homes. This would have resulted in the consolidation of the ethnic partition of the country. In addition, relocation was sometimes politically motivated and used to consolidate territorial gains made during the war. For instance, some displaced Croats from central Bosnia were encouraged to stay in western Bosnia, and new houses were constructed for them with funds provided by the Government of Croatia.[245] Other types of economic incentives, e.g. the allocation of building plots, have been given to displaced persons to encourage them to settle permanently.[246]

---

[243] See CRPC and UNHCR, *Return, Relocation and Property Rights*, 16.

[244] See International Crisis Group, *The Continuing Challenge of Refugee Return in Bosnia and Herzegovina*, 11.

[245] See International Crisis Group, *Minority Return or Mass Relocation?*, 52.

[246] See International Crisis Group, *The Continuing Challenge of Refugee Return in Bosnia and Herzegovina*, 12.

Relocation has also created further difficulties if people were relocated to empty properties which belonged to other displaced people who wanted to return. One cannot deny that, if the strategy to create the conditions for peace and security in Bosnia and Herzegovina was the reversing of ethnic cleansing, then the emphasis was rightly put on encouraging minority returns. At that stage, it was probably more appropriate to keep trying to convince both displaced persons and municipalities of the benefits of minority returns. In some villages, people reluctantly returned to their homes, but, after a year or so, they found themselves quite satisfied to be back, despite early apprehensions. In other cases, the returnees did not manage to successfully reintegrate into their former community, and sought relocation to an area where they would not be stigmatised for not belonging to the ethnic majority.

The emphasis on minority returns was challenged, even within the ranks of UNHCR itself. This strategy was criticised on the ground that, although people should be free to choose to return or relocate, international organisations only gave them the *option* to return. According to Annex 7 to the Dayton Peace Agreement, 'refugees and displaced persons have the right *freely* to return' (emphasis added), and, whether a displaced person chose to return or relocate, one must ensure that such a choice was entirely voluntary. The central question was whether we could force people who no longer wanted to live together to do so. Answering this question in the negative was interpreted as resignation and acceptance of the ethnic partition of the country. However, forcing people to return to situations in which they could face discrimination and other forms of harassment could have constituted in itself a human rights violation. The approach of international organisations involved in the return process was not always flexible enough. For instance, they could have promoted minority returns, while, at the same time, listened to the displaced persons themselves and helped them find durable solutions when they clearly did not want to return, because of the trauma suffered during the war or for other reasons. UNHCR appeared to accept that it might have to assist some voluntary relocations, whereas the Office of the High Representative was more reluctant to do so.[247]

To some extent, the debate has been settled by the sudden increase in minority returns from 2000 onwards. Five years of constant international pressure seemed to finally produce some substantial results.[248]

---

[247] See Chandler, *Bosnia*, 107–8, and Cox, 'The Right to Return Home', 628–9.
[248] See pp. 201–5 below.

Table 2 *Summary of return to Bosnia and Herzegovina (as of 31 July 2003)*

	Refugees	IDPs
Muslim–Croat Federation	383,270	320,520
Republika Srpska	49,465	189,726
Brcko District	1,964	18,710
Total for Bosnia and Herzegovina	434,699	528,956

Source: Return summary to Bosnia and Herzegovina from 1 January 1996 to 31 July 2003, http://www.unhcr.ba/return/T4-0703.pdf.

Nevertheless, although the implementation of property law has dramatically improved, some displaced persons have returned home only to resell their property. In some cases, only a part of the family, generally the older family members, have returned to the pre-war home.[249] In any case, minority returns may not have taken place on such a scale if displaced persons had been allowed to relocate in the first place.

Increased minority returns (2000–2003)

As evidenced by Figure 1 and Table 1 above, the year 2000 saw a dramatic increase in the number of minority returns. Such success is the result of a combination of international strategies which had over the years become more coordinated, more adapted to the various types of displacement, and more determined in tackling political obstruction. By 2003, around one million refugees and displaced persons had returned to their homes.

There have been numerous international bodies operating in Bosnia and Herzegovina in the post-war period. All were involved in the return process, but there were no mechanisms to coordinate their efforts. The Return and Reconstruction Task Force (RRTF) was set up in 1997 as an inter-agency body whose mandate was to address return issues in an integrated manner. The RRTF comprised the CRPC, the IOM, the OHR, the OSCE, SFOR, UNHCR, UNMIBH, the World Bank, and governmental organisations such as the EC Commission, the German Government and the US Government. Inter-agency coordination was reinforced in one

---

[249] See International Crisis Group, *The Continuing Challenge of Refugee Return in Bosnia and Herzegovina*, 11.

area of particular importance, property law implementation. As mentioned above, the Property Law Implementation Plan was set up in 1999 and has greatly improved the implementation of property laws in the last few years.[250] As of 31 July 2003, it is estimated that up to 86 per cent of property claims have been resolved.[251] This is in stark contrast to the early results which suggested that, in the state of affairs that prevailed at the time, the resolution of all property claims would take much longer. It is now expected that all property claims will be resolved in the near future.

Human displacement in the country covers many different situations, and strategies have gradually been adapted to each particular case. This has required comprehensive knowledge of the local situation. A good example of a programme developed to respond to a local situation was the Return to Central Bosnia Plan, which received political support at the Federation, cantonal and municipality levels.[252] Some displaced persons had not been displaced very far, and were still living in the same canton. It thus made sense to draw up a plan at the cantonal level. When displacement had occurred across the inter-entity boundary line, other strategies had to be used. The same applies to displacement across international boundaries, such as that between Bosnia and Herzegovina and Croatia.

With regard to the latter type of displacement, a regional approach was adopted to deal with refugee returns. In addition to its high population of internally displaced persons, Bosnia and Herzegovina also hosted 30,000 Serb refugees from Croatia who were concentrated in the northern part of the Republika Srpska, especially in urban centres such as Banja Luka.[253] Minority returns to these areas could not take place as long as these refugees did not return to Croatia. These refugees were often among the most virulent opponents to minority returns, because they often occupied the properties belonging to those who had left. Most of the housing stock had not been destroyed in the Krajina area in Croatia, and many houses were still empty, which means that refugees could return there.[254] Croatia also indirectly controlled Croat areas in

---

[250] See p. 195 above.

[251] See UNHCR, OHR, OSCE and CRPC, *Statistics – Implementation of the Property Laws in Bosnia and Herzegovina*, 31 July 2003. For more recent updates, see http://www.unhcr.ba.

[252] UNHCR, *Bosnia and Herzegovina Repatriation and Return Operation 1998*, Geneva, 19.

[253] UNHCR, *Update of UNHCR's Position on Categories of Persons 2000*, 1.

[254] See International Crisis Group, *Minority Return or Mass Relocation?*, 50.

the western part of Bosnia and Herzegovina, where very few minority returns had taken place. It therefore made no sense to target international efforts at Bosnia and Herzegovina alone, and more international pressure had to be exerted on Croatia to allow Croatian Serb refugees to return there. Croatia could also influence the level of minority returns to Croat areas of Bosnia and Herzegovina. However, despite early positive signs, the Croatian Government did not facilitate the return of Croatian Serb refugees.[255]

Within Bosnia and Herzegovina itself, more pressure was exercised by international organisations on local authorities to carry out evictions, especially in cases of double occupancy. Developments in the town of Mostar provided an interesting example of partnership between international organisations and local authorities to solve property disputes. A Double Occupancy Commission was created in 1999 which brought together local housing officials and international staff from UNHCR and OHR. Such a structure allowed the action of local authorities to be more closely monitored by international organisations. The Commission also allowed for the involvement of local actors in the process, who in turn gained some experience by working closely with international staff. Cases of double occupancy were brought to the attention of the Commission through a 'hotline'. An investigation team visited the illegal occupants, and local officials were encouraged by their international counterparts to be more active when dealing with these cases. Double Occupancy Commissions were set up in other cities as well, and have contributed to an increase in the evictions of people with multiple homes.

Increased minority returns in the Sarajevo area acted as a catalyst for the rest of the country. In the Sarajevo Declaration, which was adopted on 3 February 1998,[256] local authorities had undertaken to allow 20,000 minority returns to Sarajevo. The Sarajevo Housing Committee (SHC) was set up to supervise the implementation of property laws in the canton. It was, once again, composed of both local officials and international staff.[257] Since 1998, much progress had been made, and the increase

---

[255] See Human Rights Watch, *Broken Promises: Impediments to Refugee Return to Croatia* (Washington DC: Human Rights Watch, 2003).

[256] The Declaration is available at http://www.ohr.int/ohr-dept/rrtf/key-docs/sa-docs/default.asp?content_id=5453.

[257] See International Crisis Group, *Too Little, Too Late: Implementation of the Sarajevo Declaration*, ICG Balkans Report No. 44, Sarajevo, 9 September 1998, 23.

in minority returns to Sarajevo had a positive impact throughout the country.[258] The SHC was said to represent 'the most successful model of a co-operative initiative between the international community and local authorities'.[259]

Since local political obstruction remained one of the main obstacles to minority returns, more concerted efforts were made to deal with hard-line politicians. When these were in control of a municipality, very few minority returns took place in that municipality. In western Bosnia, some members of the HDZ (Croat nationalist party) made no secret of their determined opposition to minority returns. They even encouraged displaced Croats from central Bosnia to relocate in their area in order to ensure that no minority returns took place there.[260] The High Representative was granted the power to 'dismiss' any Bosnian official who systematically failed to comply with the provisions of the Dayton Peace Agreement.[261] This power was used occasionally against (democratically elected) officials who were undermining the return process. For instance, the Croat mayor of Stolac, south of Mostar, who would not allow Muslim families to return to his municipality, was removed from office in March 1998.[262] So far, the High Representative has removed more than thirty mayors and local officials.[263] The removal of obstructive officials remains a last resort, when all other means to ensure compliance have been exhausted. Such direct interference by the High Representative in Bosnian politics has nevertheless been criticised on the basis that this was undermining the democratisation process.[264] However, the local officials who were removed had never actually been committed to a democratic, unified and multi-ethnic country, and it seems legitimate to exclude them from the political process, especially if it allows hundreds of people to exercise their right to return home. Efforts to overcome political obstruction to minority returns were closely linked with

[258] See International Crisis Group, *Bosnia's Refugee Logjam Breaks: Is the International Community Ready?*, ICG Balkans Report No. 95, Sarajevo/Washington/DC and Brussels, 30 May 2000, 6.

[259] See OSCE et al., *Property Law Implementation Plan*, 10.

[260] See European Stability Initiative (ESI), *Interim Evaluation of RRTF Minority Return Programmes in 1999*, Berlin, September 1999, 12–13.

[261] See Cox, 'The Dayton Agreement', 218.

[262] See International Crisis Group, *Preventing Minority Return*, 15.

[263] See International Crisis Group, *The Continuing Challenge of Refugee Return in Bosnia and Herzegovina*, 9.

[264] See Chandler, *Bosnia*, 194.

efforts to ensure the protection of human rights and to support the democratisation process in Bosnia and Herzegovina.

Now that an increasing number of minority returns have taken place, it is crucial that international efforts are pursued to ensure that minority returns are sustainable in the longer term and truly contribute to (re-)creating a unified and multi-ethnic country. In particular, returnees should be provided with genuine employment opportunities. With no economic prospects in sight, they may decide to leave the area again.

Conclusion

The case study does not offer a solution to internal displacement, but it has certainly pointed to some of the successes and mistakes which were made when attempting to address IDP issues. It illustrated the inherent limits of field activities pursued in isolation from a human rights framework and goals. It demonstrated that UN field activities during the conflict were focused on providing material assistance to the civilian population, including internally displaced persons, and were not complemented by wider efforts to stop human rights abuses and/or secure asylum for those who sought to flee the country. The case study reviewed more recent efforts to return refugees and internally displaced persons to their homes in 'minority areas' and their human rights implications. These implications were to a certain extent ignored and this may explain the initial failure of such efforts to reverse ethnic cleansing.

Despite earlier doubts, one can now claim that 'the international community's focus on creating a procedure for repossessing property under local law and ensuring its implementation has been both unprecedented and amazingly successful'.[265] However, the return process has been successful because of an unprecedented international involvement which may have reflected Western guilt at the lack of political will to address the conflict in the early 1990s. The recent experience in Bosnia and Herzegovina demonstrates that, where there are sustained international efforts and commitment to the return process, displaced persons will eventually go home.

Refugees and internally displaced persons attempting to return to their homes within Bosnia and Herzegovina have encountered specific

---

[265] International Crisis Group, *The Continuing Challenge of Refugee Return in Bosnia and Herzegovina*, 39.

problems linked to the initial causes of displacement, i.e. ethnic cleansing. Extensive international involvement in the country has allowed for a better understanding of such problems. The success of the return process has also set an important precedent for establishing the right to return to one's own home. When examining the right to return of refugees and internally displaced persons, the Sub-Commission on Human Rights has referred to all the problems that had been addressed in Bosnia and Herzegovina.[266] The return strategies implemented in that country have served as a model for Kosovo where similar activities have been implemented and/or suggested.[267]

External powers have been committed to the idea of reversing the effects of the policies of ethnic cleansing and recreating a multi-ethnic country. The emphasis has therefore been put on promoting minority returns. Nevertheless, success cannot only be measured by the number of minority returns, which has been the focus, if not the obsession, of international organisations operating in the country.[268] One must also ensure that return is voluntary and conducted in safety, dignity and security. People should not be returned to situations in which their human rights are at risk. People return to their houses, but not to what they left. They are faced with a different situation,[269] and this is why efforts should now be targeted at helping them to cope with this new situation. Surely, the problem is not just about where people are living, but also about how they are living and how they are integrated into the local community. International efforts to return people to their homes have shown how difficult and costly it has been to reverse ethnic cleansing.

Finally, the case study has illustrated the importance of the link between internal displacement and issues of sovereignty. Indeed, internal displacement in Croatia and later in Bosnia and Herzegovina were symptoms of the crisis of legitimacy of the state, and the visual manifestations of conflicting claims to sovereignty. The warring parties were competing for statehood, which involved establishing control over a given territory. They believed that the only way to establish that

---

[266] See Sub-Com. Res. 2002/30, 15 August 2002.

[267] See International Crisis Group, *Return to Uncertainty: Kosovo's Internally Displaced and the Return Process*, ICG Balkans Report No. 139, Pristina and Brussels, 13 December 2002.

[268] See Ito, 'Politicisation of Minority Return', 121.

[269] See M. Stavropoulou, 'Bosnia and Herzegovina and the Right to Return in International Law' in O'Flaherty and Gisvold (eds.), *Post-War Protection Human Rights*, 123–40 at 140.

control was to ensure that only members of their own ethnic group populated the area. As a result, they forced the displacement of members of other ethnic groups. Ethnic cleansing was clearly used for the purposes of nation-state creation.[270] One can also compare the war situation with the post-war period. The former was characterised by competing claims to sovereignty, whereas the latter saw the imposition of some sort of 'international protectorate', and therefore allowed for only limited national sovereignty. This has had crucial consequences for how the international intervention could deal with internal displacement.

[270] See J. Jackson Preece, 'Ethnic Cleansing as an Instrument of Nation-State Creation: Changing State Practices and Evolving Legal Norms' (1998) 20 *Human Rights Quarterly* 817.

6 Reconceiving sovereignty and intervention

One cannot but notice the inherent tension between the references to *international* protection and *internally* displaced persons in the title of this book. This tension inevitably leads to an examination of the relationship between intervention and sovereignty. This chapter therefore looks at the problem of internal displacement within a broader conceptual framework looking at sovereignty and intervention, and how a human rights approach to the problem of internal displacement leads to a reconceiving of these two concepts with more emphasis on the notion of responsibility.

For practical, legal and moral reasons, the primary responsibility for protecting internally displaced persons should rest with the state in which they are located and not with international organisations. Central to the discussion in this chapter is the concept of state sovereignty, as the internally displaced remain under the domestic jurisdiction of their country, and, without that country's consent, usually beyond the reach of international organisations. When the state is unable (as distinct from unwilling) to protect the internally displaced, it usually requests international assistance. However, in some cases, and for reasons which will be explained, the state in question may be unwilling to protect the internally displaced and so denies international access to them. International intervention is then needed to compensate for the resulting vacuum of responsibility.

An evolving approach to the notion of sovereignty focuses on the individual and the idea of responsibility of the state to protect its population. Such an approach leads to the conclusion that, where the state is unwilling to protect the internally displaced and denies international access to them, intervention without its consent can be envisaged. A massive violation of human rights as evidenced by the number of internally displaced persons should always be interpreted as a threat to international peace and security even in the absence of transboundary effects such as refugee flows. Nevertheless, it is acknowledged at the outset that decisions to intervene are not always taken on the basis of humanitarian necessity alone.

The first section of this chapter explores the relationship between internal displacement and sovereignty. It explains why internal displacement is a characteristic of state dysfunction and how this problem has come under increased international scrutiny. The following section tries to demonstrate that the inherent link between internal displacement and human rights violations requires a reinterpretation of the notion of a threat to international peace and security. Situations justifying external intervention should include not only those producing refugee flows, but also situations of internal displacement, since mass displacement, whether external or internal, constitutes strong evidence of a grave human rights crisis. Whereas the current emphasis is put on sovereignty as responsibility for the treatment of individuals, the final section argues that sovereignty also implies responsibility of states using military power to intervene in other states. That responsibility of intervening states should include the duty to protect civilians, including internally displaced persons. Where possible, intervening states should also look beyond the provision of immediate protection to civilians and find a long-term remedy to the crisis. As this chapter seeks to place issues previously analysed within a broader conceptual framework of sovereignty, specific situations of internal displacement are adverted to but not looked at in any detail. Nevertheless, special attention is paid to the NATO-led operation in Kosovo, which offers important lessons.

Internal displacement and sovereignty issues

Internal displacement as a 'symptom of state dysfunction'[1]

Internal displacement constitutes a 'symptom of state dysfunction' to the extent that the state persecutes members of its own population and causes them to flee, or fails to protect them from persecution by non-state agents or the effects of a natural disaster which causes them to flee. It is therefore generally 'associated with the abuse or ineffective

---

[1] R. Cohen and F. M. Deng, 'Exodus Within Borders: The Uprooted Who Never Left Home' (1998) 77:4 *Foreign Affairs* 12 at 12.

exercise of sovereignty'.[2] Although it is difficult to make generalisations as situations of internal displacement vary widely, it seems that this phenomenon particularly affects states which encounter a crisis of national identity. Internal displacement often arises from challenges to central authorities taking the form of claims for autonomy or even for statehood that threaten the territorial integrity of the state. Control over territory has traditionally been seen as one of the central attributes of the sovereign state, and it follows that groups competing for the control of the state seek to gain control of territory. Thus, internal displacement often represents the physical manifestation of political challenges to the authority of the state. Nevertheless, it not only stems from weak or failed states, but also contributes to the phenomenon as it alters the ethnic and political balance in the country.

Where sovereignty and control over a defined territory are not firmly established, internal displacement is most likely to take place. For instance, as a legacy of the colonial era, most boundaries in Africa were traced without the consultation of the people directly concerned. This may explain why challenges to central authorities are especially frequent in that continent which is the most affected by internal displacement. It has also been advanced that the model of the nation-state was inappropriately imposed on African societies.[3] Others argue that some states were given all the attributes of sovereignty at the time of decolonisation, whereas they could not exercise that sovereignty effectively. These entities have been called 'quasi-states'.[4]

The most obvious difference between refugees and internally displaced persons is that the latter have not crossed an international border. As argued in Chapter 1, it is not only the occasion of border-crossing which distinguishes the two categories, but the implications of such border-crossing. Although internally displaced persons do not cross clearly visible and relatively stable international borders, they cross less visible and more fluid lines of division within the same state. These lines may divide ethnic, religious or political communities which sometimes seek secession from the state. These lines can be frontlines or lines of separation such as the Inter-Entity Boundary Line (IEBL) in Bosnia and Herzegovina.

---

[2] C. Benyani, *Internally Displaced Persons in International Law*, unpublished study, Refugee Studies Programme, Oxford, 1995, 31.

[3] See for instance J.-F. Bayart, *L'Etat en Afrique* (Paris: Fayard, 1989).

[4] See R. H. Jackson, *Quasi-States: Sovereignty, International Relations and the Third World* (Cambridge: Cambridge University Press, 1990).

This explains why the phenomenon of internal displacement is in itself a potential threat to the territorial integrity of the state, because it demonstrates the existence of these internal lines of division between communities which do not want to share the same geographical and political space.

In internal conflicts, internally displaced persons can represent valuable political pawns for the parties to the conflict. The presence of internally displaced persons can ensure the control of an area recently conquered by one party. One can draw an analogy here with former colonising states sending or encouraging settlers to migrate to the colonies. Internally displaced persons are manipulated to become weapons of war. On the other hand, some military forces target civilians who are associated with the other side with the objective of displacing or killing them (a practice referred to as ethnic cleansing).

In many cases, states are reluctant to allow international access to the internally displaced on their territory. They do not feel they have a responsibility to protect these people, and perceive them as 'adversaries'.[5] When they are associated with rebel movements, it is not in the interest of the central authorities to assist them or to let international agencies do so because it would amount to providing indirect support to the opposition movement. Similarly, rebel movements may take the same position and hinder access to internally displaced persons who are thought to support the government. Some armed groups may also in fact 'use' internally displaced persons to obtain aid from international agencies. Humanitarian assistance can thus become highly politicised. International relief for the internally displaced can also be politically sensitive if the state believes that they are used as a point of entry to address the overall political situation within the country. This has for instance been advanced by some international organisations as a reason to focus on internally displaced persons, because 'tackling the displacement problem and examining its causes and roots may provide the actor with a useful entry point towards understanding the overall situation' (i.e. the human rights situation as a whole).[6]

[5] See F. M. Deng, *Sovereignty, Responsibility and Accountability: A Framework of Protection, Assistance, and Development for the Internally Displaced*, concept paper for the Brookings Institution and Refugee Policy Group project on internal displacement, Washington DC: Brookings and Refugee Policy Group, 1995, 49–50.

[6] See UNICEF, *Expert Meeting on Gender Dimension of Internal Displacement*, New York, 14–15 June 1999, 5.

By definition, refugees have a difficult relationship with the state they have fled, but the main difference between them and the internally displaced is that refugees are out of reach from the government which seeks to stop their activities or persecute them. In contrast, internally displaced persons remain within its reach. Risks of abuse are therefore higher and protection less likely to be afforded. This renders internally displaced persons more vulnerable to persecution from the government. Access to provide protection to refugees is generally not problematic because the host state is quite willing to accept international assistance when unable or unwilling to assist refugees with its own resources. Internally displaced persons are a category of victims of human rights violations, and no surrogate protection is available to them if they cannot leave the country and if no international intervention is consented to by the government. Their situation becomes critical when they fall into what is called a vacuum of sovereignty, when the state is unable, or refuses, to assume its responsibilities towards its own population.

The crux of the matter lies in the notion of sovereignty, to which external assistance and protection to internally displaced persons poses a serious challenge.[7] The most problematic cases of internal displacement are those situations in which the state in question relies upon the norms of state sovereignty and non-intervention as a shield against international scrutiny. In such cases, most protection strategies discussed in Chapter 4 are ineffective.

The erosion of sovereignty by human rights law

Internal displacement has only become a problem of international concern as the recent development of international human rights law has exposed matters once considered to be essentially within the realm of domestic jurisdiction to international scrutiny. The principle of sovereignty continues to constitute one of the fundamental pillars of the international legal system. The United Nations is founded upon the principle of the sovereign equality of states (Article 2(1) of the UN Charter). The principle of non-intervention is closely related to the principle of sovereignty. As each state is sovereign on its territory, the UN is not allowed to interfere in its internal affairs (Article 2(7)), except for the purposes of the application of enforcement measures decided by the

---

[7] See K. Mills, *Human Rights in the Emerging Global Order: A New Sovereignty?* (London: Macmillan Press, 1998), 109.

Security Council under Chapter VII. Similarly, no state can intervene in any other state 'for any reason whatsoever'.[8]

The principle of sovereignty has traditionally been used to protect states against external interference by more powerful states, but it is being renegotiated at several levels. For one thing, the principle of non-intervention has been modified by the development of international human rights law since the Second World War. An international Bill of Rights composed of the Universal Declaration on Human Rights[9] and the two International Covenants[10] has been adopted and is supplemented by a range of human rights treaties which all grant rights to the individual and groups and impose corresponding duties on states to respect those rights.[11] Regional instruments, among which the European Convention on Human Rights[12] has established the most elaborate enforcement mechanism to date,[13] have also been adopted. One should nevertheless not overestimate the impact of weak enforcement mechanisms on the conduct of states, leading Donnelly to conclude that UN treaty monitoring procedures essentially respect sovereignty.[14] When it comes to intervention involving the use of force, the International Court of Justice famously stated that it was an inappropriate method to monitor or ensure the respect of human rights.[15] As

---

[8] Declaration on Principles of International Law Concerning Friendly Relations and Co-operation Among States in Accordance with the Charter of the United Nations, GA Res. 2625 (XXV), 24 October 1970.

[9] GA Res. 217A (III), 10 December 1948.

[10] International Covenant on Civil and Political Rights, 16 December 1966, 999 UNTS 171, and International Covenant on Economic, Social and Cultural Rights, 16 December 1966, 993 UNTS 3.

[11] Among them, the Convention on the Prevention and Punishment of the Crime of Genocide, 9 December 1948, 78 UNTS 277; Convention on the Elimination of All Forms of Racial Discrimination, 21 December 1965, 660 UNTS 195; Convention on the Elimination of All Forms of Discrimination Against Women, 18 December 1979, 19 ILM 33; Convention Against Torture and Other Cruel, Inhuman or Degrading Treatment or Punishment, 10 December 1984, 23 ILM 1027 and 24 ILM 535; and Convention on the Rights of the Child, 20 November 1989, 28 ILM 1448.

[12] European Convention for the Protection of Human Rights and Fundamental Freedoms, 4 November 1950, 213 UNTS 221.

[13] The other regional instruments are the American Convention on Human Rights, 22 November 1969, 9 ILM 673; and the African Charter on Human and Peoples' Rights, 17 June 1981, 21 ILM 58.

[14] See J. Donnelly, 'State Sovereignty and International Intervention: The Case of Human Rights', in G. M. Lyons and M. Mastanduno (eds.), *Beyond Westphalia?: State Sovereignty and International Intervention* (Baltimore: Johns Hopkins University Press, 1995), 115–46.

[15] See *Military and Paramilitary Activities in and against Nicaragua* (*Nicaragua* v. *United States*) (Merits)(1986) ICJ Reports 14, para. 268.

will be seen below, whether this remains true today is not entirely certain.

It cannot be denied that the protection of the individual's human rights can no longer be considered as a domestic matter. There has clearly been a shift from 'absolute' sovereignty to accountability for human rights abuses and this is a trend gaining momentum. Not only must the state refrain from violating human rights, but there is also a trend towards states being responsible for ensuring that human rights are not violated by non-state agents. Applying this reasoning to internal displacement, the state should not only refrain from forcibly displacing people within its territory, but should also protect them from displacement by non-state agents. Similarly, this reasoning is increasingly being applied in the refugee context (although not uniformly so): asylum can be granted not only in situations where the state is responsible for the persecution of the individual, but also where the state has failed to protect the individual from persecution by non-state agents.[16]

This development has led to a revised approach to the concept of sovereignty and more emphasis being put on notions such as legitimacy. Reisman for instance advocates a 'new constitutive, human rights-based conception of popular sovereignty'[17] whereby the sovereign's legitimacy is derived from the consent of the people. Similarly, Franck has sought to prove the existence in international law of an emerging norm of democratic governance which links sovereignty to political legitimacy.[18] It is indeed argued that the development of human rights law, and the principle of self-determination in particular, have led to a reconceiving of the concept of sovereignty. Sovereignty finds its source in the will of the people who delegate the exercise of sovereign rights to an elected government. Therefore, a government can only legitimately exercise sovereign rights on behalf of the population if it has been elected to do so. If it loses the support of the people, it thereby loses its rights to exercise sovereign rights on behalf of the people. Nevertheless, excessive emphasis should not be put on the electoral process, and one could also argue here that a government can lose its legitimacy by grossly mistreating its minorities (e.g. the treatment of Kosovo Albanians by the Serb

---

[16] See for instance R. v. *Immigration Appeal Tribunal, ex parte Shah* [1999] 2 AC 629 and *Horvath* v. *Secretary of State for the Home Department* [2000] 3 WLR 379.

[17] M. Reisman, 'Sovereignty and Human Rights in Contemporary International Law' (1990) 84 *American Journal of International Law* 866 at 870.

[18] See T. M. Franck, *Fairness in International Law and Institutions* (Oxford: Oxford University Press, 1995), 83–139.

government). This is a relevant issue for the internally displaced since they often belong to minority groups.

Concepts of human rights and democracy have thus challenged traditional notions of sovereignty, but have also led to a reinterpretation of the principle of non-intervention. Teson has drawn the most far-reaching conclusions from the new emphasis on legitimacy in international law. He claims that illegitimate governments should not be allowed to exercise their rights under international law,[19] and that the principle of non-intervention should not be applied to them. This leads to the possibility of humanitarian intervention in states controlled by illegitimate governments.[20] If a government exercises sovereign rights within a territory without the consent of the people living there, such exercise has no basis and no legitimacy. Consequently, the government should not be entitled to invoke the rule of non-intervention on behalf of the people. The right to invoke such a rule belongs to the people and it can only be exercised by a representative government. One can go further still and argue that a right of humanitarian intervention exists if a government commits grave human rights violations, regardless of whether the government has been duly elected.

A human rights-based approach to sovereignty can be useful to the extent that it allows for a reinterpretation of the rule of non-intervention. Nevertheless, there are difficulties with this approach. There are not as yet generally acceptable standards to measure the representativeness or legitimacy of a political regime. States have some international obligations to promote and respect human rights, but international law does not as yet require entities to be democratic in order to be recognised as states and participate in the international system. Surely, external intervention cannot be justified on the ground that a state is not democratic. Disruption to democracy has nevertheless been used as a ground for intervention in Haiti in 1994, although it is debatable that the absence of democracy may constitute a threat to international peace and security under Article 39 of the UN Charter.[21] Instead, intervention should depend on the scale of human rights violations. Again, there are practical difficulties associated with how we can measure that scale and

---

[19] See F. R. Teson, 'The Kantian Theory of International law' (1992) 92 *Columbia Law Review* 53 at 100.

[20] See F. R. Teson, *Humanitarian Intervention: An Inquiry into Law and Morality* (New York: Transnational Publishers, 1996, 2nd ed.).

[21] See S. Chesterman, *Just War or Just Peace? Humanitarian Intervention and International Law* (Oxford: Oxford University Press, 2001), 151–60.

to whom this task should fall. It is argued here that the Security Council should be responsible for making such a judgment when it determines threats to international peace and security, and that it should take into account the scale of displacement as an indication of the scale of human rights abuses.[22]

Arguably, states' approaches to sovereignty have not kept pace with academic thinking, and, when it comes to the development of rules in customary international law, state practice and *opinio juris* remain crucial. Despite the important theoretical developments described above, most states still resist external interference in what they consider to be domestic matters. They have also refrained from intervening in other states. The debates on internal displacement which have taken place before the Commission on Human Rights illustrate the reluctance of states to allow for a more narrow interpretation of the rule of non-intervention. Ever since the issue of internal displacement came onto the UN agenda, some states have interpreted this initiative as a disguised effort to intervene in their domestic affairs. When discussing humanitarian access to the internally displaced in 1992, the government of Sri Lanka, supported by the government of Mexico, warned that 'any international initiative on internally displaced persons must be taken subject to the paramount principle of state sovereignty, and the related principles of non-interference and non-intervention in the internal affairs of states established under the Charter of the United Nations'.[23] The Special Representative on Internally Displaced Persons has encountered similar defensive responses to his reports.[24] In a panel discussion on internal displacement organised by the Economic and Social Council (ECOSOC) in 2000, China insisted that the issue of internal displacement was 'essentially a domestic one'.[25] These concerns have not disappeared, and in 2001, ten years after the UN seized the issue of internal displacement, the Chairman of the Group of 77 made almost exactly the same comment as Sri Lanka on the importance of a request for assistance and full respect for territorial integrity

---

[22] See pp. 219–23 below.

[23] *Analytical Report of the Secretary-General on Internally Displaced Persons*, E/CN.4/1992/23, 14 February 1992, para. 95.

[24] See for instance F. M. Deng, *Protecting the Dispossessed: A Challenge for the International Community* (Washington DC: Brookings Institution, 1993), 141–8; and E. E. Ruddick, 'The Continuing Constraint of Sovereignty: International Law, International Protection, and the Internally Displaced' (1997) 77 *Boston University Law Review* 429 at 456–8.

[25] ECOSOC Press Release, 20 July 2000.

and national unity.[26] Similar remarks have been reported when some states were challenging the authority of the Guiding Principles on Internal Displacement.[27] Not surprisingly, certain states which have a serious problem of internal displacement are most reluctant to see the UN play a greater role in this area, because they fear that this would inevitably lead to addressing the root causes of displacement, i.e. a closer examination of the human rights record of the country in question.

Sovereignty as responsibility

The new focus on legitimacy as an essential attribute of state sovereignty has led modern international political theory to rethink the notion of sovereignty as involving responsibility and accountability to both domestic and external constituencies. Whereas emphasis was previously put on effective control of territory by the sovereign,[28] it is now the *nature* of that control which is prioritised. Authority is now understood to be exercised on behalf and for the benefit of the people, and one of the *raisons d'être* of the state is to protect them. Control over territory which is the essence of sovereignty should imply responsibility in the exercise of that control and responsibility for the welfare of the citizens, including the internally displaced.

For authors such as Deng, this new emphasis on sovereignty as responsibility leads to the notion of forfeiture of sovereignty. Under this conditional doctrine, if the state does not live up to its responsibilities, it would lose its legitimacy because the citizens withdraw their popular assent to it (they may however assent to the mistreatment of a minority). The state forfeits its sovereignty, which opens up the possibility of international intervention.[29] Sovereignty is therefore conditional upon whether the state lives up to its responsibilities or 'fails to uphold the social contract's promise of decent treatment'.[30] According to Deng, it

---

[26] See *Statement by Ambassador Bagher Asadi, Chairman of the Group of 77 (Islamic Republic of Iran), at the Humanitarian Affairs Segment of the Substantive Session of 2001 of the Economic and Social Council*, Geneva, 11 July 2001.

[27] See Chapter 2, pp. 71–3 above.

[28] See *Island of Palmas* case (*Netherlands* v. *United States*) (1928), Permanent Court of Arbitration, Sole Arbitrator Huber, 2 *Reports of International Arbitral Awards* 829, and the 1933 Montevideo Convention on Rights and Duties of States (1934) 165 *LNTS* 19.

[29] See Deng, *Protecting the Dispossessed*, 13, and Ruddick, 'The Continuing Constraint of Sovereignty', 462–8.

[30] See A. C. Helton, 'Forced Displacement, Humanitarian Intervention, and Sovereignty' (2000) 20:1 *SAIS Review* 61 at 72.

follows that, where the state is unable or unwilling to protect and assist the internally displaced, other states and international organisations can, possibly even have a duty to, step in.[31]

This attempt to reconceive sovereignty and responsibility is aimed at getting states to fulfil their duties towards their population. It is only by living up to their responsibilities that states can protect themselves from external interference and strengthen their sovereignty.[32] If they fail to do so, they will be more likely to draw international attention to themselves. This discourse of promoting sovereignty as responsibility serves to remind states of their responsibilities rather than criticise them, but also warns them of the potential consequences of not fulfilling their duties. This would encourage governments not to perceive the internally displaced as enemies, but as individuals to whom they have obligations.

However, to assert that a state can forfeit its sovereignty represents a bold proposal. It is difficult to insist that international intervention is justified each time a state refuses or cannot live up to its obligations. The emphasis on sovereignty as responsibility may not contribute to identifying criteria for intervention, but it may help to define strategies to improve protection and assistance to the internally displaced. These strategies should focus on how to help states meet their sovereign responsibilities towards the internally displaced.[33] Rather than providing international assistance and protection to the internally displaced, efforts should be concentrated, where possible, on assisting states to cope with crises of internal displacement by reinforcing their legal and institutional framework of protection and promoting best practices borrowed from other countries.

The discussion on sovereignty as responsibility has been taken a step further by the International Commission on Intervention and State Sovereignty (ICISS). At the initiative of the Canadian government, this twelve-member international commission was asked to contribute to the current debate on humanitarian intervention. The focus of their report has been on sovereignty as involving the 'responsibility to

---

[31] See R. Cohen and F. M. Deng, *Masses in Flight: The Global Crisis of Internal Displacement* (Washington DC: Brookings Institution, 1998), 276.

[32] See F. M. Deng, 'Frontiers of Sovereignty: A Framework of Protection, Assistance, and Development for the Internally Displaced' (1995) 8 *Leiden Journal of International Law* 247 at 268.

[33] See OCHA Internal Displacement Unit, *No Refuge: The Challenge of Internal Displacement* (New York and Geneva: United Nations, 2003), 51.

protect'.[34] Like Deng, the ICISS argues that, where a state is unwilling or unable to live up to this responsibility, action must be taken by the broader community of states in order to halt or avert a 'large scale loss of life' or a 'large scale "ethnic cleansing"'.[35] The issue of responsibility thus provides 'a linking concept that bridges the divide between intervention and sovereignty'.[36] The approach of the ICISS may appear less threatening than that of Deng to the extent that, instead of focusing on the possibility of forfeiture of sovereignty, it introduces the idea of residual responsibility to protect which would lie with the broader community of states. Nevertheless, the report of the ICISS does not develop what the 'responsibility to protect' actually entails. More emphasis could have been put on the fact that to provide protection often requires the capacity and willingness to use force against those who commit abuses against civilians, with all the risks associated with such action.

Situations of internal displacement justifying external intervention

This section seeks to demonstrate that the notion of a threat to international peace and security currently includes situations involving refugee flows, but should extend more generally to situations of grave human rights violations as evidenced by mass displacement, whether internal or external. The special case of failed states is also considered here.

Threats to international peace and security and displacement

Where international intervention is needed to protect and assist internally displaced persons in a specific situation, one inevitably asks on what legal basis this intervention can be undertaken. According to the UN Charter, states can only use force in self-defence (Article 51) or to respond to a threat to international peace and security as determined by the Security Council (Chapter VII). There have been some arguments that, since 1945, a right to use force for humanitarian purposes has emerged in customary international law. Recent years have witnessed a 'growing tolerance for various forms of humanitarian intervention'.[37] In the post-Cold War era, states have intervened to protect civilians in places such

---

[34] See International Commission on Intervention and State Sovereignty (ICISS), *The Responsibility to Protect* (Ottawa: International Development Research Centre, 2001).
[35] *Ibid.*, 32.   [36] *Ibid.*, 17.
[37] See S. A. Garrett, *Doing Good and Doing Well: An Examination of Humanitarian Intervention* (Westport, CT: Praeger, 1999), 66.

as northern Iraq, Somalia, Bosnia and Herzegovina and Kosovo. Despite increasing state practice, humanitarian intervention has not yet been clearly established as a right under international law. A so-called *devoir d'ingérence* (duty to interfere) is even more controversial.[38] I will not enter here into the debate over the existence of a possible right of humanitarian intervention in customary international law,[39] but will focus instead on the types of situations which constitute threats to international peace and security which may justify humanitarian intervention.

Acts of aggression by one state against another have traditionally been considered as constituting threats to international peace and security under Article 39 of the UN Charter. Such a determination can lead the Security Council to impose economic sanctions (Article 41) or authorise military action (Article 42). The end of the Cold War has seen a gradual extension of the notion of a threat to international peace and security. The famous Security Council Resolution 688 broke new ground by stating that the situation of the Kurds in northern Iraq constituted a threat to international peace and security.[40] According to the practice of the Security Council in the last decade, situations of grave human rights violations which are almost invariably accompanied by mass displacement can be characterised as threats to international peace and security. More recently, the Security Council went further by declaring that the following types of situation may constitute threats to international peace and security: the deliberate targeting of civilian populations in armed conflicts; the deliberate denial of humanitarian access to civilians; and the situation where refugees and internally displaced persons are under the threat of harassment or where their camps are at risk of infiltration by armed elements.[41] The Security Council has thus implicitly acknowledged that certain situations of displacement could, in themselves, constitute threats to international peace and security.

---

[38] See B. Bowring, 'The "droit et devoir d'ingérence": A Timely New Remedy for Africa?' (1995) 7 *African Journal of International and Comparative Law* 493.

[39] On this topic, see for instance F. K. Abiew, *The Evolution of the Doctrine and Practice of Humanitarian Intervention* (The Hague: Kluwer Law International, 1999); Chesterman, *Just War or Just Peace?*; L. F. Damrosch (ed.), *Enforcing Restraint: Collective Intervention in Internal Conflicts* (New York: Council on Foreign Relations Press, 1993); A. Roberts, 'Humanitarian War: Military Intervention and Human Rights' (1993) 69 *International Affairs* 429; N. S. Rodley, 'Collective Intervention to Protect Human Rights and Civilian Populations: The Legal Framework', in N. S. Rodley (ed.), *To Loose the Bands of Wickedness: International Intervention in Defence of Human Rights* (London: Brassey's, 1992), 14–42; Teson, *Humanitarian Intervention.*

[40] SC Res. 688, 5 April 1991.   [41] SC Res. 1296, 19 April 2000.

Although mass displacement is not usually the primary impetus for intervention, it often constitutes one of the reasons, as illustrated by Security Council decisions to intervene in Iraq, Somalia and Haiti.[42] Indeed, the existence of refugee flows, or the threat thereof, appears to be an important consideration in the decision to intervene. Refugee movements to the United States may explain why intervention took place in Haiti, but not in other authoritarian regimes where there were more serious human rights violations taking place.[43] Increased refugee movements to Western Europe may also explain why intervention took place in Kosovo, but not in other countries from where refugees were less likely to reach European or American borders. This must be placed in the context of a change of response to the refugee crisis from one of providing asylum to direct intervention in refugee-producing countries in an effort to contain refugee flows at their source.[44]

The exercise of the right of humanitarian intervention (if it exists in international law) does not specifically require the existence of a threat against international peace and security. As explained above, according to the ICISS, there should be evidence of massive human rights violations leading to large-scale loss of life or 'ethnic cleansing'. Nevertheless, one could still demonstrate the continuing dominance of security concerns over humanitarian concerns:[45] intervention is more likely to take place when security threats such as refugee flows appear, and not on the sole ground that grave human rights violations are being committed. Indeed, it appears that 'it is only when humanitarian outrages rise to the level of threatening peace or security – in many cases by threatening to produce massive displacement – that they become grounds for intervention'.[46] The current human rights discourse may in fact still be overruled by security concerns, especially since the events of 11 September 2001. On the other hand, it has also been argued that states only intervene in a crisis if they have an interest to do so, and therefore the issue of refugee flows connects humanitarian concerns with security issues because it provides a clear link between the two. Moreover, external

---

[42] See P. Freedman, 'International Intervention to Combat the Explosion of Refugees and Internally Displaced Persons' (1995) 9 *Georgetown Immigration Law Journal* 565 at 591.

[43] See M. Weiner, 'Bad Neighbors, Bad Neighborhoods: An Inquiry into the Causes of Refugee Flows' (1996) 21:1 *International Security* 5 at 40.

[44] See Helton, 'Forced Displacement', 66.

[45] See M. Griffith, I. Levine and M. Weller, 'Sovereignty and Suffering', in J. Harriss (ed.), *The Politics of Humanitarian Intervention* (London: Pinter, 1995), 33–90 at 35.

[46] OCHA Internal Displacement Unit, *No Refuge*, 37.

displacement 'internationalizes what might otherwise be purely domestic issues related to the causes of . . . movement'.[47]

If the same line of reasoning is applied in the context of internal displacement, it would mean that intervention can only take place if there is a risk of cross-border movement,[48] i.e. a security threat to neighbouring countries and a potential destabilisation of the region. Insisting on the existence of transboundary effects has remained the current approach.[49] When commenting on the intervention in Kosovo, the British Prime Minister Tony Blair insisted that 'when oppression produces massive flows of refugees which unsettle neighbouring countries then they can be properly described as "threats against international peace and security"'.[50] It is indeed unlikely that governments see population movements that do not have transboundary implications as threats to international peace and security. One may however note the special cases of South Africa and Rhodesia where the persistence of apartheid regimes have prompted actions under Chapter VII, and where the existence of transboundary effects was considered as secondary in the decisions for action.[51]

One may challenge the conceptual basis for the requirement of transboudary effects as one may question the cross-border element in the refugee definition.[52] The position of the ICISS is that there should be 'no distinction between those abuses occurring wholly within state borders, with no immediate cross-border consequences, and those with wider repercussions'.[53] The traditional requirement of transboundary effects demonstrates that refugees and internally displaced persons are perceived differently in security terms, and explains why they have so far produced different responses. This brings us back to the definitional issues analysed earlier and confirms the idea that, while location should be conceptually irrelevant, it plays a crucial role in determining states' responses to the problem of internal displacement. There is a need to move away from the security discourse and place the discussion within a different conceptual framework, i.e. a human rights framework which

---

[47] See A. Dowty and G. Loescher, 'Refugee Flows as Grounds for International Action' (1996) 21:1 *International Security* 43 at 69–70.

[48] See N. Geissler, 'The International Protection of Internally Displaced Persons' (1999) 11 *International Journal of Refugee Law* 451 at 473.

[49] See Rodley, 'Collective Intervention', 35–6.

[50] Tony Blair, 'Doctrine of the International Community', speech at the Economic Club, Chicago, 24 April 1999, http://www.number-10.gov.uk/output/Page1297.asp.

[51] See L. F. Damrosch, 'Introduction', in Damrosch (ed.), *Enforcing Restraint*, 10.

[52] See Chapter 1, pp. 22–4 above.   [53] ICISS, *The Responsibility to Protect*, 33.

focuses not on borders but on more relevant questions relating to human dignity.

Internal displacement and human rights violations

A wide range of human rights abuses are committed every day, and, while all of them deserve international scrutiny, only a small number potentially justify humanitarian intervention.[54] What is interesting for our purpose is the importance of internal displacement in the determination of what situations involve serious human rights abuses. As explained in the previous section, some authors only advocate humanitarian intervention in refugee-producing situations partly because they take this as evidence of security threats to neighbouring countries, but also partly because the existence of refugee flows serves as an 'index of internal disorder and as *prima facie* evidence of the violation of human rights and humanitarian standards'.[55] As internally displaced persons often flee for the same reasons as refugees, it can equally be argued that internal displacement is also evidence of the scale of human rights violations in a country.

As stated earlier, the focus should not be solely on security concerns, as this leads to an overemphasis being put on borders. If the discussion is instead centred on human rights, the critical issue should not be whether or not people cross borders, but the gravity of the human rights situation as evidenced by mass displacement. People flee the gravest threats to physical security. By the very act of fleeing, refugees *and* internally displaced persons reinforce the circumstances that may call for international intervention for the following reasons. First, displacement can result from deliberate policies of forced relocation which are major human rights violations in themselves. Where such policies are targeted at members of a particular ethnic group, they can amount to ethnic cleansing. Secondly, displacement prevents the full enjoyment of basic human rights such as the right to food, the right to shelter, the right to family life and so on. In addition, displacement creates an increased risk of human rights violations because the internally displaced are more exposed to abuses such as torture or forced recruitment.[56] Consequently, as the existence of refugee flows serves as evidence of human rights

---

[54] See Garrett, *Doing Good and Doing Well*, 57.

[55] See Dowty and Loescher, 'Refugee Flows as Grounds for International Action', 70–1.

[56] See Chapter 2, first section, above for an analysis of the various rights violated during displacement.

violations, the existence of internally displaced persons also demonstrates that serious human rights violations are being or have been committed.

Caution must nevertheless be exercised here because people also move for reasons other than human rights-related reasons. As recalled in Chapter 1, a central element in the definition of internally displaced persons is the existence of human rights violations and the evidence of forced displacement. However, a distinction must be made between the identification of a situation of internal displacement and the determination of a situation calling for external intervention. In order for a situation to justify humanitarian intervention, it must be a life-threatening situation involving massive and serious human rights violations as evidenced by mass displacement (whether internal or external). Consequently, it is difficult to argue for instance that dam construction projects displacing hundreds of thousands or millions of people[57] should justify humanitarian intervention even though the forcible relocation of minority groups takes place. Dam construction does not constitute an immediate and serious threat to physical security, in contrast with ethnic cleansing. These projects would not call for military intervention, but would certainly require other forms of international scrutiny and varying degrees of international pressure can be exercised on the state responsible for such displacement.

The special case of failed states

One needs to consider at this point the special case of failed states, in which central authority has effectively collapsed, often as a result of civil war. The situations considered here are distinct from that of a state's deliberate campaign to displace people or its refusal to protect them. There is no issue of responsibility here, or a failure to protect the internally displaced, but a collapse of state institutions which affects the *general* human rights situation. Nevertheless, large movements of population generally take place in failed states because such a phenomenon is inevitably linked to challenges to central authorities.[58] As a result, protection for internally displaced persons can also be jeopardised by the collapse of state authority, and not only by the abuse of sovereignty.[59]

---

[57] See Chapter 1, pp. 30–1 above for an example of such projects.
[58] See pp. 209–12 above.
[59] See UNHCR, *The State of World's Refugees: The Challenge of Protection* (Geneva: UNHCR, 1993), 133.

The failed state usually retains international borders which delimit its territory, but does not exercise the traditional functions of a normal state within these borders. The collapse of state authority raises difficult problems for internally displaced persons and other populations at risk because no single group effectively exercises control over the entire territory, and the warring parties may not be concerned about their fate.

Intervention in failed states may be perceived as easier to justify as it does not involve 'a case of intervention against the will of the government, but intervention when there is a lack of government'[60] and therefore an absence of legitimacy. The initial UN approach in Somalia in 1992 was to apply the traditional rule of consent to a peacekeeping operation, and each Security Council resolution referred to the request for intervention by the interim prime minister who had no real authority in the country.[61] Considering how artificial the application of the principle of consent was, this approach was subsequently abandoned.[62] Following the intervention in Somalia (1992-5), it appears that the issue of consent has turned out to be, not less, but more problematic in the case of failed states. Although no central authority can give consent to international intervention, this does not mean that no consent is needed. On the contrary, the failure of the UN/US operations in Somalia could be attributed to the lack of consent from the various warring parties and the population at large which objected to the intervention.

Beyond the issue of consent to external interference, another problem raised by intervention in failed states is that, again as illustrated in Somalia, intervention alone may not solve the humanitarian crisis. Indeed, in the longer term, what is needed is the restoration of central authorities to protect the internally displaced and other individuals. Interventions in failed states may involve more important commitments on behalf of international organisations in order to rebuild functioning institutions which will be able to respond to the needs of the internally displaced and others in the future. Nevertheless, humanitarian

---

[60] See Roberts, 'Humanitarian War', 440.

[61] See SC Res. 733, 23 January 1992, SC Res. 746, 17 March 1992, SC Res. 751, 24 April 1992, SC Res. 767, 27 July 1992 and SC Res. 775, 28 August 1992.

[62] For more detail on the intervention in Somalia, see W. Clarke and J. Herbst (eds.), *Learning from Somalia: The Lessons of Armed Humanitarian Intervention* (Boulder, CO: Westview Press, 1997); J. L. Hirsch and R. B. Oakley, *Somalia and Operation Restore Hope: Reflections on Peacekeeping and Peacemaking* (Washington DC: US Institute of Peace Press, 1995); T. Lyons, *Somalia: State Collapse, Multilateral Intervention, and Strategies for Political Reconstruction* (Washington DC: Brookings Institution, 1995); and M. Sahnoun, *Somalia: The Missed Opportunities* (Washington DC: US Institute for Peace Press, 1994).

organisations or military forces cannot and should not substitute themselves for the state or attempt to fulfil its functions, as has been the
case in Bosnia and Herzegovina and Kosovo.[63] International efforts
should instead focus on institution-building and on the restoration of
sovereignty in the hands of the local population.

Means of intervention and impact on IDP protection issues

Once the decision to intervene is taken, the discussion is not over, but
moves on to the nature, form and scale of the intervention which is
required to tackle the situation. Whereas in the discussion above the
emphasis was put on how states are responsible for the protection
of their own population, the present section shifts the focus of analysis to the intervening state(s). The Kosovo experience shows that more
attention should be paid to the impact of military intervention on IDP
protection issues. It also demonstrates that intervention is not an end
in itself and that one must look beyond.

Securing humanitarian access through international pressure and negotiation

The most problematic situations of internal displacement are those
where states refuse to acknowledge a problem of internal displacement
or deny international access to the internally displaced on the ground
that the state can cope with the problem. When confronted with such
situations, the broader community of states should attempt to secure
access to the internally displaced. Strategies falling short of military
action include international pressure on the state concerned to allow
access to the internally displaced, and/or negotiation with insurgent
groups when the internally displaced are situated in territories under
their control. Such activities depend on the provision of accurate and up-
to-date information on situations of internal displacement which can be
used against states which deny the existence of the problem. The availability of such information would also allow for early identification of
the crisis at the UN or other security organisations such as NATO.[64]

International pressure can take many forms, e.g. political and economic, but the focus here will be on specific initiatives that can be
undertaken to gain humanitarian access to the internally displaced. The
Special Representative on Internally Displaced Persons plays a crucial

---

[63] See pp. 231–2 below.   [64] See Chapter 3, pp. 105–10 above.

role in drawing attention to difficult cases of internal displacement by issuing statements of concern.[65] Some NGOs such as the US Committee for Refugees[66] also play an important role of documenting and publicising less well-known situations of internal displacement.

International pressure on the state concerned can be exercised through UN organs. So far, the response to internal displacement has been to act when requests for assistance are made by states. Nevertheless, this requirement for a request may not be adequate, especially in cases of failed states where no authority is competent to make such a request or where the internally displaced are associated with insurgent groups for which the government will not request assistance. The UN should now adopt a more pro-active stance and attempt to deal with situations where no formal request is made, but where assistance and protection for the internally displaced are still needed.[67] Diplomatic efforts directed at gaining humanitarian access to the internally displaced can be led by the Secretary-General with the assistance of the Emergency Relief Coordinator (ERC) who is the focal point in the UN system for IDP issues.[68] Pressure can also be exercised on states through the Security Council which has for instance recently called upon African states with situations of internal displacement to cooperate fully with UN efforts on the issue.[69] International pressure can also be exercised at the regional level. The European Union has for instance used its considerable leverage on trading partners or candidates for membership to improve their human rights record and in particular to allow access to the internally displaced. This has been particularly true in the case of Turkey.[70] Alternatively, cross-border operations can be undertaken to assist internally displaced persons who are situated near borders. Such operations have for instance been conducted in Burma from neighbouring Thailand.[71]

In some cases, access to the internally displaced may be hindered not by central authorities, but by insurgent groups in control of parts of the territory where the displaced are situated. If this is the case, the UN

---

[65] See *Internally Displaced Persons: Report of the Representative of the Secretary-General, Mr Francis M. Deng*, E/CN.4/2000/83, 26 January 2000, paras. 61–5.

[66] See http://www.refugees.org.

[67] See R. Cohen, *Working Paper for Conference on 'Tough Nuts to Crack': Dealing with Difficult Situations of Internal Displacement*, 28 January 1999, 9.

[68] See Chapter 3, p. 104 above.

[69] See *Presidential Statement*, S/PRST/2000/1, 13 January 2000.

[70] See R. Cohen, 'Hard Cases: Internal Displacement in Turkey, Burma and Algeria', *Forced Migration Review*, vol. 6, December 1999, 25–6.

[71] *Ibid.*, 27.

may seek to negotiate directly with those insurgent groups, although this could prove more difficult than dealing with the 'official' government. Indeed, international organisations have very little leverage over insurgent groups with whom they do not have established relations. The possibility of 'recognition' of insurgent groups by international organisations can be used as a powerful tool, although it can also have negative effects. Indeed, insurgent groups try to control 'distressed populations as a means of establishing a claim to resources designated for such persons and to the international recognition that accompanies such control'.[72] Some negotiations involving both central authorities and insurgent groups have had mixed results so far, but have temporarily secured access to some internally displaced persons. For instance, a tripartite agreement allowing Operation Lifeline Sudan was concluded in 1989 between the government, the main opposition group SPLM/SPLA (Sudan People's Liberation Movement and its military wing) and the UN.[73] Various strategies are thus available to the UN to deal with difficult situations of internal displacement, and a more pro-active approach must be adopted in order to ensure that all internally displaced persons who need international assistance and protection have access to it.

Military intervention and its limits: lessons from Kosovo

Military intervention is rarely undertaken on the sole basis that there is a crisis of internal displacement, but, as demonstrated above, it often takes place in the midst of an existing armed conflict and/or massive human rights abuses which produce internal displacement. Consequently, military intervention almost inevitably has an impact on internally displaced persons. In some cases, the stated objective of the intervention is to protect civilians who are mainly internally displaced. The NATO intervention in Kosovo in the spring of 1999, Operation Allied Force, provides a clear example of the negative impact that a military intervention can have on the protection of the internally displaced.[74]

---

[72] M. Frohart, D. Paul and L. Minear, *Protecting Human Rights: The Challenge to Humanitarian Organisations*, Occasional Paper No. 35 (Providence, RI: Thomas J. Watson Jr Institute for International Studies, 1999), 64.

[73] See H. A. Ruiz, 'The Sudan: Cradle of Displacement', in R. Cohen and F. M. Deng (eds.), *The Forsaken People: Case Studies of the Internally Displaced* (Washington DC: Brookings Institution, 1998), 139–74 at 146–9.

[74] For a general overview of the operation, see D. Kritsiotis, 'The Kosovo Crisis and NATO's Application of Armed Force Against the Federal Republic of Yugoslavia' (2000) 49 *International and Comparative Law Quarterly* 330.

As a preliminary point, it must be noted that the intervening states have the responsibility for taking the decision to intervene. There had been an exceptional building-up of pressure from NATO countries to convince public opinion of the need for military intervention in Kosovo. NATO countries tried to demonstrate that the scale of human rights violations as well as the level of displacement taking place within the province were such as to justify intervention. Western media has been accused of inflating numbers and exaggerating reports of atrocities.[75] The Kosovo Liberation Army (KLA) was also suspected of alleging mass atrocities in order to influence the decision to intervene.[76] If there is an emerging right of humanitarian intervention, it is the responsibility of the intervening states to provide evidence that the conditions exist for the exercise of that right. In other words, the intervening states must ensure that intervention is indeed justified. In addition, one may add that they should also demonstrate that such an intervention will be effective in solving the crisis. To that purpose, the ICISS believes that 'military action can only be justified if it stands a reasonable chance of success, that is, halting or averting the atrocities or suffering that triggered the intervention in the first place'.[77]

International intervention should lead to an improvement of the condition of the internally displaced. Intervention ought at least not to put them in a more difficult situation, even if only in the short term. There is doubt as to whether the NATO-led operation in Kosovo has had a 'positive humanitarian outcome'.[78] One important lesson to be drawn from the intervention is that an air operation has limited effects in terms of improving the situation of the internally displaced. Yet it had already been previously said that aerial bombing was not a practical response and had not been especially effective in the past.[79] Before the operation started, UNHCR had established a large presence inside the province,[80] and was engaged in protection and assistance activities for the internally displaced who numbered 260,000 when operations were suspended. This figure does not include the 61,000 people who had fled to the

---

[75] See A. Gillan, 'What's the Story?', London Review of Books, vol. 21, No. 11, 27 May 1999.
[76] Ibid.   [77] ICISS, The Responsibility to Protect, 37.
[78] See N. J. Wheeler, Saving Strangers: Humanitarian Intervention in International Society (Oxford: Oxford University Press, 2000), 273.
[79] See B. R. Posen, 'Military Responses to Refugee Disasters' (1996) 21:1 International Security 72 at 87.
[80] See Meeting Humanitarian Needs in Kosovo Province of the Federal Republic of Yugoslavia, HIWG/98/8, 16 November 1998.

Republic of Montenegro and the 30,000 who went to Serbia proper and who were also technically internally displaced.[81] All UN agencies and NGOs, as well as the OSCE, withdrew from the province just before the bombing operation started. Nevertheless, it must be noted that, at the height of the crisis, the Security Council urged humanitarian organisations to assist internally displaced persons within Kosovo and in other parts of the Federal Republic of Yugoslavia (Serbia and Montenegro).[82]

Once the air campaign was launched, there was no international presence in the province, and there were reports that the level of atrocities increased, and accordingly the level of displacement.[83] It is now undisputed that the bombing campaign 'accelerated' the ethnic cleansing campaign.[84] The bombing itself also contributed to displacing people who fled potential target areas.[85] During the whole period of the bombing campaign, up to one million people fled Kosovo, and, in addition, half a million were internally displaced.[86] Since the latter had no access to international assistance, most internally displaced persons lacked food and medical attention. Airdrops had been considered,[87] but were finally ruled out as too risky because they involved lower-level flights.[88] Worse, a convoy of internally displaced persons was bombed by mistake by a NATO plane on 14 April 1999.[89] Target discrimination could have been improved if pilots had flown at a lower level, but this was again probably considered too dangerous for them.[90] Not only did those who remained within the province have no access to international aid, but they were also more exposed to human rights abuses from Serb forces and to NATO bombs. Quite unusually, the internally displaced were overwhelmingly male because men, who were all potential KLA combatants, were not allowed to leave the country.

---

[81] See Statement by Mrs Sadako Ogata, United Nations High Commissioner for Refugees, to the Humanitarian Issues Working Group of the Peace Implementation Council, Geneva, 6 April 1999.

[82] SC Res. 1239, 14 May 1999, para. 2.

[83] See M. Barutciski, 'Western Diplomacy and the Kosovo Refugee Crisis', *Forced Migration Review*, vol. 5, August 1999, 9.

[84] See Wheeler, *Saving Strangers*, 269.   [85] See M. Barutciski, 'Western Diplomacy', 9.

[86] See A. Roberts, 'NATO's "Humanitarian War" over Kosovo' (1999) 41:3 *Survival* 102 at 113.

[87] See US Department of State Daily Press Briefing DPB#68, 21 May 1999, http://www.secretary.state.gov/www/briefings/9905/990521db.html.

[88] See R. Cohen and D. A. Korn, 'Failing the Internally Displaced', *Forced Migration Review*, vol. 5, August 1999, 12.

[89] See Kritsiotis, 'The Kosovo Crisis', 355.   [90] See Wheeler, *Saving Strangers*, 272.

In contrast, those who managed to flee the province, mainly women and children, were in relative safety and within the reach of humanitarian organisations. In addition, the situation of refugees in camps in Albania and the Former Yugoslav Republic of Macedonia received considerable international media coverage, whereas no foreign journalist was allowed within Kosovo where the internally displaced were. This is not to say that refugees did not deserve the attention of aid agencies and NATO forces, but that NATO countries did not have the political will to commit ground forces to assist and protect those who stayed behind. It also demonstrates that aiding the internally displaced represents a greater challenge and involves taking more risks.[91] A land operation may have caused some casualties among ground forces (and civilians), and the commitment of NATO's governments to protecting the internally displaced did not extend to risking their soldiers' lives on the ground.[92] A land operation might have led to less disparities of treatment between refugees and internally displaced persons, although aid to the latter group would still have been more difficult to deliver since it had to take place within an active war zone. However, airdrops of food and medicine could have at least been undertaken to help those trapped within Kosovo.

Beyond military intervention: post-intervention obligations

In most cases, military intervention is not sufficient to solve a crisis of internal displacement and one must look beyond military intervention to find a long-term solution to the crisis. For instance, NATO air strikes on Bosnian Serb positions and peace negotiations were only the very first step in the peace and reconstruction effort in Bosnia and Herzegovina. The use of force can only address immediate security concerns and the intervening state(s) must engage in long-term efforts to solve the political crisis that prompted their initial involvement. For the purposes of our analysis, emphasis should be put on the protection of the legal rights of returnees to ensure that refugees and internally displaced persons return home. In order to ensure that this return is sustainable, a stable social and economic environment must be promoted in return areas. The Bosnian experience has shown that establishing a strong military presence and rebuilding houses are only part of the solution.[93]

---

[91] See Cohen and Korn, 'Failing the Internally Displaced', 13.
[92] See Wheeler, *Saving Strangers*, 284.   [93] See Chapter 5, fourth section, above.

The return of refugees and internally displaced persons must not contribute to the harassment and displacement of those groups who may have been associated with their initial displacement. In the aftermath of the NATO operation in Kosovo, widespread human rights violations were committed by returning Kosovo Albanians against Serb and other minority groups in the province. As a result, around 200,000 Serbs and Roma were forcibly displaced.[94] The military presence of a NATO force, KFOR, failed to prevent this displacement or to ensure the physical security of those who remained.[95]

Post-intervention strategies have often been overlooked and underestimated in the past. This was evidenced recently by the difficulties encountered by the American and British forces in Iraq. Post-intervention strategies are crucial to the ultimate success of any military intervention, and require both political commitment and resources. Nevertheless, one must acknowledge the risks involved in any prolonged presence by the intervener in the target country.[96] While the intervening state stays on, the exercise of sovereignty is suspended. In some cases, such as Bosnia and Herzegovina or Kosovo, the territory is almost entirely administered by the UN. It is preferable that sovereignty be restored to its rightful owners as soon as possible. This was the case in East Timor, which was only briefly under UN administration before gaining independence, and more recently of Iraq. The continued presence of external actors in the country can also create local dependency on those actors.

Conclusion

This chapter has examined the problem of internal displacement within a broader conceptual framework looking at sovereignty and intervention, since ultimately the provision of international protection to the internally displaced depends on intervention in the country unable or unwilling to protect them. While traditional conceptions of sovereignty put the emphasis on borders, it was argued here that a human rights approach leads to more emphasis being put on responsibility within these borders. The notion of responsibility was therefore proposed as a way of reconciling sovereignty and intervention. It is only by placing the debate within a human rights framework that intervention becomes

---

[94] See A. C. Helton, *The Price of Indifference – Refugees and Humanitarian Action in the New Century* (Oxford: Oxford University Press, 2002), 56.
[95] See Wheeler, *Saving Strangers*, 284.   [96] See ICISS, *The Responsibility to Protect*, 44–5.

justifiable. If there is an emerging norm of humanitarian intervention on the ground of grave human rights violations, internal displacement could serve as evidence of the degree of severity of the human rights crisis.

It was argued that states should be held responsible for the human rights protection of their own population, including the internally displaced, but at the same time, intervening states are also responsible for the exercise of military power impinging on another state's sovereignty. They should therefore assume their human rights responsibilities to the whole population, but perhaps in particular to the internally displaced especially if they purport to be intervening on the latter's behalf.

In this chapter, frequent reference was made to differences of treatment between refugees and internally displaced persons which reflect differences of perceptions as well as practical differences between the problems raised by each group. In the current state of affairs, caution is still the rule when dealing with the internally displaced, and sovereignty remains the principal obstacle for their protection. Since tackling the issue of internal displacement sometimes involves overriding the sovereignty of the state concerned, few states are prepared to do so, but the trend is clearly towards more international involvement with the internally displaced. On the other hand, states are more willing to deal with refugees when these are perceived as security threats. As a result, we can witness an erosion of the sovereignty of states which refuse to deal with internally displaced persons and a corresponding reassertion of the sovereignty of states which control the admission of aliens into their territory, as explained by Dacyl:

Two contradictory tendencies may thus be identified with regard to international responses to internally versus externally displaced people of humanitarian concern. The post-Cold War responses to 'internally displaced persons' . . . seems to denote increased international concern to safeguard their human rights and simultaneous – albeit not necessarily intentional – questioning of the sanctity of the sovereignty principle with regard to the state unable to or unwilling to protect its own citizens. The post-Cold War responses to 'externally displaced persons' . . . represent in turn a substantial deterioration in respect for the protection seekers' human rights and simultaneous sharpening of the sovereign prerogatives of the host state vis-à-vis this special category of foreign citizens.[97]

---

[97] See J. Dacyl, 'Sovereignty Versus Human Rights: From Past Discourses to Contemporary Dilemmas' (1996) 9 *Journal of Refugee Studies* 136 at 159.

It remains to be seen how far these two tendencies will go. As far as internally displaced persons are concerned, improving the international response to their problems could very much depend on how serious states are when dealing with sovereignty issues and enforcing human rights generally.

Conclusions

Refugees and internally displaced persons: different frameworks of analysis

Internal displacement continues to be a topical and controversial subject. Over the last few years, there have been many discussions and studies attempting to set down a clearer picture of the situation and rights of internally displaced persons. This is no easy task because of the very complexity of the subject whose many variations militate against a single model. Newcomers to this area are often misled by their first impression of the situation of internally displaced persons which leads them to conclude that these people are essentially in the same material circumstances as refugees and should therefore benefit from the same regime of international protection. Internal displacement does not lend itself to such a simple solution. However similar their plight may be, refugees and internally displaced persons fall within two different legal concepts. It follows from this that a human rights framework of analysis must be used with regard to internally displaced persons.

Improving the analysis of the phenomenon of internal displacement and the international response to the problem should not automatically lead to the assumption that refugee protection is undermined. Protection can sometimes be ensured in-country. As long as efforts targeted at the internally displaced are accompanied by a strict requirement that borders remain open to them, the institution of asylum is not jeopardised. The improvement of IDP protection is an integral part of the general efforts to enforce international human rights law. Internally displaced persons are a special category of human rights victims. They are special because they encounter specific problems linked to the fact that they have been displaced. However, unlike refugees, they do not benefit from the surrogate protection of another state. Internally displaced persons are still located within the jurisdiction of their own state which is responsible for their protection, and may be unable or unwilling to assume this responsibility.

With regard to IDP protection, a legal definition is not a key issue, as it is for refugee protection. IDP protection is more concerned with practical protection against human rights abuses, especially in times of armed conflict. It is also more dependent on the general political situation prevailing in the country concerned. Consequently, protection measures can only offer short-term relief to the internally displaced, until the root causes of displacement are addressed. In contrast, the protection of the persecuted individual who has obtained asylum in another country is unrelated to the situation which prompted him to flee, but depends mainly on the enforcement of the legal rights contained in the 1951 Refugee Convention. As a result, this book is about human rights protection for a specific group of people and does not seek to expand the scope of refugee law to cover the internally displaced. It is only concerned with human rights and humanitarian law, as well as concrete protection measures. The methodology used was therefore to combine legal analysis with an extra-legal analysis of institutional and operational issues.

Unlike the refugee concept, the IDP concept does not require a legal category. Rather, it has served as a useful advocacy tool to raise the visibility of a special category of persons in need of international protection. Where appropriate, it can also be an operational category to which specific interpretations of general human rights and humanitarian law provisions can apply and for which specific programmes or measures can be designed. The refugee concept is also an advocacy tool and an operational category, but it is primarily a legal concept. The group classified as 'internally displaced persons' is not always an unproblematic operational category. As demonstrated on several occasions in this book, it may not always be relevant and/or practical to use the internally displaced as an operational category distinct from other human rights victims. Nevertheless, to do so can prove useful when international organisations have to deal with their specific problems. In most conflicts, internally displaced persons are more exposed to human rights abuses than non-displaced civilians and often require special protection.

Internal displacement as a human rights issue

This book has sought to analyse and understand the extent of international protection available to internally displaced persons. It has been argued here that the issue of internal displacement needs to be discussed within a wider human rights context and that an analysis of the UN's response to this problem must therefore draw on a human rights framework. To demonstrate the need for a human rights approach to the issue of internal displacement, it was explained that internally displaced persons should not be included in the same legal regime of protection as refugees, but be discussed within a wider human rights context which shifts the focus of attention from questions of location and geography to the more pertinent ones of individual/group entitlements and state obligations. Therefore, one should not try to extend refugee protection to the internally displaced, but rather to consider IDP protection within a distinct legal framework. This legal framework of protection was then identified, and it was demonstrated that it draws heavily on international human rights law and international humanitarian law. Work with internally displaced persons must be based on the relevant international legal provisions, as reflected in the Guiding Principles on Internal Displacement.

When examining the current UN response to the issue of internal displacement, it was demonstrated that this approach is deficient because UN actors' policy approaches to the problem are not sufficiently conceptually developed. UN actors must reconceptualise IDP issues in human rights terms, and this in turn should influence the IDP policy development process. A human rights approach to the IDP issue also demonstrates that UNHCR should not be given overall responsibility for the internally displaced, but rather that internally displaced persons should be the concern of all agencies. OCHA, and more specifically the Internal Displacement Unit, should promote collaboration between agencies on the IDP issue at headquarters and field levels, and ensure that work with the internally displaced is based on human rights protection goals. Field activities for internally displaced persons must be pursued within a human rights framework in order to produce effective, prompt and durable solutions to their plight. Indeed, field activities have so far been premised on the flawed assumption that assistance and protection should be distinguished from each other.

The case study on internal displacement in Bosnia and Herzegovina illustrated the inherent limits of field activities pursued in isolation from a human rights framework and goals. It demonstrated that UN field activities during the conflict were focused on providing material assistance to the civilian population, including internally displaced persons, and were not complemented by wider efforts to stop human rights abuses and secure asylum for those who sought to flee the country. The case study reviewed more recent efforts to return refugees and internally displaced persons to their homes in 'minority areas' and the human rights implications of these efforts.

The problem of internal displacement was finally examined within a broader conceptual framework looking at state sovereignty and intervention, since the provision of international protection to the internally displaced invariably depends on intervention in the country unable or unwilling to protect them. While traditional conceptions of sovereignty put the emphasis on borders, it was argued here that emphasis is now being put on responsibility to protect those living within these borders. The notion of responsibility was therefore proposed as a way of reconciling sovereignty and intervention. It was argued that states should be held responsible for the human rights protection of their own population, including the internally displaced, but, at the same time, intervening states are also responsible for the exercise of military power impinging on another state's sovereignty. Intervening states should thus live up to their human rights responsibilities to the whole population, but perhaps in particular to the internally displaced, especially if they purport to be intervening on their behalf.

In the light of all the above, it appears that it is still not possible to formulate a set of firm statements about the obligations of states, the responsibilities of international organisations and the rights of the internally displaced. As things stand today, no single and comprehensive policy response to the problem of internal displacement has been adopted. Continuing international involvement with the internally displaced may allow us, one day, to have a clearer picture of their situation and rights, but, because of the wide range of situations of internal displacement, it is unlikely that a single model of response will ever emerge. Although improvements can be made to ensure a more consistent and predictable international response to crises of internal displacement, one should also remain flexible and adapt the operational response to each situation. In any case, attention should always be paid to the protection needs of the internally displaced. In some cases, specific strategies may need to be formulated to address the protection problems they encounter. In others, there may be no need to target the internally displaced as a specific group.

Possible improvements to the UN's response to the problem of internal displacement

The UN's response to the problem of internal displacement is necessarily different in nature from its response to the refugee problem. The book has identified some directions for future action. To date, the Special Representative on Internally Displaced Persons has been a catalyst for raising awareness of the problem of internal displacement. In the past decade, there has been considerable progress in promoting the issue of internal displacement on the international agenda, but concerns for internally displaced persons now need to be translated into concrete measures.

The drafting of the Guiding Principles on Internal Displacement marked a significant step. Considering the current lack of enthusiasm for standard-setting at the United Nations, the Guiding Principles have been accepted in a remarkably short period of time. Their impact in the field still needs to be evaluated. It is crucial that initiatives to train fieldworkers in the understanding and use of the Guiding Principles continue. The Guiding Principles could prove useful as a benchmark of treatment of the internally displaced. Although non-binding, aid workers, advocates and the internally displaced have easier access to the Guiding Principles and can be confident that they reflect existing human rights and humanitarian law provisions. Nevertheless, the use of the Guiding Principles to provide protection to the internally displaced in the field is necessarily limited, and one might, for instance, wonder what difference, if any, it would have made if the document had been available during the Bosnian crisis. Considering that the internally displaced cannot be given a specific legal status, it makes little sense to have the Guiding Principles formally adopted as a legally binding international treaty. It seems unlikely that the United Nations can go beyond the drafting of the Guiding Principles, but it should pursue its efforts to disseminate them among both agencies and governments.

Recent international efforts have focused mainly upon how to improve the institutional framework of protection for the internally displaced, and in particular on the role of UNHCR. Assistance to and protection of the internally displaced should remain the responsibility of each and every UN actor. There is an increasing degree of UN activity in the field of internal displacement and agencies have started to identify the areas in which they have more expertise and experience. They need to pursue this dialogue and develop a common understanding of the IDP issue as a human rights problem, leading to common strategies to deal with it. It is incorrect to say that only UNHCR can deal with internally displaced persons. Other UN agencies, as well as the IOM and the ICRC, have developed expertise to deal with specific IDP issues.

What is needed is stronger leadership at the OCHA level to ensure that the needs of internally displaced persons, and in particular their protection needs, are covered in each crisis. The OCHA must identify as precisely as possible what each agency is mandated to do in respect of internally displaced persons and review country situations to determine the best division of labour in each crisis. As for ensuring the consistent involvement of the UN, which is one of the main criticisms of IDP advocates, the OCHA can draw attention to impending and serious crises of internal displacement and it should be more outspoken in doing so. Nevertheless, the decision to intervene may ultimately depend on the will of donor states which fund activities for the internally displaced.

Too much time and effort has been spent on debating what the best institutional arrangements are, while serious operational problems have not been directly addressed. Protection remains the most serious challenge concerning internally displaced persons. The UN should pursue efforts to clarify the notion of IDP protection. Protection must 'infuse' all programmes and activities targeted at the internally displaced, and this requires all UN bodies to be sensitised to their protection needs. Not only are the internally displaced fleeing human rights violations, but they are also more exposed to further human rights abuses as a result of their displacement, and this distinguishes them from non-displaced civilians. What UN aid agencies and peacekeeping forces need to understand is that their mere presence is not sufficient and that they need to engage in active human rights monitoring and reporting. Where possible, more forceful intervention can be made to prevent or stop human rights abuses taking place against civilians. Aid relief alone can prove counterproductive if the physical security of the populations concerned is not ensured.

Over the last few years, the UN system has made good progress in its understanding of the phenomenon of internal displacement. What it needs to do now is to translate this understanding into concrete measures. It also needs to rationalise its activities concerning internally displaced persons and promote a 'culture' of protection among all those involved with these populations in the field. Ultimately, the only effective way to respond to IDP protection problems is to address the root causes of internal displacement, and this often requires conflict resolution efforts. This book could only examine international strategies to improve IDP protection in the short to medium term. In the longer term, there is little prospect of protection without peace and stability.

Internal displacement, human rights and sovereignty

When examining internal displacement, one of the principal difficulties encountered is that it is not a clearly delimited topic of analysis because it has many links to wider debates. The central argument developed in this book is that the problem of internal displacement must be addressed conceptually in the human rights framework. However, human rights academics have very rarely addressed this issue. Those concerned with forced migration have been reluctant to address it as part of their work, focusing instead on refugees. There is however an inherent link between human rights and forced migration, as evidenced by this research. Further study of the phenomenon of internal displacement can contribute to bridging the gap between the two disciplines.

This book has analysed a specific aspect of the human rights problem and of forced migration. In particular, it has tried to explore ways of providing human rights protection in times of armed conflict and/or in situations in which the state, which is traditionally the main protector and enforcer of human rights, is unable or unwilling to play such a role with regard to a group of persons because it may not consider them worthy of its protection. The problem of internal displacement also illustrates another emerging issue in human rights: it raises the question of enforcing human rights against non-state actors. In crises of internal displacement, there is almost invariably a challenge to central authorities by insurgent groups who, in some cases, are responsible for the displacement of the internally displaced.

The phenomenon of internal displacement demonstrates the complexity of forced population movements in the post-Cold War period. Migration studies can no longer afford to ignore the study of internal displacement, which has provided the opportunity to address new forms of forced migration such as development-induced displacement or forcible relocation. Such forced movements of populations, overwhelmingly, take place within states. In addition, the study of internal displacement illustrates some of the dimensions of the new humanitarian regime which needs to deal with challenges such as negotiation with warring factions/clans, cooperation with the military, intervention in war zones, ethnic cleansing and so on, and which puts more emphasis on the link between assistance and protection. Indeed, operational involvement with the internally displaced has led humanitarian agencies to operate in difficult situations where aid alone is no longer sufficient and protection may be more crucial to the beneficiaries. The analysis of UN involvement with internally displaced persons emphasises the need to integrate human rights into humanitarian action. Due to constraints of space, the book could only touch on such important questions as the relationship between human rights and forced migration, the complexity of forced migration, the protection of civilians in armed conflict and the new humanitarian regime.

Finally, an analysis of the problem of internal displacement cannot avoid the fundamental issue of state sovereignty. The problem lies in the fact that, although the state has primary responsibility for the internally displaced, its actions can also be the cause of displacement. State sovereignty poses a challenge to solving the crisis of internal displacement: the phenomenon of internal displacement represents, in itself, a threat to the territorial integrity of the state, but international attempts to provide protection to the internally displaced also challenge a state's authority. Traditional conceptions of sovereignty have been undermined, and there is now an increasing emphasis being put on the notion of responsibility to protect.

This idea of responsibility should, however, be applied not only to states with a problem of internal displacement, but to all states, which have a duty to protect the human rights of their own people, but have also a duty not to violate (and, even, to protect) those of people in other states. Consequently, states have a responsibility not to harm civilians when intervening in other states. In addition, they should have a responsibility to keep their borders open to potential refugees as well. It is only because traditional notions of sovereignty have changed in the second half of the twentieth century that the problem of internal displacement can now be considered as a matter of international concern. Nevertheless, the availability of human rights protection still very much depends on the will of the state concerned. Likewise, international efforts to protect the internally displaced face the same constraint.

In recent times, states have seemed increasingly willing to sidestep sovereignty concerns and intervene in other states to protect internally displaced persons and other civilians. However, humanitarian intervention is only part of the answer to human rights crises. Moreover, it seems to me that states are currently redefining the notion of sovereignty in a potentially dangerous way. The classic principle of non-intervention in the internal affairs of the state is based on the principle of sovereign equality of states and serves to protect weaker states against interference from more powerful states. There is a concern that states now intervene in other states to protect human rights but, at the same time, strengthen control over their own borders. This is an indication that the age of state sovereignty, as manifested in control over territory and borders, is certainly not yet over. The analysis of international responses to internal displacement proposes a slightly different perspective on issues of sovereignty, and informs the current debate on intervention.

Although the topic of internal displacement may at first appear to be a discrete topic, this research has shown that its scope is actually quite wide and that it informs several important broader debates. The fact that it relates to so many other different issues highlights the complexity of the problem of internal displacement and explains why its analysis requires a multidimensional approach.

Annex 1
The Guiding Principles on Internal Displacement*

Introduction – Scope and Purpose

1. These Guiding Principles address the specific needs of internally displaced persons worldwide. They identify rights and guarantees relevant to the protection of persons from forced displacement and to their protection and assistance during displacement as well as during return or resettlement and reintegration.

2. For the purposes of these Principles, internally displaced persons are persons or groups of persons who have been forced or obliged to flee or to leave their homes or places of habitual residence, in particular as a result of or in order to avoid the effects of armed conflict, situations of generalized violence, violations of human rights or natural or human-made disasters, and who have not crossed an internationally recognized State border.

3. These Principles reflect and are consistent with international human rights law and international humanitarian law. They provide guidance to:
   (a) The Representative of the Secretary-General on internally displaced persons in carrying out his mandate;
   (b) States when faced with the phenomenon of internal displacement;
   (c) All other authorities, groups and persons in their relations with internally displaced persons; and
   (d) Intergovernmental and non-governmental organizations when addressing internal displacement.

4. These Guiding Principles should be disseminated and applied as widely as possible.

---

* E/CN.4/1998/53/Add.2, 11 February 1998.

Section I. General Principles

Principle 1

1. Internally displaced persons shall enjoy, in full equality, the same rights and freedoms under international and domestic law as do other persons in their country. They shall not be discriminated against in the enjoyment of any rights and freedoms on the ground that they are internally displaced.
2. These Principles are without prejudice to individual criminal responsibility under international law, in particular relating to genocide, crimes against humanity and war crimes.

Principle 2

1. These Principles shall be observed by all authorities, groups and persons irrespective of their legal status and applied without any adverse distinction. The observance of these Principles shall not affect the legal status of any authorities, groups or persons involved.
2. These Principles shall not be interpreted as restricting, modifying or impairing the provisions of any international human rights or international humanitarian law instrument or rights granted to persons under domestic law. In particular, these Principles are without prejudice to the right to seek and enjoy asylum in other countries.

Principle 3

1. National authorities have the primary duty and responsibility to provide protection and humanitarian assistance to internally displaced persons within their jurisdiction.
2. Internally displaced persons have the right to request and to receive protection and humanitarian assistance from these authorities. They shall not be persecuted or punished for making such a request.

Principle 4

1. These Principles shall be applied without discrimination of any kind, such as race, colour, sex, language, religion or belief, political or other opinion, national, ethnic or social origin, legal or social status, age, disability, property, birth, or on any other similar criteria.
2. Certain internally displaced persons, such as children, especially unaccompanied minors, expectant mothers, mothers with young children, female heads of household, persons with disabilities and elderly persons, shall be entitled to protection and assistance required by their condition and to treatment which takes into account their special needs.

Section II. Principles Relating to Protection from Displacement

Principle 5

All authorities and international actors shall respect and ensure respect for their obligations under international law, including human rights and humanitarian law, in all circumstances, so as to prevent and avoid conditions that might lead to displacement of persons.

Principle 6

1. Every human being shall have the right to be protected against being arbitrarily displaced from his or her home or place of habitual residence.
2. The prohibition of arbitrary displacement includes displacement:
   (a) When it is based on policies of apartheid, 'ethnic cleansing' or similar practices aimed at/or resulting in altering the ethnic, religious or racial composition of the affected population;
   (b) In situations of armed conflict, unless the security of the civilians involved or imperative military reasons so demand;
   (c) In cases of large-scale development projects, which are not justified by compelling and overriding public interests;
   (d) In cases of disasters, unless the safety and health of those affected requires their evacuation; and
   (e) When it is used as a collective punishment.
3. Displacement shall last no longer than required by the circumstances.

Principle 7

1. Prior to any decision requiring the displacement of persons, the authorities concerned shall ensure that all feasible alternatives are explored in order to avoid displacement altogether. Where no alternatives exist, all measures shall be taken to minimize displacement and its adverse effects.
2. The authorities undertaking such displacement shall ensure, to the greatest practicable extent, that proper accommodation is provided to the displaced persons, that such displacements are effected in satisfactory conditions of safety, nutrition, health and hygiene, and that members of the same family are not separated.
3. If displacement occurs in situations other than during the emergency stages of armed conflicts and disasters, the following guarantees shall be complied with:
   (a) A specific decision shall be taken by a State authority empowered by law to order such measures;
   (b) Adequate measures shall be taken to guarantee to those to be displaced full information on the reasons and procedures for

their displacement and, where applicable, on compensation and relocation;

(c) The free and informed consent of those to be displaced shall be sought;

(d) The authorities concerned shall endeavour to involve those affected, particularly women, in the planning and management of their relocation;

(e) Law enforcement measures, where required, shall be carried out by competent legal authorities; and

(f) The right to an effective remedy, including the review of such decisions by appropriate judicial authorities, shall be respected.

Principle 8

Displacement shall not be carried out in a manner that violates the rights to life, dignity, liberty and security of those affected.

Principle 9

States are under a particular obligation to protect against the displacement of indigenous peoples, minorities, peasants, pastoralists and other groups with a special dependency on and attachment to their lands.

Section III. Principles Relating to Protection During Displacement

Principle 10

1. Every human being has the inherent right to life which shall be protected by law. No one shall be arbitrarily deprived of his or her life. Internally displaced persons shall be protected in particular against:
    (a) Genocide;
    (b) Murder;
    (c) Summary or arbitrary executions; and
    (d) Enforced disappearances, including abduction or unacknowledged detention, threatening or resulting in death.
    Threats and incitement to commit any of the foregoing acts shall be prohibited.

2. Attacks or other acts of violence against internally displaced persons who do not or no longer participate in hostilities are prohibited in all circumstances. Internally displaced persons shall be protected, in particular, against:
    (a) Direct or indiscriminate attacks or other acts of violence, including the creation of areas wherein attacks on civilians are permitted;
    (b) Starvation as a method of combat;

(c) Their use to shield military objectives from attack or to shield, favour or impede military operations;

(d) Attacks against their camps or settlements; and

(e) The use of anti-personnel landmines.

Principle 11

1. Every human being has the right to dignity and physical, mental and moral integrity.

2. Internally displaced persons, whether or not their liberty has been restricted, shall be protected in particular against:

    (a) Rape, mutilation, torture, cruel, inhuman or degrading treatment or punishment, and other outrages upon personal dignity, such as acts of gender-specific violence, forced prostitution and any form of indecent assault;

    (b) Slavery or any contemporary form of slavery, such as sale into marriage, sexual exploitation, or forced labour of children; and

    (c) Acts of violence intended to spread terror among internally displaced persons.

    Threats and incitement to commit any of the foregoing acts shall be prohibited.

Principle 12

1. Every human being has the right to liberty and security of person. No one shall be subjected to arbitrary arrest or detention.

2. To give effect to this right for internally displaced persons, they shall not be interned in or confined to a camp. If in exceptional circumstances such internment or confinement is absolutely necessary, it shall not last longer than required by the circumstances.

3. Internally displaced persons shall be protected from discriminatory arrest and detention as a result of their displacement.

4. In no case shall internally displaced persons be taken hostage.

Principle 13

1. In no circumstances shall displaced children be recruited nor be required or permitted to take part in hostilities.

2. Internally displaced persons shall be protected against discriminatory practices of recruitment into any armed forces or groups as a result of their displacement. In particular any cruel, inhuman or degrading practices that compel compliance or punish non-compliance with recruitment are prohibited in all circumstances.

Principle 14

1. Every internally displaced person has the right to liberty of movement and freedom to choose his or her residence.
2. In particular, internally displaced persons have the right to move freely in and out of camps or other settlements.

Principle 15

Internally displaced persons have:

(a) The right to seek safety in another part of the country;
(b) The right to leave their country;
(c) The right to seek asylum in another country; and
(d) The right to be protected against forcible return to or resettlement in any place where their life, safety, liberty and/or health would be at risk.

Principle 16

1. All internally displaced persons have the right to know the fate and whereabouts of missing relatives.
2. The authorities concerned shall endeavour to establish the fate and whereabouts of internally displaced persons reported missing, and cooperate with relevant international organizations engaged in this task. They shall inform the next of kin on the progress of the investigation and notify them of any result.
3. The authorities concerned shall endeavour to collect and identify the mortal remains of those deceased, prevent their despoliation or mutilation, and facilitate the return of those remains to the next of kin or dispose of them respectfully.
4. Grave sites of internally displaced persons should be protected and respected in all circumstances. Internally displaced persons should have the right of access to the grave sites of their deceased relatives.

Principle 17

1. Every human being has the right to respect of his or her family life.
2. To give effect to this right for internally displaced persons, family members who wish to remain together shall be allowed to do so.
3. Families which are separated by displacement should be reunited as quickly as possible. All appropriate steps shall be taken to expedite the reunion of such families, particularly when children are involved. The responsible authorities shall facilitate inquiries made by family

members and encourage and cooperate with the work of humanitarian organizations engaged in the task of family reunification.

4. Members of internally displaced families whose personal liberty has been restricted by internment or confinement in camps shall have the right to remain together.

Principle 18

1. All internally displaced persons have the right to an adequate standard of living.
2. At the minimum, regardless of the circumstances, and without discrimination, competent authorities shall provide internally displaced persons with and ensure safe access to:
    (a) Essential food and potable water;
    (b) Basic shelter and housing;
    (c) Appropriate clothing; and
    (d) Essential medical services and sanitation.
3. Special efforts should be made to ensure the full participation of women in the planning and distribution of these basic supplies.

Principle 19

1. All wounded and sick internally displaced persons as well as those with disabilities shall receive to the fullest extent practicable and with the least possible delay, the medical care and attention they require, without distinction on any grounds other than medical ones. When necessary, internally displaced persons shall have access to psychological and social services.
2. Special attention should be paid to the health needs of women, including access to female health care providers and services, such as reproductive health care, as well as appropriate counselling for victims of sexual and other abuses.
3. Special attention should also be given to the prevention of contagious and infectious diseases, including AIDS, among internally displaced persons.

Principle 20

1. Every human being has the right to recognition everywhere as a person before the law.
2. To give effect to this right for internally displaced persons, the authorities concerned shall issue to them all documents necessary for the enjoyment and exercise of their legal rights, such as passports, personal identification documents, birth certificates and marriage

certificates. In particular, the authorities shall facilitate the issuance of new documents or the replacement of documents lost in the course of displacement, without imposing unreasonable conditions, such as requiring the return to one's area of habitual residence in order to obtain these or other required documents.

3. Women and men shall have equal rights to obtain such necessary documents and shall have the right to have such documentation issued in their own names.

Principle 21

1. No one shall be arbitrarily deprived of property and possessions.
2. The property and possessions of internally displaced persons shall in all circumstances be protected, in particular, against the following acts:
    (a) Pillage;
    (b) Direct or indiscriminate attacks or other acts of violence;
    (c) Being used to shield military operations or objectives;
    (d) Being made the object of reprisal; and
    (e) Being destroyed or appropriated as a form of collective punishment.
3. Property and possessions left behind by internally displaced persons should be protected against destruction and arbitrary and illegal appropriation, occupation or use.

Principle 22

1. Internally displaced persons, whether or not they are living in camps, shall not be discriminated against as a result of their displacement in the enjoyment of the following rights:
    (a) The rights to freedom of thought, conscience, religion or belief, opinion and expression;
    (b) The right to seek freely opportunities for employment and to participate in economic activities;
    (c) The right to associate freely and participate equally in community affairs;
    (d) The right to vote and to participate in governmental and public affairs, including the right to have access to the means necessary to exercise this right; and
    (e) The right to communicate in a language they understand.

Principle 23

1. Every human being has the right to education.
2. To give effect to this right for internally displaced persons, the authorities concerned shall ensure that such persons, in particular

displaced children, receive education which shall be free and compulsory at the primary level. Education should respect their cultural identity, language and religion.

3. Special efforts should be made to ensure the full and equal participation of women and girls in educational programmes.

4. Education and training facilities shall be made available to internally displaced persons, in particular adolescents and women, whether or not living in camps, as soon as conditions permit.

Section IV. Principles Relating to Humanitarian Assistance

Principle 24

1. All humanitarian assistance shall be carried out in accordance with the principles of humanity and impartiality and without discrimination.

2. Humanitarian assistance to internally displaced persons shall not be diverted, in particular for political or military reasons.

Principle 25

1. The primary duty and responsibility for providing humanitarian assistance to internally displaced persons lies with national authorities.

2. International humanitarian organizations and other appropriate actors have the right to offer their services in support of the internally displaced. Such an offer shall not be regarded as an unfriendly act or an interference in a State's internal affairs and shall be considered in good faith. Consent thereto shall not be arbitrarily withheld, particularly when authorities concerned are unable or unwilling to provide the required humanitarian assistance.

3. All authorities concerned shall grant and facilitate the free passage of humanitarian assistance and grant persons engaged in the provision of such assistance rapid and unimpeded access to the internally displaced.

Principle 26

Persons engaged in humanitarian assistance, their transport and supplies shall be respected and protected. They shall not be the object of attack or other acts of violence.

Principle 27

1. International humanitarian organizations and other appropriate actors when providing assistance should give due regard to the protection needs and human rights of internally displaced persons and take appropriate measures in this regard. In so doing, these organizations and actors should respect relevant international standards and codes of conduct.

2. The preceding paragraph is without prejudice to the protection responsibilities of international organizations mandated for this purpose, whose services may be offered or requested by States.

Section V. Principles Relating to Return, Resettlement and Reintegration

Principle 28

1. Competent authorities have the primary duty and responsibility to establish conditions, as well as provide the means, which allow internally displaced persons to return voluntarily, in safety and with dignity, to their homes or places of habitual residence, or to resettle voluntarily in another part of the country. Such authorities shall endeavour to facilitate the reintegration of returned or resettled internally displaced persons.

2. Special efforts should be made to ensure the full participation of internally displaced persons in the planning and management of their return or resettlement and reintegration.

Principle 29

1. Internally displaced persons who have returned to their homes or places of habitual residence or who have resettled in another part of the country shall not be discriminated against as a result of their having been displaced. They shall have the right to participate fully and equally in public affairs at all levels and have equal access to public services.

2. Competent authorities have the duty and responsibility to assist returned and/or resettled internally displaced persons to recover, to the extent possible, their property and possessions which they left behind or were dispossessed of upon their displacement. When recovery of such property and possessions is not possible, competent authorities shall provide or assist these persons in obtaining appropriate compensation or another form of just reparation.

Principle 30

All authorities concerned shall grant and facilitate for international humanitarian organizations and other appropriate actors, in the exercise of their respective mandates, rapid and unimpeded access to internally displaced persons to assist in their return or resettlement and reintegration.

Bibliography

Abiew, F. K., *The Evolution of the Doctrine and Practice of Humanitarian Intervention* (The Hague: Kluwer Law International, 1999)

Adelman, H., 'Humanitarian Intervention: The Case of the Kurds' (1992) 4 *International Journal of Refugee Law* 4

Albert, S., *Les réfugiés bosniaques en Europe* (Paris: Montchrestien, 1995)

Alderman, H., 'What Is the Place of IDP Research in Refugee Studies?', in Norwegian University of Science and Technology, *Researching Internal Displacement: State of the Art*, Conference Report, 7–8 February 2003, Trondheim, Norway

Alston, P., 'The Downside of Post-Cold-War Complexity: Comments on Hathaway' (1995) 8 *Journal of Refugee Studies* 302

Amnesty International, *'Who's Living in My House?' Obstacles to the Safe Return of Refugees and Displaced People* (London: Amnesty International, 1997)

All the Way Home: Safe 'Minority Returns' as a Just Remedy and for a Secure Future (London: Amnesty International, 1998)

Bosnia-Herzegovina: Waiting on the Doorstep: Minority Returns to Eastern Republika Srpska (London: Amnesty International, 2000)

Arulanantham, A. T., 'Restructured Safe Havens: A Proposal for Reform of the Refugee Protection System' (2000) 22 *Human Rights Quarterly* 1

Askin, K. D., 'Sexual Violence in Decisions and Indictments of the Yugoslav and Rwandan Tribunals: Current Status' (1999) 93 *American Journal of International Law* 97

Bagshaw, S., 'Internally Displaced Persons at the Fifty-Fourth Session of the United Nations Commission on Human Rights, 16 March–24 April 1998' (1998) 10 *International Journal of Refugee Law* 548

Developing the Guiding Principles on Internal Displacement: The Role of a Global Public Policy Network, Case Study for the UN Vision Project on Global Public Policy Network, http://www.gppi.net/cms/ public/ 86880753f4f7e096dd8b747195113f6cbagshaw% 20gpp%202000.pdf.

Internally Displaced Persons and Political Participation: The OSCE Region, Occasional Paper, Brookings Institution Project on Internal Displacement, Washington DC, September 2000

Barber, B., 'Feeding Refugees, or War? The Dilemma of Humanitarian Aid' (1997) 76:4 *Foreign Affairs* 8

Barutciski, M., 'The Reinforcement of Non-Admission Policies and the Subversion of UNHCR: Displacement and Internal Assistance in Bosnia-Herzegovina, 1992–1994' (1996) 8 *International Journal of Refugee Law* 49

'Politics Overrides Legal Principles: Tragic Consequences of the Diplomatic Intervention in Bosnia-Herzegovina (1991–1992)' (1996) 11 *American University Journal of International Law and Policy* 767

'Tension Between the Refugee Concept and the IDP Debate', *Forced Migration Review*, vol. 3, December 1998

'Western Diplomacy and the Kosovo Refugee Crisis', *Forced Migration Review*, vol. 5, August 1999

'A Critical View on UNHCR's Mandate Dilemmas' (2002) 14 *International Journal of Refugee Law* 365

J.-F. Bayart, *L'Etat en Afrique* (Paris: Fayard, 1989)

A. Bayefsky and M. W. Doyle, *Emergency Return: Principles and Guidelines* (Princeton: Center of International Studies, Princeton University, 1999)

Beigbeder, Y., *Le Haut Commissariat des Nations Unies pour les réfugiés* (Paris: Presses Universitaires de France, 1999)

Benyani, C., *Internally Displaced Persons in International Law*, unpublished study, Refugee Studies Programme, Oxford, 1995

Human Rights Standards and the Free Movement of People Within States (Oxford: Oxford University Press, 2000)

G. Bettocchi with R. Freitas, 'A UNHCR Perspective', *Forced Migration Review*, vol. 17, May 2003

Borgen, J., *The Protection of Internally Displaced Persons by NRC: Platforms, Concepts and Strategies* (Oslo: Norwegian Refugee Council, 1994)

Bougarel, X., *Bosnie: anatomie d'un conflit* (Paris: La Découverte, 1996)

Bowring, B., 'The "droit et devoir d'ingérence": A Timely New Remedy for Africa?' (1995) 7 *African Journal of International and Comparative Law* 493

Brandrup, P., 'The Task Force of the Inter-Agency Standing Committee: Strive for a Coherent Response', in ICRC, *Internally Displaced Persons, Symposium, Geneva, 23–25 October 1995* (Geneva: ICRC, 1996), 68–72

R. Brett and E. Lester, 'Refugee Law and International Humanitarian Law: Parallels, Lessons and Looking Ahead' (2001) 843 *International Review of the Red Cross* 713

Brookings Institution, *Report of the Conference on Internal Displacement in Asia, Bangkok, Thailand, 22–24 February 2000*, http://www.brookings.edu/fp/projects/idp/conferences/asia200002_summary.htm

Summary Report of the Regional Workshop on Internal Displacement in the South Caucasus, Tsibili, Georgia, 10–12 May 2000, http://www.brookings.edu/fp/projects/idp/conferences/georgia200005/summary.htm

Summary Report of the International Colloquy on the Guiding Principles on Internal Displacement, Vienna, Austria, September 2000, http://www.brook.edu/fp/projects/idp/conferences/vienna20009/summary.htm

International Symposium on the Mandate of the Representative of the UN Secretary-General on Internally Displaced Persons: Taking Stock and Charting the Future, Vienna, Austria, 12–13 December 2002, http://www.brookings.edu/dybdocroot/fp/projects/idp/conferences/ViennaReport.pdf

Brownlie, I., 'Recognition in Theory and Practice' (1982) 53 *British Yearbook of International Law* 197

von Buchwald, U., *Response Systems of Non-Governmental Organisations to Assistance and Protection Needs of the Internally Displaced Persons*, draft report, Norwegian Refugee Council, Geneva, March 1996

S. L. Burg and P. S. Shoup, *The War in Bosnia-Herzegovina: Ethnic Conflict and International Intervention* (Armonk, NY: M. E. Sharpe, 2000)

Campbell, D., 'Apartheid Cartography: The Political Anthropology and Spatial Effects of International Diplomacy in Bosnia' (1999) 18 *Political Geography* 395

Carens, J. H., 'Aliens and Citizens: The Case for Open Borders' (1987) 49 *Review of Politics* 251

Carey, C. M., 'Internal Displacement: Is Prevention Through Accountability Possible? A Kosovo Case Study' (1999) 49 *American University Law Review* 243

Caritas Internationalis and Friends World Committee for Consultation (Quakers), *Internally Displaced Persons: Joint Oral Statement to the Commission on Human Rights*, 9 April 1998

J. Y. Carlier, D. Vanheule, K. Hullmann and C. Pena Galiano (eds.), *Who's a Refugee? A Comparative Case Law Study* (The Hague: Kluwer Law International, 1997)

Carnegie Endowment for International Peace, *Report of the International Migration Policy Breakfast Briefing: Fixing Responsibility for the Internally Displaced*, 2 March 2000, http://www.ceip.org/programs/migrat/IDPbrief.htm

Castel, J., 'Rape, Sexual Assault and the Meaning of Persecution' (1992) 4 *International Journal of Refugee Law* 39

Cernea, M. M., 'Understanding and Preventing Impoverishment from Displacement: Reflections on the State of Knowledge' (1995) 8 *Journal of Refugee Studies* 245

Chandler, D., *Bosnia: Faking Democracy After Dayton* (London: Pluto Press, 1999)

Chesterman, S., *Just War or Just Peace? Humanitarian Intervention and International Law* (Oxford: Oxford University Press, 2001)

Chimni, B. S., 'The Incarceration of Victims: Deconstructing Safety Zones', in N. Al-Naumi and R. Meese (eds.), *International Legal Issues Arising from the United Nations Decade of International Law* (The Hague: Martinus Nijhoff, 1995), 823–54

Clarance, W. D., 'Open Relief Centres: A Pragmatic Approach to Emergency Relief and Monitoring During Conflict in a Country of Origin' (1991) 3 *International Journal of Refugee Law* 320

'Field Strategy for the Protection of Human Rights' (1997) 9 *International Journal of Refugee Law* 229

Clark, L., 'Internal Refugees – The Hidden Half', in US Committee for Refugees, *World Refugee Survey 1988* (Washington DC: USCR, 1988)

'Internally Displaced Persons: Framing the Issues', speech given at the Georgetown Symposium on Internally Displaced Persons, Washington DC, 15–18 October 1989

W. Clarke and J. Herbst (eds.), *Learning from Somalia: The Lessons of Armed Humanitarian Intervention* (Boulder, CO: Westview Press, 1997)

Cohen, R., *UN Human Rights Bodies Should Deal with the Internally Displaced*, presentation given at a meeting organised for delegates to the Commission on Human Rights by the Quaker United Nations Office and the World Council of Churches, Geneva, 7 February 1990

'International Protection for Internally Displaced Persons', in L. Henkin and J. L. Hargrove (eds.), *Human Rights: An Agenda for the Next Century*, Studies in Transnational Legal Policy, No. 26 (Washington DC: American Society of International Law, 1994), 17–48

International Protection for Internally Displaced Persons: Next Steps, Refugee Policy Group Focus Paper No. 2, Washington DC, 1994

'Protecting the Internally Displaced', in US Committee for Refugees, *World Refugee Survey 1996* (Washington DC: USCR, 1996)

'Internally Displaced Persons: An Extended Role for UNHCR', Discussion Paper for UNHCR, International Conference on 'People of Concern', 21–24 November 1996

'Protecting Internally Displaced Women and Children', in Norwegian Refugee Council, *Rights Have No Borders: Worldwide Internal Displacement* (Oxford: Norwegian Refugee Council/Global IDP Survey, 1998), 63–74

'The Guiding Principles on Internal Displacement: A New Instrument for International Organisations and NGOs', *Forced Migration Review*, vol. 2, August 1998

Working Paper for Conference on 'Tough Nuts to Crack': Dealing with Difficult Situations of Internal Displacement, 28 January 1999

'Hard Cases: Internal Displacement in Turkey, Burma and Algeria', *Forced Migration Review*, vol. 6, December 1999

'The Development of International Standards to Protect Internally Displaced Persons', in A. F. Bayefsky and J. Fitzpatrick (eds.), *Human Rights and Forced Displacement* (The Hague: Kluwer Law International, 2000), 76–85

R. Cohen and J. Cuénod, *Improving Institutional Arrangements for the Internally Displaced* (Washington DC: Brookings Institution and Refugee Policy Group, 1995)

R. Cohen and F. M. Deng, 'Exodus Within Borders: The Uprooted Who Never Left Home' (1998) 77:4 *Foreign Affairs* 12

Masses in Flight: The Global Crisis of Internal Displacement (Washington DC: Brookings Institution, 1998)

(eds.), *The Forsaken People: Case Studies of the Internally Displaced* (Washington DC: Brookings Institution, 1998)

R. Cohen, F. M. Deng and G. Sanchez-Garzoli, 'Internal Displacement in the Americas: Some Distinctive Features', Brookings–City University of New York (CUNY) Project on Internal Displacement, Occasional Paper, May 2001

R. Cohen and D. A. Korn, 'Failing the Internally Displaced', *Forced Migration Review*, vol. 5, August 1999

I. Cohn and G. Goodwin-Gill, *Child Soldiers: The Role of Children in Armed Conflict* (Oxford: Oxford University Press, 1994)

Centre on Housing Rights and Evictions, *Housing and Property Restitution for Refugees and Internally Displaced Persons: International, Regional and National Legal Resources* (Geneva: COHRE, 2001)

Commission on Human Security, *Human Security Now* (New York, 2003)

Contat Hickel, M., 'Protection of Internally Displaced Persons Affected by Armed Conflict: Concept and Challenges' (2001) 843 *International Review of the Red Cross* 699

de Courten, J., 'The ICRC's Focus: Access to Victims of Armed Conflict and Internal Disturbances', in ICRC, *Internally Displaced Persons, Symposium, Geneva, 23–25 October 1995* (Geneva: ICRC, 1996), 84–7

Courtland Robinson, W., *Risks and Rights: The Causes, Consequences, and Challenges of Development-Induced Displacement*, Brookings Institution occasional paper, May 2003

Cox, M., 'The Right to Return Home: International Intervention and Ethnic Cleansing in Bosnia and Herzegovina' (1998) 47 *International Comparative Law Quarterly* 599

'The Dayton Agreement in Bosnia and Herzegovina: A Study of Implementation Strategies' (1999) 70 *British Yearbook of International Law* 201

CRPC and UNHCR, *Return, Relocation and Property Rights: A Discussion Paper*, Sarajevo, December 1997

Cullet, P., 'Human Rights and Displacement: The Indian Supreme Court Decision on Sardar Sarovar in International Perspective' (2001) 50 *International and Comparative Law Quarterly* 973

S. A. Cunliffe and M. Pugh, 'The Politicization of UNHCR in the Former Yugoslavia' (1997) 10 *Journal of Refugee Studies* 134

'UNHCR as Leader in Humanitarian Assistance: A Triumph of Politics over Law?', in F. Nicholson and P. Twomey (eds.), *Refugee Rights and Realities: Evolving International Concepts and Regimes* (Cambridge: Cambridge University Press, 1999), 175–199

Cutts, M., 'The Humanitarian Operation in Bosnia, 1992–95: Dilemmas in Negotiating Humanitarian Access', UNHCR Working Paper No. 8, May 1999

Dacyl, J., 'Sovereignty Versus Human Rights: From Past Discourses to Contemporary Dilemmas' (1996) 9 *Journal of Refugee Studies* 136

Damrosch, L. F. (ed.), *Enforcing Restraint: Collective Intervention in Internal Conflicts* (New York: Council on Foreign Relations Press, 1993)

Deng, F. M., *Protecting the Dispossessed: A Challenge for the International Community* (Washington DC: Brookings Institution, 1993)

   War of Visions: Conflicts of Identities in the Sudan (Washington DC: Brookings Institution, 1995)

   Sovereignty, Responsibility and Accountability: A Framework of Protection, Assistance, and Development for the Internally Displaced, concept paper for the Brookings Institution and Refugee Policy Group Project on Internal Displacement, Washington DC, 1995

   'Frontiers of Sovereignty: A Framework of Protection, Assistance, and Development for the Internally Displaced' (1995) 8 *Leiden Journal of International Law* 247

   'The International Protection of the Internally Displaced' (1995) *International Journal of Refugee Law*, Special issue 74

   'Dealing with the Displaced: A Challenge to the International Community' (1995) 1 *Global Governance* 45

   'The Global Challenge of Internal Displacement' (2001) 5 *Washington University Journal of Law and Policy* 141

F. M. Deng and J. Kunder, *The Consolidated Appeals and IDPs: The Degree to Which UN Consolidated Inter-Agency Appeals for the Year 2000 Support Internally Displaced Populations*, Brookings Institution and UNICEF, August 2000, http://www.brook.edu/views/papers/ deng/200008CAP.htm

F. Deng and D. McNamara, 'International and National Responses to the Plight of IDPs', *Forced Migration Review*, vol. 10, April 2001

Donnelly, J., 'State Sovereignty and International Intervention: The Case of Human Rights', in G. M. Lyons and M. Mastanduno (eds.), *Beyond Westphalia?: State Sovereignty and International Intervention* (Baltimore: Johns Hopkins University Press, 1995), 115–46

A. Dowty and G. Loescher, 'Refugee Flows as Grounds for International Action' (1996) 21:1 *International Security* 43

Dubernet, C., *The International Containment of Displaced Persons: Humanitarian Spaces Without Exit* (Aldershot: Ashgate, 2001)

The Economist, 'When is a Refugee Not a Refugee?', 3 March 2001, 23–5

A. Eide, A. Rosas and T. Meron, 'Combating Lawlessness in Grey Zone Conflicts Through Minimum Humanitarian Standards' (1995) 89 *American Journal of International Law* 215

European Stability Initiative (ESI), *Interim Evaluation of RRTF Minority Return Programmes in 1999*, Berlin, September 1999

Farha, L., 'Women's Rights to Land, Property and Housing', *Forced Migration Review*, vol. 7, April 2000

Feldmann, A., 'Rational Ambivalence: The UNHCR Responses to Internal
    Displacement Emergencies', unpublished paper presented at the
    International Studies Association Convention, Los Angeles, 15–18 March
    2000
Feller, E., 'Statement by the Director, UNHCR Department of International
    Protection, to the 18th Meeting of the UNHCR Standing Committee, 5 July
    2000' (2000) 12 *International Journal of Refugee Law* 401
Fitzpatrick, J., *Human Rights in Crisis: The International System for Protecting Human
    Rights During States of Emergency* (Philadelphia: University of Pennsylvania
    Press, 1994)
    'Human Rights and Forced Displacement: Converging Standards', in A. F.
    Bayefsky and J. Fitzpatrick (eds.), *Human Rights and Forced Displacement* (The
    Hague: Kluwer Law International, 2000), 3–25
J. Fitzpatrick and R. Bonoan, 'Cessation of Refugee Protection', in E. Feller, V.
    Türk and F. Nicholson (eds.), *Refugee Protection in International Law: UNHCR's
    Global Consultations on International Protection* (Cambridge: Cambridge
    University Press, 2003), 491–544
Forsythe, D., 'UNHCR's Mandate: The Politics of Being Non-Political', UNHCR
    Working Paper No. 33, March 2001
Franck, T. M., *Fairness in International Law and Institutions* (Oxford: Oxford
    University Press, 1995)
Freedman, P., 'International Intervention to Combat the Explosion of Refugees
    and Internally Displaced Persons' (1995) 9 *Georgetown Immigration Law
    Journal* 565
Frelick, B., '"Preventive Protection" and the Right to Seek Asylum: A
    Preliminary Look at Bosnia and Croatia' (1992) 4 *International Journal of
    Refugee Law* 439
    'Assistance Without Protection: Feed the Hungry, Clothe the Naked, and
    Watch Them Die', in US Committee for Refugees, *World Refugee Survey 1997*
    (Washington DC: USCR, 1997), 24
    'Aliens in Their Own Land: Protection and Durable Solutions for Internally
    Displaced Persons', in US Committee for Refugees, *World Refugee Survey 1998*
    (Washington DC: USCR, 1998)
M. Frohart, D. Paul and L. Minear, *Protecting Human Rights: The Challenge to
    Humanitarian Organisations*, Occasional Paper No. 35 (Providence, RI:
    Thomas J. Watson Jr Institute for International Studies, 1999)
P. T. Gan, 'Caught in the Crossfire: Strengthening International Protection for
    Internally Displaced Persons Due to Internal Armed Conflict' (1994) 39
    Ateneo Law Journal 1
Garling, M., *The UNHCR and Internal Displacement: A Fresh Look*, Geneva, May 1999
    'Protection for Property Rights: A Partial Solution? The Commission for Real
    Property Claims of Displaced Persons and Refugees (CRPC) in Bosnia and
    Herzegovina' (2000) 19:3 *Refugee Survey Quarterly* 64
Garrett, S. A., *Doing Good and Doing Well: An Examination of Humanitarian
    Intervention* (Westport, CT: Praeger, 1999)

Garvey, J., 'The New Asylum-Seekers: Addressing Their Origin', in D. A. Martin (ed.), *The New Asylum-Seekers: Refugee Law in the 1980s, the Ninth Sokol Colloquium on International Law* (Dordrecht: Martinus Nijhoff Publishers, 1988), 181–94

Geissler, N., *Der völkerrechtliche Schutz der Internally Displaced Persons: eine Analyse des normativen und institutionellen Schutzes der IDPs im Rahmen innerer Unruhen und nicht-internationaler Konflikte* (Berlin: Duncker & Humblot, 1999)

'The International Protection of Internally Displaced Persons' (1999) 11 *International Journal of Refugee Law* 451

Georgetown Symposium on Internally Displaced Persons, 15–18 October 1989, Summary of Discussion (unpublished document)

Gibney, M., T. Apodaca and J. McCann, 'Refugee Flows, the Internally Displaced and Political Violence: An Explanatory Analysis', unpublished paper, Purdue University, 1994

Gillan, A., 'What's the Story?', *London Review of Books*, vol. 21, No. 11, 27 May 1999

Glenny, M., *The Fall of Yugoslavia* (London: Penguin Books, 1993)

Global IDP Database, *Internal Displacement in the OSCE Region*, Geneva, September 2001

Profile of Internal Displacement: Bosnia and Herzegovina, January 2003

Global IDP Survey, *Internally Displaced People: A Global Survey* (London: Earthscan Publications Ltd, 1998)

Internally Displaced People: A Global Survey (London: Earthscan Publications Ltd, 2002, 2nd ed.)

Goldman, R. K., 'International Human Rights and Humanitarian Law and the Internally Displaced', in A. A. Cançado Trindade (ed.), *The Modern World of Human Rights: Essays in Honour of Thomas Buergenthal* (San José, Costa Rica: Inter-American Institute of Human Rights, 1996), 517–48

'Codification of International Rules on Internally Displaced Persons' (1998) 324 *International Review of the Red Cross* 463

Goodwin-Gill, G., '*Non-Refoulement* and the New Asylum Seekers' (1986) 26 *Virginia Journal of International Law* 897

'The Language of Protection' (1989) 1 *International Journal of Refugee Law* 17

'Asylum: The Law and Politics of Change' (1995) 7 *International Journal of Refugee Law* 1

The Refugee in International Law (Oxford: Clarendon Press, 1996, 2nd ed.)

'Refugee Identity and Protection's Fading Prospect', in F. Nicholson and P. Twomey (eds.), *Refugee Rights and Realities: Evolving International Concepts and Regimes* (Cambridge: Cambridge University Press, 1999), 220–49

'UNHCR and Internal Displacement: Stepping into a Legal and Political Minefield', *World Refugee Survey 2000* http://www.refugees.org/world/articles/wrs00_unhcr.htm

'The Individual Refugee, the 1951 Convention and the Treaty of Amsterdam', in E. Guild and C. Harlow (eds.), *Implementing Amsterdam: Immigration and Asylum Rights in EC Law* (Oxford: Hart Publishing, 2001), 141–63

Gow, J., *Triumph of the Lack of Will: International Diplomacy and the Yugoslav War* (New York: Columbia University Press, 1997)

Gowlland-Debbas, V. (ed.), *The Problem of Refugees in the Light of Contemporary International Law Issues* (The Hague: Martinus Nijhoff Publishers, 1995)

Grahl-Madsen, A., *Territorial Asylum* (Stockholm: Almqvist & Wiksell International, 1980)

Grecic, V., 'Refugees and Internally Displaced Persons in the Former Yugoslavia in the Light of Dayton and Paris Agreements', in *Refuge*, vol. 16, No. 5, November 1997

Greenwood, C., 'Customary Law Status of the 1977 Geneva Protocols', in A. J. M. Delissen and G. J. Tanja (eds.), *Humanitarian Law of Armed Conflict: Challenges Ahead: Essays in Honour of Frits Karlshoven* (Dordrecht: Martinus Nijhoff, 1991), 93–114

M. Griffith, I. Levine and M. Weller, 'Sovereignty and Suffering', in J. Harriss (ed.), *The Politics of Humanitarian Intervention* (London: Pinter, 1995), 33–90

Hakata, K., *La protection internationale des personnes déplacées à l'intérieur de leur propre pays*, thèse de doctorat en droit, Université de Genève, February 1998
  'Vers une protection plus effective des "personnes déplacées à l'intérieur de leur propre pays"' (2002) *Revue Générale de Droit International Public* 619–44

Hartling, P., 'The Concept and Definition of "refugee" – Legal and Humanitarian Aspects' (1979) 48 *Nordisk Tidsskrift for International Ret* 125

Harvey, C., *Seeking Asylum in the UK: Problems and Prospects* (London: Butterworths, 2000)

Hathaway, J., 'A Reconsideration of the Underlying Premise of Refugee Law' (1990) 31 *Harvard International Law Journal* 129
  The Law of Refugee Status (Toronto: Butterworths, 1991)
  'Reconceiving Refugee Law as Human Rights Protection', in K. E. Mahoney and P. Mahoney (eds.), *Human Rights in the Twenty-First Century: A Global Challenge* (Dordrecht: Martinus Nijhoff Publishers, 1993), 659–78

J. C. Hathaway and M. Forster, 'Internal Protection/Relocation/Flight Alternative as an Aspect of Refugee Status Determination', in E. Feller, V. Türk and F. Nicholson (eds.), *Refugee Protection in International Law: UNHCR's Global Consultations on International Protection* (Cambridge: Cambridge University Press, 2003), 357–417

J. Hathaway and R. A. Neve, 'Making International Refugee Law Relevant Again: A Proposal for Collectivised and Solution-Oriented Protection' (1997) 10 *Harvard Human Rights Journal* 115

Held, D. (ed.), *States and Societies* (Oxford: Martin Robertson & Co. Ltd, 1983)

Helle, D., 'Enhancing the Protection of Internally Displaced Persons', in Norwegian Refugee Council, *Rights Have No Borders: Worldwide Internal Displacement* (Oxford: Norwegian Refugee Council/Global IDP Survey, 1998), 31–51

Helton, A. C., 'Forced Displacement, Humanitarian Intervention, and Sovereignty' (2000) 20:1 *SAIS Review* 61

The Price of Indifference – Refugees and Humanitarian Action in the New Century (Oxford: Oxford University Press, 2002)

Henkin, A. H. (ed.), *Honoring Human Rights and Keeping the Peace: Lessons from El Salvador, Cambodia and Haiti* (Washington DC: Alpen Institute, 1995)

Higgins, R., 'The New United Nations and Former Yugoslavia' (1993) 69 *International Affairs* 465

J. L. Hirsch and R. B. Oakley, *Somalia and Operation Restore Hope: Reflections on Peacekeeping and Peacemaking* (Washington DC: US Institute of Peace Press, 1995)

Hofmann, R., 'Internally Displaced Persons as Refugees' (1993) 35 *Acta Juridica Hungarica* 179

'International Humanitarian Law and the Law of Refugees and Internally Displaced Persons', in European Commission, *Law in Humanitarian Crisis*, vol. 1 (Brussels: European Commission, 1995), 249–309

Holborn, L. W., *Refugees: A Problem of Our Time: The Work of the United Nations High Commissioner for Refugees, 1951–1972*, vol. I (Metuchen, NJ: Scarecrow Press, 1975)

Holbrooke, R., *To End a War* (New York: The Modern Library, 1999)

Statement at Cardozo Law School on Refugees and Internally Displaced Persons, USUN press release #44 (00), 28 March 2000

'A Borderline Difference', *Washington Post*, 8 May 2000

van Houtte, H., 'Mass Property Claim Resolution in a Post-War Society – The Commission for Real Property Claims in Bosnia and Herzegovina (CRPC)' (1999) 48 *International and Comparative Law Quarterly* 625

Howland, T., 'Mirage, Magic, or Mixed Bag? The United Nations High Commissioner for Human Rights' Field Operation in Rwanda' (1999) 21 *Human Rights Quarterly* 1

Human Rights Law Centre/University of Sarajevo, *Legal and Factual Obstacles Before Return of Refugees and Displaced Persons to the Sarajevo Canton*, September 1998

Human Rights Watch, *The Lost Agenda: Human Rights and UN Field Operations* (New York: Human Rights Watch, 1993)

Bosnia-Herzegovina: The Fall of Srebrenica and the Failure of UN Peacekeeping (Washington DC: Human Rights Watch, 1995)

Broken Promises: Impediments to Refugee Return to Croatia (Washington DC: Human Rights Watch, 2003)

Human Rights Watch/Africa, *Failing the Internally Displaced: The UNDP Displaced Persons Program in Kenya* (New York: Human Rights Watch/Africa, 1997)

Hyndman, P., 'Preventive, Palliative, or Punitive? Safe Spaces in Bosnia-Herzegovina, Somalia, and Sri Lanka' (2003) 16 *Journal of Refugee Studies* 167

Inter-Agency Standing Committee, 'Protection of Internally Displaced Persons', Inter-Agency Standing Committee policy paper, New York, December 1999

Supplementary Guidance to Humanitarian/Resident Co-ordinators on Their Responsibilities in Relation to IDPs, 29 March 2000

Senior Inter-Agency Network to Reinforce the Operational Response to Situations of Internal Displacement, New York, 15 September 2000

Growing the Sheltering Tree: Protecting Rights Through Humanitarian Action (New York: UNICEF, 2002)

International Commission on Intervention and State Sovereignty (ICISS), *The Responsibility to Protect* (Ottawa: International Development Research Centre, 2001)

International Committee of the Red Cross (ICRC), *Persons Displaced Within Their Own Countries as a Result of Armed Conflict or Disturbances*, working document prepared by the ICRC, Geneva, 1991

Internally Displaced Persons, Symposium, Geneva, 23–25 October 1995 (Geneva: ICRC, 1996)

'Internally Displaced Persons: The Mandate and Role of the International Committee of the Red Cross' (2000) 838 *International Review of the Red Cross* 491

International Council of Voluntary Agencies (ICVA), *A Discussion Paper on Future Options for an Institutional Response to Internally Displaced Persons*, Geneva, 30 January 2001

Some NGO Views on an Institutional Response to Internally Displaced Persons, Geneva, 26 March 2001

International Crisis Group (ICG), *Going Nowhere Fast: Refugees and Internally Displaced Persons in Bosnia*, ICG Balkans Report No. 23, Sarajevo, 1 May 1997

Minority Return or Mass Relocation?, ICG Balkans Report No. 33, Sarajevo, 14 May 1998

Too Little, Too Late: Implementation of the Sarajevo Declaration, ICG Balkans Report No. 44, Sarajevo, 9 September 1998

Preventing Minority Return in Bosnia and Herzegovina: The Anatomy of Hate and Fear, ICG Balkans Report No. 73, Sarajevo, 2 August 1999

Is Dayton Failing?: Bosnia Four Years After the Peace Agreement, ICG Balkans Report No. 80, Sarajevo, 28 October 1999

Bosnia's Refugee Logjam Breaks: Is the International Community Ready?, ICG Balkans Report No. 95, Sarajevo/Washington/Brussels, 30 May 2000

The Continuing Challenge of Refugee Return in Bosnia and Herzegovina, ICG Balkans Report No. 137, Sarajevo/Brussels, 13 December 2002

Return to Uncertainty: Kosovo's Internally Displaced and the Return Process, ICG Balkans Report No. 139, Pristina/Brussels, 13 December 2002

International Law Association, Report of the Committee on Internally Displaced Persons, in International Law Association, *Report of the Sixty-Seventh Conference Held at Helsinki, 12 to 17 August 1996* (London: ILA, 1996)

International Organisation for Migration (IOM), *Internally Displaced Persons*, contribution of the IOM to the 3 February 1993 meeting of the IASC (Geneva: IOM, 1993)

The Reintegration of Internally Displaced Vulnerable Groups in the IOM's Assistance Programme (Geneva: IOM, 1993)

Internally Displaced Persons: IOM Policy and Programmes (Geneva: IOM, 1997)

Statement by IOM to the Commission on Human Rights, Geneva, April 1998

Ito, A., 'Politicisation of Minority Return in Bosnia and Herzegovina – The First Five Years Examined' (2001) 13 *International Journal of Refugee Law* 98

Jackson, R. H., *Quasi-States: Sovereignty, International Relations and the Third World* (Cambridge: Cambridge University Press, 1990)

Jackson Preece, J., 'Ethnic Cleansing as an Instrument of Nation-State Creation: Changing State Practices and Evolving Legal Norms' (1998) 20 *Human Rights Quarterly* 817

Jeannet, S., 'Recognition of the ICRC's Long-Standing Rule of Confidentiality – An Important Decision by the International Criminal Tribunal for the Former Yugoslavia' (2000) 838 *International Review of the Red Cross* 403

Kälin, W., 'Guiding Principles on Internal Displacement', paper presented at the Overseas Development Institute, London, 20 July 1998

'The Guiding Principles on Internal Displacement – Introduction' (1998) 10 *International Journal of Refugee Law* 557

Guiding Principles on Internal Displacement: Annotations (Washington DC: American Society of International Law and the Brookings Institution, 2000)

'How Hard is Soft Law? The Guiding Principles on Internal Displacement and the Need for a Normative Framework', presentation at Roundtable Meeting, Ralph Bunche Institute for International Studies, City University of New York Graduate Center, 19 December 2002

Kenny, K. E., 'Formal and Informal Innovations in the United Nations Protection of Human Rights: The Special Rapporteur on the Former Yugoslavia' (1995) 48 *Austrian Journal of Public International Law* 19

'Introducing the Sustainability Principle to Human Rights Operations' (1997) 4 *International Peacekeeping* 61

When Needs Are Rights: An Overview of UN Efforts to Integrate Human Rights in Humanitarian Action, Occasional Paper No. 38 (Providence, RI: Thomas J. Watson Jr Institute for International Studies, 2000)

Kjærum, M., 'The Evolving Role of UNHCR in the Broader UN Perspective', in V. Gowlland and K. Samson (eds.), *Problems and Prospects of Refugee Law* (Geneva: Graduate Institute of International Studies, 1991), 105–12

Kleine-Ahlbrandt, S. T. E., *The Protection Gap in the International Protection of Internally Displaced Persons: The Case of Rwanda* (Geneva: Institut Universitaire des Hautes Etudes Internationales, 1996)

'The Kibeho Crisis: Towards a More Effective System of International Protection of IDPs', *Forced Migration Review*, vol. 2, August 1998

Korn, D. A., *Exodus Within Borders: An Introduction to the Crisis of Internal Displacement* (Washington DC: Brookings Institution, 1999)

Kourula, P., *Broadening the Edges: Refugee Definition and International Protection Revisited* (The Hague: Martinus Nijhoff Publishers, 1997)

Krill, F., 'The ICRC's Policy on Refugees and Internally Displaced Civilians' (2001) 843 *International Review of the Red Cross* 607

Kritsiotis, D., 'Reappraising Policy Objections to Humanitarian Intervention'
     (1998) 19 *Michigan Journal of International Law* 1005
     'The Kosovo Crisis and NATO's Application of Armed Force Against the
     Federal Republic of Yugoslavia' (2000) 49 *International and Comparative Law
     Quarterly* 330
Kumar, R., *Divide and Fall? Bosnia and the Annals of Partition* (London: Verso, 1997)
Kunder, J., *The Needs of Internally Displaced Women and Children: Guiding Principles
     and Considerations*, New York, Office of Emergency Programmes, Working
     Paper Series, September 1998
     The US Government and Internally Displaced Persons: Present, But Not Accounted for,
     Brookings Institution and the US Committee for Refugees, Washington DC,
     November 1999
Lambrecht, C. W., *NGO Response Patterns to the Assistance, Protection and
     Development Needs of the Internally Displaced*, Norwegian Refugee Council,
     Geneva, July 1996
Landgren, K., 'Safety Zones and International Protection: A Dark Grey Area'
     (1995) 7 *International Journal of Refugee Law* 436
E. Lauterpacht and D. Bethlehem, 'The Scope and Content of the Principle of
     Non-Refoulement: Opinion', in E. Feller, V. Türk and F. Nicholson (eds.), *Refugee
     Protection in International Law: UNHCR's Global Consultations on International
     Protection* (Cambridge: Cambridge University Press, 2003), 87–177
S. Lautze, B. D. Jones and M. Duffield, *Strategic Humanitarian Coordination in the
     Great Lakes Region 1996–1997: An Independent Study for the Inter-Agency Standing
     Committee*, New York, March 1998
Lavoyer, J. P., 'Refugees and Internally Displaced Persons: International
     Humanitarian Law and the Role of the ICRC' (1995) 305 *International Review
     of the Red Cross* 162
     'Protection under International Humanitarian Law', in ICRC, *Internally
     Displaced Persons, Symposium, Geneva, 23–25 October 1995* (Geneva: ICRC, 1996),
     26–36
     'Guiding Principles on Internal Displacement: A Few Comments on the
     Contribution of International Humanitarian Law' (1998) 324 *International
     Review of the Red Cross* 467
     'Forced Displacement: The Relevance of International Humanitarian Law', in
     A. F. Bayefsky and J. Fitzpatrick (eds.), *Human Rights and Forced Displacement*
     (The Hague: Kluwer Law International, 2000), 50–65
Lawyers Committee for Human Rights, *Protection by Presence? The Limits of United
     Nations Safekeeping Activities in Croatia*, Discussion Paper, New York,
     September 1993
Leckie, S., 'Resolving Kosovo's Housing Crisis: Challenges for the UN Housing
     and Property Directorate', *Forced Migration Review*, vol. 7, April 2000
     'Housing and Property Issues for Refugees and Internally Displaced Persons
     in the Context of Return: Key Considerations for UNHCR Policy and
     Practice' (2000) 19:3 *Refugee Survey Quarterly* 5

Lee, L. T., 'Legal Status of Internally Displaced Persons' (1992) 86 *ASIL Proceedings* 630

'Draft Declaration of Principles of International Law on Internally Displaced Persons' (1996) 90 *ASIL Proceedings* 555

'Internally Displaced Persons and Refugees: Toward a Legal Synthesis?' (1996) 9 *Journal of Refugee Studies* 27

'Strengthening Legal Protection in Internal Conflicts' (1997) 3 *ILSA Journal of International and Comparative Law* 529

'The London Declaration of International Law Principles on Internally Displaced Persons: Its Significance and Implications' (2001) 14 *Journal of Refugee Studies* 70

'The London Declaration of International Law Principles on Internally Displaced Persons' (2001) 95 *American Journal of International Law* 454

X. Leus, J. Wallace and A. Loretti, 'Internally Displaced Persons' (2001) 16:3 *Prehospital and Disaster Medicine* 75

Lewis, C. E., 'Dealing with the Problem of Internally Displaced Persons' (1992) 6 *Georgetown Immigration Law Journal* 693

Loescher, G., *Beyond Charity: International Co-operation and the Global Refugee Crisis* (Oxford: Oxford University Press, 1993)

The UNHCR and World Politics: A Perilous Path (Oxford: Oxford University Press, 2001)

G. Loescher and L. Monaham (eds.), *Refugees and International Relations* (Oxford: Oxford University Press, 1989)

Lyons, T., *Somalia: State Collapse, Multilateral Intervention, and Strategies for Political Reconstruction* (Washington DC: Brookings Institution, 1995)

MacDonald, F., 'Legal Protection of the Vulnerable: The Case of Older IDPs', *Forced Migration Review*, vol. 14, July 2002

Macklin, A., 'Refugee Women and the Imperatives of Categories' (1995) 17 *Human Rights Quarterly* 213

Malanczuk, P., 'The Kurdish Crisis and Allied Intervention in the Aftermath of the Second Gulf War' (1991) 2 *European Journal of International Law* 114

Malcolm, N., *Bosnia: A Short Story* (London: Papermac, 1996, 2nd ed.)

Martin, D. A., 'The Refugee Concept: On Definitions, Politics, and the Careful Use of a Scarce Resource', in H. Adelman (ed.), *Refugee Policy: Canada and the United States* (North York, Ontario: York Lanes Press Ltd, 1991), 30–51

Martin, I., 'A New Frontier: The Early Experience and Future of International Human Rights Field Operations' (1998) 16 *Netherlands Quarterly of Human Rights* 121

Maselen, S., 'The Implications of the 1996 Land-Mines Protocol for Refugees and the Internally Displaced' (1996) 8 *International Journal of Refugee Law* 383

A. Mawson, R. Dodd and J. Hilary, *War Brought Us Here: Protecting Children Displaced Within Their Own Countries by Conflict* (London: Save the Children, 2000)

J. McLean and T. Greene, 'Turmoil in Tajikistan: Addressing the Crisis of Internal Displacement', in R. Cohen and F. M. Deng (eds.), *The Forsaken*

People: Case Studies of the Internally Displaced (Washington DC: Brookings Institution, 1998), 313–58

McNamara, D., 'UNHCR's Perspective', in ICRC, *Internally Displaced Persons, Symposium, Geneva, 23–25 October 1995* (Geneva: ICRC, 1996), 59–67

Information Note by the UN Special Coordinator of the Senior Inter-Agency Network on Internal Displacement, 13 September 2000

Interim Report from the Special Co-ordinator of the Network on Internal Displacement, 9 April 2001

Médecins sans frontières, *Populations in Danger 1995, a Médecins sans frontières Report* (London: Médecins sans frontières UK, 1995)

Meindersma, C., 'Legal Issues Surrounding Population Transfers in Conflict Situations' (1994) 41 *Netherlands International Law Review* 31

Melander, G., 'Internally Displaced Persons', in G. Alfredsson and P. Macalister-Smith (eds.), *The Living Law of Nations: Essays on Refugees, Minorities, Indigenous Peoples and the Human Rights of Other Vulnerable Groups in Memory of Atle Grahl-Madsen* (Kehl am Rhein: Engel, 1996), 69–74

Mendiluce, J. M., 'War and Disaster in the Former Yugoslavia: The Limits of Humanitarian Action', *World Refugee Survey 1994*, http://www.refugees.org/world/articles/yugoslavia_wrs94.htm

Mercier, M., *Crimes Without Punishment: Humanitarian Action in the Former Yugoslavia* (London: Pluto Press, 1995)

Meron, T., *Human Rights in Internal Strife: Their International Protection* (Cambridge: Grotius Publications, 1987)

Human Rights and Humanitarian Norms as Customary Law (Oxford: Clarendon Press, 1989)

Messina, C., 'From Migrants to Refugees: Russian, Soviet and Post-Soviet Migration' (1994) 6 *International Journal of Refugee Law* 620

Mills, K., *Human Rights in the Emerging Global Order: A New Sovereignty?* (London: Macmillan Press, 1998)

L. Minear and R. C. Kent, 'Rwanda's Internally Displaced: A Conundrum Within a Conundrum', in R. Cohen and F. M. Deng (eds.), *The Forsaken People: Case Studies of the Internally Displaced* (Washington DC: Brookings Institution, 1998), 57–95

L. Minear, J. Clark, R. Cohen, D. Gallagher, I. Guest and T. G. Weiss, *Humanitarian Action in the Former Yugoslavia: The UN's Role 1991–1993*, Occasional Paper No. 18 (Providence, RI: Thomas J. Watson Jr Institute for International Studies and Refugee Policy Group, 1994).

L. Minear and T. G. Weiss, *Mercy under Fire: War and the Global Humanitarian Community* (Boulder: Westview, 1995)

Mooney, E. D., 'Presence, Ergo Protection? UNPROFOR, UNHCR and the ICRC in Croatia and Bosnia and Herzegovina' (1995) 7 *International Journal of Refugee Law* 407

'Internal Displacement and the Conflict in Abkhazia: International Responses and Their Protective Effect' (1996) 3 *International Journal on Group Rights* 197

Internally Displaced Persons: The Role of OHCHR, paper presented at the informal meeting of experts on measures to ensure international protection to all who need it, Geneva, 11 May 1998

'In-Country Protection: Out of Bounds for UNHCR?', in F. Nicholson and P. Twomey (eds.), *Refugee Rights and Realities: Evolving International Concepts and Regimes* (Cambridge: Cambridge University Press, 1999), 200–19

'Principles of Protection for Internally Displaced Persons' (2001) 38:6 *International Migration* 81

Morris, N., 'Protection Dilemmas and UNHCR's Response: A Personal View from Within UNHCR' (1997) 9 *International Journal of Refugee Law* 492

Moussalli, M., 'The Evolving Functions of the Office of the High Commissioner for Refugees', in V. Gowlland and K. Samson (eds.), *Problems and Prospects of Refugee Law* (Geneva: Graduate Institute of International Studies, 1991), 81–103

K. Musalo, J. Moore and R. A. Boswell, *Refugee Law and Policy: Cases and Materials* (Durham, NC: Carolina Academic Press, 1997)

Nanda, V. P., 'International Law and the Refugee Challenge: Mass Expulsion and Internally Displaced People' (1992) 28 *Willamente Law Review* 791

Nash, A. E. (ed.), *Human Rights and the Protection of Refugees under International Law* (South Halifax, NS: Institute for Research and Public Policy, 1988)

K. Newland and D. Waller Meyers, 'Peacekeeping and Refugee Relief' (1999) 5 *International Peacekeeping* 15

Norwegian Refugee Council, *Institutional Arrangements for Internally Displaced Persons: The Ground Level Experience* (Oslo: Norwegian Refugee Council, 1995)

Rights Have No Borders: Worldwide Internal Displacement (Oxford: Norwegian Refugee Council/Global IDP Survey, 1998)

Norwegian Refugee Council and Refugee Policy Group, *Norwegian Government Roundtable Discussion on United Nations Human Rights Protection for Internally Displaced Persons, Nyon, Switzerland, February 1993* (Washington DC: Refugee Policy Group, 1993)

Norwegian University of Science and Technology, *Researching Internal Displacement: State of the Art*, Conference Report, 7–8 February 2003, Trondheim, Norway

O'Ballance, E., *Civil War in Bosnia, 1992–94* (London: Macmillan Press Ltd, 1995)

L. Obregón and M. Stavropoulou, 'In Search of Hope: The Plight of Displaced Colombians', in R. Cohen and F. M. Deng (eds.), *The Forsaken People: Case Studies of the Internally Displaced* (Washington DC: Brookings Institution, 1998), 399–453

Office for the Coordination of Humanitarian Assistance (OCHA), *Handbook for Applying the Guiding Principles on Internal Displacement*, 1999

Manual on Field Practice in Internal Displacement: Examples from UN Agencies and Partner Organisations of Field-Based Initiatives Supporting Internally Displaced Persons, Inter-Agency Standing Committee Policy Paper Series No. 1, 1999

OCHA Internal Displacement Unit, *Protection Coalition on Internal Displacement – Terms of Reference*, http://www.reliefweb.int/ idp/docs/references/ ToRProtCoalition240702.pdf

No Refuge: The Challenge of Internal Displacement (New York and Geneva: United Nations, 2003)

OCHA Internal Displacement Unit and the Brookings Institution-SAIS Project on Internal Displacement, *The Protection Survey*, http://www.reliefweb.int/idp/docs/references/ProtSurvProp.pdf

Office of the High Commissioner for Human Rights (OHCHR), *Internally Displaced Persons: Compilation and Analysis of Legal Norms* (New York and Geneva: United Nations, 1998)

Ogata, S., Statement of the United Nations High Commissioner for Refugees to the International Meeting on Humanitarian Aid for Victims of the Conflict in the Former Yugoslavia, Geneva, 29 July 1992

'Refugees: Challenge of the 1990s', Statement of the United Nations High Commissioner for Refugees, New School for Social Research, New York, 11 November 1992

'The Interface Between Peacekeeping and Humanitarian Action', Statement of the United Nations High Commissioner for Refugees at the International Colloquium on New Dimensions of Peacekeeping at the Graduate Institute of International Studies, Geneva, 11 March 1994

Statements of the United Nations High Commissioner for Refugees at the Humanitarian Issues Working Group of the International Conference on Former Yugoslavia, Geneva, 10 October 1995 and 13 May 1996

'UNHCR in the Balkans: Humanitarian Action in the Midst of War', in W. Biermann and M. Vadset (eds.), *UN Peacekeeping in Trouble: Lessons Learned from the Former Yugoslavia* (Aldershot: Ashgate, 1998), 186–99

Statement by the United Nations High Commissioner for Refugees, to the Humanitarian Issues Working Group of the Peace Implementation Council, Geneva, 6 April 1999

'Protecting People on the Move', Address by the United Nations High Commissioner for Refugees, sponsored by the Center for the Study of International Organization, New York, 18 July 2000

Oraa, J., *Human Rights in States of Emergency in International Law* (Oxford: Clarendon Press, 1992)

OSCE, UNMIBH, OHR, UNHCR and CRPC, *Property Law Implementation Plan: Inter-Agency Framework Document*, October 2000

Osterdahl, I., 'By All Means, Intervene! The Security Council and the Use of Force under Chapter VII of the UN Charter in Iraq (to Protect the Kurds), in Bosnia, Somalia, Rwanda and Haiti' (1997) 66 *Nordic Journal of International Law* 241

Oswald, B. M., 'The Creation and Control of Places of Protection During United Nations Peace Operations' (2001) 844 *International Review of the Red Cross* 1013

Paul, D., *An Integrated, Strategic Approach to the Protection of Internally Displaced Persons*, 14 November 2000, http://www.1chr.org/conference/MEMOPaul.htm

Pax International, *Internally Displaced Persons – A Discussion Paper*, Washington DC, March 2002, http://www.paxinternational.org/discuss

G. Peress and E. Stover, *The Graves: Forensic Efforts in Srebrenica and Vukovar* (Zurich: Scalo, 1998)

Petrasek, D., 'New Standards for the Protection of Internally Displaced Persons:
    A Proposal for a Comprehensive Approach' (1995) 14:1&2 *Refugee Survey
    Quarterly* 285
    'Moving Forward on the Development of Minimum Humanitarian Standards'
    (1998) 92 *American Journal of International Law* 557
Phuong, C., 'Refugees and Internally Displaced Persons: Conceptual Differences
    and Similarities' (2000) 18 *Netherlands Quarterly of Human Rights* 215
    '"Freely to Return": Reversing Ethnic Cleansing in Bosnia and Herzegovina'
    (2000) 13 *Journal of Refugee Studies* 165
    'At the Heart of the Return Process: Solving Property Issues in Bosnia and
    Herzegovina', *Forced Migration Review*, vol. 7, April 2000
    'Improving the United Nations Response to Crises of Internal Displacement'
    (2002) 13 *International Journal of Refugee Law* 491
Plattner, D., 'The Protection of Displaced Persons in Non-International Armed
    Conflicts' (1993) 291 *International Review of the Red Cross* 567
Plender, R., 'The Legal Basis of International Jurisdiction to Act with Regard to
    the Internally Displaced' (1994) 6 *International Journal of Refugee Law* 345
Popovic, E., 'The Impact of International Human Rights Law on the Property
    Law of Bosnia and Herzegovina' in M. O'Flaherty and G. Gisvold (eds.),
    Post-War Protection of Human Rights in Bosnia and Herzegovina (The Hague:
    Martinus Nijhoff Publishers, 1998), 141–56
Posen, B. R., 'Military Responses to Refugee Disasters' (1996) 21:1 *International
    Security* 72
Ramcharan, B. G., 'Early-Warning at the United Nations: The First Experiment'
    (1989) 1 *International Journal of Refugee Law* 379
Refugee Policy Group, *Human Rights Protection for Internally Displaced Persons: An
    International Conference, June 24–25, 1991* (Washington DC: Refugee Policy
    Group, 1991)
Regensburg, K., 'Refugee Law Reconsidered: Reconciling Humanitarian
    Objectives with the Protectionist Agendas of Western Europe and the
    United States' (1996) 29 *Cornell International Law Journal* 225
N. Reindorp and P. Wiles, *Humanitarian Coordination: Lessons from Recent Field
    Experience*, study commissioned by the Office for the Coordination of
    Humanitarian Assistance and the Overseas Development Institute, London,
    June 2001
Reisman, M., 'Sovereignty and Human Rights in Contemporary International
    Law' (1990) 84 *American Journal of International Law* 866
Rich, R., 'Recognition of States: The Collapse of Yugoslavia and the Soviet
    Union' (1993) 4 *European Journal of International Law* 36
Rieff, D., *Slaughterhouse: Bosnia and the Failure of the West* (New York: Simon &
    Schuster, 1995)
Roberts, A., 'Humanitarian War: Military Intervention and Human Rights'
    (1993) 69 *International Affairs* 429
    'NATO's "Humanitarian War" over Kosovo' (1999) 41:3 *Survival* 102

A. Roberts and R. Guelff, *Documents on the Laws of War* (Oxford: Oxford University Press, 2000, 3rd ed.)

Roch, M. P., 'Forced Displacement in the Former Yugoslavia: A Crime under International Law?' (1995) 14 *Dickinson Journal of International Law* 1

Rodhe, D., *A Safe Area: Srebrenica: Europe's Worst Massacre Since the Second World War* (New York: Simon & Schuster, 1997)

Rodley, N. S., 'Collective Intervention to Protect Human Rights and Civilian Populations: The Legal Framework', in N. S. Rodley (ed.), *To Loose the Bands of Wickedness: International Intervention in Defence of Human Rights* (London: Brassey's, 1992), 14–42

Rosand, E., 'The Right to Return under International Law Following Mass Dislocation: The Bosnia Precedent?' (1998) 19 *Michigan Journal of International Law* 1091

  'The Right to Compensation in Bosnia: An Unfulfilled Promise and a Challenge to International Law' (2000) 33 *Cornell International Law Journal* 113

Rose, M., 'Field Coordination of UN Humanitarian Assistance, Bosnia, 1994', in J. Whitman and D. Pocock (eds.), *After Rwanda: The Coordination of UN Humanitarian Assistance* (London: Macmillan, 1996), 149–60

Ruddick, E. E., 'The Continuing Constraint of Sovereignty: International Law, International Protection, and the Internally Displaced' (1997) 77 *Boston University Law Review* 429

Rudge, P., *The Need for a More Focused Response: European Donor Policies Toward Internally Displaced Persons*, Brookings Institution, Norwegian Refugee Council and US Committee for Refugees, January 2002

Russell, S., 'Sexual Orientation and Refugee Claims Based on "membership of a Particular Social Group" under the 1951 Refugee Convention', in F. Nicholson and P. Twomey (eds.), *Current Issues of UK Asylum Law and Policy* (Aldershot: Ashgate, 1998), 133–51

Sahnoun, M., *Somalia: The Missed Opportunities* (Washington DC: US Institute for Peace Press, 1994)

Sandoz, Y., 'The Establishment of Safety Zones for Persons Displaced Within Their Country of Origin', in N. Al-Naumi and R. Meese (eds.), *International Legal Issues Arising from the United Nations Decade of International Law* (The Hague: Martinus Nijhoff, 1995), 899–927

van Selm-Thorburn, J., *Refugee Protection in Europe: Lessons of the Yugoslav Crisis* (The Hague: Martinus Nijhoff, 1998)

Senior Inter-Agency Network on Internal Displacement, *Mission to Ethiopia and Eritrea, 16–21 October 2000, Findings and Recommendations*

  Mission to Burundi, 18–22 December 2000, Findings and Recommendations

Shacknove, A. E., 'Who Is a Refugee?' (1985) 95 *Ethics* 274

Sheridan, L. M. E., 'Institutional Arrangements for the Coordination of Humanitarian Assistance in Complex Emergencies of Forced Migration' (2000) 14 *Georgetown Immigration Law Journal* 941

L. Silber and A. Little, *Yugoslavia: Death of a Nation* (New York: Penguin Books, 1997)

Simpson, J. H., *Refugees: A Preliminary Report of a Survey* (London: Royal Institute of International Affairs, 1938)

Stavropoulou, M., 'The Right Not to be Displaced' (1994) 9 *American University Journal of International Law and Policy* 689

'Bosnia and Herzegovina and the Right to Return in International Law' in M. O'Flaherty and G. Gisvold (eds.), *Post-War Protection of Human Rights in Bosnia and Herzegovina* (The Hague: Martinus Nijhoff Publishers, 1998), 123–40

'Displacement and Human Rights: Reflections on UN Practice' (1998) 20 *Human Rights Quarterly* 515

S. Steil and D. Yuefang, 'Policies and Practices in Three Gorges Resettlement: A Field Account', *Forced Migration Review*, vol. 12, January 2002

Stein, M., 'The Three Gorges: The Unexamined Toll of Development-Induced Displacement', *Forced Migration Review*, vol. 1, January–April 1998

Suhrke, A., 'Reflections on Regime Change', in Norwegian University of Science and Technology, *Researching Internal Displacement: State of the Art*, Conference Report, 7–8 February 2003, Trondheim, Norway

Sumit, S., *International Law of Internally Displaced Persons: The Role of UNHCR*, MPhil dissertation, Jawaharlal Nehru University, New Delhi, 1995

'Exiled at Home: The International Regime of Internal Displacement' (1998) 38 *Indian Journal of International Law* 182

Teson, F. R., 'The Kantian Theory of International Law' (1992) 92 *Columbia Law Review* 53

Humanitarian Intervention: An Inquiry into Law and Morality (New York: Transnational Publishers, 1996, 2nd ed.)

Tharakan, S. (ed.), *The Nowhere People: Response to Internally Displaced Persons* (Bangalore: Books for Change, 2002)

Thompson, M., *A Paper House: The Ending of Yugoslavia* (London: Hutchinson Radius, 1992)

Tiso, C. T., 'Safe Haven Refugee Programs: A Method of Combating International Refugee Crises' (1994) 8 *Georgetown Immigration Law Journal* 575

Tolley, H., *The UN Commission on Human Rights* (Boulder: Westview Press, 1987)

M. J. Toole and R. J. Waldman, 'The Public Health Aspects of Complex Emergencies and Refugee Situations' (1997) 18 *Annual Review of Public Health* 283

Tuitt, P., *False Images: The Law's Reconstruction of the Refugee* (London: Pluto Press, 1996)

Türk, V., 'The Role of UNHCR in the Development of International Refugee Law', in F. Nicholson and P. Twomey (eds.), *Refugee Rights and Realities: Evolving Concepts and Regimes* (Cambridge: Cambridge University Press, 1999), 153–74

UNDP, *UNDP and Internally Displaced Persons*, draft of 7 May 1997, Geneva

Integrating Human Rights with Sustainable Development: A UNDP Policy Document, New York, January 1998, available at http://magnet.undp.org

Sharing New Ground in Post-Conflict Situations: The Role of UNDP in Support of Reintegration Programmes, DP/2000/14, 9 February 2000

UNHCR, *Handbook on Procedures and Criteria for Determining Refugee Status* (Geneva: UNHCR, 1979)

The State of the World's Refugees: The Challenge of Protection (Geneva: UNHCR, 1993)

UNHCR's Operational Experience with Internally Displaced Persons (Geneva: UNHCR, 1994)

Refugee Children: Guidelines on Protection and Care (Geneva: UNHCR, 1994)

Working in a War Zone: A Review of UNHCR's Operations in Former Yugoslavia, EVAL/YUG/14, April 1994

The State of the World's Refugees: In Search of Solutions (Geneva: UNHCR, 1995)

The CIS Conference on Refugees and Migrants, Regional Conference to Address the Problems of Refugees, Displaced Persons, Other Forms of Involuntary Displacement and Returnees in the Countries of the Community of Independent States and Relevant Neighbouring Countries, European Series, vol. 2, No. 1, January 1996 (Geneva: UNHCR 1996)

International Legal Standards Applicable to the Protection of Internally Displaced Persons: A Reference Manual for UNHCR Staff (Geneva: UNHCR, 1996)

The State of World's Refugees: A Humanitarian Agenda (Geneva: UNHCR, 1997)

Bosnia and Herzegovina: Repatriation and Return Operation 1997 (Geneva: UNHCR, 1997)

Bosnia and Herzegovina: Repatriation and Return Operation 1998 (Geneva: UNHCR, 1998)

Update of UNHCR's Position on Categories of Persons from Bosnia and Herzegovina Who Are in Continued Need of International Protection, May 1999

Open Cities Initiative, Sarajevo, 1 August 1999

The Kosovo Refugee Crisis: An Independent Evaluation of UNHCR's Emergency Preparedness and Response, EPAU/2000/001, February 2000

Update of UNHCR's Position on Categories of Persons from Bosnia and Herzegovina in Need of International Protection, August 2000

Angola 2000: A Real-Time Assessment of UNHCR's IDP Intervention, Geneva, 15 November 2000

The State of World's Refugees: Fifty Years of Humanitarian Action (Geneva: UNHCR, 2000)

UNHCR's Programme for Internally Displaced People in Angola: A Joint Danida/UNHCR Review, EPAU/2001/04, May 2001

Update of UNHCR's Position on Categories of Persons from Bosnia and Herzegovina in Need of International Protection, September 2001

Statistical Yearbook 2002: Trends in Displacement, Protection and Solutions (Geneva: UNHCR, 2004)

Guidelines on International Protection: Gender-Related Persecution Within the Context of Article 1A(2) of the 1951 Convention and/or Its 1967 Protocol Relating to the Status of Refugees, 7 May 2002, reproduced in (2002) 14 *International Journal of Refugee Law* 457

UNHCR and Internally Displaced Persons in Angola: A Programme Continuation Review, EPAU/2002/03, May 2002

UNHCR's Programme for Internally Displaced Persons in Sri Lanka: Report of a Joint Appraisal Mission by the UK Department for International Development and UNHCR, EPAU/2002/04, May 2002

Protection and Solutions in Situations of Internal Displacement: Learning from UNHCR's Operational Experience, EPAU/2002/10, August 2002

Evaluation of UNHCR's Programme for Internally Displaced Persons in Colombia, EPAU/2003/03, May 2003

Sexual and Gender-Based Violence Against Refugees, Returnees and Internally Displaced Persons: Guidelines for Prevention and Response, May 2003

UNHCR, Brookings Institution and OAU, Internal Displacement in Africa: Report of a Workshop Held in Addis Ababa, Ethiopia, 19–20 October 1998

UNHCR and ICVA, Oslo Declaration and Plan of Action (Geneva: UNHCR, 1995)

UNHCR, OHR, OSCE and CRPC, Statistics – Implementation of the Property Laws in Bosnia and Herzegovina, 31 July 2003

UNICEF, Internally Displaced Children: The Role of UNICEF, discussion paper on programme issues related to internally displaced persons (New York: UNICEF, date of publication unknown)

Enhanced Monitoring and Reporting: UNICEF's Observations and Recommendations, Panel discussion on monitoring and reporting, Centre for Refugee Studies Conference on human rights and forced displacement, York University, Toronto, 7–9 May 1998

Mission to Sri Lanka with a View to Develop Best Practices to Internal Displacement, New York, Office of Emergency Programmes, Working Paper Series, August 1998

The Gender Dimension of Internal Displacement: Concept Paper and Annotated Bibliography, New York, Office of Emergency Programmes, Working Paper Series, September 1998

Expert Meeting on Gender Dimension of Internal Displacement, New York, 14–15 June 1999

Mission to Colombia with a View to Develop Best Practices to Internal Displacement, New York, Office of Emergency Programmes, Working Paper Series, December 1999

Good Practices Report on the Integration of Human Rights Protection and Humanitarian Assistance, December 1999

US Committee for Refugees (USCR), East of Bosnia: Refugees in Serbia and Montenegro (Washington DC: USCR, 1993)

World Refugee Survey 1997 (Washington DC: USCR, 1997)

US General Accounting Office, Internally Displaced Persons Lack Effective Protection, Report to the Chairman and the Ranking Minority Member, Committee on Foreign Relations, US Senate, Washington DC, August 2001

Verghese, J. P., 'Rights of Persons Displaced Within Their Own Country (with Special References to Tribal Population)', in World Congress on Human Rights,

10–15 December 1990 (New Delhi: School of International Studies, Jawaharlal Nehru University, 1990)

Vincent, M., 'Internally Displaced Persons: Rights and Status', *Forced Migration Review*, vol. 8, August 2000

M. Vincent and B. R. Sørensen, *Caught Between Borders: Response Strategies of the Internally Displaced* (London: Pluto Press in association with Norwegian Refugee Council, 2001)

Waters, T. W., 'The Naked Land: The Dayton Accords, Property Disputes, and Bosnia's Real Constitution' (1999) 40 *Harvard International Law Journal* 517

Weiner, M., 'Bad Neighbors, Bad Neighborhoods: An Inquiry into the Causes of Refugee Flows' (1996) 21:1 *International Security* 5

Weis, P., 'Le concept de réfugié en droit international' (1960) 87 *Journal de Droit International* 569

Weiss, T. G., 'UN Responses in the Former Yugoslavia: Moral and Operational Choices' (1994) 8 *Ethics and International Affairs* 1

'Whither International Efforts for Internally Displaced Persons?' (1999) 36 *Peace Research* 363

'Internal Exiles: What Next for Internally Displaced Persons?' (2003) 24 *Third World Quarterly* 429

T. G. Weiss and A. Pasic, 'Reinventing UNHCR: Enterprising Humanitarians in the Former Yugoslavia, 1991–1995' (1997) 3 *Global Governance* 41

'Dealing with the Displacement and Suffering Caused by Yugoslavia's Wars', in R. Cohen and F. M. Deng (eds.), *The Forsaken People* (Washington DC: Brookings Institution, 1998), 175–231

Wheeler, N. J., *Saving Strangers: Humanitarian Intervention in International Society* (Oxford: Oxford University Press, 2000)

J. Whitman and D. Pocock (eds.), *After Rwanda: The Coordination of United Nations Humanitarian Assistance* (London: Macmillan, 1996)

Wichert, T., *Internally Displaced Persons – Discussion Paper*, Quaker United Nations Office, Geneva, April 1995

'Human Rights, Refugees and Internally Displaced Persons: The UN Commission on Human Rights', *Refugee*, vol. 16, No. 5, November 1997, 41

Woodward, S., *Balkan Tragedy: Chaos and Dissolution after the Cold War* (Washington DC: Brookings Institution, 1995)

World Commission on Dams, *Dams and Development: A New Framework for Decision-Making* (London: Earthscan Publications, 2000)

World Food Programme, *WFP's IDP Review: WFP – Reaching People in Situations of Displacement*, discussion paper, version II, April 2000

Consolidated Framework of WFP Policies – An Updated Version, May 2003

World Health Organization, *Internally Displaced Persons, Health and WHO*, paper presented to the Humanitarian Affairs Segment of ECOSOC, New York, 19–20 July 2000

Young, K., 'UNHCR and ICRC in the Former Yugoslavia: Bosnia-Herzegovina' (2001) 843 *International Review of the Red Cross* 781

A. R. Zolberg, A. Suhrke and S. Aguayo, *Escape from Violence: Conflict and the Refugee Crisis in the Developing World* (New York: Oxford University Press, 1989)

N. L. Zucker and N. F. Zucker, 'The Uneasy Troika in US Refugee Policy: Foreign Policy, Pressure Groups and Resettlement Costs' (1989) 2 *Journal of Refugee Studies* 359

WEBSITES

United Nations, http://www.un.org

Office of the High Commissioner for Human Rights, http://www.unhchr.ch

Office of the High Commissioner for Refugees, http://www.unhcr.ch

United Nations Development Programme, http://www.undp.org

United Nations Children's Fund, http://www.unicef.org

World Food Programme, http://www.wfp.org

International Committee of the Red Cross, http://www.icrc.org

International Organization for Migration, http://www.iom.int

World Bank, http://www.worldbank.org

World Health Organization, http://www.who.int/en/

OCHA IDP Unit, http://www.reliefweb.int/idp/

Global IDP Project, http://www.idpproject.org

Brookings-SAIS Project on Internal Displacement,
    http://www.brookings.edu/fp/projects/idp/idp.htm

Office of the High Commissioner for Refugees in Bosnia and Herzegovina,
    http://www.unhcr.ba

Office of the High Representative in Bosnia and Herzegovina, http://www.ohr.int

Commission for Real Property Claims of Displaced Persons and Refugees,
    http://www.crpc.org.ba/new/en/main.htm

International Crisis Group, http://www.crisisweb.org/home/index.cfm

Index

The Search for Good Governance in Africa
Making Constitutions in the States of the Commonwealth
Peter Slinn and John Hatchard

Transboundary Damage in Internationtal Law
Hanqin Xue

European Criminal Procedures
Edited by Mireille Delmas-Marty and John Spencer

The Accountability of Armed Opposition Groups in International Law
Liesbeth Zegveld

Sharing Transboundary Resources
International Law and Optimal Resource Use
Eyal Benvenisti

International Human Rights and Humanitarian Law
Renè Provost

Remedies Against International Organisations
Basic Issues
Karel Wellens

Diversity and Self-Determination in International Law
Karen Knop

The Law of Internal Armed Conflict
Lindsay Moir

International Commercial Arbitration and African States
Amazu A. Asouzu

The Enforceability of Promises in European Contract Law
James Gordley

International Law in Antiquity
David J. Bederman

Money-Laundering
Guy Stessens